Prince of Programming

Beginner's Guide

A.C. THOMAS

Disclaimer
This book is provided for educational purposes only. The author and publisher make no guarantees regarding the accuracy or completeness of the information contained herein and assume no responsibility for errors or omissions. The code examples and explanations are provided "as is," without warranty of any kind. The author and publisher shall not be liable for any loss or damage arising from the use of this material.

All trademarks and registered trademarks mentioned in this book are the property of their respective owners.

C# and .NET are trademarks of Microsoft Corporation.

ISBN: 978-1-0674563-0-6
First Edition

Overview

Table of Contents

Contents

Chapter 2

Chapter 3

Chapter 4

Bonus I

Chapter 5

Chapter 7

Chapter 8

Chapter 9

Bonus III

I

Introduction

"Everyone should learn to code because it teaches you how to think." — Steve Jobs

About This Book

This book teaches you how to program with the help of C#. Unlike many programming books that try to be "complete" and cover as much as possible we removed all unnecessary clutter and only included what someone learning how to code need to know.

You'll learn the core fundamentals, the essential 20% of concepts that handle 80% of real-world programming. Each concept comes with clear code examples, detailed comments, and expected output right on the page, so you can learn anywhere. On the bus, at the beach, or lying in bed and know what to expect when you write code. Because learning should be fun, not a march through boring source code. Also, the examples are game-themed with a back story, so imagine a text-based game where a captured Prince in a dungeon is trying to escape and rescue his Princess.

Chapters build naturally on one another, one concept at a time, explained clearly, followed by practice. Examples use simple console applications to remove visual distractions, letting you focus on the code. The skills you learn are the same ones used in professional apps, enterprise systems, and even games, you're just learning them without the noise.

By the end, you'll understand the fundamentals every programmer relies on: variables, logic, loops, functions, classes and proper program structure. You'll have a strong foundation, the ability to continue learning on your own, and the mindset to think like a programmer. Breaking problems into pieces, debugging effectively, and building software that work.

Who This Book Is For

I originally set out to find something I could use to help teach my son how to program. After searching, I realized there really wasn't a resource that focused on strong fundamentals while still being fun and engaging. So, I decided to create one.

You don't need any prior programming experience to use this book. If you have never written a line of code, or are not even sure what code really is, you are exactly who this book was written for. We start at the beginning and assume nothing. You will learn step by step, focusing on understanding why things work instead of just copying code and hoping for the best. Concepts are introduced one at a time, helping you move from "Why are we doing this?" to "Oh, that actually makes sense."

This book is beginner friendly, but it is also valuable for intermediate developers. If you taught yourself programming and have already built a few projects, this book will help strengthen your foundation and sharpen the way you think about problem solving and code structure.

You don't need advanced math skills or an expensive computer to get started. What you do need is curiosity, a little patience when things don't work the first time, and the willingness to keep going. Those qualities matter far more than any technical background.

What You'll Be Able to Do by the End

By the time you finish this book, you'll have something more valuable than a list of memorized syntax, you'll understand how programmers think. When you face a problem, you'll automatically start breaking it down into smaller, manageable pieces. When your code doesn't work (and it won't, sometimes), you'll know how to investigate systematically instead of randomly changing things and hoping for the best. You will know where to start and how to structure your approach.

You will understand the core principles that underpin all programming, regardless of language: how to store and manipulate information, how to make programs respond intelligently to different situations, how to avoid repeating yourself, and how to organize code so it stays manageable as it grows. These aren't all C#-specific tricks, they're fundamental concepts that translate to any programming language or platform you might work with in the future.

More practically, you'll be able to write real, working programs. Useful tools that solve actual problems. You'll be comfortable reading other people's code and understanding what it does. You'll know how to search for solutions when you get stuck (a critical skill that professionals use daily). And you'll have the foundation needed to dive into any specialization you're interested in: web applications, game development, mobile apps, data analysis, whatever catches your interest.

Why C#?

Why not Python, which some might say is "easier"? Or JavaScript, which runs in browsers? Or C++, used for high-performance games?

C# hits the sweet spot. It's powerful enough to build professional software. You'll find it at many enterprise companies use it. It's also clean and readable, without the confusing syntax that makes some languages hard to learn.

It's strongly typed, which means you tell the computer what kind of data you're working with. That might sound strict at first, but it actually helps catch mistakes early. Think of it as guardrails while you're learning, keeping you away from mysterious errors later.

C# is incredibly versatile. Desktop apps? Web apps? Mobile apps with Xamarin? Games? Some game engines like Unity, Godot, Stride and MonoGame support it. Plus, C# is cross-platform, running on Windows, macOS, and Linux, so your skills aren't tied to a single operating system.

C# tools are excellent! Visual Studio and Visual Studio Code are free, powerful, and help you learn as you go by catching errors and suggesting fixes.

Finally, once you know C#, picking up other languages is much easier. The syntax may change slightly, but the core concepts stay the same. Learn C# well, and you'll have skills that transfer across the programming world.

Acknowledgments

Writing this book has been a long and rewarding process, and I am thankful to everyone who helped make it possible.

First and foremost, I want to thank my wonderful wife. Her love, support, and encouragement kept me going through the late nights. Her belief in me and in this project made all the difference.

To my children, thank you for putting up with the hours I spent working instead of playing co-op games with you. Your energy, curiosity, and enthusiasm reminded me why this work matters. My son helped me shape many of the programming concepts in this book, and my daughters, whose hugs and cheerful presence provided just the right motivation when I needed it.

This book is for all of you, and because of all of you.

About the Author

I started programming when I was about ten years old, piecing together computers from scavenged spare parts and teaching myself how to make them do something useful. What began as curiosity quickly turned into a lifelong passion for building things and figuring out how they work.

After earning a degree in Information Technology, I spent my career working with a variety of software companies, learning new technologies and programming languages along the way. I've worked on everything from GIS systems and web applications to flight procedure design software and large-scale enterprise SaaS microservices. Every project brought new challenges, and every challenge was an opportunity to learn something new.

Along the way, while leading many teams, I discovered that I enjoy helping others grow just as much as I enjoy writing code. I've mentored many developers, reviewed more pull requests than I can count, and learned that the best software is built when people learn together. This book comes from a long-held desire to give back, share what I've learned, and make the journey of learning to program a little more enjoyable.

Resources for This Book

All source code and supplemental materials for this book are available online.

Website: https://www.PrinceOfProgramming.com
Source Code: https://github.com/PrinceOfProgrammingBook/BeginnersGuide

The website may contain updates, errata, and additional resources. The GitHub repository includes all code examples from the book, organized by chapter.

These resources may evolve over time to reflect updates, fixes, and improvements.

II

Before You Start

"The best way to predict the future is to invent it." — Alan Kay

Getting Ready for Your Journey

Welcome to the training grounds. Before you jump into writing code, let's take a few minutes to understand how this book works. Think of this as the tutorial level, the part where you learn the controls before facing your first spike trap. Knowing how to navigate this book will make your learning journey smoother and help you get the most out of every chapter.

This isn't the kind of book where you absolutely must read every word in order (though that's definitely a good way to do it). Some sections you'll breeze through, others you'll want to spend more time on. That's normal. This chapter explains how the book is structured, what all those icons and sidebars mean, and when it's okay to move forward even if you don't understand everything perfectly yet.

Don't forget about the **Glossary** and **Index** at the back, they're there to make your life easier. The glossary gives quick, plain-language explanations of terms you might want to revisit, while the index helps you jump straight to the exact topic, concept, or keyword you're looking for without flipping through chapters. Whether you're stuck on a term, refreshing your memory, or hunting for that one example you *know* you saw earlier, these sections can save you time and frustration.

Let's get you oriented.

The Story of Our Prince

You're probably wondering why the book is named *"Prince of Programming"*. Everyone loves a good adventure right, so why not use coding examples that follow the story of a Prince on an adventure?

Here's our back story for our Prince:

(Inspired by Classic Arabian Nights Tales)

In an ancient Arabian desert kingdom, the sultan's palace, intrigue and dark magic, a young prince finds himself trapped in a deadly struggle for love and power. He is in love with the Sultan's daughter, but their future is threatened by the Sultan's most trusted advisor, the Evil Vizier, a sorcerer determined to claim the throne for himself.

When the Vizier learns that the prince could marry the princess and ruin his plans, he acts swiftly. Using deception and dark magic, he has the prince captured and thrown into a vast dungeon hidden beneath the palace. There, the Vizier intends to keep him imprisoned until he can force the princess into marriage and secure his rule.

The dungeon is a brutal maze of twisting corridors, patrolling guards, and deadly traps: spike pits, swinging blades, and heavy metal gates controlled by ancient switches. To survive, the prince must run, jump, climb, and carefully plan every move where one mistake could be fatal. But it's not all death and gloom, hidden are some magic potions to help the Prince when he's injured and somewhere the Prince can find a sword he will need to fight his way back to save the Princess.

This dungeon becomes the backdrop for the examples throughout the book. The story will continue at the end of each chapter before you get to the fun experiment. As the prince navigates traps and puzzles, you'll practice the same skills needed to learn programming: thinking clearly, solving problems, handling unexpected situations, and choosing the right actions at the right time.

Imagine a text-based game with a mix of Aladdin and Indiana Jones: racing against a ticking clock, navigating deadly traps with precise timing. That's the vibe we're going for in this book, learning to program while having a little adventure along the way.

How to Read This Book

The Basic Structure

Each chapter opens with an inspiring quote and an illustration of the Prince in action, setting the tone for what's ahead. This is followed by a brief introduction explaining what you'll learn and why it matters, then a table listing the core programming concepts covered. The main content teaches these concepts clearly with code examples, comments, and expected output, building from simple to complex. At the end, you'll find a Fun Experiment which is a small coding challenge to practice what you just learned (with a sample solution provided).

Icons and Sidebars

Trivia Block

 **Trivia:**

Before diving into the actual content, every chapter includes a trivia block with fascinating facts that loosely connect to what you're about to learn. These aren't random, they're chosen to spark your curiosity and get your brain warmed up.

Pro Tip Block

 **Pro Tip:**

"Pro Tips" contain helpful information that goes beyond the basics. These might explain why professionals do something a certain way, share common shortcuts, or give you some insight into how something works under the hood. You don't need to memorize Pro Tips to move forward, but they'll deepen your understanding.

Throughout the content, you'll see various icons highlighting specific types of information.

Here's what each one means:

 **Do this:**

When you see this icon, pay attention. It's highlighting the correct way to do something. The best practice, the recommended approach, or a technique you should make a habit of using. Think of these as the right moves in a sword fight.

 **Don't do this:**

This icon warns you about common mistakes or bad habits to avoid. These are the traps and pitfalls that trip up beginners (and sometimes experienced programmers too). Learning what not to do is just as important as learning what to do.

 **Important:**

When you see this icon, stop and make sure you understand what it's saying. These are critical concepts, common sources of confusion, or important warnings. Missing these can lead to frustration later.

Code Examples and Output

Every code example in this book follows the same format to make it easy to identify, read and understand:

The code itself is in a clearly marked block, with comments (lines starting with //) explaining what each part does:

```
// This is a comment explaining what the code does
int princeHealth = 100;                  // The Prince starts with full health
princeHealth = princeHealth - 20;        // He takes damage from a spike trap
Console.WriteLine("Prince health: " + princeHealth);
```

Below that, you will usually see the expected output. This is what you should see when you run the code. This means you can follow along and understand what's happening even if you're not sitting at a computer.

Expected Output:

```
Prince health: 80
```

When you see code samples, don't just skim over them quickly as something only a computer needs to care about. The names used for variables and methods combined with the comments are part of the explanation and is written in such a way that it's easy to read and understand. Code comments usually start with double forward slashes "//", if you see them, read them!

Read Front to Back vs. Skip Around

The short answer: Start from the beginning and work your way through in order, at least for your first read.

The longer answer: This book is designed to build knowledge progressively. Each chapter assumes you've understood the previous ones. If you skip Chapter 3 and jump to Chapter 7, you'll likely encounter concepts that were explained earlier, and you might get a bit lost if you don't know those concepts already.

That said, programming isn't a perfectly linear journey. Sometimes you'll need to review an earlier concept, and that's completely normal. The structure of this book makes it easy to flip back and refresh your memory on specific topics.

Here's a good approach
- **First time through:** Read chapters in order, front to back. Work through the examples, try the Fun Experiments, and don't skip ahead until you understand the current chapter.
- **When reviewing:** Use the Core Concepts tables at the start of each chapter to quickly find what you need. The Glossary of the book at the end are also great for quick reference.

- **When stuck:** If something in a later chapter doesn't make sense, there's a good chance you need to review an earlier concept. Don't be afraid to go back, that's how we learn.
- **After you've finished once:** Feel free to skip around and use the book as a reference. By then, you'll have the foundation and context to jump to specific topics as needed.

When It's Okay to Move On

You don't need to understand everything 100% perfectly before moving to the next chapter!

Learning to program is like learning to ride a bike. You can read about balance and momentum and steering all you want, but the real understanding comes from actually doing it. Sometimes a concept will not fully click until you have seen it used in a few different ways, or until you have tried (and failed) to use it yourself a few times.

You should move on when:
- You understand the main concept, even if some details are fuzzy
- You can follow the code examples and predict what they'll do (roughly)
- You've attempted the Fun Experiment, even if your solution wasn't perfect
- You feel like you're spending more time confused than learning

You should not move on when:
- The code examples look like complete gibberish
- You can't explain the main concept in your own words at all
- You skipped the previous chapter entirely
- Everything from the last three chapters is still a mystery

Think of it this way: if our Prince story was a real game when the user needs the Prince to jump across a pit, he doesn't need to understand the physics of projectile motion. The user just needs to know when to press the jump button and roughly how far he'll go. The deeper understanding comes with practice.

If you find yourself stuck on a concept for too long, sometimes the best thing to do is mark it with a bookmark, move forward, and come back to it later. Often, seeing how something is used in the next chapter will make the previous concept suddenly click.

 **Important:**

If you find yourself completely lost multiple chapters in a row, stop and go back. There's a foundational concept you missed somewhere, and moving forward will only make things worse. It's better to spend an extra day on Chapter 3 until it makes sense than to muddle through to Chapter 10 understanding nothing.

 **Pro Tip:**

Keep a notebook (physical or digital) while you read. When something doesn't quite make sense, write it down. Often, the act of writing the question helps you understand it better. And if it doesn't, you'll have a list of specific questions to revisit or ask someone about later.

That's it for the ground rules. You know how the book is structured, what the icons mean, and how to approach your reading. Now let's get into the actual programming. The dungeon awaits.

Final Note About Debugging

As you work through this book, you'll be writing code and running examples. Most of the time, if you follow the examples carefully, everything will work as expected. But here's the reality of programming: sometimes things don't work, and you'll need to figure out why.

Maybe you made a small typo, or get curious and try changing something to see what happens. Maybe you'll start experimenting with your own ideas. When that happens (and it will), your code might not behave the way you expect. That's completely normal and actually a sign you're learning!

When you run into problems and need help figuring out what's going wrong, flip to "**Appendix A - Debugging**". This chapter is packed with techniques for investigating and fixing issues in your code. You don't need to read it right now; it will make more sense once you've written some code and understand the basics. But keep it in mind as your troubleshooting guide.

Think of **Appendix A** as your emergency toolkit. You don't need to carry it with you everywhere, but when something breaks, you'll be glad you know where it is.

For now, just follow along with the examples in each chapter. If something doesn't work and you can't figure out why, that's when you visit the debugging appendix. By the end of this book, when you start writing your own programs from scratch, those debugging skills will become essential tools you'll use every day.

III

Getting Started

"Give me six hours to chop down a tree and I will spend the first four sharpening the axe." — Abraham Lincoln

Before you can bring your ideas to life in code, you need the right tools and knowledge to get started. This chapter is all about setting up your programming environment and understanding the fundamental workflow that every developer uses: writing code, compiling it into something your computer can execute, and running it to see the results. Whether you're building the next viral mobile app, creating automation tools that save hours of repetitive work, or developing the backend systems that power websites visited by millions, this same basic process applies. Every piece of software you've ever used, from your web browser to your favorite music streaming app all started exactly where you are now, with a developer setting up their tools and writing their first lines of code.

You'll also learn one of the most crucial skills in programming: how to read and fix errors. Professional developers don't write perfect code on the first try. They write code, encounter errors, read what went wrong, and fix it. This cycle happens hundreds of times a day, and mastering it is what separates someone who can write code from someone who can build real software. By the end of this chapter, you'll have a working development environment, you'll understand how your code transforms into a running program, and you'll know how to troubleshoot the inevitable mistakes that every programmer makes. These fundamentals will serve you whether you're coding for fun, building tools for yourself, or starting a career in software development.

Core Concepts Covered

✓ Setting up a professional development environment
✓ Understanding the software development workflow
✓ The compilation process and how code becomes executable programs
✓ Reading and interpreting error messages
✓ Debugging and troubleshooting techniques
✓ File systems and project organization
✓ The relationship between source code and compiled applications

---

Welcome, New Programmer

 **Trivia:**

Almost every programmer's first program prints "Hello, World!" on screen. This tradition started in 1978 with the book "The C Programming Language" by Brian Kernighan and Dennis Ritchie. Before that, programming tutorials used boring examples like calculating interest rates. "Hello, World!" became iconic because it's simple enough for absolute beginners but proves your programming environment works. Millions of programmers across decades and hundreds of languages have started their journey with these exact two words.

Okay so let's sharpen our axe before we get chopping! Before we can make the Prince jump over spike traps or battle guards, we need to get our tools ready. Think of this like preparing your inventory before heading into a dungeon – you wouldn't go fight the final boss with a wooden stick, right?

Choosing Your Development Environment

Before we dive into installation, let's talk about your options for writing C# code. You need to pick ONE tool and stick with it throughout this book. Here's some of your options:

Option 1: Visual Studio Community (RECOMMENDED for Windows)

If you're running Windows, this is your best choice. Visual Studio is Microsoft's full-featured IDE (Integrated Development Environment), and it's designed specifically for C# development. It requires the least amount of setup and configuration, which means you can focus on learning to code instead of fighting with tools.

Why Visual Studio is best for beginners on Windows:
- Everything works immediately after installation – no extra setup needed
- Console applications run in their own windows automatically

- Creating different project types (Console, Windows Forms, etc.) is simple and wizard-driven
- Has a built-in visual designer for Windows Forms (which we'll use in a bonus chapter)
- Debugging tools are built-in and work seamlessly
- IntelliSense (code suggestions) works perfectly out of the box
- It's what professional C# developers use

The downside: It's big (10-20GB) and only runs on Windows.

Option 2: Visual Studio Code (For Other Operating Systems or Lightweight Needs)

VS Code is a lighter-weight code editor that works on Windows, Mac, and Linux. If you're NOT on Windows, or if your computer doesn't have enough space for Visual Studio, VS Code is your next best option.

Things to know about VS Code:
- Works on all operating systems (Windows, Mac, Linux)
- You'll need to install the C# Dev Kit extension to get full C# support
- Console applications don't run in their own window – they run in the integrated Terminal panel
- Debugging requires additional configuration (launch.json and tasks.json files)
- Creating Windows Forms projects requires command-line .NET calls and manual setup
- There's NO visual designer for Windows Forms – you'd have to code UI elements manually
- Each project may need configuration files to compile and run properly

VS Code is powerful and many professionals use it, but it adds complexity that can be frustrating when you're trying to learn programming basics.

Option 3: Command Line + Text Editor (Minimalist Approach)

This old-school method works on any operating system and teaches you exactly what's happening under the hood. You use any text editor (Notepad, Sublime Text, etc.) to write code, then compile and run it using command-line tools.

 **This is best for:**
- Understanding the fundamentals of how compilation works
- Working on very low-powered computers
- Developers who prefer minimal tools

 **This is NOT ideal for:**
- Beginners who want a smooth learning experience
- Anyone who wants to create Windows Forms applications

- People who need visual debugging tools

Option 4: JetBrains Rider (Professional Alternative)

Rider is a paid IDE (though free for students) that works on Windows, Mac, and Linux. It's excellent and has most of the features of Visual Studio, but it costs money after the trial period. If you're already a Rider user, it will work fine for this book, but we won't cover it specifically since Visual Studio Community is free and does everything we need.

Our Recommendation

1. **If you're on Windows:** Install Visual Studio Community (Option 1)
2. **If you're on Mac or Linux:** Install VS Code with the C# Dev Kit (Option 2)
3. **If you want to learn the fundamentals:** Use Command Line + Text Editor (Option 3)

✋ **Important:** Its best to pick one tool and stick with it throughout this entire book! Don't switch back and forth or you'll confuse yourself. All three do the same thing – they let you write and run C# code. The difference is in the interface and convenience.

Visual Studio Community

(OPTION 1: RECOMMENDED for Windows)

Visual Studio is Microsoft's full-featured IDE. It's powerful, professional, and makes C# development as smooth as possible. Think of Visual Studio as a fully equipped workshop – everything you need is right there, organized and ready to use.

Installing Visual Studio Community

Step 1: Download Visual Studio

1. Go to: `https://visualstudio.microsoft.com/downloads/`
2. Under "Community", click the "Free Download" button
3. Wait for the installer to download (it's small, around 3-4MB)

Step 2: Run the Installer

1. Double-click the downloaded file (`VisualStudioSetup.exe`)
2. Click "Yes" if Windows asks for permission
3. The Visual Studio Installer will launch

Step 3: Select Workloads

This is important! Visual Studio can install components for many types of development. You need to tell it what you want:

1. On the "Workloads" tab, check this box:
   - o **".NET desktop development"** (this is the main one you need!)
2. On the right side, you'll see "Installation details". The default selections should be fine for console applications.
3. Click "Install"
4. Wait... this will take a while (15-30 minutes depending on your internet speed)
5. You might need to restart your computer when it's done

 **Pro Tip:**

Visual Studio is HUGE – the full installation can be 10-20GB or more. Make sure you have enough space on your hard drive. If you're short on space, consider using VS Code instead, though you'll sacrifice some convenience.

Creating a New Console Application in Visual Studio

Visual Studio has a powerful project creation wizard that makes getting started incredibly easy.

Step 1: Launch Visual Studio

1. Open Visual Studio Community
2. You'll see a start window with several options

Step 2: Create a New Project

1. Click "Create a new project"
2. You'll see a list of project templates

Step 3: Choose Console App

1. In the search box at the top, type: `console`
2. Select **Console App** with the C# tag
3. **IMPORTANT:** Make sure it does NOT say "(.NET Framework)"
4. Click "Next"

Step 4: Configure Your Project

1. Give your project a name (like `HelloPrince`)
2. Choose where to save it (Documents is fine)
3. Check "Place solution and project in the same directory" (keeps things tidy)
4. Click "Next"
5. Leave Framework at default .NET 10.0 or higher and click Create.

Visual Studio will create your project and open it automatically. You'll see several panels and windows – the main code editor in the center, Solution Explorer on the right, and other helpful tools. Don't worry if it looks overwhelming at first!

Understanding Other Project Types:

While we're focusing on Console Apps for learning, Visual Studio can create other types:

- o **Windows Forms App** – Traditional Windows applications with buttons, windows, and menus (we'll use this later for graphics)
- o **WPF Application** – Modern Windows apps with fancier graphics and animations
- o **Class Library** – Reusable code packages that other projects can reference

For now, stick with Console Apps! They're perfect for learning the fundamentals.

Important: Always select projects for modern **.NET** (versions 8.0, 9.0, 10.0, etc.) and NOT **.NET Framework**. The .NET Framework is older and Microsoft isn't developing it anymore. Modern .NET is faster, cross-platform, and has all the latest features.

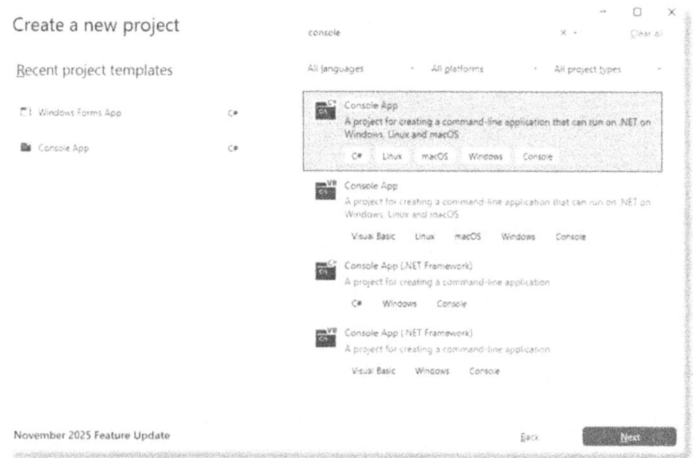

Opening Existing Projects in Visual Studio

Method 1: Through Visual Studio

1. Launch Visual Studio
2. On the start window, click "Open a project or solution"
3. Navigate to your project folder
4. Select the `.csproj` file (or `.sln` file if there is one)
5. Click "Open"

Method 2: From Windows Explorer

1. Navigate to your project folder
2. Find the `.csproj` file or `.sln` file
3. Double-click it

4. Visual Studio will launch and open the project

Method 3: Recent Projects

1. Launch Visual Studio
2. On the start window, you'll see a list of recent projects on the right
3. Click on the one you want to open

What's the difference between .csproj and .sln files?

- `.csproj` – The project file. Contains settings for a single project.
- `.sln` – The solution file. Can contain multiple projects working together.

For most of your learning, you'll work with single projects, so opening the `.csproj` file is fine. Visual Studio automatically creates a `.sln` file when you create a project.

Running Your Code in Visual Studio

Visual Studio makes running your code incredibly easy. Here are your options:

Method 1: Using the Start Button (Easiest)

1. Look at the top toolbar
2. You'll see a green "play" button (▷) with text next to it showing your project name (like "HelloPrince")
3. Click it!
4. A console window will appear with your program's output

Method 2: Using the Menu

1. Click **Debug → Start Without Debugging** (or press `Ctrl+F5`)
2. Your program compiles and runs in a console window
3. The window stays open after the program finishes so you can read the output

Method 3: Using the Keyboard

- Press `Ctrl+F5` to run without debugging (recommended while learning)
- Press `F5` to run with debugging (for when you're hunting bugs later)

 **Pro Tip:**

Use `Ctrl+F5` (Start Without Debugging) while you're learning. The `F5` (Start Debugging) option is for when you need to find and fix errors, which we'll cover in the debugging section later. Starting without debugging is faster and the console window automatically stays open so you can read your program's output.

Your First Program in Visual Studio

Let's create a simple program to test everything:

1. Create a new Console App called HelloPrince (using the steps above)
2. Visual Studio will open with your Program.cs file already displayed in the center
3. You'll see this default code:

```
// See https://aka.ms/new-console-template for more information
Console.WriteLine("Hello, World!");
```

4. Replace it with:

```
Console.WriteLine("==================================");
Console.WriteLine("  Welcome to the Palace Dungeons");
Console.WriteLine("==================================");
Console.WriteLine("");
Console.WriteLine("The Prince awakens in darkness...");
Console.WriteLine("He must find a way to escape!");
```

5. Save the file (Ctrl+S)
6. Click the green Start button (or press Ctrl+F5)

Expected output:

A console window will pop up showing this text, and it will say "Press any key to close this window..." at the bottom. Perfect! You just wrote and ran your first C# program!

To make it more readable the relevant output will be displayed like this:

```
==================================
  Welcome to the Palace Dungeons
==================================

The Prince awakens in darkness...
He must find a way to escape!
```

Visual Studio Code

(OPTION 2: For Mac, Linux, or Lightweight Windows Setup)

VS Code is a lightweight, cross-platform code editor. While it's more flexible than Visual Studio, it requires more setup and configuration. This is your best option if you're on Mac or Linux.

Installing VS Code and .NET SDK

Step 1: Download VS Code
1. Open your web browser
2. Go to: `https://code.visualstudio.com`
3. Click the big download button (it'll automatically detect your operating system)
4. Wait for the download to finish (about 90MB)

Step 2: Install VS Code

On Windows:
1. Find the downloaded file (probably in your Downloads folder) called something like `VSCodeSetup.exe`
2. Double-click it
3. Click "Yes" when Windows asks for permission
4. Follow the installation wizard:
   - Accept the license agreement
   - Choose the default installation location
   - **IMPORTANT:** On the "Select Additional Tasks" screen, check these boxes:
     - "Add 'Open with Code' action to Windows Explorer file context menu"
     - "Add 'Open with Code' action to Windows Explorer directory context menu"
     - "Add to PATH"
   - Click Install
5. Click Finish when done

On Mac:
1. Open the downloaded `.dmg` file
2. Drag VS Code to your Applications folder
3. Open VS Code from Applications

On Linux:

1. Follow the instructions on the VS Code website for your specific distribution (Ubuntu, Fedora, etc.)
2. The site provides specific commands for different package managers

Step 3: Download and install the .NET SDK

1. Go to: `https://dotnet.microsoft.com/download`
2. Click "Download .NET SDK" – get the latest version (currently .NET 8.0 or newer)
3. Download the installer for your operating system
4. Run the installer and follow the prompts
5. Wait for it to finish (takes a minute or two)

Step 4: Verify Everything Works

On Windows:

1. Press the Windows key
2. Type "cmd" or "command prompt"
3. Press Enter

On Mac:

1. Press Cmd+Space to open Spotlight
2. Type "terminal"
3. Press Enter

On Linux:

1. Open your terminal application (varies by distribution)

In the terminal window, type:

```
dotnet --version
```

If you see a version number like `10.0.100` or similar, you're good to go! If you see an error saying 'dotnet' is not recognized, you might need to restart your computer or terminal.

Installing the C# Dev Kit Extension

VS Code by itself is just a text editor. To make it work well for C# development, you need to install the C# Dev Kit extension.

Step 1: Open the Extensions Panel

1. Launch VS Code
2. Look at the left sidebar – you'll see several icons

3. Click on the Extensions icon (it looks like four squares with one floating away) OR press `Ctrl+Shift+X` (Windows/Linux) or `Cmd+Shift+X` (Mac)

Step 2: Install the C# Dev Kit

1. In the search box at the top, type: `C# Dev Kit`
2. You'll see "C# Dev Kit" by Microsoft appear in the results
3. Click on it, then click the green "Install" button
4. This will also automatically install the base "C#" extension – that's perfect!
5. Wait a minute or two for it to install

Step 3: Restart VS Code

1. Close VS Code completely
2. Open it again
3. You might see a notification asking to install additional components – click "Install" if you see this

Now VS Code has C# superpowers! However, remember that you'll still need to configure some things as you go, unlike Visual Studio which works immediately.

Pro Tip:

The C# Dev Kit includes debugging tools and a solution explorer, but you'll still need to set up `launch.json` and `tasks.json` files for more complex debugging scenarios. For the console applications in this book, the default setup should work fine.

Creating a New Project in VS Code

Method 1: Using the Command Palette

1. Press `Ctrl+Shift+P` (Windows/Linux) or `Cmd+Shift+P` (Mac) to open the Command Palette
2. Type: `.NET: New Project`
3. Press Enter
4. Select "Console App" from the list
5. Choose where to save your project (your Desktop or Documents folder is fine)
6. Give it a name like `HelloPrince`
7. Select the default `.sln` and press enter when it confirms your path.
8. VS Code will create the project and open it automatically

Method 2: Using the Terminal (Works on All Operating Systems)

1. In VS Code, click **Terminal → New Terminal** (or press `Ctrl+`` `)
2. Navigate to where you want to create your project:

```
cd Desktop
```

(Use `cd Documents` for Documents folder, etc.)

3. Create a new console project:

```
dotnet new console -n HelloPrince
```

4. Navigate into your new project:

```
cd HelloPrince
```

5. Open the project in VS Code:

```
code .
```

(The dot means "current folder")

Understanding Project Types:

*   **Console Application** (`dotnet new console`) – Runs in the terminal window. Perfect for learning the basics and text-based programs.
*   **Windows Forms App** (`dotnet new winforms`) – Creates apps with graphical windows and buttons. **Note:** This only works on Windows, and VS Code doesn't have a visual designer for it. You'd have to write all the UI code manually. We'll cover this in a bonus chapter with specific instructions for VS Code users.
*   **Class Library** (`dotnet new classlib`) – Creates reusable code that other projects can use, not a standalone program.

For now, stick with Console Applications!

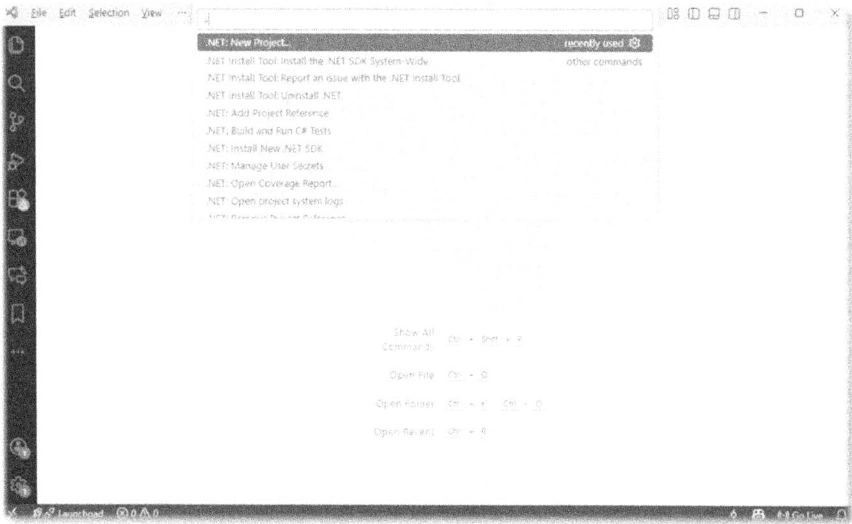

Opening Existing Projects in VS Code

Method 1: Through VS Code
1. Click File → Open Folder
2. Navigate to your project folder (the one containing the `.csproj` file)
3. Click "Select Folder" (Windows/Linux) or "Open" (Mac)

Method 2: From File Explorer/Finder

Windows:

1. Navigate to your project folder in Windows Explorer
2. Right-click the folder
3. Select "Open with Code"

Mac:

1. Open Terminal
2. Navigate to your project folder: `cd path/to/your/project`
3. Type: `code .`

Method 3: From the Terminal
1. Open your terminal application
2. Navigate to your project folder:

```
cd path/to/your/project
```

3. Type:

```
code .
```

Running Your Code in VS Code

With the C# Dev Kit installed, you have several ways to run your code:

Method 1: Using the Run Button
4. Open your `Program.cs` file
5. Look at the top-right corner of VS Code
6. You'll see a "play" button (▷) that says "Run" when you hover over it
7. Click it!
8. Your program will compile and run, and you'll see the output in the Terminal panel at the bottom

Method 2: Using the Terminal (Most Reliable)
1. Make sure you're in your project folder
2. Click **Terminal** → **New Terminal** (if you don't have one open)

3. Type:

```
dotnet run
```

4. Your program compiles and runs, showing output in the same Terminal window

Method 3: Using Debug (F5)

1. Press F5 on your keyboard
2. If prompted, select "C#" as the environment
3. Your program will compile and run
4. Output appears in the Debug Console (not a separate window like Visual Studio)

   **Important Note About Console Output:**

Unlike Visual Studio, VS Code doesn't open your console applications in a separate window. Instead, the output appears in the integrated Terminal or Debug Console panel at the bottom of VS Code. This is fine for learning, but it's different from what you'd see if you were using Visual Studio or running the `.exe` file directly.

   **Pro Tip:**

The `dotnet run` method in the Terminal is the most reliable way to run console apps in VS Code. It's explicit, clear, and you see exactly what's happening. The Run button and F5 debugging are convenient but sometimes require additional configuration files.

Your First Program in VS Code

Let's create a simple program to test everything:

1. Create a new Console Application called `HelloPrince` (using either method above)
2. Open the `Program.cs` file from the Explorer panel on the left
3. You should see this default code:

```
// See https://aka.ms/new-console-template for more information
Console.WriteLine("Hello, World!");
```

4. Replace it with:

```
Console.WriteLine("===================================");
Console.WriteLine("  Welcome to the Palace Dungeons");
Console.WriteLine("===================================");
Console.WriteLine("");
Console.WriteLine("The Prince awakens in darkness...");
Console.WriteLine("He must find a way to escape!");
```

5. Save the file (Ctrl+S or Cmd+S)

6. Open the Terminal (Terminal → New Terminal)
7. Make sure you are in the `.csproj` folder
8. Type:

```
dotnet run
```

Expected output:

If you see this output in the Terminal panel, congratulations! VS Code is fully set up and ready to go!

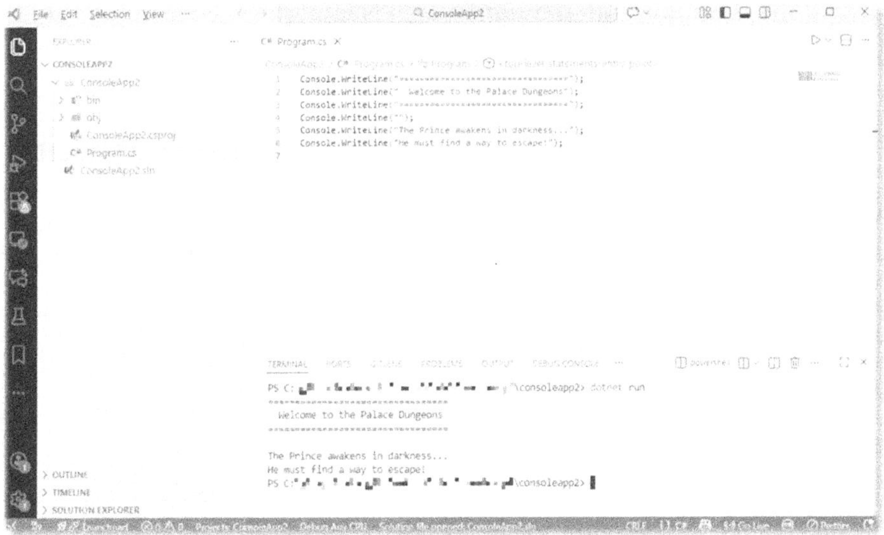

To make output more recognizable the relevant output will be displayed like this:

```
===================================
  Welcome to the Palace Dungeons
===================================

The Prince awakens in darkness...
He must find a way to escape!
```

A Note About Windows Forms in VS Code

One of the bonus chapters in this book covers creating graphical applications using Windows Forms. This is straightforward in Visual Studio (which has a built-in visual designer), but it's a bit more complex in VS Code.

Windows Forms relies heavily on a visual designer, automatic layout code generation, and tight integration with Windows-specific build tools. All this are provided in full with Visual Studio but intentionally absent from VS Code since VS Code is also written for other operating systems that works differently. As a result, every control, layout decision, and event hookup must be written and maintained manually in code, increasing both the amount of boilerplate and the chance of errors, especially for beginners.

Command Line + Text Editor

(OPTION 3: Minimalist Approach)

This is the old-school, minimalist approach. It works on any operating system and teaches you exactly what's happening when you compile and run code. You can use any text editor you like – even basic ones like Notepad on Windows, TextEdit on Mac, or nano on Linux.

What You Need

1. **The .NET SDK** (install this the same way as shown in the VS Code section above for your operating system)
2. **Any text editor** – Notepad, TextEdit, Notepad++, Sublime Text, Atom, or even VS Code without extensions

Creating and Running Projects

All the same `dotnet` commands from the VS Code section work here!

The commands are identical regardless of your operating system:

- `dotnet new console -n ProjectName` – Create a new console project
- `dotnet run` – Compile and run your project
- `dotnet build` – Just compile without running

Refer back to the VS Code section for full details on these commands.

Quick Workflow

On Windows:

1. Open Command Prompt:
   - Press Windows key
   - Type "cmd"
   - Press Enter
2. Create a project:

```
cd Desktop
dotnet new console -n HelloPrince
cd HelloPrince
```

3. Edit your code:

```
notepad Program.cs
```

4. Run your code:

```
dotnet run
```

On Mac:

1. Open Terminal:
    o Press Cmd+Space
    o Type "terminal"
    o Press Enter
2. Create a project:

```
cd Desktop
dotnet new console -n HelloPrince
cd HelloPrince
```

3. Edit your code:

```
open -e Program.cs
```

(This opens TextEdit. You can also use `nano Program.cs` or `vim Program.cs` if you prefer)

4. Run your code:

```
dotnet run
```

On Linux:

1. **Open your terminal** (varies by distribution)
2. **Create a project:**

```
cd Desktop
dotnet new console -n HelloPrince
cd HelloPrince
```

3. **Edit your code:**

```
nano Program.cs
```

(Or use `vim`, `gedit`, `kate`, or whatever text editor you prefer)

4. **Run your code:**

```
dotnet run
```

That's it! The command line approach is simple and direct. You're using the same .NET tools that VS Code and Visual Studio use behind the scenes – you're just typing the commands yourself.

 **Pro Tip:**

This method teaches you what's really happening. When you click the "Run" button in VS Code or Visual Studio, they're just executing `dotnet run` for you. Understanding the commands gives you superpowers when things go wrong, and it works identically on Windows, Mac, and Linux!

Running Future Code Examples

Throughout this book, whenever you see code examples, just follow these steps for whatever IDE or option you decided on:

1. **Create** a new Console Application:
   - Name it appropriately (like `Chapter2Example` or `VariablesTest`)
2. **Open** the `Program.cs` file
3. **Replace** or update the existing code with the example code from the book
4. **Save** the file (Ctrl+S or Cmd+S)
5. **Run** it

 **Pro Tip:**

Name your projects meaningfully – `LoopsExample`, `MethodsTest`, `VariablesChallenge`, etc. You'll thank yourself later when you have 20 projects and need to find the right one! Create a main folder like `C:\CodingProjects` or `Documents\LearningCSharp` and put all your projects inside to stay organized.

Understanding Files and Compilation

Now that you know how to create and run programs with your chosen tool, let's understand what's actually happening behind the scenes. This is important regardless of which option you chose!

What is a File?

A **file** is just a container that stores information on your computer. Think of it like a chest in a game that holds something very specific.

Files come in different types:

- `.txt` – Plain text files (like a note or letter)
- `.cs` – C# code files (what you just created!)
- `.exe` – Executable files on Windows (programs you can run)
- `.dll` – Dynamic Link Library (compiled code that programs use)
- `.jpg` / `.png` – Image files
- `.mp3` – Audio files
- `.csproj` – C# project file (contains settings and references)
- `.sln` – Solution file (groups multiple projects together)

The part after the dot is called the **file extension** and it tells your computer (and you) what kind of data is inside.

Your `Program.cs` file is a C# source code file. Right now it's just text that humans can read. Your computer can't run it directly – it needs to be **compiled** first.

The Compilation Process

Compiling is the process of turning your human-readable code into an executable file that your computer can actually run. Think of it like this: you write instructions in English (well, C#), and the compiler translates those instructions into machine language that your computer's processor understands.

Here's what happens step by step:
1. **You write code** in C# (the `.cs` file) – human-readable
2. **You run your code** (click Run button, press Ctrl+F5, or type `dotnet run`)
3. **The compiler reads your code** and checks for syntax errors
4. **If there are no errors**, it translates your code into **Intermediate Language (IL)**
5. **The IL code is packaged** into a `.dll` or `.exe` file
6. **When you run the program**, the .NET runtime converts IL into actual machine code for your specific processor
7. **Your program executes!**

 **Pro Tip:**

C# uses a two-step compilation process. First, your code is compiled to Intermediate Language (IL), which is like a universal language. Then, when you run your program, the .NET runtime compiles IL to actual machine code for your specific computer (x86, x64, ARM, etc.). This is why C# programs can run on Windows, Mac, and Linux – the IL code is the same, but the final machine code is different for each platform! Pretty clever, right?

Where Does the Compiled Code Go?

When you compile your code, several folders are created automatically:

```
YourProject/
├── bin/
│   └── Debug/
│       └── net10.0/
│           ├── YourProject.exe (Windows) or YourProject (Mac/Linux)
│           ├── YourProject.dll
│           └── (other files)
├── obj/
│   └── (temporary compilation files)
└── Program.cs
```

- `bin` (binary) – Contains your final executable files
- `Debug` – The configuration (Debug vs Release)
- `Net10.0` – The .NET version you're targeting
- `obj` (object) – Temporary files used during compilation

When you run your program using any of the methods above, it automatically finds the executable in `bin/Debug/net10.0` and runs it.

 **Pro Tip:**

You can also compile in "Release" mode which creates a faster, smaller executable without debugging information. When you want to share your application with someone, you'd compile in Release mode by using `dotnet build -c Release` or `dotnet publish`.

Understanding Errors and Warnings (Visual Studio)

Let's talk about something every programmer deals with constantly: errors! Don't worry – making mistakes is a totally normal part of programming. In fact, professional developers spend a huge chunk of their time fixing errors. The difference between a beginner and a pro isn't that the pro doesn't make mistakes – it's that the pro knows how to read error messages and fix them quickly.

Think of errors like the spikes and traps our Prince might face. The first time you encounter them, they might kill you. But once you learn to recognize them and know how to deal with them, they become just another obstacle you can jump over.

A Quick Note About the Examples Below

The code examples in this section show common errors, but don't worry if you don't understand what the code does yet. We'll explain everything in the next chapters. You don't need to type this code in right now, though feel free to break things if you're curious. I know reading about errors before writing real code seems about as exciting as reading the instruction manual for a microwave. But when you're three hours into debugging and suddenly remember "wait, semicolons are a thing," you'll be thanking past you for reading this.

The Error List Panel in Visual Studio

Visual Studio has an incredibly helpful feature called the Error List. This panel shows you ALL the errors and warnings in your code at once, and it's your best friend when debugging.

How to open the Error List:
1. Look at the bottom of Visual Studio
2. You should see a tab called "Error List"
3. If you don't see it, go to **View → Error List**

What you'll see in the Error List:
The Error List shows three types of messages:
1. **Errors** (round red "x" icon) – These MUST be fixed before your code will run. The compiler stops and refuses to create an executable if there are errors.
2. **Warnings** (triangle yellow "!" icon) – These are potential problems that won't stop your code from running, but might cause issues later. You should pay attention to warnings!
3. **Messages** (round blue "i" icon) – These are just informational and usually safe to ignore.

Reading an error message:
Each error in the list shows:
- **Description** – What's wrong
- **File** – Which file has the error
- **Line** – The line number where the error is
- **Column** – Sometimes even the exact character position

Example error:

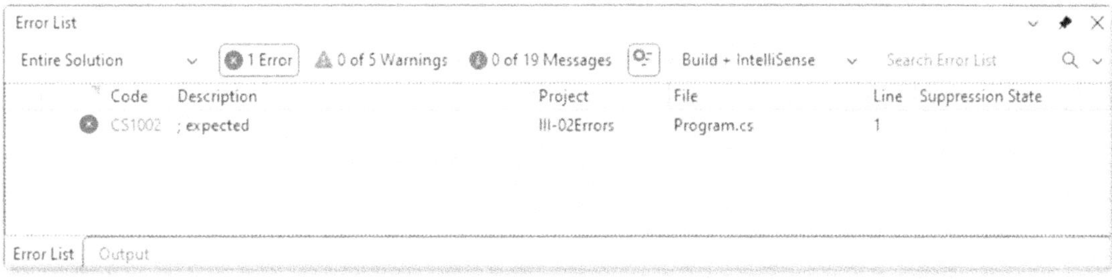

This tells you: "You're missing a semicolon on line 1."

How to jump to an error:

- Double-click any error in the Error List
- Visual Studio will immediately take you to that line in your code
- The cursor will be positioned right where the problem is

 **Pro Tip:**

Fix errors one at a time, starting from the top of the Error List. Sometimes one error causes several other "fake" errors below it. Fix the first error, and the others might disappear!

The Most Common Beginner Errors

Let's look at the errors you'll probably encounter in your first few days of programming:

Error 1: Missing Semicolon

This is THE classic beginner mistake. Every statement in C# needs to end with a semicolon (;). Forgetting it is like forgetting to close a door – things just don't work right.

 **Broken code:**

```
Console.WriteLine("Hello")
Console.WriteLine("World");
```

Error message you'll see:

Code	Description	Line
CS1002	; expected	1

 **Fixed code:**

```
Console.WriteLine("Hello");
Console.WriteLine("World");
```

Every line that does something (a statement) needs that semicolon at the end. Think of it like ending a sentence with a period.

Error 2: Misspelling or Wrong Capitalization

C# is case-sensitive, which means `Console` and `console` are completely different things. If you misspell something or get the capitalization wrong, C# won't know what you're talking about.

 **Broken code:**

```
console.WriteLine("Hello");  // lowercase 'c'
Console.Writeline("World");  // lowercase 'l' in Line
```

Error message you'll see:

Code	Description	Line
CS0103	The name 'console' does not exist in the current context	1
CS0117	'Console' does not contain a definition for 'Writeline'	2

 **Fixed code:**

```
Console.WriteLine("Hello");
Console.WriteLine("World");
```

Always match the capitalization exactly. When in doubt, let IntelliSense (the auto-complete feature) help you – if you type `Con` and press Tab, it will complete `Console` for you correctly.

Error 3: Missing or Mismatched Quotes

Strings (text) need to be wrapped in double quotes ("). If you forget the closing quote or use the wrong type of quote, C# gets confused.

 **Broken code:**

```
Console.WriteLine("Hello World);        // missing closing quote
Console.WriteLine('Hello World');        // single quotes instead of double
Console.WriteLine("Hello World');        // mixed quotes
```

Error messages you'll see:

Code	Description	Line
CS1010	Newline in constant	1
CS1003	Syntax error, ',' expected	1
CS1012	Too many characters in character literal	2
CS1026	) expected	2
CS1010	Newline in constant	3
CS1026	) expected	3
CS1002	; expected	3

 **Fixed code:**

```
Console.WriteLine("Hello World");
```

Always use double quotes for strings, and make sure every opening quote has a matching closing quote.

Note: As you can see from above examples, sometimes you will see multiple errors from just one simple mistake. Look at the first one and see if you can fix the problem there first then the other fake errors will also disappear.

Error 4: Missing Parentheses or Braces

Methods (like `WriteLine`) need parentheses `()` to work. You also need braces `{}` to group code together (we'll learn more about this later). Forgetting them causes errors.

 **Broken code:**

```
Console.WriteLine "Hello";          // missing parentheses
Console.WriteLine("Hello"           // missing closing parenthesis
```

Error message you'll see:

Code	Description	Line
CS0201	Only assignment, call, increment, decrement, await, and new object expressions can be used as a statement	1
CS1002	; expected	1
CS1026	) expected	2
CS1002	; expected	2

 **Fixed code:**

```
Console.WriteLine("Hello");
```

Think of parentheses as the hands that hold the information you're passing to a method.

Error 5: Typos in Keywords

C# has special words like `using`, `namespace`, `class`, etc. If you misspell these, the compiler won't understand your code.

 **Broken code:**

```
Consol.WriteLine("Hello");          // 'Console' misspelled
```

Error message you'll see:

Code	Description	Line
CS0103	The name 'Consol' does not exist in the current context	1

 **Fixed code:**

```
Console.WriteLine("Hello");
```

Reading Error Messages

Here's the most important advice I can give you:

READ THE ERROR MESSAGES!

Seriously, this is where beginners make their biggest mistake. When you see an error, your first instinct might be to panic or randomly change things hoping it will work. Don't do that! The error message is trying to help you.

The anatomy of a good error message:

Let's look at a real error:

Code	Description	File	Line
CS1002	; expected	Program.cs	5

This error is telling you:

- **What's wrong:** A semicolon is expected
- **Where it's wrong:** Program.cs, Line 5
- **Error code:** CS1002 (you can Google this for more info)

How to use error messages:
1. **Read the description carefully** – It usually tells you exactly what's wrong
2. **Go to the line number** – The error shows you where to look
3. **Look at the surrounding code** – Sometimes the actual mistake is on the line BEFORE the error
4. **Google the error code** – If you don't understand the message, search for "C# CS1002" and you'll find explanations and examples

 **Pro Tip:**

Error messages sometimes point to the line AFTER the actual mistake. If you're missing a semicolon on line 5, the error might appear on line 6 because that's where the compiler realized something was wrong. Always check the line above the error too!

Warnings Are Important Too!

Don't ignore warnings! They're like those little health warnings in a game – they won't stop you immediately, but they might cause problems later.

Common warnings you'll see:

Warning: Variable is assigned but its value is never used

```csharp
int health = 100;  // You created this variable but never used it
```

Warning message you'll see:

Code	Description	Line	Column
CS0219	The variable 'health' is assigned but its value is never used	1	5

This warning tells you that you're wasting memory or might have forgotten to use something you intended to use.

Warning: Unreachable code detected

```
Console.WriteLine("This prints");
return;
Console.WriteLine("This will never execute");  // Warning here!
```

Warning message you'll see:

Code	Description	Line	Column
CS0162	Unreachable code detected	5	1

This tells you that some of your code can never run because you return (exit) before reaching it.

While warnings won't stop your program from compiling, they often point to logic errors or sloppy code. Fix them when you can!

There are many more but I think you get the point.

Quick Troubleshooting Checklist

When you get an error, go through this checklist:

1. **Read the error message carefully** – What is it telling you?
2. **Go to the line number** – Double-click the error in the Error List
3. **Check for common mistakes**:
    - Missing semicolon at the end of the line?
    - Misspelled word or wrong capitalization?
    - Missing or mismatched quotes?
    - Missing opening or closing parenthesis/brace?
4. **Check the line above too** – The error might actually be there
5. **Save and try compiling again** – Sometimes Visual Studio needs a refresh
6. **Google the error code** – Other people have had the same error!

 **Pro Tip:**

Get comfortable with errors. They're not failures – they're the compiler helping you learn. Every error you fix makes you a better programmer!

Fun Experiment: Create Your Own Message

Now it's your turn!

The Prince's Journey: Discovery

The story so far…

As the Prince's eyes adjust to the dim torchlight of the dungeon, he stumbles upon a grim sight, the skeletal remains of a previous prisoner, long forgotten in this forsaken place. Clutched in the bones is a rusty but sturdy sword, perhaps the last possession of some noble soul who tried and failed to escape.

The Prince pulls the blade free, feeling its weight in his hand. It's not much, but it's something, a tool, a weapon, a symbol of hope. Before he can venture deeper into the Vizier's maze of death traps and guards, he needs to test himself. Can he wield this sword effectively? Does he have the skill to face what lies ahead? He looks around the chamber and decides to practice, to prove to himself that he's ready for the challenges that await.

The Challenge

Using whichever tool you set up, create a program that:

1. Displays a title for your own imaginary game
2. Shows at least 3 lines of text describing the game
3. Makes it look interesting using equal signs (=), asterisks (*), or other characters to create borders

Try building this yourself first!

Example Answer

Here's one way to solve it:

```
Console.WriteLine("                                           ");
Console.WriteLine("        ESCAPE FROM CASTLE DOOM            ");
Console.WriteLine("                                           ");
Console.WriteLine("");
Console.WriteLine("You are trapped in a haunted castle.");
Console.WriteLine("Solve puzzles to find the exit.");
Console.WriteLine("Watch out for ghost guards!");
Console.WriteLine("");
Console.WriteLine("Press any key to begin your adventure...");
```

Expected output:

```
  ESCAPE FROM CASTLE DOOM


You are trapped in a haunted castle.
Solve puzzles to find the exit.
Watch out for ghost guards!

Press any key to begin your adventure...
```

Feel free to get creative! Try different characters like asterisks (*), hashes (#), or dashes (-) to make borders. The goal is to make something that looks cool when it runs.

 **Pro Tip:**

You can find cool Unicode box-drawing characters by searching "unicode box drawing" in Google. Characters like ╔, ═, ║, ╚, ╝ and ╗ can make your console output look really professional! Just copy and paste them into your code. They work on all operating systems.

Wrap-up: What You've Learned

Congratulations! You've taken your first steps into the world of programming.

Key Takeaways

- **Chose and set up your development environment** – Whether Visual Studio, VS Code, or Command Line, you're ready to code
- **Installed the necessary tools** – .NET SDK and your chosen editor/IDE
- **Learned about different project types** – Mainly console apps, with a brief look at other options
- **Created your first C# project** – Using wizards, commands, or the command line
- **Wrote and ran your first program** – You made text appear on screen!
- **Understood the compilation process** – How your code becomes a runnable program
- **Learned how to read and fix errors** – The essential skill for every programmer
- **Understood files and extensions** – What they are and why they matter
- **Learned your workflow for future examples** – The process you'll use throughout this book

You might not feel like you've learned a lot yet, but trust me – you've just cleared the first level. In our Prince game, that first level where you learn to run, jump, and pull yourself up onto ledges? That's what you just did. Now you have the basic tools to start building something awesome.

There is a Debugging Appendix closer to the end of the book that go into more detail on how you can find other bugs like logic bugs. Feel free to page there when you get stuck playing with the examples and you can't figure out what the problem is.

Next up, we'll dive into the actual structure of C# code and start making things way more interactive. Get ready – it's about to get fun!

Chapter 1

Code structure

"First, solve the problem. Then, write the code." — John Johnson

Welcome to your first real look at code! Before you can tell a computer what to do, you need to understand how to speak its language. Just like how English has rules about sentences, paragraphs, and punctuation, programming languages have their own structure. In this chapter, you'll learn how C# code is organized, where things go, why they go there, and how to make your code readable not just for the computer, but for other humans (including future you). Every piece of software you've ever used, from your favorite apps to the operating system running on your phone, follows these same fundamental organizational principles. Whether someone's building a music streaming service, a photo editing app, or a weather forecasting system, they all start with the same basic code structure you're about to learn.

You'll also discover why programmers are obsessed with things like formatting, naming, and comments. It might seem picky at first, but here's the truth: code is read far more often than it's written. Professional developers spend most of their time reading and understanding existing code, not writing new code from scratch. A well-structured file with clear names and helpful comments can mean the difference between fixing a bug in five minutes or spending hours trying to figure out what's going on. The habits you build now like organizing your code cleanly, choosing descriptive names, and writing thoughtful comments will save you countless headaches down the road and make you a better programmer from day one.

Core Concepts Covered

- ✓ How programming languages organize code into hierarchical structures
- ✓ Reading and executing code sequentially from top to bottom
- ✓ Using visual formatting and indentation to communicate code organization
- ✓ Documenting code intent for human readers while the computer ignores it
- ✓ Following naming conventions to make code predictable and professional
- ✓ Understanding the difference between code that runs and code that explains

---

The Anatomy of Code

 **Trivia:**

The classic side-scroller Prince of Persia written by Jordan Mechner in 1989 was coded mostly in Assembly, which is like programming with stone tools, and yet the result blew minds. You, on the other hand, have **C#**, a modern, shiny sword compared to that old stick he used. So, let's start your own hero's journey into code!

Alright, let's crack open a C# file and see what makes it tick. Think of code like a recipe, but instead of making cookies, you're telling the computer exactly what to do. And just like how recipes have a specific format (ingredients first, then instructions), code has a structure too.

Here's the most basic C# program, the legendary "Hello World" but slightly modified for our own Prince's story:

```
using System;

namespace PrinceOfProgramming
{
    class Game
    {
        static void Main(string[] args)
        {
            Console.WriteLine("The Prince awakens...");
        }
    }
}
```

Expected Output:

```
The Prince awakens...
```

Now, I know what you're thinking: "That's a lot of weird words just to say 'The Prince awakens...'" You're not wrong! But each part has a purpose. Let's break it down piece by piece.

Breaking Down the Code Palace

The `using` Directive

```
using System;
```

Think of `using` like opening your toolbox before starting a project. `System` is a collection of pre-built tools (we call them "libraries") that Microsoft gives you for free. In this case, we need `System` because it contains `Console`, which lets us write text to that black screen (we'll get to that in a bit).

In game terms, imagine you're about to start building a level for your Prince. You'd need access to your sprite editor, your tile map tools, and your animation frames. The `using` statement is like saying, "Hey, I'm going to need my animation tools for this level."

The `namespace` Keyword

```
namespace PrinceOfProgramming
{
    // Everything else goes in here
}
```

A namespace is like a folder that keeps your code organized. When game developers work on a game, they usually have different folders for enemy sprites, player animations, and level designs. A namespace does the same thing in code, it groups related stuff together.

Namespaces help prevent confusion. Imagine you create something called `Timer` for your program, but Microsoft also has something called `Timer`. How does the computer know which one you mean? Namespaces solve this problem by giving everything a "last name":

```
using System.Timers.Timer;        // Microsoft's Timer
using MyGame.Timer;               // Your Timer
```

For now, you can name it whatever you want. I called mine `PrinceOfProgramming` because, well, we're learning to program while thinking about that awesome Prince.

Notice those curly braces: { }? They're super important! Everything between an opening "{" and closing "}" belongs together. Think of them like the walls of a room where everything inside the room is part of that room.

 **Pro Tip:**

The standard convention is to name namespaces after your project or company. For example, Microsoft uses `Microsoft.Something`, while a company's inventory software might use `MyCorp.Inventory`. This helps everyone know where code came from.

The `class` Keyword

```
class Game
{
    // Your code goes here
}
```

A class is like a blueprint. In our Prince game we should have a blueprint for "Guard" to define how guards look, how they move, how much health they have, and what happens when they get hit by your sword. Every guard in our game is then created from that same blueprint. More about classes later.

For now, just know that `class Game` is our main blueprint, and we'll put all our starting code inside it.

Pro Tip:

Class names should start with a capital letter and describe what the class represents. `Game`, `Player`, `Enemy`, and `TreasureChest` are all good class names. `thing`, `stuff`, or `code1` are terrible names. Future you will thank you for using good names.

The `Main` Method

```
static void Main(string[] args)
{
    Console.WriteLine("The Prince awakens...");
}
```

Here's the big one: `Main` is where your program starts. Every C# program needs exactly one `Main` method, and when you run your program, the computer says, "Okay, where's the `Main` method?" and starts there.

Think of `Main` as the "START" button on any program. When you boot up a game, the game doesn't randomly jump to level 7, it starts at the beginning and runs in order. Same with your code!

Don't worry too much about `static void` and `string[] args` right now. For now, just know they need to be there. We'll cover what they mean later when it makes more sense.

Inside `Main`, we have:

```
Console.WriteLine("The Prince awakens...");
```

`Console.WriteLine` is a command that writes text to the console (that black screen where your program runs) and then moves to the next line. Whatever you put inside the quotation marks will appear on the screen. It's like the text boxes in old adventure games!

Top to Bottom: The Code Execution Highway

Here's a crucial concept: **code runs from top to bottom, one line at a time**, just like reading a book. The computer doesn't skip around unless you specifically tell it to.

Let's see this in action:

```
namespace PrinceOfProgramming
{
    class Game
    {
        static void Main(string[] args)
        {
            Console.WriteLine("Level 1: The Prison");
            Console.WriteLine("You pull the lever...");
            Console.WriteLine("The gate slowly opens.");
            Console.WriteLine("You step forward into the darkness.");
        }
    }
}
```

Expected Output:

```
Level 1: The Prison
You pull the lever...
The gate slowly opens.
You step forward into the darkness.
```

As we can see from the output Line 1, then line 2, then line 3, then line 4. Always starting at the top and going down in sequence.

This is how all programs and games that to react to user input work. For example, every frame a game need to:

1. Check for player input
2. Update the Prince's position
3. Check for collisions
4. Update enemy positions
5. Draw everything on screen
6. Wait until it's time for the next frame
7. Repeat

Your code works the same way, step by step and in order.

 **Pro Tip:**

The computer is incredibly literal. It does *exactly* what you tell it to do, in *exactly* the order you tell it. If your code isn't working, 99% of the time it's because you told the computer to do the wrong thing, not because the computer messed up. This is actually good news—it means bugs are fixable!

Curly Braces: The Indentation Dance

Curly braces are your code's fences. They show exactly where things start and end. I personally like lining up my opening and closing braces so they're easy to follow. Other styles exist, and that's okay, but clear code is always better than clever-looking code:

```
namespace PrinceOfProgramming
{
    class Game
    {
        static void Main(string[] args)
        {
            Console.WriteLine("Good alignment!");
        }
    }
}
```

See how each { has a matching } directly below it? And notice how everything inside is indented (pushed to the right)? This isn't just to look pretty, it helps you see the structure at a glance.

Here's what bad formatting looks like:

```
namespace PrinceOfProgramming { class Game { static void Main(string[] args) {
Console.WriteLine("This works but hurts to read"); } } }
```

Technically, this runs fine. The computer doesn't care about spacing. But humans? We care a LOT. Reading this is like trying to play a game when all the walls and floors look the same. Technically possible, but why would you do that to yourself?

Imagine you're building a trap mechanism. There are pressure plates that trigger spikes. In code, that might look like:

```
if (princeLandsOnPressurePlate)
{
    TriggerSpikes();
    PlaySound("spikes.wav");
    _princeHealth = _princeHealth - 1;
}
```

The braces show you that all three things happen *only* when the Prince lands on the pressure plate. Good formatting makes it obvious what belongs together.

Comments: Notes to Your Future Self

Comments are lines in your code that the computer completely ignores. They're for us humans, for you when you come back to your code later and think, "What was I doing here?". And yes, for other humans as well when you work in a team, so don't use comments that only you can understand.

There are two types of comments in C#:

Single-Line Comments

```
// This is a comment. The computer ignores this line completely.
Console.WriteLine("This runs!"); // You can also put comments at the end of lines
```

Everything after // on that line is ignored.

Multi-Line Comments

```
/*
This is a multi-line comment.
I can write as much as I want here.
The computer will ignore all of this.
Useful for longer explanations!
*/
Console.WriteLine("This runs!");
```

Everything between /* and */ is ignored, even if it spans multiple lines.

When to Use Comments

Comments are great for explaining *why* you did something, not *what* you did. Here's an example:

 **Bad comment:**

```
// Add 1 to health
health = health + 1;
```

We can already see you're adding 1 to health. The comment doesn't help.

 **Good comment:**

```
// The Prince starts with 3 health, but play testers kept dying on Level 1
// so we are secretly giving player 1 extra health here
health = health + 1;
```

Now *that's* useful information!

Where to Place Comments

Good comments live right above or next to the code they're explaining:

```
// Check if the prince landed on a spike trap
if (currentTileType == "spikes")
{
    princeHealth = princeHealth - 1;  // Ouch!
}
```

Avoid putting comments far away from what they explain, that will make things confusing when you're scrolling around. And when code gets modified it might even lose its position and then it's really confusing.

When NOT to Use Comments

Keep this in mind, the best code barely needs comments because it should explain itself. When you decide on the name for a variable, method or class, always try to give it a name that explains exactly what its purpose is.

Here we need a comment because code is unclear:

```
int t = 60;  // Time limit in seconds
```

Here the code is self-explanatory!

```
int timeLimitInSeconds = 60;
```

The second version doesn't need a comment because the variable name tells you everything! This is called "clean code", code that reads like English and require no comments to explain what it is or what's its doing.

Pro Tip:

If you find yourself writing many comments to explain what your code does, it might mean your code is too complicated. Try using better variable names or breaking complex code into smaller, simpler pieces. Comments should explain the "why," not the "what."

The Commenting-Out Trick

Sometimes you want to temporarily skip some code without deleting it. Just comment it out!

```
Console.WriteLine("Level 1 starts...");
// Console.WriteLine("Playing intro music..."); // Not ready yet, add this later
Console.WriteLine("The gate opens.");
```

When writing code this is super common. Sometimes you just want to test using a different method, just comment current method and add the new one. You can just remove the comments when you're done and the code will be like it was before. Or in our Prince's case, maybe you're testing a level and don't want to sit through the intro cut scene every time. Just comment it out temporarily!

Naming Conventions: The Rules of the Road

Programmers follow certain naming rules to keep things consistent. It's like how in English, we start sentences with capital letters, it's a convention that makes code easier to read.

PascalCase

Used for classes, methods, and namespaces. Every word starts with a capital letter and when it has multiple words then each new word is capitalized (you can't use spaced in names):

```
class EnemyGuard        // Good!
class enemyguard        // Nope
class enemy_guard       // Also nope for classes
```

camelCase

Used for variables (we'll cover these in the next chapter). First word is lowercase, then every word after starts with a capital:

```
int princeHealth        // Good!
int PrinceHealth        // Nope, that's PascalCase
int prince_health       // Nope, that's snake_case (used in Python, not C#)
```

Make Names Descriptive

Your code should read almost like English.

Compare these:

 **Bad naming**

```
int h;
int e;
string n;
```

vs.

 **Good naming**

```
int playerHealth;
int enemyHealth;
string playerName;
```

Which one would you rather come back to a few weeks later when you want to start using those variables?

>  **Pro Tip:**
>
> If you find yourself adding numbers to variable names (like `guard1`, `guard2`, `guard3`), you're probably doing something wrong. There's usually a better way (we'll learn about collections later). The exception is if the numbers mean something specific, like `level1Boss` vs. `level2Boss`.

The Console: Your Testing Ground

Now let's talk about that "`black screen`" aka the console. You might be wondering, "Why are we using this boring text window. It would be so much nicer if we had good looking windows, buttons or controls, maybe even some graphics and sound like when we play as the Prince?"

Great question! The console is like a software developer's sketchpad with many uses.

What Is the Console?

The console (also called a terminal or command prompt) is a text-based window where your program can display output and receive input. It's been around since before graphical user interfaces existed. Remember those old green-text computer screens from 1980s movies.

```
Console.WriteLine("This text appears in the console!");
```

When you run this, a black window pops up with white text. Simple, but incredibly useful.

Why We Use the Console for Learning

Here's why well be using console programs:

1. **Zero Distractions**

    When you're learning the fundamentals like variables, loops and logic you want to focus on the *thinking* part, not on "Why is my sprite showing up in the wrong place?" or "How do I load this image file?"

    When writing a program, you want to make sure it does what it's intended to do. What's the use of having a window with some controls show up but the program crashes the moment you try to click on a button? In a real game for our Prince we don't need to start by drawing the Prince. We first start with logic like this: "If the player is falling, increase falling speed. If falling speed is too high, the player dies." That logic works the same whether it's displayed as fancy graphics or just text that says "You fell and died."

2. Instant Feedback

Want to see if your code works? Run it, and BOOM! instant text output. No need to compile textures, load sprite sheets, or set up a rendering pipeline. You get immediate results:

```
Console.WriteLine("Guard health: 5");
Console.WriteLine("You attack!");
Console.WriteLine("Guard health: 4");
```

Expected Output:

```
Guard health: 5
You attack!
Guard health: 4
```

See? You just simulated combat without drawing a single pixel.

3. Easy Debugging

When something goes wrong (and trust me, things *will* go wrong), the console makes it easy to see what's happening. You can print out values to check your work:

```
int princeHealth = 3;
// Check if it's what you expect
Console.WriteLine("Prince health is: " + princeHealth);
```

This is exactly how professional developers debug their code, even in massive enterprise software and you guessed it games. They print values to logs to see what's going on behind the scenes.

4. The Core Is the Same

Notice that the logic you write for console programs is *exactly the same* as the logic in graphical applications or games. Whether you display "Guard defeated!" in a console or show a fancy animation of a guard falling down, the underlying code is identical:

```
Console.WriteLine("Guard defeated!");
// Console version
// OR
// PlayDefeatAnimation();// Graphics version
```

The `if` statement, the comparison, the logic, it's all the same. We're just using text output instead of graphics for now.

5. Real Programs and even Games Started Here

Many complex software systems start with the console. Creating spikes (doing research and experiments) to see if what they are planning to do will work or not.

Even modern indie hits like Undertale and Hollow Knight started with developers testing their game logic in simple forms before adding the fancy graphics. Toby Fox (creator of

Undertale) prototyped combat mechanics and dialogue systems before ever drawing Flowey's creepy face.

Console vs. Windows vs. Graphics

Think of it this way:

Console Program:

- You enter the dungeon.
- Do you go left or right?
- You press the left button
- You found a health potion!

Application with graphics:

- Shows dungeon room with animated torches
- Displays two doorways
- Player clicks left door
- Shows potion pickup animation

Same logic, different presentation. We'll tinker with some graphics later in a bonus chapter, but for now, the console lets us focus on the thinking part of programming. And this is all you need to learn to program like a pro!

 **Pro Tip:**

Many professional developers still write console programs for testing algorithms, processing data, or creating tools. Command-line utilities are everywhere in game development—build scripts, asset converters, level generators. Learning console programming isn't a step backward; it's learning a tool you'll use forever.

Fun Experiment: Chronicling the Journey

Time to put this knowledge to work!

The Prince's Journey: Finding His Voice

The story so far…

The Prince steadies himself, sword in hand, and begins to navigate the twisting corridors of the dungeon. Stone pillars loom like silent sentries, and passages branch off in every direction. Some leading deeper into darkness, others perhaps toward freedom.

As he moves cautiously forward, testing each step, he realizes something crucial: he needs to understand the layout of this place. Where did he start? Which passages has he already explored? Where might the exit be? Before he can map out an escape route or plan his next move, he must first learn to chronicle his journey, to create a record of his progress through this labyrinth.

He pauses in a quiet alcove, catches his breath, and decides to document the beginning of his tale. If nothing else, should he fall, perhaps someone will find his story and know that he tried.

The Challenge

Create a program that tells a short story about the Prince entering the first level of the dungeon. Use at least 5 `Console.WriteLine` statements, add some comments explaining parts of your story, and make sure your braces are properly aligned.

Try to include:

1. A title for your level
2. Some action happening
3. At least one comment explaining something interesting
4. Proper indentation and brace alignment

Give it a shot before looking at the example answer!

Example Answer

Here's one way to solve it:

```csharp
using System;

namespace PrinceOfProgramming
{
    class Game
    {
        static void Main(string[] args)
        {
            // The beginning of the Prince's journey
            Console.WriteLine("=== LEVEL 1: THE DUNGEONS ===");
            Console.WriteLine("");

            Console.WriteLine("You land gracefully in a dark corridor.");
            Console.WriteLine("The stone floor is cold beneath your feet.");

            // In the actual game, this is where the famous running jump
            // animation would play
            Console.WriteLine("You take a running leap across a chasm...");
            Console.WriteLine("And barely catch the ledge on the other side!");

            Console.WriteLine("");
            Console.WriteLine("Your adventure begins now, Prince.");
        }
    }
}
```

Expected Output:

```
=== LEVEL 1: THE DUNGEONS ===

You land gracefully in a dark corridor.
The stone floor is cold beneath your feet.
You take a running leap across a chasm...
And barely catch the ledge on the other side!

Your adventure begins now, Prince.
```

Notice how the empty `Console.WriteLine("")` adds a blank line for spacing? That's a simple way to make your output more readable!

Wrap-Up: What You've Learned

Congratulations! You just learned the fundamental structure of C# code.

Key Takeaways

- **Code files have a specific structure** with `using` statements, namespaces, classes, and methods
- **The `using` statement lets you access tools** from .NET, external libraries, or your own namespaces
- **Namespaces organize your code** like folders and let you share classes between different files
- **The `Main` method is where every program starts:** It's your application's start button
- **Code runs from top to bottom,** one line at a time, just like reading a book
- **Curly braces { } define scope** and group code together, and we always line them up vertically
- **Comments are for humans**, not computers. We use `//` for single lines and `/* */` for multiple lines
- **Good comments explain "why," not "what"** and clean code should be self-explanatory, not full of comments to try and tell what each variable stores.
- **Naming conventions matter:** We use *PascalCase* for classes and methods and *camelCase* for variables
- **Good names are descriptive,** for example `playerHealth` beats `h` every time
- **The console is your testing ground,** it lets you focus on logic without graphics getting in the way
- **Console programs teach the same skills** as graphical application or games, just without the visual complexity

Think of this as your "code map". Just like how most game levels have a layout, your code has a structure. Master this structure, and you have just picked up the sword you need to get to the next level!

Chapter 2

Variables

"The measure of intelligence is the ability to change." — Albert Einstein

Imagine you're using Spotify and you press play on your favorite song. The app needs to remember which song you're listening to, how far into it you are, your volume level, whether shuffle is on, and dozens of other pieces of information all at the same time. Or think about Instagram: when you scroll through your feed, the app is constantly tracking which post you're viewing, how many likes it has, who posted it, and whether you've already liked it yourself. Every piece of software you use daily, be it your web browser keeping track of open tabs or your phone's calculator remembering your last calculation, they all rely on one fundamental concept: storing and managing information that can change.

This is what variables are all about. They're the foundation of all programming, the basic building blocks that let software remember things and work with data. Without variables, programs would be like a person with no memory, not able to track anything, respond to anything, or do anything useful. In this chapter, you'll learn how to create these memory containers, what types of information they can hold, how to work with different kinds of data, and the rules about where and when you can use them. Master variables, and you're well on your way to understanding how all software really works under the hood.

Core Concepts Covered

✓   Creating named containers to store information your program needs to remember
✓   Understanding different categories of data and choosing the right container for each
✓   Converting between different data types when needed
✓   Working with text and manipulating it in useful ways
✓   Getting input from users and making programs interactive
✓   Tracking time and creating time-based behaviors
✓   Organizing related values into meaningful groups
✓   Understanding where data exists and how long it lives in your program
✓   All types share a common foundation and how to work with any type of data

The Program's Brain Cells

 **Trivia:**

Programmers in the 1960s-70s stored years using only two digits (like "99" for 1999) to save memory — every byte was precious. This seemed fine until people realized that on January 1, 2000, computers would think it was 1900. Banks might calculate you owe 100 years of interest, power grids might shut down, and planes might think their maintenance was overdue by a century. The world spent an estimated $300 billion updating variables from two digits to four digits.

Think about any game when you'd open a potion bottle and your health would instantly go from "basically dead" to "ready to fight guards again"? That potion didn't just magically appear, the game was tracking your health the entire time using something called a **variable**. Variables are basically labeled boxes where your program stores information it needs to remember.

Variables are the foundation of everything you'll ever code. Without them, your program would be like a game character with amnesia that is forgetting everything the moment it happens. Let's look at how these magical boxes work.

Different Data, Different Types

Think of variables as different sized containers for different types of stuff. You wouldn't store your sword in a potion bottle, right? Same deal with variables, different types is needed for different data.

Basic Variable Types

Type	What It Stores	Example Values	Common Uses
int	Whole numbers (integers)	42, -7, 0, 1000	Age, score, level number, enemy count
double	Decimal numbers	3.14, -2.5, 127.89	Pi, damage multiplier, precise positions
float	Decimal numbers (less precise)	5.5f, 1.25f	Quick calculations, less precise than double
bool	True or false	true, false	Is deleted? Is door locked? Is player alive?
char	Single character	'A', '5', '!'	Keyboard input, simple text symbols (In single quotes)
string	Text (multiple characters)	"Hello", "Prince"	Name, messages, dialogue (In double quotes)

These are the basic types you'll use most often. There are many more types and if you want to see them you can take a look in the Quick Reference chapter at the end of the book, but for now this is all you'll need.

Let's see them in action:

```
int playerHealth = 100;
int currentLevel = 3;
int enemiesDefeated = 0;

double playerSpeed = 5.5;
double damageMultiplier = 1.25;

float jumpHeight = 2.5f;

bool hasSword = true;
bool isAlive = true;
bool doorIsLocked = false;

char playerInput = 'A';
char rank = 'S';

string playerName = "Prince";
string message = "The door opens with a creak";
```

These just store values, so there is no output yet, but we'll use them soon!

In most games your health would be an `int`, whether you're hanging from a ledge would be a `bool`, and your exact position on screen might be a `double` for smooth movement.

>  **Pro Tip:**
>
> Notice that float values have an f after the number (like 2.5f)? That tells C# it's a float and not a double. Most of the time, just use double—it's more accurate and you don't need the f. Use float only when you're doing heavy 3D graphics and need to save memory for example.

Naming Things: The Hardest Problem in Programming

Here's the deal: you can name variables almost anything, but that doesn't mean you should. Let's compare:

 **Bad Names:**

```
int x = 100;
int a = 3;
bool b = true;
double spd = 5.5;
string n = "Prince";
```

What does these mean? No clue. You'll forget in five minutes, and anyone else looking at your code will be completely lost. Even abbreviations like spd can be confusing, is it speed or spawned or maybe special damage?

 **Good Names:**

```
int playerHealth = 100;
int currentLevel = 3;
bool hasSword = true;
double movementSpeed = 5.5;
string playerName = "Prince";
```

NOW we're talking! These names tell you exactly what they're storing. When you're debugging at 2 AM trying to figure out why the Prince keeps falling through the floor, you'll thank yourself for using clear names.

Naming Rules in C#:
- Start with a letter or underscore (not a number)
- Use camelCase for variables (firstWordLowercase, restCapitalized)
- No spaces (use camelCase instead: playerHealth not player health)
- Be descriptive but not ridiculously long (enemyCount is better than theNumberOfEnemiesCurrentlyInTheRoom)
- Avoid single letters except maybe for loops (which we'll cover later)

Imagine working on some code and seeing variable with names like this:

```
int x = 5;  // What is x? The prince's health? The level number? A secret?
```

vs.

```
int guardAttackDamage = 5;  // Ah! That's how much damage a guard's sword does!
```

See the difference? Good names make your code readable, which means you can actually understand what you wrote last week!

 **Pro Tip:**

If you can't come up with a good name for a variable, that might mean you don't fully understand what it's supposed to do. Take a moment to think about its purpose—the right name will help you (and others) understand your code better.

Strings: Your Text Holder

Okay, time for one of the most useful types: **strings**. A string stores any text, words, sentences, messages, anything made of characters. Think of every message in any game ("Press Button to Continue") any dialogue box, those are all strings.

Creating Strings

Here's a few examples of how to set some string values. These do nothing more than just storing the text inside the string variable so there will be no output yet.

```
string playerName = "Prince";
string message = "The door opens with a creak";
string gameTitle = "Prince of Programming";
```

Concatenation (Joining Strings with +)

You can stick strings together using the + operator:

```
string playerName = "Prince";
string message = "Welcome, " + playerName + "!";
Console.WriteLine(message);
```

Expected Output:

```
Welcome, Prince!
```

This works, but it gets messy fast when you're combining lots of things:

```
int health = 100;
int level = 3;
string status = "Player: "+ playerName + " | Health: " + health + " | Level: " + level;
Console.WriteLine(status);
```

Expected Output:

```
Player: Prince | Health: 100 | Level: 3
```

See how cluttered that looks with all those plus signs and quotes? There's a better way called string interpolation.

String Interpolation (The Better Way)

Instead of all those plus signs, use string interpolation with $ and curly braces:

```
string playerName = "Prince";
int playerHealth = 100;
int level = 3;
string status = $"Player: {playerName} | Health: {playerHealth} | Level: {level}";
Console.WriteLine(status);
```

Expected Output:

```
Player: Prince | Health: 100 | Level: 3
```

Way cleaner and easier to read, right? The $ before the quotes tells C# "I'm going to put variables inside this string," and anything in {} gets replaced with the variable's value.

Here's another example of what you might see in our Prince's adventure:

```
int timeRemaining = 45;
string urgentMessage = $"You have {timeRemaining} minutes to save the princess!";
Console.WriteLine(urgentMessage);
```

Expected Output:

```
You have 45 minutes to save the princess!
```

Escaping Special Characters

Sometimes you need to include special characters in your strings. For example, we use quotes to tell C# that the next text is inside a string. But what if we want to have quotes inside our string? C# will think you are stopping the string and throw a syntax error.

In cases like these, and other we use the backslash \ as our escape character, to tell C# to use character as the actual text:

```
string dialogue = "The guard shouts, \"Stop right there!\"";
Console.WriteLine(dialogue);
```

Expected Output:

```
The guard shouts, "Stop right there!"
```

Here are some common escape sequences:
- \" - Double quote
- \n - New line (like pressing Enter)
- \t - Tab
- \\ - Backslash itself

Example with new lines:

```
string gameOver = "GAME OVER\nYou were crushed by spikes\nBetter luck next time!";
Console.WriteLine(gameOver);
```

Expected Output:

```
GAME OVER
You were crushed by spikes
Better luck next time!
```

You can also create multi-line strings that don't need all the special new line characters using the @ symbol (called a verbatim string):

```
string asciiArt = @"
   /\
  /  \
 / /\ \
/ ____ \
/_/    \_\
";
Console.WriteLine(asciiArt);
```

Expected Output:

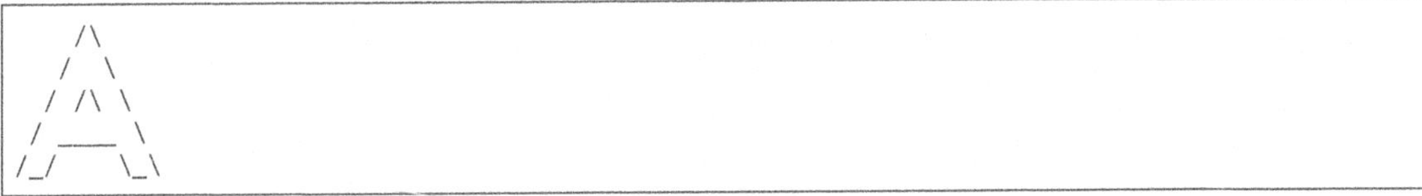

Common String Methods

Strings come with built-in superpowers (methods) that let you manipulate them.

To use them just add a dot (.) to the end of the string variable name and the helper method you want to use:

```
string weapon = "Sword";

// Make it LOUD (Uppercase)
string loud = weapon.ToUpper();
Console.WriteLine(loud);

// Make it quiet (Lowercase)
string quiet = weapon.ToLower();
Console.WriteLine(quiet);

// How long is it?
int length = weapon.Length;
Console.WriteLine($"The word is {length} characters long");

// Check if it contains something
bool hasSword = weapon.Contains("Sword");
Console.WriteLine($"Has sword: {hasSword}");

// Replace parts of it
string newWeapon = weapon.Replace("Sword", "Dagger");
Console.WriteLine(newWeapon);

// Remove extra spaces
string messy = "  Prince  ";
string clean = messy.Trim();
Console.WriteLine($"Before: '{messy}'");
Console.WriteLine($"After: '{clean}'");
```

Expected Output

```
SWORD
sword
The word is 5 characters long
Has sword: True
Dagger
Before: '  Prince  '
After: 'Prince'
```

These methods are incredibly useful. Imagine checking if a player typed "NORTH" or "north" or "North". If you use normal C# comparison it will see the difference in casing (upper-case and lower-case letters).

For all these you can use .ToLower() to make them all the same before comparing:

```
Console.WriteLine("Which direction? (North, South, East, West)");
string input = Console.ReadLine();
string direction = input.ToLower();

if (direction == "north")
{
    Console.WriteLine("You head north into the darkness...");
}
```

Expected Output: if you type "NORTH" or "North" or "north")

```
Which direction? (North, South, East, West)
NORTH
You head north into the darkness...
```

Well look into the `if` statement later but it just checks if a condition is true. In this case it checks if two values are the same using the `==` equals to operator. More about this in the Logic chapter!

 **Pro Tip:**

Strings in C# are **immutable**, which means once you create them, they can't be changed. When you do `weapon.ToUpper()`, it doesn't change the original—it creates a NEW string. This is actually a good thing for preventing bugs, but if you need to build up a long string piece by piece (like generating a complex game map), look into `StringBuilder` later on.

Console Input: Interacting with The User

Until now far we've been using hardcoded values in our variables. But most programs including games need to be interactive!

That's where `Console.ReadLine()` is used to let the user provide input:

```
Console.WriteLine("What is your name, brave adventurer?");
string playerName = Console.ReadLine();
Console.WriteLine($"Welcome, {playerName}!");
```

Expected Output: (if you type "Ali")

```
What is your name, brave adventurer?
Ali
Welcome, Ali!
```

`Console.ReadLine()` stops and waits for the player to type something and press Enter. Whatever they type gets stored in your variable as a string.

Here's a simple interaction:

```
Console.WriteLine("Enter a command (LOOK, TAKE, JUMP):");
string command = Console.ReadLine();
string cleanCommand = command.ToUpper().Trim();

if (cleanCommand == "LOOK")
{
    Console.WriteLine("You see a dusty corridor with ancient stone walls.");
}
else if (cleanCommand == "TAKE")
{
```

```
    Console.WriteLine("You pick up the golden sword!");
}
else if (cleanCommand == "JUMP")
{
    Console.WriteLine("You leap across the gap!");
}
else
{
    Console.WriteLine("Unknown command.");
}
```

Expected Output: (if you type " look ")

```
Enter a command (LOOK, TAKE, JUMP):
  look
You see a dusty corridor with ancient stone walls.
```

Notice how we used `.ToUpper().Trim()`? This means no matter how the player types it, either "look", "LOOK" or even " Look " with spaces, it will all work!

 **Pro Tip:**

`Console.ReadLine()` always returns a string, even if the player types a number. If you need to use that number for calculations, you'll need to convert it (coming up next!).

Type Casting: When Variables Switch Roles

Here's a common problem: you ask the player "How much health do you have?" and they type "100". But `Console.ReadLine()` gives you the *text* "100" (string type), not the *number* 100 (int type). You can't do math with text! So you need to convert the text to a number format first.

This is where **type casting** (also called **conversion** or **parsing**) comes in. You convert the text into a number. C# gives us several ways to do this, and each has its place.

Parse Method (The Direct Approach)

The `Parse` method takes a string and converts it directly to the type you need:

```
Console.WriteLine("Enter your starting health:");
string healthText = Console.ReadLine();
int health = int.Parse(healthText);

Console.WriteLine($"Your health is {health}");
health = health + 50;
Console.WriteLine($"After drinking a potion, your health is {health}");
```

Expected Output: (if you type "100")

```
Enter your starting health:
100
Your health is 100
After drinking a potion, your health is 150
```

You will notice that each type has its own Parse method:

```
int wholeNumber = int.Parse("42");
double decimalNumber = double.Parse("3.14");
float smallDecimal = float.Parse("2.5");
bool isTrue = bool.Parse("true");

Console.WriteLine($"Integer: {wholeNumber}");
Console.WriteLine($"Double: {decimalNumber}");
Console.WriteLine($"Float: {smallDecimal}");
Console.WriteLine($"Boolean: {isTrue}");
```

Expected Output:

```
Integer: 42
Double: 3.14
Float: 2.5
Boolean: True
```

What Happens If They Type Garbage?

If someone types "pizza" when you ask for a number, `int.Parse()` will crash your program with an error. For now, just trust your players to type numbers when you ask for numbers. We'll learn how to handle bad input safely in the Exception Handling chapter.

Boxing (Converting Between Value Types)

I know it sounds like it, but there's no fighting involved here. Sometimes you need to convert between different number types. This is called **boxing** (when converting to a more general type) or **unboxing** (when converting to a specific type):

```
int playerHealth = 100;
double preciseHealth = playerHealth;  // int to double (automatic, no problem)
Console.WriteLine($"Precise health: {preciseHealth}");

double playerSpeed = 5.75;
int roundedSpeed = (int)playerSpeed;  // double to int (needs explicit cast)
Console.WriteLine($"Rounded speed: {roundedSpeed}");
```

Expected Output:

```
Precise health: 100
Rounded speed: 5
```

Notice that when converting from `double` to `int`, you need to put the type in parentheses like `(int)`. This is because you're losing information (the decimal part). C# wants you to be explicit about it so you know what's happening.

> **Pro Tip:**
>
> When converting from `double` to `int`, it doesn't round—it just chops off the decimal part. So, 5.9 becomes 5, not 6. If you want to round properly, use `Math.Round()` which we'll cover in the Logic section.

Convert Class (The Flexible Approach)

The `Convert` class is like a Swiss Army knife for type conversion. It's more forgiving than Parse and handles some edge cases better:

```
string numberText = "42";
int number = Convert.ToInt32(numberText);
Console.WriteLine($"Converted number: {number}");

string decimalText = "3.14";
double decimalValue = Convert.ToDouble(decimalText);
Console.WriteLine($"Converted decimal: {decimalValue}");

string boolText = "true";
bool boolValue = Convert.ToBoolean(boolText);
Console.WriteLine($"Converted boolean: {boolValue}");
```

Expected Output:

```
Converted number: 42
Converted decimal: 3.14
Converted boolean: True
```

The cool thing about `Convert` is that it can also handle `null` (empty/nothing) values better:

```
string emptyText = "";
// int resultParse = int.Parse(emptyText);   // This will crash!

string nullText = null;
int resultWithNull = Convert.ToInt32(nullText);   // This returns 0 instead of crashing!
Console.WriteLine($"Result: {resultWithNull}");
```

Expected Output:

```
Result: 0
```

Here's a practical example using all three approaches:

```
Console.WriteLine("=== CHARACTER CREATION ===");
```

```csharp
// Using Parse for direct conversion
Console.WriteLine("Enter your starting level (1-10):");
int level = int.Parse(Console.ReadLine());

// Using Convert for safety
Console.WriteLine("Enter your strength stat:");
string strengthInput = Console.ReadLine();
int strength = Convert.ToInt32(strengthInput);

// Using casting for number type conversion
double experiencePoints = 1547.89;
int displayExp = (int)experiencePoints;

Console.WriteLine($"\nCharacter Stats:");
Console.WriteLine($"Level: {level}");
Console.WriteLine($"Strength: {strength}");
Console.WriteLine($"Experience: {displayExp} XP");
```

Expected Output: *(if you type "5" and "18")*

```
=== CHARACTER CREATION ===
Enter your starting level (1-10):
5
Enter your strength stat:
18

Character Stats:
Level: 5
Strength: 18
Experience: 1547 XP
```

When to Use Each:

- **Parse**: When you're sure the input is valid and want it to crash if it's not (helps you find bugs)
- **Casting**: When converting between number types (int to double, double to int, etc.)
- **Convert**: When you want a bit more safety and don't mind default values for bad input

 **Pro Tip:**

There's also `int.TryParse()` which doesn't crash if the input is invalid — it just returns `false`. But that's a bit advanced for now. Stick with `Parse` and `Convert` for now.

Date and Time Types

Most programs need to work with dates and time. Games also track time to for example know how long you've been playing, when events happen, cooldown timers etc. If our Prince game for example only gave you 60-minutes to save the princess, then we have two main types in C# to work with time: **DateTime** and **TimeSpan**.

DateTime Type (Specific Points in Time)

A `DateTime` represents a specific moment, for example "January 15, 2025 at 3:45 PM" or "right now":

```csharp
DateTime now = DateTime.Now;
Console.WriteLine($"Current time: {now}");

DateTime gameStartTime = new DateTime(2025, 1, 15, 14, 30, 0);
Console.WriteLine($"Game started: {gameStartTime}");
```

Expected Output: *(will vary based on when you run it)*

```
Current time: 11/22/2025 10:45:23 AM
Game started: 1/15/2025 2:30:00 PM
```

You can access different parts of a DateTime:

```csharp
DateTime now = DateTime.Now;
Console.WriteLine($"Year: {now.Year}");
Console.WriteLine($"Month: {now.Month}");
Console.WriteLine($"Day: {now.Day}");
Console.WriteLine($"Hour: {now.Hour}");
Console.WriteLine($"Minute: {now.Minute}");
Console.WriteLine($"Second: {now.Second}");
```

Example Output:

```
Year: 2025
Month: 11
Day: 22
Hour: 10
Minute: 45
Second: 23
```

In a game, you might use DateTime to track when the player started a level:

```csharp
DateTime levelStartTime = DateTime.Now;
Console.WriteLine($"Level started at: {levelStartTime}");
Console.WriteLine("Fighting guards...");
Console.WriteLine("Solving puzzles...");
DateTime levelEndTime = DateTime.Now;
Console.WriteLine($"Level completed at: {levelEndTime}");
```

Example Output:

```
Level started at: 11/22/2025 10:45:23 AM
Fighting guards...
Solving puzzles...
Level completed at: 11/22/2025 10:47:15 AM
```

TimeSpan Type (Durations of Time)

A `TimeSpan` represents a length of time, for example "5 minutes" or "30 seconds". You can create them directly or by subtracting two DateTimes:

```
TimeSpan fiveMinutes = TimeSpan.FromMinutes(5);
Console.WriteLine($"Duration: {fiveMinutes}");

TimeSpan thirtySeconds = TimeSpan.FromSeconds(30);
Console.WriteLine($"Duration: {thirtySeconds}");

TimeSpan oneHour = new TimeSpan(1, 0, 0);  // hours, minutes, seconds
Console.WriteLine($"Duration: {oneHour}");
```

Expected Output:

```
Duration: 00:05:00
Duration: 00:00:30
Duration: 01:00:00
```

Here's something cool, you can subtract DateTimes to get a TimeSpan:

```
DateTime levelStart = DateTime.Now;
Console.WriteLine("Prince enters the dungeon...");
// Imagine some gameplay happens here
DateTime levelEnd = DateTime.Now.AddMinutes(2);  // Simulating 2 minutes passing

TimeSpan timeTaken = levelEnd - levelStart;
Console.WriteLine($"Level completed in: {timeTaken.TotalMinutes} minutes");
Console.WriteLine($"Or: {timeTaken.TotalSeconds} seconds");
```

Expected Output:

```
Prince enters the dungeon...
Level completed in: 2 minutes
Or: 120 seconds
```

Let's create a countdown timer for our Prince's escape:

```
int timeLimit = 60;  // 60 minutes to save the princess
DateTime gameStart = DateTime.Now;
DateTime deadline = gameStart.AddMinutes(timeLimit);

Console.WriteLine($"You have {timeLimit} minutes to save the princess!");
Console.WriteLine($"Current time: {gameStart}");
Console.WriteLine($"Deadline: {deadline}");

TimeSpan remaining = deadline - DateTime.Now;
Console.WriteLine($"Time remaining: {remaining.TotalMinutes:F1} minutes");
```

Expected Output:

```
You have 60 minutes to save the princess!
Current time: 11/22/2025 10:45:23 AM
Deadline: 11/22/2025 11:45:23 AM
Time remaining: 60.0 minutes
```

You can format TimeSpan values to show just what you need:

```csharp
TimeSpan playTime = new TimeSpan(2, 34, 15);  // 2 hours, 34 minutes, 15 seconds
Console.WriteLine($"Total play time: {playTime}");
Console.WriteLine($"Just hours: {playTime.Hours}");
Console.WriteLine($"Just minutes: {playTime.Minutes}");
Console.WriteLine($"Just seconds: {playTime.Seconds}");
Console.WriteLine($"Total in minutes: {playTime.TotalMinutes:F2}");
```

Expected Output:

```
Total play time: 02:34:15
Just hours: 2
Just minutes: 34
Just seconds: 15
Total in minutes: 154.25
```

Here's a practical example tracking ability cooldowns:

```csharp
DateTime lastSpecialAttack = DateTime.Now;
TimeSpan cooldownDuration = TimeSpan.FromSeconds(10);

Console.WriteLine("You use your special attack!");
Console.WriteLine($"Used at: {lastSpecialAttack}");

// Check if we can use it again
DateTime canUseAgainAt = lastSpecialAttack.Add(cooldownDuration);
TimeSpan timeUntilReady = canUseAgainAt - DateTime.Now;

if (timeUntilReady.TotalSeconds > 0)
{
    Console.WriteLine($"Special attack cooling down...");
    Console.WriteLine($"Ready in: {timeUntilReady.TotalSeconds:F1} seconds");
}
else
{
    Console.WriteLine("Special attack is ready!");
}
```

Expected Output:

```
You use your special attack!
Used at: 11/22/2025 10:45:23 AM
Special attack cooling down...
Ready in: 10.0 seconds
```

 **Pro Tip:**

For simple countdown timers in games, you'll often use a `Stopwatch` class (which we'll learn about later), but `DateTime` and `TimeSpan` are perfect for tracking when things happened and calculating durations.

Enums: Giving Names to Numbers

Okay, this is where things get cool. Sometimes you need to track states or options, and using numbers gets confusing fast. Check this out:

 **The Confusing Way:**

```csharp
int direction = 0;  // What does 0 mean? Up? Down? Left?
int direction = 1;  // And what's 1?
int direction = 2;  // I'm already lost...
```

 **The Clear Way with Enums:**

```csharp
enum Direction
{
    Up,
    Down,
    Left,
    Right
}

Direction playerDirection = Direction.Right;
Console.WriteLine($"The prince is moving {playerDirection}");
```

Expected Output:

```
The prince is moving Right
```

An **enum** (short for enumeration) lets you give meaningful names to numbers. Behind the scenes, `Direction.Up` is actually 0, `Direction.Down` is 1, and so on. But you don't need to remember that, you can just use the names!

Here's an example for our Prince's adventure:

```csharp
enum GameState
{
    MainMenu,
    Playing,
    Paused,
    GameOver
}

GameState currentState = GameState.Playing;

if (currentState == GameState.Playing)
{
    Console.WriteLine("The adventure continues!");
}
else if (currentState == GameState.Paused)
{
    Console.WriteLine("Game is paused. Press P to resume.");
}
```

Expected Output:

```
The adventure continues!
```

Enums make your code way more readable. Instead of `if (state == 2)`, you write `if (currentState == GameState.GameOver)`. Future you will be grateful. As we continue you will notice that a lot of what a programmer do is to ensure they can work on code later without needing to relearn what the code is doing.

In SimCity, the game tracks whether each zone is residential, commercial, or industrial. That's a perfect use for an enum:

```csharp
enum ZoneType
{
    Residential,
    Commercial,
    Industrial,
    Park
}

ZoneType newZone = ZoneType.Residential;
Console.WriteLine($"Building a {newZone} zone");
```

Expected Output:

```
Building a Residential zone
```

You can also manually set the backing numbers if you want:

```csharp
enum EnemyType
{
    Guard = 1,
    SkeletonWarrior = 2,
    Boss = 10
}

EnemyType currentEnemy = EnemyType.SkeletonWarrior;
int enemyValue = (int)currentEnemy;
Console.WriteLine($"Fighting: {currentEnemy}");
Console.WriteLine($"Enemy difficulty: {enemyValue}");
```

Expected Output:

```
Fighting: SkeletonWarrior
Enemy difficulty: 2
```

 **Pro Tip:**

Enums are great for anything that has a fixed set of options: Days of the week, months, difficulty levels, directions, item types, enemy types, quest status, etc. If you find yourself using magic numbers (a number where you don't know what it means) like `if (status == 3)`, that's a sign you should probably be using an `enum` instead!

Tuples: Sometimes Variables Need a Buddy

Sometimes you need to return or store multiple related values together, but creating a whole new class seems like overkill.

That's where **tuples** are handy, they're like a quick package deal for grouping things together:

```csharp
(string name, int health) player = ("Prince", 100);
Console.WriteLine($"Player: {player.name}, Health: {player.health}");
```

Expected Output:

```
Player: Prince, Health: 100
```

You can also create tuples without naming the parts:

```csharp
(string, int, bool) playerInfo = ("Prince", 100, true);
Console.WriteLine($"Name: {playerInfo.Item1}");
Console.WriteLine($"Health: {playerInfo.Item2}");
Console.WriteLine($"Has Sword: {playerInfo.Item3}");
```

Expected Output:

```
Name: Prince
Health: 100
Has Sword: True
```

But named tuples are way more readable, so use those when you can.

You can also deconstruct tuples into separate variables:

```csharp
(string enemyName, int enemyHealth, int attackPower) enemy = ("Guard", 50, 15);

// Deconstruct the tuple
string name = enemy.enemyName;
int health = enemy.enemyHealth;
int attack = enemy.attackPower;

Console.WriteLine($"Enemy: {name}");
Console.WriteLine($"Health: {health}");
Console.WriteLine($"Attack: {attack}");
```

Expected Output:

```
Enemy: Guard
Health: 50
Attack: 15
```

Or even shorter:

```
(string enemyName, int enemyHealth, int attackPower) enemy = ("Guard", 50, 15);
(string name, int health, int attack) = enemy;

Console.WriteLine($"{name} has {health} HP and {attack} attack power");
```

Expected Output:

```
Guard has 50 HP and 15 attack power
```

 **When to Use Tuples:**

- When you need to quickly group a few related values
- When creating a full class would be overkill
- For temporary data structures
- For returning multiple values from a method (we'll cover methods later!)

 **When NOT to Use Tuples:**

- When you have more than 4-5 values (gets messy)
- When the data represents an important concept that deserves its own class
- When you need to add behavior/methods to the data

 **Pro Tip:**

Tuples are super handy for quick and dirty data grouping, but if you find yourself passing the same tuple structure around a lot, that's a sign you should probably create a proper class for it. We'll learn about classes soon!

Null Types: Handling *"Nothing"* in C#

Sometimes a variable needs to represent "nothing" or "no value." That's where **null** comes in. But there's a catch: basic types like `int`, `double`, and `bool` can't be null, they always have to have a value. If you need them to be able to hold "nothing," you need to make them **nullable** by adding a ? after the type.

Regular Types cannot be set to null:

```csharp
int playerHealth = 100;
playerHealth = null;  // This won't work! Compiler error!
```

However nullable types can be set to `null`!:

```csharp
int? playerHealth = 100;
playerHealth = null;  // This works!

if (playerHealth == null)
{
    Console.WriteLine("Health is unknown");
}
else
{
    Console.WriteLine($"Health: {playerHealth}");
}
```

Expected Output:

```
Health is unknown
```

Here's an example where null makes some sense as a value:

```csharp
int? lastCheckpointLevel = null;  // Player hasn't reached a checkpoint yet

Console.WriteLine("Starting new game...");
if (lastCheckpointLevel == null)
{
    Console.WriteLine("No checkpoint found. Starting from Level 1.");
}
else
{
    Console.WriteLine($"Resuming from checkpoint at Level {lastCheckpointLevel}");
}

// Later in the game...
lastCheckpointLevel = 5;
Console.WriteLine($"Checkpoint saved at Level {lastCheckpointLevel}!");
```

Expected Output:

```
Starting new game...
No checkpoint found. Starting from Level 1.
Checkpoint saved at Level 5!
```

You can check if a nullable type has a value using the `HasValue` property:

```csharp
int? enemyCount = null;

if (enemyCount.HasValue)
{
    Console.WriteLine($"There are {enemyCount.Value} enemies");
}
else
{
```

```
    Console.WriteLine("Enemy count unknown");
}

enemyCount = 3;

if (enemyCount.HasValue)
{
    Console.WriteLine($"There are {enemyCount.Value} enemies");
}
```

Expected Output:

```
Enemy count unknown
There are 3 enemies
```

There's also a cool shorthand called the **null-coalescing operator** (??) that gives you a default value if something is null:

```
int? savedHealth = null;
int actualHealth = savedHealth ?? 100;   // If savedHealth is null, use 100

Console.WriteLine($"Health: {actualHealth}");
```

Expected Output:

```
Health: 100
```

Variable Types

It's good to know that all variables are categorized as **value types** or **reference types**.
Value types like `int`, `double`, and `bool` hold their own copy of the data. Changing one does **not** affect another.
Reference types like `string`, `class`, and `array` hold a reference to the data. Two variables can point to the same object, so changing one affects the other.

Look at it this way, **value types** are like everyone getting your own cookie, when you eat your cookie, the other person still has a full cookie! **Reference types**, on the other hand, are like both holding the same cookie, when someone takes a bite, the cookie changes for both.

Strings and other reference types can be null by default:

```
string playerName = null;   // This works fine

if (playerName == null)
{
    Console.WriteLine("No player name set");
}

playerName = "Prince";
Console.WriteLine($"Player: {playerName}");
```

Expected Output:

```
No player name set
Player: Prince
```

When to Use Null:
- When a value might not exist yet (no checkpoint saved)
- When you need to distinguish between "zero" and "nothing" (0 gold vs. unknown gold amount)
- When a value is optional

Pro Tip:

In modern C#, there's also something called "nullable reference types" which helps you avoid null errors with strings and objects. But that's more advanced. For now, just remember: basic types need a ? to be nullable, and null means "no value."

Var: Letting C# Figure Out the Type

Here's a shortcut: you don't always have to write out the full type name. C# can figure it out for you using the var keyword.

When you use var, you're telling C# "Look at what I'm assigning and figure out the type yourself."

```
var playerHealth = 100;        // C# knows this is an int
var playerName = "Prince";     // C# knows this is a string
var hasSword = true;           // C# knows this is a bool

Console.WriteLine($"{playerName} has {playerHealth} health. Has sword: {hasSword}");
```

Expected Output:

```
Prince has 100 health. Has sword: True
```

Behind the scenes, var playerHealth = 100; is exactly the same as int playerHealth = 100;. C# just fills in the type for you.

You can use var when C# can clearly tell what type the variable should be.

 **This Works:**

```
var score = 500;
var message = "Level Complete!";
var gameTime = DateTime.Now;
```

 **This Doesn't Work:**

```
var playerHealth;  // ERROR! C# doesn't know what type this should be
playerHealth = 100;
```

You must assign a value when you declare with `var`.

It saves typing, especially with long type names:

```
// Without var
DateTime gameStartTime = DateTime.Now;

// With var - cleaner
var gameStartTime = DateTime.Now;
```

You'll notice I don't use `var` much in this book. That's intentional! I want you to see the actual types so you learn what everything is. Both are correct, but explicit types make it crystal clear what each variable is when you're learning.

 **Pro Tip:**

Use `var` when the type is obvious (like `var name = "Prince";`), and use explicit types when it helps clarity. As you gain experience, you'll develop your own style!

Object: The Root of All Types

It's important to know that **everything is also an** `object`, literally everything. Even simple types like `int`, `bool`, and `string` are secretly objects under the hood.

Every single type in C# inherits from a base type called `Object` (or `object` in lowercase, they're the same thing). This means every type automatically gets certain capabilities that come from `Object`.

What Object Gives You:
- `ToString()`: Converts the object to a string representation
- `GetType()`: Returns the type of the object
- `Equals()`: Checks if two objects are equal
- `GetHashCode()`: Returns a hash code for the object

Let us look at some examples:

```
int number = 42;
string text = "Hello";
bool isAlive = true;

// All of these have methods from Object
Console.WriteLine(number.ToString());
```

```
Console.WriteLine(text.GetType());
Console.WriteLine(isAlive.GetHashCode());
```

Expected Output (Hash code will differ):

```
42
System.String
12479570
```

Because everything inherits from `Object`, you can write methods that accept ANY type as arguments:

```csharp
static void PrintAnything(object thing)
{
    Console.WriteLine($"You gave me: {thing}");
    Console.WriteLine($"Its type is: {thing.GetType()}");
}

// Usage:
PrintAnything(42);
PrintAnything("Hello");
PrintAnything(true);
PrintAnything(3.14);
```

Expected Output:

```
You gave me: 42
Its type is: System.Int32
You gave me: Hello
Its type is: System.String
You gave me: True
Its type is: System.Boolean
You gave me: 3.14
Its type is: System.Double
```

 **Pro Tip:**

When you call `Console.WriteLine()` with any object, it automatically calls that object's `ToString()` method. That's why you can print numbers, strings, Booleans and even custom types we'll learn about later since they all have `ToString()`. This is inherited from Object!

Finding out what type an object is

When you pass items around as objects you will need a way to figure out what type the object is before you can use it.

Here are the two most common ways to check types:

1. `GetType()`: Called on an instance, returns the actual runtime type
2. `typeof()`: Used with a type name, returns the type information

Let's see them in action:

```csharp
int playerHealth = 100;

// GetType() - used on instances
Type healthType = playerHealth.GetType();
Console.WriteLine($"Health type: {healthType.Name}");

// typeof() - used with type names
Type intType = typeof(int);
Console.WriteLine($"Int type: {intType.Name}");

// Check if they're the same
Console.WriteLine($"Same type? {healthType == intType}");
```

Expected Output:

```
Health type: Int32
Int type: Int32
Same type? True
```

Pro Tip:

There are also **is** and **as** keywords for type checking and casting which we'll learn about in the Inheritance chapter. Both approaches have their uses, and understanding explicit casting like this gives you fundamental knowledge for working with objects in C#.

Casting back from Object

Now that we know how to find out what type an `object` really is, we can use that information to convert objects back to their original type in order to use them:

```csharp
static void ProcessGameValue(object thing)
{
    if (thing.GetType() == typeof(int))
    {
        int number = (int)thing;   // Cast it back to int
        Console.WriteLine($"Health value: {number}");
    }
    else if (thing.GetType() == typeof(string))
    {
        string text = (string)thing;
        Console.WriteLine($"Message: {text}");
    }
    else if (thing.GetType() == typeof(bool))
    {
        bool flag = (bool)thing;
        Console.WriteLine($"Status: {flag}");
    }
    else
    {
        Console.WriteLine($"Unknown type: {thing.GetType().Name}");
    }
```

```
}

// Usage:
ProcessGameValue(100);
ProcessGameValue("Level Complete!");
ProcessGameValue(true);
ProcessGameValue(3.14);
```

Expected Output:

```
Health value: 100
Message: Level Complete!
Status: True
Unknown type: Double
```

The ability to treat everything as `object` is what makes generic collections like `List` possible. It's also how serialization works (saving objects to files), how debuggers inspect your variables, and how many frameworks can work with types they've never seen before.

When to Use Object

Rarely in your own code! Use specific types whenever possible (`int`, `string`, `bool`, etc.). Object is mostly useful in advanced scenarios like:

- Building frameworks or libraries that work with any type
- Working with collections before you learn about generics
- Interfacing with older code written before modern C# features

For now, just understand that everything is an object under the hood. It's a core concept that makes C# work the way it does.

Fun Experiment: The Guardian's Riddle

Alright, this was a mouth full, time to put everything together! Let's create a more complex text adventure that uses some of the concepts we've learned.

The Prince's Journey: The Potion's Price

The story so far...

After what feels like hours of cautious exploration, the Prince arrives at a stone platform overlooking a lower chamber. Below, bathed in an eerie green glow, sits a crystal bottle containing a shimmering potion. His wounds ache from earlier falls, and he knows such magic could mean the difference between survival and death in the trials ahead. But the dungeon has already taught him to be wary, nothing here is given freely.

As he carefully descends to examine the bottle more closely, he notices ancient mechanisms embedded in the walls and a massive sealed door across the chamber. Runes glow faintly on a stone pedestal nearby, and he realizes this is no random cache. The Vizier, or perhaps those who built this prison long ago, left this as a test. To claim the potion and unlock the path forward, he must first prove he can think clearly under pressure. The Prince takes a deep breath, steadies his mind, and approaches the pedestal to face whatever challenge awaits.

The Challenge

Create a program that:

1. Asks the player for their name
2. Asks them to choose a starting health value
3. Records the start time using `DateTime`
4. Uses an `enum` to track the current state (Exploring, Fighting, Resting)
5. Have the player find an item and stores the item info in a tuple (item name, value, weight)
6. Displays a door puzzle with a numeric code
7. If they enter the correct code (1357), calculate how long it took them using `TimeSpan`
8. Use string interpolation for all messages
9. Use at least one nullable type for an optional item

Try building this yourself first! Challenge yourself to make it fun and interactive.

Example Answer

Here's one way to solve it:

```csharp
using System;

enum GameState
{
    Exploring,
    Fighting,
    Resting,
    Completed
}

class Program
{
    static void Main()
    {
        Console.WriteLine("                                      ");
        Console.WriteLine("      THE PRINCE'S DUNGEON QUEST       ");
        Console.WriteLine("                                      ");
        Console.WriteLine();

        // Get player info
        Console.WriteLine("What is your name, brave adventurer?");
        string playerName = Console.ReadLine();

        Console.WriteLine($"\nWelcome, {playerName}!");
        Console.WriteLine("Enter your starting health (50-100):");
        string healthInput = Console.ReadLine();
        int playerHealth = Convert.ToInt32(healthInput);
```

```csharp
// Track game start time
DateTime gameStartTime = DateTime.Now;
Console.WriteLine($"\nGame started at: {gameStartTime:HH:mm:ss}");

// Game state tracking
GameState currentState = GameState.Exploring;

// Optional magic potion (nullable)
int? magicPotionCharges = null;

Console.WriteLine($"\n{playerName} enters the ancient dungeon...");
Console.WriteLine($"Health: {playerHealth}");
Console.WriteLine($"Status: {currentState}");

// Finding an item - using tuple
Console.WriteLine("\nYou spot a glowing chest in the corner!");
Console.WriteLine("Open it? (yes/no)");
string openChest = Console.ReadLine().ToLower();

(string itemName, int value, double weight) foundItem = ("Ancient Sword",
    500, 3.5);

if (openChest == "yes")
{
    Console.WriteLine($"\nYou found: {foundItem.itemName}!");
    Console.WriteLine($"Value: {foundItem.value} gold");
    Console.WriteLine($"Weight: {foundItem.weight} kg");

    Console.WriteLine("\nThere's also a dusty potion with 3 charges. " +
        "Take it? (yes/no)");
    string takePot = Console.ReadLine().ToLower();

    if (takePot == "yes")
    {
        magicPotionCharges = 3;
        Console.WriteLine("Magic potion acquired!");
    }
}

// Change state
currentState = GameState.Fighting;
Console.WriteLine($"\n⚔  A skeleton guard blocks your path!");
Console.WriteLine($"Status: {currentState}");

if (magicPotionCharges.HasValue && magicPotionCharges > 0)
{
    Console.WriteLine($"Use magic potion? You have {magicPotionCharges} " +
        $"charges. (yes/no)");
    string usePot = Console.ReadLine().ToLower();

    if (usePot == "yes")
    {
        magicPotionCharges = magicPotionCharges - 1;
        Console.WriteLine(" Magic blast! The skeleton is destroyed!");
        Console.WriteLine($"Potion charges remaining: " +
            $"{magicPotionCharges ?? 0}");
    }
    else
    {
        Console.WriteLine("You defeat the skeleton in combat!");
        playerHealth = playerHealth - 20;
```

```csharp
            Console.WriteLine($"You took 20 damage. Health: {playerHealth}");
    }
}
else
{
    Console.WriteLine("You defeat the skeleton in combat!");
    playerHealth = playerHealth - 20;
    Console.WriteLine($"You took 20 damage. Health: {playerHealth}");
}

// Rest phase
currentState = GameState.Resting;
Console.WriteLine($"\nYou find a safe alcove to rest.");
Console.WriteLine($"Status: {currentState}");
Console.WriteLine("Restoring 10 health...");
playerHealth = playerHealth + 10;
Console.WriteLine($"Current health: {playerHealth}");

// The door puzzle
currentState = GameState.Exploring;
DateTime puzzleStartTime = DateTime.Now;

Console.WriteLine($"\n{playerName} approaches a massive stone door.");
Console.WriteLine("Ancient runes glow on its surface...");
Console.WriteLine("There's a numeric keypad with worn numbers.");
Console.WriteLine("\nEnter the 4-digit code:");

string codeInput = Console.ReadLine();
int enteredCode = int.Parse(codeInput);
int correctCode = 1357;

DateTime puzzleEndTime = DateTime.Now;
TimeSpan puzzleDuration = puzzleEndTime - puzzleStartTime;

if (enteredCode == correctCode)
{
    currentState = GameState.Completed;
    Console.WriteLine("\n✦ *CLICK* ✦");
    Console.WriteLine("The ancient mechanisms grind to life!");
    Console.WriteLine("The massive door slowly swings open...");
    Console.WriteLine($"\n{playerName} steps through into the light...");

    // Calculate total game time
    TimeSpan totalGameTime = DateTime.Now - gameStartTime;

    Console.WriteLine("\n╔══════════════════════════╗");
    Console.WriteLine("║        QUEST COMPLETED!        ║");
    Console.WriteLine("╚══════════════════════════╝");
    Console.WriteLine($"Player: {playerName}");
    Console.WriteLine($"Final Health: {playerHealth}");
    Console.WriteLine($"Status: {currentState}");
    Console.WriteLine($"Puzzle solved in: {puzzleDuration.TotalSeconds:F1} " +
        $"seconds");
    Console.WriteLine($"Total time: {totalGameTime.TotalMinutes:F1} minutes");

    if (magicPotionCharges.HasValue)
    {
        Console.WriteLine($"Magic potion charges left: {magicPotionCharges}");
    }
    else
    {
```

```
                Console.WriteLine("No magic items remaining");
            }
        }
        else
        {
            Console.WriteLine("\n⚠  *BZZT* ⚠");
            Console.WriteLine("The keypad flashes red!");
            Console.WriteLine("Poison gas fills the room!");

            int trapDamage = 30;
            playerHealth = playerHealth - trapDamage;

            Console.WriteLine($"You took {trapDamage} damage!");
            Console.WriteLine($"Final health: {playerHealth}");
            Console.WriteLine($"\nYou solved the puzzle in " +
                $"{puzzleDuration.TotalSeconds:F1} seconds");
            Console.WriteLine("But the wrong code sealed your fate...");
            Console.WriteLine("\nGAME OVER");
        }

        Console.WriteLine("\nPress any key to exit...");
        Console.ReadLine();
    }
}
```

Expected Output: *(if you enter "Aladdin", "100", "yes", "yes", "yes", and "1357")*

```
┌─────────────────────────────────────────┐
│    THE PRINCE'S DUNGEON QUEST            │
└─────────────────────────────────────────┘

What is your name, brave adventurer?
Aladdin

Welcome, Aladdin!
Enter your starting health (50-100):
70

Game started at: 20:21:46

Aladdin enters the ancient dungeon...
Health: 70
Status: Exploring

You spot a glowing chest in the corner!
Open it? (yes/no)
yes

You found: Ancient Sword!
Value: 500 gold
Weight: 3.5 kg

There's also a dusty potion with 3 charges. Take it? (yes/no)
yes
Magic potion acquired!

??  A skeleton guard blocks your path!
Status: Fighting
Use magic potion? You have 3 charges. (yes/no)
yes
```

```
?? Magic blast! The skeleton is destroyed!
Potion charges remaining: 2

You find a safe alcove to rest.
Status: Resting
Restoring 10 health...
Current health: 80

Aladdin approaches a massive stone door.
Ancient runes glow on its surface...
There's a numeric keypad with worn numbers.

Enter the 4-digit code:
1357

? *CLICK* ?
The ancient mechanisms grind to life!
The massive door slowly swings open...

Aladdin steps through into the light...

    ┌─────────────────────────────┐
    │        QUEST COMPLETED!      │
    └─────────────────────────────┘
Player: Aladdin
Final Health: 80
Status: Completed
Puzzle solved in: 9.8 seconds
Total time: 0.7 minutes
Magic potion charges left: 2

Press any key to exit...
```

See how much you've learned? You're now tracking complex states, managing time, using tuples to store item data, handling optional items with nullable types, and creating an engaging interactive experience. You're really programming now!

Wrap-up: What You've Learned

You've just leveled up your coding skills significantly!

Key Takeaways

- **Basic Variable Types** - You know the fundamental types in C# (`int`, `double`, `float`, `bool`, `char`, `string`) and when to use each one based on what data you need to store.
- **Naming** - You understand that good variable names make your code readable and maintainable. You use camelCase and descriptive names that explain what the variable represents.
- **Strings** - You can combine strings with concatenation (+) or interpolation (`$"{}"`), handle special characters with escaping (`\"`), use verbatim strings (`@""`), and manipulate text with methods like `.ToUpper()`, `.ToLower()`, `.Contains()`, `.Replace()`, and `.Trim()`.

- **Console Input** - You can get player input with `Console.ReadLine()` and make your programs interactive, cleaning up input with string methods.
- **Type Casting** - You can convert between types using `Parse` for direct string-to-number conversion, explicit casting for number type conversions like `(int)`, and the `Convert` class for more flexible conversions with better null handling.
- **DateTime and TimeSpan** - You can track specific moments in time with `DateTime`, calculate durations with `TimeSpan`, measure how long things take.
- **Enums** - You can create meaningful names for related values instead of using confusing numbers, making your code self-documenting for states, directions, item types, and more.
- **Tuples** - You can quickly group related values together using tuples with named or unnamed fields, perfect for returning multiple values or creating lightweight data structures.
- **Nullable Types** - You understand that some variables might need to represent "no value" using null, and you can make value types nullable with `?`, check for null values, and provide defaults with the `??` operator.
- **Var Keyword** - You know that `var` lets C# infer the type automatically, making code cleaner when the type is obvious, though explicit types are often clearer when learning.
- **Object Type** - You understand that every type in C# inherits from Object, giving all types common capabilities like `ToString()` and `GetType()`. You can use object to accept any type of data, check what type something really is using `GetType()` and `typeof()`, and cast objects back to their specific types when needed.

These are the building blocks of every program you'll ever write. In all programs all these concepts are used to track every detail required. In our examples we tracked the Prince's position, health, time remaining etc. but it's also used in all every applications to track all kinds of information. Now you know how to do it yourself!

Logic

"When you have eliminated the impossible, whatever remains, however improbable, must be the truth." — Arthur Conan Doyle

Ever wondered how your favorite apps know exactly what to do in any situation? How Netflix decides which show to recommend, how your phone knows when to switch from light mode to dark mode, or how a self-driving car determines whether it's safe to change lanes? The answer is "logic"! The fundamental ability of programs to make decisions based on conditions. Without logic, software would be nothing more than a mindless robot following the same steps over and over, regardless of what's happening around it. Logic is what transforms code from a simple recipe into an intelligent system that can adapt, respond, and make choices.

In this chapter, you'll learn how to teach your programs to think. You'll discover how to compare values, combine multiple conditions to make complex decisions, and perform the mathematical calculations that power everything from physics simulations to financial calculations. These aren't just game mechanics, it's the core building blocks of every piece of software you've ever used. Whether it's a weather app deciding if it should send you an umbrella reminder, Spotify determining if you've listened to enough songs to trigger a new playlist recommendation, or a fitness tracker calculating whether you've hit your daily step goal, it all comes down to the concepts you're about to learn.

Core Concepts Covered

✓   Making decisions based on conditions and comparisons
✓   Combining multiple conditions to create complex logic
✓   Choosing between different paths of execution
✓   Performing mathematical operations and calculations
✓   Understanding how programs evaluate truth and make choices
✓   Creating flexible code that responds to different situations

Welcome to the Brain of Your "Game"

 **Trivia:**

George Boole invented Boolean logic (true/false, yes/no, 1/0) in 1847 as a way to solve philosophical arguments using mathematics. He died in 1864, never knowing his work would become the foundation of all computer programming 100 years later. Every if-statement, every decision a computer makes, uses Boolean logic. The AND, OR, and NOT operations he invented are built into every computer chip on Earth.

So, you've learned about variables, the boxes where we keep our stuff. Now it's time to make decisions with it. This is where your code stops being a boring list of instructions and starts acting like it has a brain.

Think about our Prince running toward a pit, the game needs to decide, "Is he jumping? No? Then he falls and dies." Or when a guard swings a sword: "Did it hit the Prince? Yes? Subtract health. No? Keep playing." Every single moment is filled with tiny decisions happening faster than you can blink.

Let's learn how to make our code think and make choices. Let's dive in!

If statement: The Decision Maker

The `if` conditional statement is like asking a question and doing something based on the answer. Imagine a game constantly asking: "Is the Prince touching the floor? If yes, let him run. If no, make him fall."

Here's the basic structure:

```
if (condition)
{
    // Do something if the condition is true
}
```

Let's look at an example from our Prince's adventure:

```
int princeHealth = 3;
bool guardAttacked = true;

if (guardAttacked)
{
    princeHealth = princeHealth - 1;
    Console.WriteLine("Ouch! The guard hit you!");
    Console.WriteLine("Health remaining: " + princeHealth);
}

Console.WriteLine("You continue your journey...");
```

Expected Output:

```
Ouch! The guard hit you!
Health remaining: 2
You continue your journey...
```

See how the code inside the curly braces {} only runs if `guardAttacked` is true? If it were false, the code would skip right over it and just print "You continue your journey..."

When playing an action game, every time an enemy attack, there's an if statement checking "Did the attack connect?" If yes, reduce health. This happens many times per second. Same thing for any other program, for example if you want to check if the budget is less than the expense… but that sounds boring let's rather keep with the game theme.

If-Else: Two Paths Forward

Sometimes you need to do one thing if the condition is true, and something completely different if it's false.

That's where `else` condition statement comes in:

```
int potionDistance = 2;

if (potionDistance <= 1)
{
    Console.WriteLine("You grab the health potion! +1 Health");
}
else
{
    Console.WriteLine("The potion is too far away. You need to get closer.");
}
```

Expected Output (*if potionDistance is 2*):

```
The potion is too far away. You need to get closer.
```

When the Prince tries to grab a ledge, the game checks "Is he close enough to the ledge?" If yes, he grabs it. Else, he falls. That's life-or-death decision-making powered by if-else!

Else-If: Multiple Choices

What if you have more than two possibilities? Welcome to `else if` conditional statement. Now you can chain as many as you need:

```
int princeHealth = 1;

if (princeHealth <= 0)
{
    Console.WriteLine("GAME OVER - The Prince has fallen!");
}
else if (princeHealth == 1)
{
    Console.WriteLine("Warning! Critical health - Find a potion!");
}
else if (princeHealth == 2)
{
    Console.WriteLine("Health is low. Be careful!");
}
else
{
    Console.WriteLine("Health is good. Keep going!");
}
```

Expected Output

```
Warning! Critical health - Find a potion!
```

Pro Tip:

The order matters! The code checks each condition from top to bottom and stops at the first one that is true. So put your most specific conditions first.

Let's assume the Evil Vizier used his magic to bring some old bones in the dungeon to life as skeletons to fight you, in a game with graphics when you approach: Is it dead (bones lying on ground)? Is it rising (animation starting)? Is it attacking? Is it just standing? Each state needs different behavior, and that's what else-if chains handle perfectly.

Comparison Operators: How to Ask Questions

To make decisions, you need to compare things. Here are your tools:

Operator	Meaning	Example
==	Equal to	health == 3
!=	Not equal to	health != 0
>	Greater than	score > 1000
<	Less than	lives < 3
>=	Greater than or equal	level >= 5
<=	Less than or equal	time <= 60

Let's see them in action:

```
int princeLevel = 8;
int bossLevel = 10;

if (princeLevel < bossLevel)
{
    Console.WriteLine("The boss is too powerful! Train more before fighting.");
}

if (princeLevel >= 10)
{
    Console.WriteLine("You're strong enough to face the final boss!");
}
else
{
    Console.WriteLine($"Current level: {princeLevel}. You need level 10 to proceed.");
}
```

Expected Output:

```
The boss is too powerful! Train more before fighting.
Current level: 8. You need level 10 to proceed.
```

Every collision uses comparisons. "Is the Prince's X position greater than the pit's X position AND less than the pit's X position + width?" If yes, he's standing on solid ground. These comparisons happen constantly.

Logical Operators: Combining Conditions

Sometimes one condition isn't enough and you need to check multiple things at once. That's where logical operators shine.

AND Operator (&&)

Both conditions must be true for the whole thing to be true:

```
bool hasKey = true;
bool doorIsLocked = true;

if (hasKey && doorIsLocked)
{
    Console.WriteLine("You use the key to unlock the door!");
    Console.WriteLine("The path forward is open.");
}
```

Expected Output:

```
You use the key to unlock the door!
The path forward is open.
```

In our Prince's back-story we mentioned the dungeon had some ancient switches that can open or close some gates. The code can check: "Is the player standing on the switch AND is the gate currently closed?" Both must be true to trigger an opening animation.

OR Operator (||)

Only ONE of the conditions needs to be true:

```
bool foundPotion = false;
bool foundFountain = true;

if (foundPotion || foundFountain)
{
    Console.WriteLine("Your health is restored!");
}
else
{
    Console.WriteLine("No healing items found. Stay alert!");
}
```

Expected Output:

```
Your health is restored!
```

When checking if the Prince should die, the game asks: "Is health zero OR did he fall into spikes OR did he fall too far?" Any one of these means game over.

NOT Operator (!)

Flips true to false and false to true. It's like saying "the opposite of.":

```
bool guardIsAlive = false;

if (!guardIsAlive)
{
    Console.WriteLine("The path is clear. You can proceed safely.");
}
```

Expected Output:

```
The path is clear. You can proceed safely.
```

You can also use ! with other operators for example the equals sign to change it to NOT equals to:

```
int treasureChests = 5;

if (treasureChests != 0)
{
    Console.WriteLine($"You still have {treasureChests} chests to find!");
}
```

Expected Output:

```
You still have 5 chests to find!
```

When coding enemy AI, you might check "if the player is NOT in attack range, then patrol." The NOT operator is super handy for these inverse checks.

Combining All of Them

You can combine these operators to create complex logic:

```
int princeHealth = 2;
bool hasShield = true;
bool guardAttacking = true;

if (guardAttacking && (princeHealth > 1 || hasShield))
{
    Console.WriteLine("Guard attacks, but you defend successfully!");
    if (hasShield)
    {
        Console.WriteLine("Your shield blocks the attack.");
    }
    else
    {
        princeHealth--;
        Console.WriteLine("You dodge, but it was close! Health: " + princeHealth);
    }
}
```

Expected Output:

```
Guard attacks, but you defend successfully!
Your shield blocks the attack.
```

 **Pro Tip:**

Notice the parentheses ()? They group conditions together, just like in math. The code checks "Is the guard attacking AND (does the prince have more than 1 health OR does he have a shield)." Parentheses make your logic clear and work the way you intend.

Switch Statements: The Menu of Choices

When you have lots of possible values for one variable and you want to do different things for each value, `switch` statements are cleaner than a giant chain of if-else statements.

Here's the old-school format that still works and it's a bit easier to read and use when you are new to a switch:

```csharp
int levelNumber = 3;

switch (levelNumber)
{
    case 1:
        Console.WriteLine("Level 1: The Palace Entrance");
        Console.WriteLine("Watch out for loose tiles!");
        break;
    case 2:
        Console.WriteLine("Level 2: The Prison Cells");
        Console.WriteLine("Guards patrol these corridors.");
        break;
    case 3:
        Console.WriteLine("Level 3: The Tower");
        Console.WriteLine("Careful with those spike traps!");
        break;
    default:
        Console.WriteLine("Unknown level. Starting from the beginning...");
        break;
}
```

Expected Output:

```
Level 3: The Tower
Careful with those spike traps!
```

Important: You MUST include `break;` at the end of each case. It tells the code "I'm done with this case, exit the switch." Forget it and your code won't compile. (Okay, technically you can do fancy fall-through stuff, but let's not get crazy yet.)

The `default` case is like the `else` in an if statement where it runs if none of the other cases match.

Think about what happens when a player presses different keys in a game. Press ↑ to jump, ← to run left, → to run right, ↓ to crouch, Space to attack. Each key is a different case in a switch statement deciding what animation to play.

Switch Expressions

C# has a newer, shorter way to write switches using expressions:

```
string enemyType = "guard";

string attackMessage = enemyType switch
{
    "guard" => "The guard swings his sword!",
    "skeleton" => "The skeleton lunges with its blade!",
    "sorcerer" => "sorcerer unleashes dark magic!",
    _ => "An unknown enemy appears!"
};

Console.WriteLine(attackMessage);
```

Expected Output:

```
The guard swings his sword!
```

This is way more compact. The `=>` is like an arrow pointing from the case to what should happen. The underscore `_` is the default case.

Pro Tip:

Use the old-style switch when you need to run multiple lines of code for each case. Use switch expressions when you're assigning a single value based on another value—it's cleaner and easier to read.

When to Use Switch vs. If-Else

Use Switch Statements when:

- You're checking one variable against several specific values
- You have more than 3-4 possible values to check
- The values are simple (numbers, strings, or enums)

```
string itemPickedUp = "sword";

switch (itemPickedUp)
{
```

```
    case "sword":
        Console.WriteLine("Attack power increased!");
        break;
    case "potion":
        Console.WriteLine("Health restored!");
        break;
            case "key":
        Console.WriteLine("You can now unlock doors.");
        break;
}
```

Use If-Else when:

- You're checking different variables or complex conditions
- You need range checks (like `health > 50`)
- You're combining multiple conditions with AND/OR

```
int health = 75;
bool hasArmor = true;

if (health > 50 && hasArmor)
{
    Console.WriteLine("You're in good shape for battle!");
}
```

Many different application and games used switch statements for handling user input (which key was pressed) and if statements in a game for physics checks (is the player falling? is there a floor beneath?).

Math Operators: Making the Numbers Dance

Time to do some calculations! Applications and games are full of math, calculating totals, positions, velocities, scores, you name it.

Basic Operations

Operator	Operation	Example	Result
+	Addition	5 + 3	8
-	Subtraction	5 - 3	2
*	Multiplication	5 * 3	15
/	Division	10 / 2	5
%	Modulus (remainder)	10 % 3	1

Let's see them in action:

```csharp
int score = 1000;
int bonusPoints = 250;
int totalScore = score + bonusPoints;

Console.WriteLine("Base score: " + score);
Console.WriteLine("Bonus points: " + bonusPoints);
Console.WriteLine("Total score: " + totalScore);

int lives = 5;
int livesLost = 2;
int remainingLives = lives - livesLost;

Console.WriteLine("Lives remaining: " + remainingLives);

int damage = 10;
int criticalMultiplier = 3;
int criticalDamage = damage * criticalMultiplier;

Console.WriteLine("Critical hit! Damage: " + criticalDamage);
```

Expected Output

```
Base score: 1000
Bonus points: 250
Total score: 1250
Lives remaining: 3
Critical hit! Damage: 30
```

Every time the Prince jumps, a game could calculate it's vertical position using addition (going up) and subtraction (falling down). Your X position changes with addition (moving right) or subtraction (moving left). It's all basic math! Of course, you can also do basic math to add and subtract expenses and income for the month to display a total.

Division: Watch Out for Integers!

Here's something tricky that catches everyone at first:

```csharp
int totalDamage = 7;
int numberOfHits = 2;
int averageDamage = totalDamage / numberOfHits;

Console.WriteLine("Average damage per hit: " + averageDamage);
```

Expected Output:

```
Average damage per hit: 3
```

Wait, what? 7 divided by 2 is 3.5, not 3! What's going on? When you divide two integers, C# gives you back an integer. It just chops off the decimal part, no rounding, it just cuts it off.

If you want the real answer with decimals then you need to make sure it is a type that can handle fractions like `double`:

```
double totalDamage = 7;
double numberOfHits = 2;
double averageDamage = totalDamage / numberOfHits;

Console.WriteLine("Average damage per hit: " + averageDamage);
```

Expected Output:

```
Average damage per hit: 3.5
```

Pro Tip:

Sometimes you WANT integer division. Like if you're calculating how many complete steps the Prince can take before running out of stamina: `int steps = stamina / staminaPerStep;` You don't care about partial steps!

Modulus: The Remainder Wizard

The modulus operator % gives you the remainder after division. It's weirdly useful in many different calculations, but let's see how it can help our Prince!

```
int number = 10;
int divisor = 3;
int remainder = number % divisor;

Console.WriteLine($"{number} divided by {divisor} leaves a remainder of {remainder}");
```

Expected Output:

```
10 divided by 3 leaves a remainder of 1
```

Cool Uses:

1. **Alternating patterns** - Check if even or odd:

```
int tileNumber = 5;

if (tileNumber % 2 == 0)
{
    Console.WriteLine("Light tile");
}
else
{
    Console.WriteLine("Dark tile");
}
```

Expected Output:

```
Dark tile
```

2. **Wrapping around** - Make something loop:

```csharp
int frameNumber = 47;
int animationFrames = 8;
int currentFrame = frameNumber % animationFrames;

Console.WriteLine($"Animation frame: {currentFrame}");
```

Expected Output:

```
Animation frame: 7
```

Let's assume the skeleton's falling-apart animation has, let's say, 10 frames. If the game needs to loop that animation, it uses modulus: `currentFrame = frameCounter % 10.` When frameCounter hits 10, it wraps back to 0. Magic!

3. **Every Nth time** - Do something periodically:

```csharp
int gameFrame = 180;

if (gameFrame % 60 == 0)
{
    Console.WriteLine("One second has passed! (at 60 FPS)");
}
```

If a game runs at 60 frames per second, and you want a torch to flicker every half-second, you check `if (frameCount % 30 == 0)`. Easy!

Shorthand Operators: Write Less, Do More

Programmers are lazy (in a good way) and we like shortcuts!

Here are the most common ones:

Increment (++) and Decrement (--)

Rather than typing: `health = health + 1;` you can just type: `health++;` to add or subtract 1 to your existing value:

```csharp
int health = 5;

health++;  // Same as: health = health + 1
Console.WriteLine("Health after increment: " + health);

health--;  // Same as: health = health - 1
Console.WriteLine("Health after decrement: " + health);
```

Expected Output:

```
Health after increment: 6
Health after decrement: 5
```

It's very useful, sometimes you just would want to add one to you existing value for example counting the repetitions in a loop: `cnt++` , or you collect a coin in a game: `coins++`. Every time you take damage: `health--`. It can be used anywhere!

Compound Assignment Operators

Similar to the increment and decrement above, sometimes we want to add more than 1 to the existing value, so rather than typing: `score = score + 50;` you can just type: `score += 50;`.

Same goes for other operators like when you want to multiple or even divide by itself:

```csharp
int score = 100;

score += 50;   // Same as: score = score + 50
Console.WriteLine("Score after bonus: " + score);

score -= 20;   // Same as: score = score - 20
Console.WriteLine("Score after penalty: " + score);

int damage = 10;
damage *= 2;   // Same as: damage = damage * 2
Console.WriteLine("Double damage: " + damage);

int lives = 10;
lives /= 2;   // Same as: lives = lives / 2
Console.WriteLine("Lives halved: " + lives);
```

Expected Output:

```
Score after bonus: 150
Score after penalty: 130
Double damage: 20
Lives halved: 5
```

 **Pro Tip:**

There's even %= for modulus! `frameCounter %= 60;` keeps a counter cycling between 0 and 59.

When the Prince drinks a healing potion: `health += potionStrength`. When he takes fall damage: `health -= fallDistance / 2`. Clean and clear!

Math Methods: Your Calculator Functions

C# has a bunch of built-in math functions in the `Math` class you can use.

Here are the most useful ones (check the comments and output at end to see what they do):

```csharp
// Absolute value (distance from zero)
int negativeNumber = -15;
int positive = Math.Abs(negativeNumber);
Console.WriteLine($"Absolute value of {negativeNumber} is {positive}");

// Maximum and Minimum
int health1 = 45;
int health2 = 70;
int maxHealth = Math.Max(health1, health2);
int minHealth = Math.Min(health1, health2);
Console.WriteLine($"Highest health: {maxHealth}");
Console.WriteLine($"Lowest health: {minHealth}");

// Power (exponents)
double @base = 2;
double exponent = 3;
double result = Math.Pow(@base, exponent);
Console.WriteLine($"{@base} to the power of {exponent} is {result}");

// Square root
double number = 16;
double squareRoot = Math.Sqrt(number);
Console.WriteLine($"Square root of {number} is {squareRoot}");

// Rounding
double damage = 15.7;
double roundedDamage = Math.Round(damage);
Console.WriteLine($"Rounded damage: {roundedDamage}");

double flooredDamage = Math.Floor(damage);
Console.WriteLine($"Floored damage: {flooredDamage}");

double ceilingDamage = Math.Ceiling(damage);
Console.WriteLine($"Ceiling damage: {ceilingDamage}");
```

Expected Output

```
Absolute value of -15 is 15
Highest health: 70
Lowest health: 45
2 to the power of 3 is 8
Square root of 16 is 4
Rounded damage: 16
Floored damage: 15
Ceiling damage: 16
```

 **Pro Tip:**

Notice the @ before the "@base" variable. This is because "base" is a C# reserved keyword and therefore it does not know how to handle it. The @ tells the compiler: "treat the following text as an identifier, not a keyword." This works for variable names, parameters, properties, classes, etc.

Some more useful `Math` methods:

- **Abs:** Converts negative numbers to positive (removes the negative sign). Useful when calculating distance between two objects where you only care about how far apart they are, not which direction.
- **Max/Min:** Returns the larger or smaller of two numbers. Useful for capping values within limits, like preventing health from exceeding maximum or ensuring values don't drop below zero.
- **Pow:** Raises a number to a power (multiplies a number by itself a certain number of times). For example, $2^3 = 2 \times 2 \times 2 = 8$. Useful for exponential growth calculations like compound damage multipliers, experience point scaling, or calculating areas and volumes.
- **Sqrt:** Calculates the square root of a number (what number multiplied by itself gives you this value). Helpful when calculating distances between two points using the Pythagorean theorem, or determining velocities and speeds in physics calculations.
- **Round/Floor/Ceiling:** Converts decimal numbers to whole numbers in different ways. Round picks the nearest integer, Floor always rounds down, Ceiling always rounds up. Useful when you need whole number values for things like health, damage, or pixel positions on screen.

Putting It All Together: A Battle Scene

Let's combine what we've learned so far:

```csharp
Console.WriteLine("=== DUNGEON BATTLE ===\n");

int princeHealth = 5;
int guardHealth = 3;
bool princeHasShield = true;
int turnCounter = 0;

Console.WriteLine("A guard appears! Battle begins!\n");

// Turn 1
turnCounter++;
Console.WriteLine($"--- Turn {turnCounter} ---");

if (turnCounter % 2 == 1)
{
    Console.WriteLine("Prince's turn to attack!");
    int princeAttackDamage = 2;
```

```csharp
    guardHealth -= princeAttackDamage;
    Console.WriteLine($"The Prince strikes! Guard health: {guardHealth}");
}

// Turn 2
turnCounter++;
Console.WriteLine($"\n--- Turn {turnCounter} ---");

if (turnCounter % 2 == 0)
{
    Console.WriteLine("Guard's turn to attack!");
    int guardAttackDamage = 1;

    if (princeHasShield)
    {
        Console.WriteLine("The Prince blocks with his shield!");
    }
    else
    {
        princeHealth -= guardAttackDamage;
        Console.WriteLine($"Hit! Prince health: {princeHealth}");
    }
}

// Turn 3
turnCounter++;
Console.WriteLine($"\n--- Turn {turnCounter} ---");
Console.WriteLine("Prince's turn to attack!");

int criticalChance = 7;
bool isCritical = criticalChance % 3 == 1;

if (isCritical)
{
    int criticalDamage = 3;
    guardHealth -= criticalDamage;
    Console.WriteLine($"CRITICAL HIT! Guard health: {guardHealth}");
}
else
{
    int normalDamage = 1;
    guardHealth -= normalDamage;
    Console.WriteLine($"Normal attack. Guard health: {guardHealth}");
}

// Check battle result
Console.WriteLine("\n--- BATTLE RESULT ---");

if (guardHealth <= 0 && princeHealth > 0)
{
    Console.WriteLine("Victory! The guard is defeated!");
    Console.WriteLine($"Prince health remaining: {princeHealth}");
}
else if (princeHealth <= 0 && guardHealth > 0)
{
    Console.WriteLine("Defeat! The Prince has fallen!");
}
else if (princeHealth <= 0 && guardHealth <= 0)
{
    Console.WriteLine("Both fighters have fallen!");
```

```
}
else
{
    Console.WriteLine("Battle continues...");
    Console.WriteLine($"Prince: {princeHealth} HP | Guard: {guardHealth} HP");
}
```

Expected Output:

```
=== DUNGEON BATTLE ===

A guard appears! Battle begins!

--- Turn 1 ---
Prince's turn to attack!
The Prince strikes! Guard health: 1

--- Turn 2 ---
Guard's turn to attack!
The Prince blocks with his shield!

--- Turn 3 ---
Prince's turn to attack!
CRITICAL HIT! Guard health: -2

--- BATTLE RESULT ---
Victory! The guard is defeated!
Prince health remaining: 5
```

Look at everything happening here:

- Variables tracking health
- If statements deciding who attacks
- Modulus determining turn order
- Boolean logic for shields
- Subtraction for damage
- Comparison operators checking battle results
- Compound conditions with && and ||

This is the kind of logic that can be used for any program and basically powers every combat system in every game ever made!

Fun Experiment: The Skeleton Guardian's Gauntlet

Let use our logic before we forget it!

The Prince's Journey: The Guardian Awakens

The story so far...

The Prince pushes open the heavy iron door, and it groans shut behind him with a resounding clang that echoes through the chamber. Before him stretches a long corridor lined with decorative tiles, their patterns barely visible in the flickering torchlight. At the far end, he can see another door, perhaps its the way forward, perhaps his path to freedom? But as he takes his first step, a grinding sound fills the air. From a shadowed alcove, bones begin to rattle and assemble themselves, drawn together by the Vizier's dark magic...

A skeletal warrior rises, clutching a rusted blade, its empty eye sockets glowing with an unnatural green light. The Prince grips his sword tighter and realizes with growing dread that the corridor itself is the trap. Sharp metal spikes thrust up from certain floor tiles at regular intervals, creating a deadly pattern he must navigate. To reach the exit, he must move forward carefully, timing his steps to avoid the spikes while the undead guardian advances. There's no turning back now, the door behind him is sealed. He must face both the magic-animated bones and the Vizier's mechanical trap if he hopes to survive this gauntlet.

The Challenge

Create a spike trap puzzle for out Prince!

1. The Prince starts at position 0
2. There's a spike trap at position 5
3. The Prince moves forward each turn (add 1 to his position)
4. If he steps on the spikes (position equals 5), reduce his health by 2
5. If he has a shield AND steps on spikes, he only takes 1 damage
6. The Prince starts with 3 health
7. The goal is at position 8
8. Use if statements to check the position
9. Use math operators to calculate movement and damage

Bonus Challenges:
- Add a message when he reaches each position
- Make spikes appear every 3 tiles using modulus
- Add a potion at position 3 that heals 1 health if picked up

Give it a shot! Try to solve it yourself before looking at the example answer below.

Example Answer

Here's one way to solve it:

```
Console.WriteLine("=== SPIKE TRAP GAUNTLET ===\n");

int princePosition = 0;
```

```csharp
int princeHealth = 3;
bool hasShield = true;
int goalPosition = 8;
bool hasPotion = false;

Console.WriteLine($"Starting position: {princePosition}");
Console.WriteLine($"Starting health: {princeHealth}");
Console.WriteLine($"Shield equipped: {hasShield}\n");

// Move through each position
while (princePosition < goalPosition)
{
    princePosition++;
    Console.WriteLine($"--- Moving to position {princePosition} ---");

    // Check for potion at position 3
    if (princePosition == 3 && !hasPotion)
    {
        Console.WriteLine("You found a health potion!");
        princeHealth++;
        hasPotion = true;
        Console.WriteLine($"Health restored to: {princeHealth}");
    }

    // Check for spike trap (every 3 tiles)
    if (princePosition % 3 == 2)
    {
        Console.WriteLine("SPIKE TRAP!");

        if (hasShield)
        {
            princeHealth -= 1;
            Console.WriteLine("Your shield absorbs some damage!");
            hasShield = false; // Shield breaks after one use
        }
        else
        {
            princeHealth -= 2;
            Console.WriteLine("The spikes pierce you!");
        }

        Console.WriteLine($"Current health: {princeHealth}");

        if (princeHealth <= 0)
        {
            Console.WriteLine("\nGAME OVER - The Prince has perished!");
            break;
        }
    }
    else
    {
        Console.WriteLine("Safe tile. Moving forward...");
    }

    Console.WriteLine();
}

// Check if we reached the goal
if (princePosition >= goalPosition && princeHealth > 0)
{
    Console.WriteLine("=== SUCCESS! ===");
```

```
    Console.WriteLine($"You reached the goal with {princeHealth} health remaining!");
}
```

Expected Output:

```
=== SPIKE TRAP GAUNTLET ===

Starting position: 0
Starting health: 3
Shield equipped: True

--- Moving to position 1 ---
Safe tile. Moving forward...

--- Moving to position 2 ---
SPIKE TRAP!
Your shield absorbs some damage!
Current health: 2

--- Moving to position 3 ---
You found a health potion!
Health restored to: 3
Safe tile. Moving forward...

--- Moving to position 4 ---
Safe tile. Moving forward...

--- Moving to position 5 ---
SPIKE TRAP!
The spikes pierce you!
Current health: 1

--- Moving to position 6 ---
Safe tile. Moving forward...

--- Moving to position 7 ---
Safe tile. Moving forward...

--- Moving to position 8 ---
SPIKE TRAP!
The spikes pierce you!
Current health: -1

GAME OVER - The Prince has perished!
```

Experiment with the start variable values. How long can our Prince survive?

What's Happening:

- We use a `while` loop (don't worry, we'll learn how to use loops soon!) to move forward
- Modulus `%` creates spike traps at positions 2, 5, 8 (every position where position % 3 == 2)
- If statements check for traps and potions
- Math operators calculate damage and healing
- Boolean logic determines shield effectiveness

Wrap-Up: What You've Learned

Congratulations! You've just learned how to give your code a brain. This is a massive milestone in your programming journey and you've moved beyond just storing data and can make your programs actually think and respond to different situations.

Key Takeaways

- **Make decisions** with if, else if, and else statements to create branching paths in your code
- **Compare values** using ==, !=, >, <, >=, <= to evaluate conditions and check relationships between data
- **Combine conditions** with AND (&&), OR (||), and NOT (!) to create sophisticated logic that checks multiple things at once
- **Handle multiple choices** with switch statements in both classic and modern expression styles
- **Perform calculations** with +, -, *, /, and % to manipulate numbers and calculate game values
- **Use shorthand** operators like ++, --, +=, -=, *=, /= to write cleaner, more efficient code
- **Apply math functions** like Math.Max, Math.Min, Math.Sqrt, Math.Abs, and rounding functions to solve complex problems
- **Understand modulus** and harness its power for creating patterns, cycles, and determining divisibility
- **Build complex logic** by combining all these elements together into decision-making systems

Every program you've ever used uses this stuff constantly. In a game it could be checking whether Mario hit a block, if your Sim is hungry, or if our Prince successfully grabbed a ledge, it all comes down to logic, comparisons, and math.

Think about what you can do now that you couldn't do before. Your programs can adapt to different situations, respond to user input in meaningful ways, calculate values on the fly, and make choices based on complex conditions. You're not just writing instructions anymore; you're creating systems that can think.

Chapter 4

Loops

"Repetition is the mother of learning." — Latin Proverb

Every program you've ever used from streaming your favorite music to scrolling through social media relies on repetition. When Spotify plays your playlist, it loops through each song. When Instagram loads your feed, it loops through posts. When your web browser displays a page, it loops through every element to render it on screen. Without loops, programmers would need to write the same code thousands or even millions of times. Loops are the fundamental tool that lets computers do what they do best: perform repetitive tasks tirelessly and perfectly, every single time.

But loops aren't just about saving typing, they're about unlocking computational power. They let you process enormous amounts of data (think of Netflix analyzing viewing habits for millions of users), create responsive experiences (your phone's interface updating 60 times per second), and solve problems that would be impossible to tackle manually. Understanding loops means understanding how to harness a computer's ability to work at superhuman speeds. Once you master loops, you'll see them everywhere, and you'll start thinking in terms of patterns and repetition which is a fundamental shift in how you approach problem-solving.

Core Concepts Covered

- ✓ Repetition and iteration as fundamental programming patterns
- ✓ Choosing the right repetition structure for different scenarios
- ✓ Processing collections of data efficiently
- ✓ Early termination and conditional skipping for optimization
- ✓ Understanding performance implications of nested repetition
- ✓ Managing program flow with controlled repetition

Doing the Same Thing Again (On Purpose)

 **Trivia:**

In 1982, Soviet satellites detected five US nuclear missiles launching toward Russia. Officer Stanislav Petrov noticed the system kept reporting exactly five missiles—not the hundreds expected in a real attack. Suspecting a computer error stuck in a false loop, he didn't report it as genuine. He was right—sunlight on clouds had triggered false detections. His decision prevented nuclear retaliation that could have started World War III!

Alright, so you've learned variables, you can make decisions with if-else statements, and you can do math. However, real programs need to do stuff **over and over again**. Like, a LOT!

Think about the Prince running through a dungeon. Every single frame (assuming it's 60 times per second) the computer will need to:

- Check if the player pressed a button
- Update the Prince's position
- Check for collisions with walls, spikes, or guards
- Draw everything on the screen
- Play sound effects

Imagine writing that code 60 times just to get one second of gameplay. Then multiply that by the hundreds of seconds a player might spend in a level. Your program would be millions of lines long! This is where **loops** come to the rescue.

Loops let you tell the computer: "Hey, do this thing multiple times" or "Keep doing this until something happens." They're absolutely essential for games, and basically every program you'll ever write.

Without loops, you'd have to write something like this to check 5 rooms:

```
Console.WriteLine("Checking room 1...");
Console.WriteLine("Checking room 2...");
Console.WriteLine("Checking room 3...");
Console.WriteLine("Checking room 4...");
Console.WriteLine("Checking room 5...");
```

But what if you need to check 100 rooms? Or 1000? You'd be typing forever! With loops, you can do all of that with just a few lines of code. Almost like magic!

Choosing the Right Loop: When to Use Which

C# gives you four main types of loops, and each one has its special purpose. Think of them like different tools in your development toolkit:

- `foreach` - "Do this for each item in a collection" (Best for going through lists of things)
- `for` - "Do this an exact number of times" (Best when you know how many iterations you need)
- `while` - "Keep doing this as long as something is true" (Best for game loops and unknown durations)
- `do-while` - "Do this once, then keep going if something is true" (Best for menus and when you need at least one iteration)

Let's explore each one and see where they shine.

Quick Detour: Arrays Sneak Peek

To really show you the power of loops, we need to use something called an **array** which we'll cover in the Collections chapter coming up soon. We could not cover collections earlier because Loop's are pretty important to explain collections properly. It's a bit of a chicken-and-egg situation. But here's the super quick version so you can understand the examples below.

An array is just a list of values stored together under one name. Instead of having `room1`, `room2`, `room3` as separate variables, you can have one array called `rooms` that holds all of them.

The two square brackets `[ ]` after the type basically tells you, and C# that it's an array. Then when you instantiate it you either specify the size (count of items it will hold) or the actual values.

You can create an array like this:

```
int[] numbers = { 1, 2, 3, 4, 5 };  // A list of numbers
string[] rooms = { "Entrance", "Hallway", "Treasure Room" };  // A list of rooms
```

A **2D array** (two-dimensional) is like a grid or table that has rows AND columns. Here you will see a comma between the two square brackets [,] that basically allows you to specify the column and grid size when you instantiate the 2D array.

Think of it like a spreadsheet with rows and columns:

```
// Creates a 3-row by 4-column grid of true/false values
bool[,] hasTrap = new bool[3, 4];
hasTrap[0, 2] = true;  // Put a trap at row 0, column 2
```

Don't worry if this seems confusing right now. We'll cover that soon. For now, just know that `hasTrap[row, col]` lets us check if there's a trap at a specific grid position. Now let's see loops in action!

The Foreach Loop: Processing Collections

The `foreach` loop is your buddy when you have a collection of items and you want to do something with each one. No counting, no tracking indexes, just "for each item, do this."

Imagine you have a collection of health potions scattered across the level. You want to check each potion to see if the Prince is close enough to pick it up:

```
string[] potionLocations = { "Room 1", "Room 3", "Room 5", "Room 8" };

Console.WriteLine("Searching for health potions...\n");

foreach (string location in potionLocations)
{
    Console.WriteLine("Found a health potion in " + location);
}

Console.WriteLine("\nAll potions located!");
```

Expected Output:

```
Searching for health potions...

Found a health potion in Room 1
Found a health potion in Room 3
Found a health potion in Room 5
Found a health potion in Room 8

All potions located!
```

The `foreach` loop automatically goes through every item in `potionLocations`. The variable `location` holds the current item (first "Room 1", then "Room 3", and so on). You don't need to worry about counting or tracking your position, C# handles that for you.

Here's another example with numbers to check damage from multiple guards:

```csharp
int[] guardDamage = { 10, 15, 20, 10, 25 };
int totalDamage = 0;

Console.WriteLine("Calculating damage from all guards...\n");

foreach (int damage in guardDamage)
{
    Console.WriteLine("Guard dealt " + damage + " damage");
    totalDamage += damage;
}

Console.WriteLine("\nTotal damage taken: " + totalDamage);
Console.WriteLine("Ouch! Better find those health potions!");
```

Expected Output:

```
Calculating damage from all guards...

Guard dealt 10 damage
Guard dealt 15 damage
Guard dealt 20 damage
Guard dealt 10 damage
Guard dealt 25 damage

Total damage taken: 80
Ouch! Better find those health potions!
```

Foreach loops are everywhere in programming! Processing emails in your inbox, displaying items in an online shopping cart, updating all open documents in a word processor, or checking every file in a folder. Our Prince would use foreach to check all enemies on the screen (updating their positions and attacks), process all collectible items (potions, keys, swords), update every trap in the level, or even check all animation frames when performing moves.

 **Pro Tip:**

The `foreach` loop is "read-only" for the collection—you can't add or remove items while you're looping through them. If you tried to destroy an enemy while looping through all enemies with foreach, C# would throw an error. For that, you'd need a regular `for` loop. But foreach is cleaner and easier to read when you just need to look at or use each item.

The For Loop: Counting and Precise Control

The `for` loop is your go-to when you know exactly how many times you want to repeat something, or when you need precise control over the counter. It's got three parts packed into one line:

1. **Initialization** - Set up a counter variable
2. **Condition** - Keep going while this is true
3. **Update** - Change the counter after each iteration

Let's say our Prince needs to search through 5 rooms in the dungeon to find a health potion:

```csharp
int totalRooms = 5;
bool foundPotion = false;

for (int roomNumber = 1; roomNumber <= totalRooms; roomNumber++)
{
    Console.WriteLine("Searching room " + roomNumber + "...");

    if (roomNumber == 3)
    {
        foundPotion = true;
        Console.WriteLine("Found a health potion in room 3!");
    }
}

if (foundPotion)
{
    Console.WriteLine("Time to heal up!");
}
else
{
    Console.WriteLine("No potions found. Better be careful...");
}
```

Expected Output:

```
Searching room 1...
Searching room 2...
Searching room 3...
Found a health potion in room 3!
Searching room 4...
Searching room 5...
Time to heal up!
```

Let's decode that first line:

```csharp
for (int roomNumber = 1; roomNumber <= totalRooms; roomNumber++)
```

- `int roomNumber = 1`: Start at room 1
- `roomNumber <= totalRooms`: Keep going until we've checked all 5 rooms
- `roomNumber++`: Add 1 to roomNumber after each loop (so we go 1, 2, 3, 4, 5)

The for loop is super flexible. You can count backwards, skip numbers, or use any pattern you want:

```csharp
// Counting down a timer
Console.WriteLine("Door closing in...");
for (int seconds = 5; seconds > 0; seconds--)
{
    Console.WriteLine(seconds + "...");
}
Console.WriteLine("Door sealed! You're trapped!");
```

Expected Output:

```
Door closing in...
5...
4...
3...
2...
1...
Door sealed! You're trapped!
```

For loops are perfect when you know the exact count, for example displaying pages in a PDF viewer (page 1 of 50, page 2 of 50...), processing rows in a spreadsheet, creating calendar grids (7 days across, 5 weeks down), or loading assets during a progress bar (1/100, 2/100, 3/100...).

For our Prince we can use for loops to draw the dungeon grid (each tile, row by row), count down timer-based traps (gate closing in 5... 4... 3...), cycle through sword attack animations frame by frame, or check collision with each wall segment in the level.

 **Pro Tip:**

The variable used in the for loop; `roomNumber` only exists inside the loop. If you tried to use it after the loop ends, C# would give you an error. This is called **scope**, and it helps prevent bugs. If you need the final value outside the loop, declare the variable before the loop starts.

The While Loop: Conditional Repetition

The `while` loop is probably the simplest to understand. It says: "While this condition is true, keep running this code."

Imagine the Prince is being chased by a guard. He needs to keep running while the guard is still chasing him:

```csharp
bool guardIsChasing = true;
int distanceRan = 0;

while (guardIsChasing)
{
    Console.WriteLine("Prince is running! Distance: " + distanceRan + " meters");
    distanceRan++;

    if (distanceRan >= 10)
    {
        guardIsChasing = false;
        Console.WriteLine("The Prince escaped! The guard gave up.");
    }
}

Console.WriteLine("Safe! Time to catch your breath.");
```

Expected Output:

```
Prince is running! Distance: 0 meters
Prince is running! Distance: 1 meters
Prince is running! Distance: 2 meters
Prince is running! Distance: 3 meters
Prince is running! Distance: 4 meters
Prince is running! Distance: 5 meters
Prince is running! Distance: 6 meters
Prince is running! Distance: 7 meters
Prince is running! Distance: 8 meters
Prince is running! Distance: 9 meters
The Prince escaped! The guard gave up.
Safe! Time to catch your breath.
```

See what happened? The loop kept running as long as `guardIsChasing` was true. Each time through the loop (we call this an **iteration**), the Prince ran a bit further. Once he hit 10 meters, we set `guardIsChasing` to false, and the loop stopped.

Here's an example with user input:

```csharp
string playerAction = "";

Console.WriteLine("You're in a dark dungeon room. What do you do?");
Console.WriteLine("(Type 'search', 'wait', or 'exit')\n");

while (playerAction != "exit")
{
    Console.Write("> ");
    playerAction = Console.ReadLine().ToLower();

    if (playerAction == "search")
    {
        Console.WriteLine("You search the room and find a rusty key.");
    }
    else if (playerAction == "wait")
    {
        Console.WriteLine("You wait. Nothing happens. It's still dark.");
    }
    else if (playerAction == "exit")
    {
        Console.WriteLine("You leave the dungeon room.");
    }
    else
    {
        Console.WriteLine("You can't do that. Try something else.");
    }
}

Console.WriteLine("On to the next room!");
```

Expected Output (example interaction):

```
You're in a dark dungeon room. What do you do?
(Type 'search', 'wait', or 'exit')

> search
You search the room and find a rusty key.
```

```
> wait
You wait. Nothing happens. It's still dark.
> exit
You leave the dungeon room.
On to the next room!
```

While loops handle unknown durations perfectly, waiting for a file download to complete, keeping a chat application running until the user logs out, retrying network connections until successful, or processing data until you reach the end of a file.

For our Prince the main game loop could run with `while (gameIsRunning)`, keeping everything active until the player quits. We could also use while loops when our Prince is being chased (run while guard is following), falling down pits (fall while not touching ground), or in combat (fight while both combatants are alive).

Pro Tip:

Be careful with while loops! If the condition never becomes false, you've created an **infinite loop** and your program will freeze. Like if you forgot to increase `distanceRan` in our first example; our Prince would be running in place forever like a broken animation. Always make sure something in your loop can change the condition to false.

The Do-While Loop: Execute First, Check Later

The `do-while` loop is like the while loop's more determined cousin. It's different because it **always runs at least once** before checking the condition.

Imagine the Prince steps on a trap door and falls into a pit. He's definitely falling at least once, but he'll keep falling while there are more floors below:

```
int currentFloor = 3;
int fallDistance = 0;

do
{
    Console.WriteLine("Falling through floor " + currentFloor + "!");
    fallDistance += 10;
    currentFloor--;
} while (currentFloor > 0);

Console.WriteLine("Landed! Fell a total of " + fallDistance + " feet.");
Console.WriteLine("Ouch! Lost some health.");
```

Expected Output:

```
Falling through floor 3!
Falling through floor 2!
Falling through floor 1!
Landed! Fell a total of 30 feet.
Ouch! Lost some health.
```

The key difference: the condition (`currentFloor > 0`) is checked **after** the code runs, not before. So even if `currentFloor` started at 0, our Prince would still fall once.

Here's a good real-world use case, a menu system:

```
string menuChoice = "";

do
{
    Console.WriteLine("\n=== DUNGEON MENU ===");
    Console.WriteLine("1. Start Game");
    Console.WriteLine("2. View High Scores");
    Console.WriteLine("3. Quit");
    Console.Write("Choose an option: ");

    menuChoice = Console.ReadLine();

    if (menuChoice == "1")
    {
        Console.WriteLine("Starting game...");
    }
    else if (menuChoice == "2")
    {
        Console.WriteLine("High Scores: 1. Jordan - 5000 pts");
    }
    else if (menuChoice == "3")
    {
        Console.WriteLine("Thanks for playing!");
    }
    else
    {
        Console.WriteLine("Invalid choice. Try again.");
    }

} while (menuChoice != "3");
```

Expected Output (*example interaction*):

```
=== DUNGEON MENU ===
1. Start Game
2. View High Scores
3. Quit
Choose an option: 2
High Scores: 1. Jordan - 5000 pts

=== DUNGEON MENU ===
1. Start Game
2. View High Scores
3. Quit
Choose an option: 1
Starting game...
```

```
=== DUNGEON MENU ===
1. Start Game
2. View High Scores
3. Quit
Choose an option: 3
Thanks for playing!
```

Do-while loops are great for validation, for example showing a login form at least once, then keep showing it while credentials are wrong. ATM machines use this pattern: display the menu at least once, then keep showing it until the user selects "exit." Great for any "try then retry if needed" scenario.

For our Prince its perfect for menu systems (show options at least once), tutorial prompts ("Press any key to continue" which is display it at least once), and trap sequences (trigger the trap once, then keep checking if more traps activate). Also useful for falling mechanics where our Prince falls at least one floor, then continues falling while there are more floors below.

 **Pro Tip:**

If you find yourself writing `while (true)` which is an infinite loop (coming soon) and then use `break` to exit, consider if a do-while loop would be clearer. They're often more readable because the exit condition is right there at the bottom where you can see it.

Breaking Out: The Break Statement

Sometimes you need to escape a loop early, like when our Prince finds a secret door and doesn't need to keep searching. That's where `break` is used, it immediately exits the loop and continues with whatever code comes after:

```csharp
int switchesToCheck = 10;

for (int switchNumber = 1; switchNumber <= switchesToCheck; switchNumber++)
{
    Console.WriteLine("Testing switch " + switchNumber + "...");

    if (switchNumber == 4)
    {
        Console.WriteLine("This switch opened the secret door!");
        break; // Exit the loop immediately
    }
}

Console.WriteLine("Moving through the secret door...");
```

Expected Output:

```
Testing switch 1...
Testing switch 2...
Testing switch 3...
Testing switch 4...
This switch opened the secret door!
Moving through the secret door...
```

Notice how the loop stopped at switch 4, even though we told it to check 10 switches? The break keyword immediately exits the loop and continues with whatever code comes after it.

Here's a more practical example searching for an item in a treasure room:

```csharp
string[] treasureItems = { "Gold Coin", "Ruby", "Old Book", "Magic Sword", "Diamond" };
bool foundSword = false;

Console.WriteLine("Searching the treasure room for a sword...\n");

foreach (string item in treasureItems)
{
    Console.WriteLine("Found: " + item);

    if (item == "Magic Sword")
    {
        Console.WriteLine("That's the sword! No need to keep searching.");
        foundSword = true;
        break;
    }
}

if (foundSword)
{
    Console.WriteLine("\nEquipped the Magic Sword!");
}
```

Expected Output:

```
Searching the treasure room for a sword...

Found: Gold Coin
Found: Ruby
Found: Old Book
Found: Magic Sword
That's the sword! No need to keep searching.

Equipped the Magic Sword!
```

Break saves processing time everywhere. Searching for a contact in your phone (stop once found), finding a specific file in a folder structure (exit once located), or stopping a spell-checker when it finds the first error. Any time you're looking for something specific and don't need to keep searching after you find it.

We use break when our Prince searches treasure rooms (found the sword, now stop looking!), detecting which switch opens the secret door (found it, no need to test the others), checking for collisions (hit a spike, stop checking other objects this frame), or scanning for the nearest enemy to target.

 **Pro Tip:**

If you have nested loops (a loop inside another loop), `break` only exits the innermost loop. If you need to break out of multiple loops, you might need a flag variable or a different approach. We'll talk about nested loops in just a bit.

Skipping Ahead: The Continue Statement

What if you want to skip the rest of the current iteration but keep looping? That's what `continue` does. It jumps straight to the next iteration without running the rest of the code in the loop.

Let's say our Prince is checking rooms for traps, but some rooms are locked and he can't enter them:

```csharp
int[] roomNumbers = { 1, 2, 3, 4, 5, 6, 7, 8 };
int[] lockedRooms = { 2, 5, 7 };

foreach (int room in roomNumbers)
{
    // Check if this room is locked
    bool isLocked = false;
    foreach (int lockedRoom in lockedRooms)
    {
        if (lockedRoom == room)
        {
            isLocked = true;
            break;
        }
    }

    if (isLocked)
    {
        Console.WriteLine("Room " + room + " is locked. Skipping...");
        continue; // Skip to the next room
    }

    Console.WriteLine("Room " + room + " - Searching for traps...");
    Console.WriteLine("Room " + room + " is safe!");
}
```

Expected Output:

```
Room 1 - Searching for traps...
Room 1 is safe!
Room 2 is locked. Skipping...
Room 3 - Searching for traps...
Room 3 is safe!
```

```
Room 4 - Searching for traps...
Room 4 is safe!
Room 5 is locked. Skipping...
Room 6 - Searching for traps...
Room 6 is safe!
Room 7 is locked. Skipping...
Room 8 - Searching for traps...
Room 8 is safe!
```

When a room is locked, `continue` skips the rest of that iteration and jumps to the next value of `room`.

Here's another example with guard patrol where it skips updating guards that are already defeated:

```csharp
int[] guardHealth = { 100, 0, 50, 0, 75, 100 };

Console.WriteLine("Updating all guards...\n");

for (int i = 0; i < guardHealth.Length; i++)
{
    if (guardHealth[i] == 0)
    {
        Console.WriteLine($"Guard {i + 1} is defeated. Skipping update.");
        continue;
    }

    Console.WriteLine($"Guard {i + 1} is active (Health: {guardHealth[i]})");
    Console.WriteLine($"Guard {i + 1} is patrolling...");
}

Console.WriteLine("\nAll active guards updated!");
```

Expected Output:

```
Updating all guards...

Guard 1 is active (Health: 100)
Guard 1 is patrolling...
Guard 2 is defeated. Skipping update.
Guard 3 is active (Health: 50)
Guard 3 is patrolling...
Guard 4 is defeated. Skipping update.
Guard 5 is active (Health: 75)
Guard 5 is patrolling...
Guard 6 is active (Health: 100)
Guard 6 is patrolling...

All active guards updated!
```

Continue improves efficiency by skipping unnecessary work. Processing emails but skipping spam, backing up files but skipping temporary ones, or validating form fields but skipping empty optional fields. It's all about "skip the ones that don't need processing."

For our Prince its perfect for updating enemies (skip the defeated ones, they don't need AI updates), rendering objects (skip off-screen items, no point drawing what players can't see), checking locked doors (skip them and try the next one), or processing treasure chests (skip the empty or already-opened ones).

Pro Tip:

Don't overuse `break` and `continue`. Sometimes they make code clearer, but sometimes they make it harder to follow—especially for someone reading your code later (including future you). If you find yourself using them constantly, there might be a better way to structure your loop. Always aim for readability first!

Going Faster: Introduction to Parallel Loops

Now, here's something cool but a bit more advanced. Don't worry about using this soon but it's good to know it exist. Normally, loops run one iteration at a time, in order. But modern computers have multiple processor cores that can do different things at the same time. **Parallel loops** let you take advantage of this by running multiple loop iterations simultaneously.

Imagine you have 1000 rooms to search for treasure, and you have 4 guards helping you. Instead of having one guard search all 1000 rooms one by one, you could have all 4 guards search different rooms at the same time! That's what parallel loops do.

Here's a simple example:

```csharp
using System.Threading.Tasks;

int[] roomNumbers = { 1, 2, 3, 4, 5, 6, 7, 8, 9, 10 };

Console.WriteLine("Searching rooms in parallel...\n");

Parallel.ForEach(roomNumbers, room =>
{
    Console.WriteLine("Searching room " + room + "...");
    // Imagine some complex search logic here
});

Console.WriteLine("\nAll rooms searched!");
```

Expected Output (order might vary!):

```
Searching rooms in parallel...

Searching room 1...
Searching room 3...
Searching room 2...
Searching room 5...
Searching room 4...
Searching room 7...
Searching room 6...
```

```
Searching room 8...
Searching room 9...
Searching room 10...

All rooms searched!
```

Notice how the rooms might not be searched in order? That's because multiple rooms are being searched at the same time by different processor cores. The exact order depends on which core finishes first.

 **When NOT to use parallel loops:**

- When the order matters (like drawing pixels on screen from left to right)
- When iterations are very quick (the overhead of parallelization isn't worth it)
- When your code modifies shared variables (this can cause bugs called "race conditions")
- When you're just learning stick with regular loops until you're comfortable!

 **When parallel loops can help:**

- Processing thousands of objects independently
- Loading multiple assets at once
- Complex calculations that don't depend on each other
- Large-scale simulations (like in SimCity with thousands of citizens)

 **Pro Tip:**

Parallel loops are powerful but can make debugging harder since things happen in unpredictable order. Only use them when you have a real performance problem and you've measured that they actually help. As they say in game development: "Premature optimization is the root of all evil." Get your program working first, then make it fast if needed!

For now, just know that parallel loops exist. When you get more experienced and you're working on something that needs to process tons of data quickly, you can come back to this concept. Regular loops will handle 99% of what you need when you're starting out.

Nested Loops: Grids and Multi-Dimensional Thinking

Let's spice it up a bit! You can put loops **inside** other loops. This is called **nesting**, and it's super useful for grid-based games.

Imagine the dungeon is a grid: 4 rooms wide and 3 rooms tall. We want to check every single room:

```csharp
int dungeonWidth = 4;
int dungeonHeight = 3;

Console.WriteLine("Mapping the dungeon...\n");

for (int row = 1; row <= dungeonHeight; row++)
{
    for (int column = 1; column <= dungeonWidth; column++)
    {
        Console.Write("[Room " + row + "," + column + "] ");
    }
    Console.WriteLine(); // New line after each row
}

Console.WriteLine("\nAll rooms mapped!");
```

Expected Output:

```
Mapping the dungeon...

[Room 1,1] [Room 1,2] [Room 1,3] [Room 1,4]
[Room 2,1] [Room 2,2] [Room 2,3] [Room 2,4]
[Room 3,1] [Room 3,2] [Room 3,3] [Room 3,4]

All rooms mapped!
```

Here's what's happening: for **each** row, we loop through **all** the columns. When row = 1, we go through columns 1, 2, 3, 4. Then row = 2, and we go through columns 1, 2, 3, 4 again.

Let's make this more game-like by placing traps randomly:

```csharp
int gridWidth = 5;
int gridHeight = 4;
bool[,] hasTrap = new bool[gridHeight, gridWidth];

// Place some traps
hasTrap[0, 2] = true; // Row 1, Column 3
hasTrap[1, 1] = true; // Row 2, Column 2
hasTrap[2, 4] = true; // Row 3, Column 5
hasTrap[3, 0] = true; // Row 4, Column 1

Console.WriteLine("Dungeon Layout (X = trap, . = safe):\n");

for (int row = 0; row < gridHeight; row++)
{
    for (int col = 0; col < gridWidth; col++)
    {
        if (hasTrap[row, col])
        {
            Console.Write("X ");
        }
        else
        {
            Console.Write(". ");
        }
```

```
    }
    Console.WriteLine();
}
```

Expected Output:

```
Dungeon Layout (X = trap, . = safe):

. . X . .
. X . . .
. . . . X
X . . . .
```

Grids and tables are everywhere, spreadsheet applications (rows and columns), image editors (every pixel in a photo), chess games (each square on the board), or seat selection on airline booking sites (rows of seats). Anytime you have data organized in rows and columns, you'll use nested loops.

For our Prince the dungeon is a grid! Nested loops draw every tile (floor, walls, spikes), check every grid square for collisions, generate random dungeon layouts (place items in each grid cell), update every position in the level, or even implement the path finding AI (check all possible paths through the grid).

Pro Tip:

Be careful with nested loops and their performance impact! If you have a loop with 100 iterations inside another loop with 100 iterations, that's 10,000 total iterations (100×100). This might be okay, but if you nest three loops with 1000 iterations each, that's 1 BILLION iterations. Your program will freeze faster than our Prince in a time-stop trap. Always think about how many times your nested loops will actually run. We call this **computational complexity**, and it matters a lot for performance.

Avoiding the Eternal Trap: Infinite Loops

Sometimes you **want** an infinite loop (like for a game's main loop), but usually they're bugs that freeze your program.

Here's what they look like:

```
// DON'T RUN THIS! It will freeze your program
// while (true)
// {
//     Console.WriteLine("Trapped forever!");
// }
```

Or the sneaky kind that looks like it should end but doesn't:

```
// This looks like it should end, but it won't
// int guardDistance = 10;
// while (guardDistance > 0)
// {
//     Console.WriteLine("Guard is approaching...");
//     // Oops! We forgot to decrease guardDistance
//     // This will run forever
// }
```

 **Pro Tip:**

If you accidentally create an infinite loop, your program will freeze and stop responding. In Visual Studio Code or most development environments, you can press **Ctrl+C** in the console (or Command+C on Mac) to kill the program. Don't panic—we've all done it! It's a rite of passage.

Intentional infinite loops

Sometimes we want loops to keep going:

```
bool gameRunning = true;

while (gameRunning)
{
    // Handle player input
    // Update game objects
    // Draw everything
    // Check if player pressed ESC to quit

    if (playerPressedEscape)
    {
        gameRunning = false;
    }
}

Console.WriteLine("Thanks for playing!");
```

That while loop runs thousands or millions of times during a gaming session. The condition (gameRunning) is controlled by game logic, when the player quits, you set it to false and the game ends gracefully.

> **Pro Tip:**
>
> Always ask yourself: "What makes this loop stop?" If you can't immediately answer that question while writing the loop, you might have an infinite loop waiting to happen. Double-check your exit conditions!

Common Loop Patterns and Best Practices

Here are some patterns you'll use over and over when writing applications:

Counting Up:

```csharp
for (int i = 0; i < 10; i++)
{
    // Runs 10 times: 0, 1, 2, 3, 4, 5, 6, 7, 8, 9
}
```

Counting Down:

```csharp
for (int i = 10; i > 0; i--)
{
    // Runs 10 times: 10, 9, 8, 7, 6, 5, 4, 3, 2, 1
}
```

Skipping Values:

```csharp
for (int i = 0; i < 10; i += 2)
{
    // Runs 5 times: 0, 2, 4, 6, 8
}
```

Processing an Array:

```csharp
string[] rooms = { "Entrance", "Hallway", "Treasure Room" };

// Method 1: Using foreach (simpler, cleaner)
foreach (string room in rooms)
{
    Console.WriteLine(room);
}

// Method 2: Using for with index (when you need the position)
for (int i = 0; i < rooms.Length; i++)
{
    Console.WriteLine("Room " + i + ": " + rooms[i]);
}
```

Searching Until Found:

```csharp
string[] items = { "Key", "Potion", "Sword", "Shield" };
bool foundSword = false;

foreach (string item in items)
```

```
{
    if (item == "Sword")
    {
        foundSword = true;
        break;
    }
}
```

Fun Experiment: The Systematic Search

Time to put your loop skills to the test! Create a simple dungeon crawler where our Prince walks through rooms looking for items and the exit.

The Prince's Journey: Climbing Through Repetition

The story so far...

The Prince's muscles burn as he pulls himself onto a stone ledge, the sound of metal spikes slamming into the floor below still ringing in his ears. He had barely made it, one more second and those deadly traps would have impaled him. Now, standing on this higher platform, he looks ahead and his heart sinks. Before him stretches a long passage with multiple chambers, each doorway identical to the last. The Vizier's dungeon is designed to confuse and exhaust escapees, making them wander endlessly through repetitive corridors until they collapse from fatigue or stumble into a trap. But the Prince notices something the Vizier might not have expected: patterns. The rooms follow a sequence. Some are empty, some contain items he desperately needs, and some harbor dangers. If he can systematically explore each chamber in order, keeping his wits about him and remembering what he finds in each, he might finally piece together the path forward. He grips his sword, takes a steadying breath, and prepares to move through the passage methodically, room by room, determined not to miss anything that could aid his escape.

The Challenge

1. Our Prince needs to explore 12 rooms in a dungeon
2. Use a for loop to go through each room (1 through 12)
3. In room 3, he finds a sword (print a message)
4. In room 5, he finds a health potion (print a message)
5. In room 8, he encounters a guard (print a message)
6. In room 11, he finds a key (print a message)
7. In room 12, he finds the exit and escapes!
8. For all other rooms, print that the room is empty

Bonus Challenge:

- Keep track of how many items our Prince has collected using a counter variable that you increment each time he finds something.

Try this on your own first! Then check the example answer below to see one way to solve it.

Example Answer

Here's one way to solve the challenge:

```csharp
int totalRooms = 12;
int itemsCollected = 0;
bool hasSword = false;
bool hasKey = false;

Console.WriteLine("The Prince enters the dungeon...\n");

for (int roomNumber = 1; roomNumber <= totalRooms; roomNumber++)
{
    Console.WriteLine("=== Room " + roomNumber + " ===");

    if (roomNumber == 3)
    {
        Console.WriteLine("Found a sword! Now you can fight!");
        hasSword = true;
        itemsCollected++;
    }
    else if (roomNumber == 5)
    {
        Console.WriteLine("Found a health potion! Feeling refreshed.");
        itemsCollected++;
    }
    else if (roomNumber == 8)
    {
        if (hasSword)
        {
            Console.WriteLine("A guard blocks the path!");
            Console.WriteLine("Drew your sword and defeated the guard!");
        }
        else
        {
            Console.WriteLine("A guard blocks the path!");
            Console.WriteLine("You have no weapon! The guard defeats you.");
            Console.WriteLine("\n*** GAME OVER ***");
            break; // Exit the loop - game ended
        }
    }
    else if (roomNumber == 11)
    {
        Console.WriteLine("Found a rusty key! Wonder what it opens...");
        hasKey = true;
        itemsCollected++;
    }
    else if (roomNumber == 12)
    {
        if (hasKey)
        {
            Console.WriteLine("Found a locked door - the exit!");
            Console.WriteLine("Used the key to unlock it. Freedom!");
        }
        else
        {
            Console.WriteLine("Found a locked door - the exit!");
```

```
                Console.WriteLine("But you don't have a key! Still trapped.");
        }
    }
    else
    {
        Console.WriteLine("The room is empty. Moving on...");
    }

    Console.WriteLine();
}

Console.WriteLine("=== Adventure Summary ===");
Console.WriteLine("Rooms explored: " + totalRooms);
Console.WriteLine("Items collected: " + itemsCollected);

if (hasKey && hasSword)
{
    Console.WriteLine("Status: VICTORIOUS! You escaped the dungeon!");
}
else
{
    Console.WriteLine("Status: The adventure continues...");
}
```

Expected Output (*successful run*):

```
The Prince enters the dungeon...

=== Room 1 ===
The room is empty. Moving on...

=== Room 2 ===
The room is empty. Moving on...

=== Room 3 ===
Found a sword! Now you can fight!

=== Room 4 ===
The room is empty. Moving on...

=== Room 5 ===
Found a health potion! Feeling refreshed.

=== Room 6 ===
The room is empty. Moving on...

=== Room 7 ===
The room is empty. Moving on...

=== Room 8 ===
A guard blocks the path!
Drew your sword and defeated the guard!

=== Room 9 ===
The room is empty. Moving on...

=== Room 10 ===
The room is empty. Moving on...

=== Room 11 ===
Found a rusty key! Wonder what it opens...
```

```
=== Room 12 ===
Found a locked door - the exit!
Used the key to unlock it. Freedom!

=== Adventure Summary ===
Rooms explored: 12
Items collected: 3
Status: VICTORIOUS! You escaped the dungeon!
```

This solution uses a for loop to go through all 12 rooms, checking what's in each one with if-else statements. Notice how we use Boolean variables (`hasSword`, `hasKey`) to remember what our Prince has collected, and an integer counter (`itemsCollected`) to track the total. The `break` statement stops the game early if our Prince encounters a guard without a sword. Pretty cool how loops, variables, and conditionals all work together!

Wrap-Up: What We Learned

Loops are your best friends in programming. They let you repeat code without typing it thousands of times, and they're essential for games and applications where things need to happen over and over.

Key Takeaways

- **Foreach loops** are the cleanest way to process every item in a collection, no counting needed
- **For loops** give you precise control with a counter and perfect when you know exactly how many times to repeat
- **While loops** run as long as a condition is true, ideal for game loops and unknown durations
- **Do-while loops** guarantee at least one execution which is great for menus and validation
- **Break** exits a loop immediately. Use it when you've found what you're looking for
- **Continue** skips to the next iteration. Use it to bypass items that don't need processing
- **Parallel loops** can speed up processing by using multiple CPU cores, but add complexity
- **Nested loops** work with grids and multi-dimensional data. Works great for tile-based games
- Always watch out for **infinite loops** as they'll freeze your program

Every application uses loops constantly. Email apps loop through messages. Spreadsheets loop through cells. Web browsers loop through page elements…

The best part? You now understand the fundamental concept that makes computers powerful, automation through repetition. Without loops, computers would be glorified calculators. With loops, they become the amazing tools we use every day.

Graphics

"Art is the elimination of the unnecessary." — Pablo Picasso

Graphics are where programming transforms from abstract logic into something you can actually *see*. Every application you interact with - from your web browser to your favorite game to the weather app on your phone - uses graphics programming to turn data into visual information. When Spotify shows you album artwork, when Google Maps renders a route, when your video editor displays a timeline, that's all graphics code converting numbers and instructions into pixels on your screen. Learning to work with graphics isn't just about making games look pretty; it's about understanding how to communicate information visually, create user interfaces people want to use, and bring your ideas to life in ways that text alone never could.

In this chapter, we're diving into the world of visual programming using Windows' built-in graphics system called GDI+. You'll learn how colors work at a fundamental level (spoiler: they're just numbers), how to draw shapes and create animations, and most importantly, how to make things move on screen using the same core loop concept that powers everything from vintage arcade games to modern applications. We'll also explore randomness - a crucial tool for creating variety and unpredictability in both games and practical applications. By the end of this chapter, you won't just understand how graphics work; you'll be able to create your own visual programs that respond, animate, and come alive.

Core Concepts Covered

- ✓ How computers represent and mix colors using numerical values
- ✓ Drawing basic shapes and controlling their appearance
- ✓ Creating animation through repeated drawing cycles
- ✓ Understanding the update-draw loop pattern used in interactive applications
- ✓ Generating unpredictable values for variety and dynamic behavior
- ✓ Managing timing and frame rates for smooth visual updates
- ✓ Coordinate systems and positioning elements on screen

Welcome to the Visual Zone!

 **Trivia:**

The original Toy Story (1995) took 800,000 computer hours to render—about 91 years if one computer did it alone. Pixar used 117 computers running 24/7 for months, each looping through billions of calculations per frame to figure out lighting, shadows, and reflections. Some complex frames took 13 hours just to calculate a single second of film!

So, you've conquered loops and you're probably thinking, "Cool, I can print stuff to the console a hundred times. But when do I get to make something that looks, you know, *not boring*?"

Well, my friend, welcome to your first bonus chapter! We're going to take those loops you just learned and use them to draw actual graphics on the screen. Think of it like this, in a real game with graphics and animation if our Prince was running through those dungeons, it can't just printing "Prince moved right" to a console. It will need to draw him pixel by pixel, frame by frame, using loops to paint the world.

 **Pro Tip:**

Modern game engines like Unity or Unreal handle most of this graphics stuff for you, but understanding how to draw things directly teaches you what's happening under the hood. Plus, some of the most creative indie games (like Undertale) still use simple 2D drawing techniques!

Quick Note Before We Start

Heads up: this bonus chapter uses some concepts like methods, classes, and events that we haven't covered in detail yet. Don't worry if some of the code looks confusing or you're not sure why things are structured the way they are, that's okay!

If you find yourself scratching your head thinking "Wait, what's `Timer_Tick` doing?" or "Why are we using `protected override`?", you have two options:

1. **Keep going anyway** - Just follow along, type the code, see the cool graphics, and don't stress about understanding every detail. Sometimes the best way to learn is to experiment first and understand later.
2. **Come back later** - Skip this chapter for now and return after you've read the chapters on Methods, Classes, and Events. Everything will make a lot more sense then!

Think of it like trying to beat a tough level in a game before you've collected all the health potions - you can try it now and have fun, or come back when you're more powered up. Either way works!

It's good to see how loops can create animations and how graphics programming works. The specific syntax details will click into place as you continue through the book.

✋ **Important:** This chapter's examples are Windows-only! If you're coding on a Mac or Linux, you can still read along and learn using the example output provided.

Why Windows Only?

You might be wondering: "Wait, I thought C# works everywhere?" And you'd be right! C# itself is cross-platform, but **Windows Forms** (the framework we're about to use) is a Windows-specific technology. It talks directly to the Windows operating system to create windows, buttons, and graphics.

These days, if you want to make cross-platform graphics apps, you'd use technologies like:
- **Avalonia UI** - works on Windows, Mac, and Linux
- **MAUI** - Microsoft's newer cross-platform framework
- **Game engines** like Unity or Godot

But for learning the basics of drawing graphics and understanding how loops create animations, Windows Forms is perfect. It's simple, it's fast to set up, and it teaches the core concepts that apply everywhere.

Setting Up Your Visual Playground

To draw graphics, we need a window to draw on. That means we're switching from a boring console app to a **Windows Forms** app. Don't worry, it's easier than you think.

Creating a Windows Forms Project in Visual Studio

If you're using Visual Studio (the full version, not VS Code), here's how to create your graphics project:

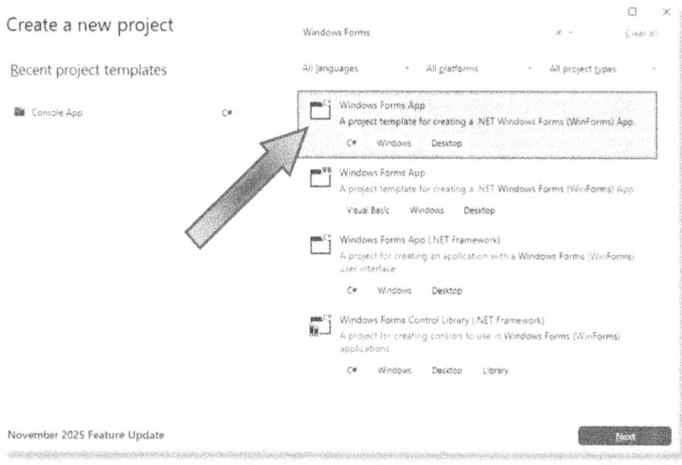

1. Open Visual Studio
2. Click "Create a new project"
3. In the search box, type "Windows Forms"
4. Select "Windows Forms App (.NET)" (make sure it says C# and not VB)
5. Click "Next"
6. Name your project "GraphicsPlayground"
7. Choose where to save it
8. Click "Next"
9. Select the latest .NET version (probably .NET 10)
10. Click "Create"

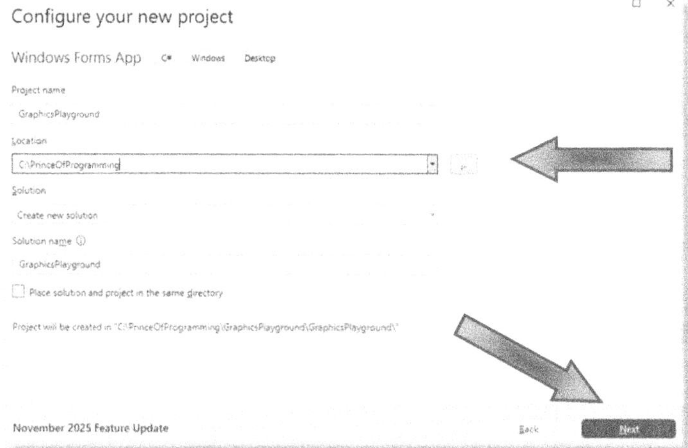

Visual Studio will create your project and automatically open `Form1.cs` in designer view. You'll see a gray window with a grid - that's your canvas! You can switch between the designer view and the code view by clicking the tabs at the top or right-clicking the file in Solution Explorer.

To run your app, just press **F5** or click the green "Start" button at the top.

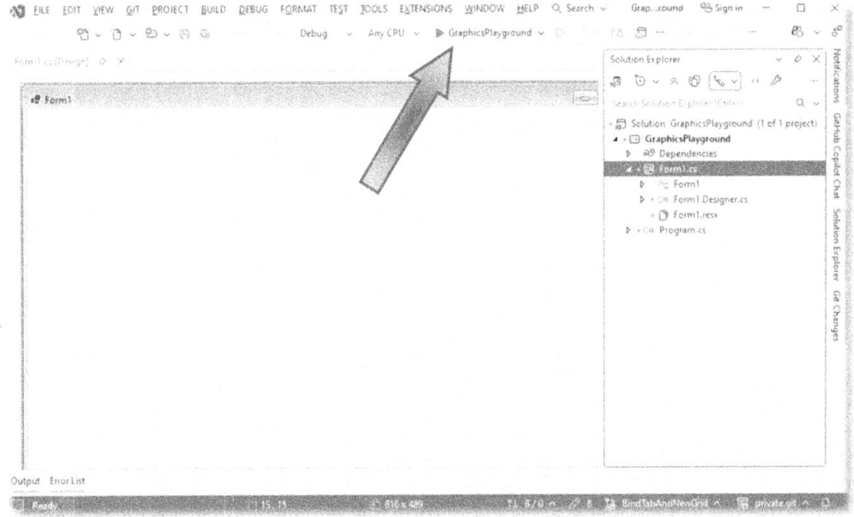

Creating a Windows Forms Project in VS Code

If you're using VS Code, the process is a bit more manual but still straightforward.

1. First, open your terminal in VS Code (View → Terminal, or just press `Ctrl+``).
2. Type this command and hit Enter:

```
dotnet new winforms -n GraphicsPlayground
```

This creates a new Windows Forms project called "GraphicsPlayground". Think of it like starting a new game save file.

3. Now navigate into your new project folder:

```
cd GraphicsPlayground
```

4. And open it in VS Code:

```
code .
```

If VSCode ask you if you trust the authors of the files in the folder select "Yes" since well be trusting our own code… this time ;).

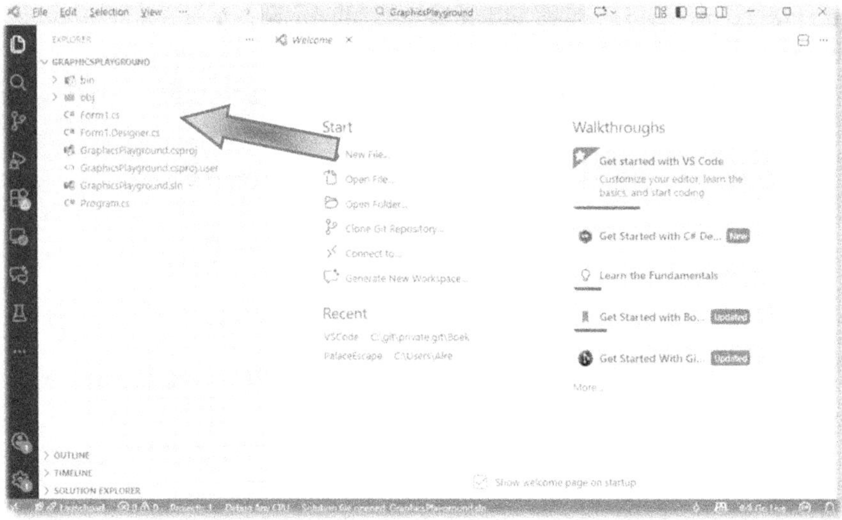

Your project folder will have a file called `Form1.cs` - that's your canvas! Open it up.

5. To run your app, type this in the terminal:

```
dotnet run
```

Expected Output:

A blank window appears. It's like that moment when you first load up a game and see the menu screen!

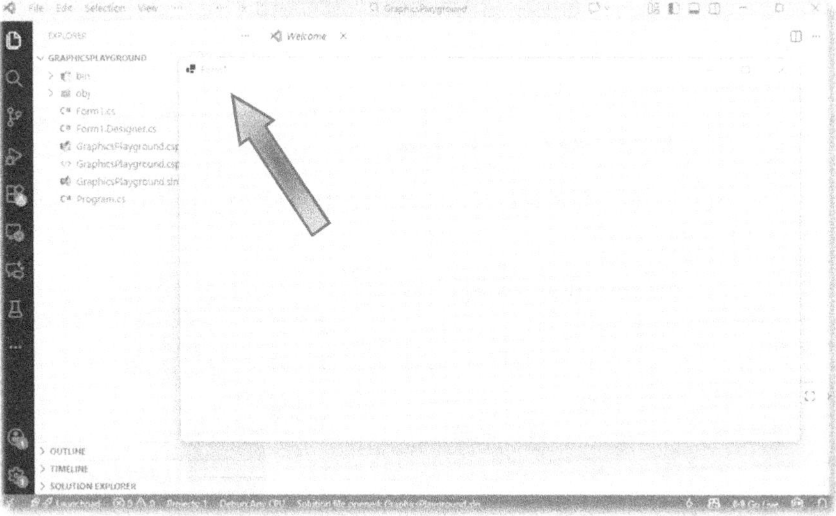

 **Pro Tip:**

If VS Code asks you to install recommended extensions for C# when you open the project, say yes! It'll make your life much easier with features like auto-complete and error highlighting.

What is GDI+ Anyway?

Before we start drawing, let's talk about what we're actually using. **GDI+** stands for "Graphics Device Interface Plus" - a very technical-sounding name for "the thing that lets you draw stuff on Windows."

The Simple Explanation

Think of GDI+ as your art supplies kit. When you want to draw something on your computer screen, you can't just directly change pixels (well, you *can*, but it's really complicated). Instead, you tell GDI+: "Hey, draw me a circle here" or "Fill this rectangle with red" and GDI+ handles all the complicated pixel-pushing for you.

It's like how in SimCity, you didn't place individual bricks - you clicked a zone tool and the game handled building the actual structures. GDI+ is similar: you give high-level commands, and it handles the low-level details.

What GDI+ Can Do

GDI+ provides tools for:

- **Drawing shapes** - circles, rectangles, lines, polygons, curves
- **Filling shapes** - solid colors, gradients, patterns, textures
- **Drawing text** - with different fonts, sizes, and styles
- **Drawing images** - loading and displaying pictures
- **Transformations** - rotating, scaling, and moving graphics
- **Alpha blending** - making things transparent or semi-transparent

Where GDI+ is Used

You might think: "This is old tech, right?" Well, yes and no. While modern games use more advanced graphics APIs like DirectX or OpenGL, GDI+ is still used for:

- **Business applications** - charts, graphs, and data visualization
- **Simple games** - 2D indie games, puzzle games, card games
- **UI elements** - custom buttons, progress bars, dashboard displays
- **Image editing tools** - basic drawing programs
- **Prototyping** - quickly testing game ideas before moving to a full engine

Most 2D games use graphics routines which are conceptually similar to GDI+. The developer told the computer "draw this shape here" and the hardware handled it.

The Basics: Brushes and Pens

In GDI+, you draw using two main tools:

- **Pen**: Used for drawing outlines and lines
    - Like a pencil or marker
    - Has a color and thickness
    - Used with `Draw` methods: `DrawLine`, `DrawRectangle`, `DrawEllipse`
- **Brush**: Used for filling shapes
    - Like a paint bucket
    - Has a color (and can have patterns or gradients)
    - Used with `Fill` methods: `FillRectangle`, `FillEllipse`, `FillPolygon`

Think of it like this: if you're drawing a circle, the **pen** draws the outline, and the **brush** fills the inside.

Pro Tip:

In Wolfenstein 3D, John Carmack had to write his own graphics routines from scratch to draw the 3D walls. With GDI+, Microsoft has done all that hard work for you, so you can focus on making cool stuff instead of fighting with pixels!

The Minimum GDI+ Setup (Speed Run Edition)

You know how in speedruns, players skip all the cutscenes and get straight to the action? That's what we're doing here. Here's the minimum code to get a window that you can draw on.

Open `Form1.cs` and replace everything with this:

```
using System;
using System.Drawing;
using System.Windows.Forms;

namespace GraphicsPlayground
{
    public partial class Form1 : Form
    {
        public Form1()
        {
            Text = "Graphics Demo";
            Size = new Size(800, 600);
            DoubleBuffered = true; // Prevents flickering - trust me on this
        }
```

```csharp
        protected override void OnPaint(PaintEventArgs e)
        {
            base.OnPaint(e);
            Graphics g = e.Graphics;

            // YOUR DRAWING CODE GOES HERE


        }
    }
}
```

Now open `Program.cs` and make sure it looks something like this (Visual Studio usually creates this for you already):

```csharp
namespace GraphicsPlayground
{
    internal static class Program
    {
        /// <summary>
        ///  The main entry point for the application.
        /// </summary>
        [STAThread]
        static void Main()
        {
            // To customize application configuration such as
            // set high DPI settings or default font,
            // see https://aka.ms/applicationconfiguration.
            ApplicationConfiguration.Initialize();
            Application.Run(new Form1());
        }
    }
}
```

Run your app (F5 in Visual Studio, or `dotnet run` in VS Code terminal).

Expected Output:

A blank window appears with the title "Graphics Demo". It's like that moment when you first load up an application or a game and see the menu!

What's happening here?

- `Form1` is your window (like the window for any windows application or game)
- `OnPaint` is a special method that gets called whenever Windows needs to draw your window
- `Graphics g` is your paintbrush that you'll use to draw everything
- `DoubleBuffered = true` is a trick that prevents your graphics from flickering (we won't go into the details now, but it's like how old games used page flipping to make animations smooth)

Pro Tip:

The `OnPaint` method gets called automatically whenever your window needs to be redrawn - when you first open it, when you resize it, when another window was covering it and moves away, etc. You never call it directly since Windows calls it for you.

Colors: Mixing Your Palette

In the old days when computers still were lucky to have a display with more than one color game used a limited color palette. Modern computers can display millions of colors, and we create them using the **RGB** color model.

RGB: Red, Green, Blue

Every color on your screen is made by mixing three colors: Red, Green, and Blue. Each color has a value from 0 to 255 (that's 256 possible values because we start counting at 0).

- **0** means "none of this color"
- **255** means "maximum of this color"

Think of it like mixing paint, but with light instead!

Here's a few examples of creating our own colors:

```
// Creating colors
Color red = Color.FromArgb(255, 0, 0);      // Full red, no green, no blue
Color green = Color.FromArgb(0, 255, 0);    // No red, full green, no blue
Color blue = Color.FromArgb(0, 0, 255);     // No red, no green, full blue

Color purple = Color.FromArgb(128, 0, 128); // Half red, no green, half blue
Color white = Color.FromArgb(255, 255, 255);// All colors at maximum
Color black = Color.FromArgb(0, 0, 0);      // No color at all

Color orange = Color.FromArgb(255, 165, 0); // Full red, some green, no blue
Color teal = Color.FromArgb(0, 128, 128);   // No red, half green, half blue
```

Pro Tip:

C# has built-in colors you can use: `Color.Red`, `Color.Green`, `Color.Blue`, `Color.Yellow`, etc. But making custom colors with RGB gives you way more options!

Alpha: The Invisible Component

There's actually a **fourth** value called **Alpha** that controls transparency:

```csharp
// Alpha is the FIRST parameter in FromArgb when you use 4 values
Color transparentRed = Color.FromArgb(128, 255, 0, 0); // Half-transparent red
Color invisibleBlue = Color.FromArgb(0, 0, 0, 255);    // Completely invisible blue
Color solidGreen = Color.FromArgb(255, 0, 255, 0);     // Fully opaque green
```

- **Alpha = 0**: Completely invisible (like the Prince when he drinks that invisible potion... wait, wrong game)
- **Alpha = 255**: Completely solid
- **Alpha = 128**: Half-transparent (perfect for ghost effects!)

Transparency is used for things like:

- Fading effects when you die
- Semi-transparent UI windows that don't completely block the game
- Ghost enemies (like in *Another World*)
- Water and glass effects
- Particle effects like smoke or magic spells

Try adding this to your `OnPaint` method to see colors in action:

```csharp
protected override void OnPaint(PaintEventArgs e)
{
    base.OnPaint(e);
    Graphics g = e.Graphics;

    // Draw some colored rectangles
    g.FillRectangle(new SolidBrush(Color.FromArgb(255, 0, 0)), 50, 50, 100, 100);
    g.FillRectangle(new SolidBrush(Color.FromArgb(0, 255, 0)), 100, 100, 100, 100);
    g.FillRectangle(new SolidBrush(Color.FromArgb(0, 0, 255)), 150, 150, 100, 100);

    // Draw a semi-transparent purple rectangle over them
    g.FillRectangle(new SolidBrush(Color.FromArgb(128, 128, 0, 128)), 75, 75, 150,150);
}
```

Expected Output:

Three solid-colored squares (red, green, blue) overlapping each other, with a semi-transparent purple square on top showing the colors beneath it.

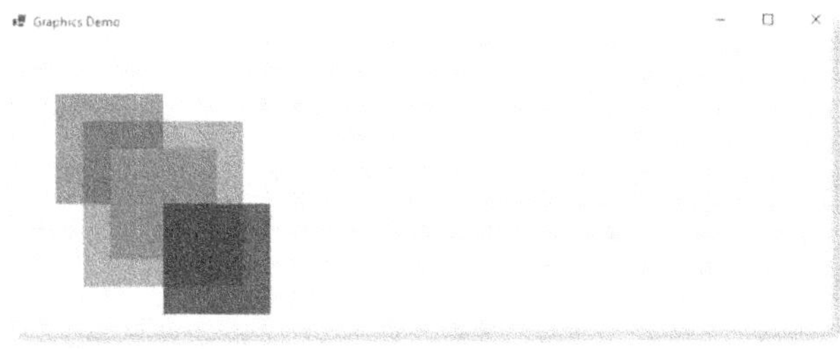

Drawing Basic Shapes

Alright, time to put paint to canvas! GDI+ gives us methods to draw basic shapes. Let's look at the main ones.

Drawing Circles (Actually, Ellipses)

```csharp
protected override void OnPaint(PaintEventArgs e)
{
    base.OnPaint(e);
    Graphics g = e.Graphics;

    // Create a brush for filling (like a paint bucket)
    Brush redBrush = new SolidBrush(Color.Red);

    // Draw a filled circle
    // Parameters: brush, x, y, width, height
    g.FillEllipse(redBrush, 100, 100, 50, 50);

    // Create a pen for outlines (like a pencil)
    Pen bluePen = new Pen(Color.Blue, 3); // Color and thickness

    // Draw a circle outline
    g.DrawEllipse(bluePen, 200, 100, 50, 50);

    redBrush.Dispose();
    bluePen.Dispose();
}
```

Expected Output:

A red filled circle at position (100, 100) and a blue circle outline at (200, 100). Both are 50 pixels wide and tall.

Coordinates: The screen uses X and Y coordinates, just like in math class, but with one twist - (0, 0) is the **top-left** corner! X increases going right, Y increases going **down**.

Why "Ellipse" and not "Circle"? An ellipse is the mathematical name for an oval shape. A circle is just a special case of an ellipse where the width equals the height.

If you make width and height different, you get an oval!

```
// This is a circle (width = height)
g.FillEllipse(redBrush, 100, 100, 50, 50);

// This is an oval (width ≠ height)
g.FillEllipse(redBrush, 200, 100, 80, 50);
```

Drawing Rectangles

```
protected override void OnPaint(PaintEventArgs e)
{
    base.OnPaint(e);
    Graphics g = e.Graphics;

    // Filled rectangle
    Brush greenBrush = new SolidBrush(Color.Green);
    g.FillRectangle(greenBrush, 300, 100, 80, 60); // x, y, width, height

    // Rectangle outline
    Pen yellowPen = new Pen(Color.Yellow, 2);
    g.DrawRectangle(yellowPen, 400, 100, 80, 60);

    greenBrush.Dispose();
    yellowPen.Dispose();
}
```

Expected Output:

A green filled rectangle and a yellow rectangle outline appear on your window.

Drawing Lines

```
protected override void OnPaint(PaintEventArgs e)
{
    base.OnPaint(e);
    Graphics g = e.Graphics;

    Pen greenPen = new Pen(Color.Green, 2);
    Pen redPen = new Pen(Color.Red, 2);
    Pen bluePen = new Pen(Color.Blue, 2);

    // Draw a line from point A to point B
    // Parameters: pen, x1, y1, x2, y2
    g.DrawLine(greenPen, 50, 50, 150, 150);
```

```csharp
    // Draw a horizontal line
    g.DrawLine(redPen, 200, 100, 400, 100);

    // Draw a vertical line
    g.DrawLine(bluePen, 500, 50, 500, 200);

    greenPen.Dispose();
    redPen.Dispose();
    bluePen.Dispose();
}
```

Expected Output:

A diagonal green line from point (50, 50) to point (150, 150), a horizontal red line, and a vertical blue line.

Pro Tip:

Always clean up your pens and brushes when you're done with them by calling `.Dispose()`, or better yet, use the `using` statement. Otherwise, you can leak memory like a dungeon sewer with no pipes!

Example: `using Brush redBrush = new SolidBrush(Color.Red);`

Random Type: Your New Best Friend

Think about our Prince's adventure, we want some spike traps to be in random locations. And guards should randomly patrol a corridor. In programming, we use something called a **Random** object to generate unpredictable numbers.

Think of it like rolling dice in a tabletop game where you never know what you'll get, but it's always within a certain range.

How to Use Random

First, you need to **create** a Random object (we call this "instantiating", fancy word for "making a new one"):

```
Random random = new Random();
```

 **Important:** You should only create ONE Random object in your program and reuse it. Creating multiple Random objects too quickly can actually give you the same "random" numbers. It's like having a loaded die!

Now you can use it to get random numbers:

```
// Get a random number between 0 and 99
int randomNumber = random.Next(100);

// Get a random number between 50 and 150
int randomInRange = random.Next(50, 151); // Note: upper bound is EXCLUSIVE

// Get a random decimal between 0.0 and 1.0
double randomDecimal = random.NextDouble();
```

> ### Pro Tip:
>
> The upper bound in `Next(min, max)` is **exclusive**, meaning it won't include that number. So `Next(1, 7)` gives you 1 through 6, perfect for simulating a dice roll!

Where Random Gets Used in Games

- **Loot drops**: Did you get a health potion or a sword from that chest? Random decides!
- **Enemy spawning**: Where does the next goblin appear? Random!
- **Critical hits**: Did your attack do double damage? Random!
- **Procedural generation**: Games like Minecraft use random numbers to generate entire worlds
- **Particle effects**: Those sparkles when Prince picks up a potion? Each particle moves randomly

Here's an example:

```
Random rng = new Random();

// Simulating a health potion drop (30% chance)
int dropChance = rng.Next(100); // 0-99
if (dropChance < 30)
{
    Console.WriteLine("A health potion appeared!");
}
else
{
```

```
    Console.WriteLine("No drops this time.");
}

// Random damage between 10 and 25
int damage = rng.Next(10, 26);
Console.WriteLine($"You dealt {damage} damage!");

// Random position for enemy spawn
int enemyX = rng.Next(0, 800);
int enemyY = rng.Next(0, 600);
Console.WriteLine($"Enemy spawned at ({enemyX}, {enemyY})");
```

Expected Output:

```
A health potion appeared!
You dealt 18 damage!
Enemy spawned at (423, 187)
```

(Results will vary each time you run it, but that's the point!)

Using Random with Graphics

Random is perfect for creating visual variety. Here's an example that draws circles at random positions with random colors:

```
protected override void OnPaint(PaintEventArgs e)
{
    base.OnPaint(e);
    Graphics g = e.Graphics;

    Random rng = new Random();

    // Draw 20 random circles
    for (int i = 0; i < 20; i++)
    {
        // Random position
        int x = rng.Next(0, this.ClientSize.Width - 50);
        int y = rng.Next(0, this.ClientSize.Height - 50);

        // Random size
        int size = rng.Next(20, 60);

        // Random color
        int r = rng.Next(0, 256);
        int g2 = rng.Next(0, 256);
        int b = rng.Next(0, 256);
        Color randomColor = Color.FromArgb(r, g2, b);

        // Draw it
        using (Brush brush = new SolidBrush(randomColor))
        {
            g.FillEllipse(brush, x, y, size, size);
        }
    }
}
```

Expected Output:

Twenty circles of random sizes, colors, and positions scattered across your window. Every time you resize the window (which triggers a repaint), you'll get a completely different pattern!

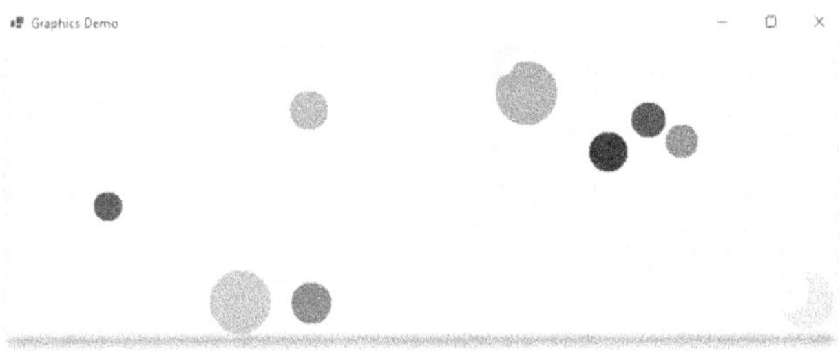

 **Pro Tip:**

Notice we're creating the Random object inside `OnPaint` for the example? This is not ideal when `OnPaint` gets called frequently, its unnecessary and you might get similar random numbers. A better approach is to make Random a field of the Form class so it persists between paint calls.

Working with Timers

Before we combine random and graphics into animations, we need to talk about **Timers**. A timer is like an alarm clock that goes off repeatedly at regular intervals. In games and animations we should try to use the same time between frames to ensure it is displayed correctly on all computers even with different hardware.

Most games update's the screen about 60 times per second. It needs to check for input, move characters, draw everything, wait a bit, then do it all again. So that's what we'll do!

Creating and Using a Timer

Here's how to set up a basic timer:

```
// Create a new timer
System.Timers.Timer myTimer = new System.Timers.Timer();

// Set how often it "ticks" (in milliseconds)
myTimer.Interval = 100; // 100ms = 0.1 seconds = 10 times per second

// Tell it what to do each time it ticks
myTimer.Elapsed += MyTimer_Elapsed;
```

```
// Start the timer
myTimer.Start();

// Keep the console app running so we can see the ticks
Console.WriteLine("Timer started. Press Enter to stop...");
Console.ReadLine();
myTimer.Stop();
```

Then we need a method that handles what happens each tick:

```
//Then you need a method that handles what happens each tick:
static void MyTimer_Elapsed(object sender, System.Timers.ElapsedEventArgs e)
{
    // This code runs every 100 milliseconds
    Console.WriteLine("Tick!");
}
```

Expected Output:

"Tick!" appears in the console 10 times per second until you stop the program by pressing Enter.

 **Pro Tip:**

Notice we used `Elapsed` instead of `Tick`? That's because `System.Timers.Timer` (for console apps) uses `Elapsed`, while `System.Windows.Forms.Timer` (for graphics apps) uses `Tick`. Also, console apps need something like `Console.ReadLine()` to keep running, otherwise the program would end immediately!

Timer Intervals: How Fast Should It Tick?

The `Interval` property controls how many milliseconds pass between ticks.

Here are some common values:

```
System.Timers.Timer slowTimer = new System.Timers.Timer();
slowTimer.Interval = 1000; // 1 second (1 tick per second)

System.Timers.Timer mediumTimer = new System.Timers.Timer();
mediumTimer.Interval = 100; // 0.1 seconds (10 ticks per second)

System.Timers.Timer fastTimer = new System.Timers.Timer();
fastTimer.Interval = 16; // ~0.016 seconds (about 60 ticks per second -
                         // typical game frame rate!)
```

Where Timers can be Used:

- **Games**: Wolfenstein 3D aimed for 70 FPS (about 14ms intervals), and modern games typically target 60 FPS (16ms) or 30 FPS (33ms), Prince of Persia ran at 12 FPS (about 83ms between frames)
- **Auto-save features**: Save your document every 5 minutes (300,000ms)
- **Status updates**: Check server connection every 30 seconds (30,000ms)
- **Animations**: Fade effects, progress bars, loading spinners (usually 16-50ms for smooth motion)
- **Clocks**: Digital clock displays updating every second (1000ms)
- **Notifications**: Check for new emails or messages periodically (60,000ms for every minute)

Complete Timer Example

Here's a simple program that counts up every second and displays it in the window title:

```csharp
public partial class Form1 : Form
{
    private int counter = 0;

    public Form1()
    {
        Text = "Counter: 0";
        Size = new Size(400, 300);

        System.Windows.Forms.Timer countTimer = new System.Windows.Forms.Timer();
        countTimer.Interval = 1000; // Once per second
        countTimer.Tick += CountTimer_Tick;
        countTimer.Start();
    }

    private void CountTimer_Tick(object sender, EventArgs e)
    {
        counter++;
        Text = $"Counter: {counter}";
    }
}
```

Expected Output:

A window opens with the title "Counter: 0". Every second, the number increases: "Counter: 1", "Counter: 2", "Counter: 3", and so on.

Starting and Stopping Timers

You can control your timer with these methods:

```
_countTimer.Start();                // Begin ticking
_countTimer.Stop();                 // Stop ticking (you can start it again later)
_countTimer.Enabled = true;         // Another way to start
_countTimer.Enabled = false;        // Another way to stop
```

This is useful when you want to pause your game or animation. To make this work you can add the following code to the earlier example code.

First you will need to add the KeyPress event to the form to let it know what it should call if a key was pressed. Don't worry about events for now, well cover that later.

```csharp
public Form1()
{
    KeyPress += Form1_KeyPress;

    // Rest of the code as above
}
```

Then we add the event method to capture the key presses and stop or start the timer:

```csharp
private void Form1_KeyPress(object sender, KeyPressEventArgs e)
{
    if (e.KeyChar == 'p' || e.KeyChar == 'P')
    {
        if (_countTimer.Enabled)
        {
            _countTimer.Stop();
            this.Text = "PAUSED";
        }
        else
        {
            _countTimer.Start();
            this.Text = "Running";
        }
    }
}
```

Expected Output:

A window opens with the title "Counter: 0". Every second, the number increases untill you press 'p' then it pauses the counter and write "PAUSED" to the form title. Pressing 'p' again starts the counter again.

 **Pro Tip:**

Always remember that the timer runs on the same thread as your UI. If your `Tick` event handler takes too long to execute (like if you're doing heavy calculations), it can make your window feel unresponsive. Keep your tick handlers fast and efficient!

Now that you understand timers, we can use them to create smooth animations by updating our graphics on each tick!

Loops and Graphics: Animation Basics

Now here's where loops and graphics come together beautifully. Every game you've ever played is just a loop that runs over and over:

1. Update game state (move characters, check collisions, etc.)
2. Draw everything to the screen
3. Wait a tiny bit
4. Repeat

This is called the "**game loop**", and it's basically how all animations, games and graphic intensive applications work.

Creating Simple Animation

Let's create a program that uses a timer (which is just a repeating loop) to animate something:

```
namespace GraphicsPlayground
{
    public partial class Form1 : Form
    {
        private int circleX = 50;
        private int circleY = 50;
        private int speedX = 5;
        private int speedY = 3;

        public Form1()
        {
            this.Text = "Bouncing Circle";
            this.Size = new Size(800, 600);
            this.DoubleBuffered = true;

            // Set up a timer that ticks 60 times per second
            System.Windows.Forms.Timer timer = new System.Windows.Forms.Timer();
            timer.Interval = 16; // roughly 60 FPS (1000ms / 60 = 16.67ms)
            timer.Tick += Timer_Tick;
            timer.Start();
        }

        private void Timer_Tick(object sender, EventArgs e)
```

```csharp
    {
        // Move the circle
        circleX += speedX;
        circleY += speedY;

        // Bounce off edges
        if (circleX < 0 || circleX > this.ClientSize.Width - 50)
        {
            speedX = -speedX; // Reverse horizontal direction
        }

        if (circleY < 0 || circleY > this.ClientSize.Height - 50)
        {
            speedY = -speedY; // Reverse vertical direction
        }

        // Redraw the window
        this.Invalidate();
    }

    protected override void OnPaint(PaintEventArgs e)
    {
        base.OnPaint(e);
        Graphics g = e.Graphics;

        // Clear background
        g.Clear(Color.Black);

        // Draw the circle
        using (Brush brush = new SolidBrush(Color.Cyan))
        {
            g.FillEllipse(brush, circleX, circleY, 50, 50);
        }
    }
}
}
```

Expected Output:

A cyan circle bounces around the window, reversing direction when it hits the edges. It's like a very simple version of Pong!

What's Happening Here:

1. **The Timer**: This is like the game loop in any animation or game. Every 16 milliseconds (about 60 times per second), the `Timer_Tick` method runs.

2. **Movement**: Each tick, we update the circle's position by adding `speedX` and `speedY`.

3. **Collision Detection**: We check if the circle hit the edges, and if so, we reverse its direction by flipping the sign of the speed.

4. **Redrawing**: `Invalidate()` tells Windows "Hey, my window needs to be redrawn!" which triggers the `OnPaint` method. And voilà!

Note: You might have noticed we wrote `this.Text` and `this.Size` instead of just `Text` and `Size`. The "`this`" keyword refers to "the current object" - in this case, the Form itself. It's like saying "my own Text property" or "my own Size property." Most of the time, you can leave out the "`this.`" part because C# knows what you mean. Writing just `Text = "Bouncing Circle"` works perfectly fine. Some programmers like using `this` everywhere to be super clear, while others think it clutters the code. Both approaches work! In this book, we'll usually skip the `this` to keep things cleaner, but you'll see it in code examples online, so it's good to know what it means.

Fun Experiment: The Potion's Visions

Time to combine everything! We're going to create a program that draws growing circles in random spots with changing colors. It'll look like a trippy screensaver from the 90s, basically our evil Vizier's enchanted potion.

The Prince's Journey: Magic Unveiled

The story so far...

The Prince uncorks the crystal bottle and tilts his head back, letting the glowing liquid pour down his throat. Immediately, warmth floods through his body and his wounds begin to close, his strength returns, the ache in his muscles fades away. But something unexpected happens. The potion doesn't just heal his body; it awakens something in his mind. The torchlight on the dungeon walls begins to shimmer and pulse with colors he's never seen before. Rings of light bloom from the flames, expanding outward in mesmerizing patterns, each one shifting through a spectrum of brilliant hues before fading away and being replaced by another.

The Prince realizes this is no ordinary healing potion, it's been enchanted with the Vizier's magic, perhaps meant to disorient or entrance anyone who drinks it. But the Prince has a strong will and purpose. Instead of succumbing to the hypnotic display, he watches carefully, studying the patterns, the colors, the way each ring grows and transforms. If he can understand how the Vizier's magic creates these illusions, perhaps he can recognize and resist other enchantments that surely await him deeper in the dungeon. He steadies himself against a pillar and focuses on the swirling lights, determined to master this magic rather than be mastered by it.

The Challenge

Create a program that:

1. Draws circles at random positions on the screen
2. Each circle starts small and grows larger
3. The circle's color gradually shifts as it grows
4. When a circle reaches a certain size, start a new one somewhere else
5. Use a loop concept (via timer) to create the animation

Hints:

- You'll need a Random object to pick random positions
- Use a Timer to create the animation effect
- Change the color by incrementing one of the RGB values
- Store the current circle's position, size, and color as fields in your Form class

Example Solution

Here's one way to solve it. Notice how we use the timer (which is conceptually a loop) to create the animation effect!

```csharp
using System;
using System.Drawing;
using System.Windows.Forms;

namespace GraphicsPlayground
{
    public partial class Form1 : Form
    {
        private Random random;
        private int circleX;
        private int circleY;
        private int radius;
        private int redValue;

        public Form1()
        {
            Text = "Hypnotic Circles - Press Any Key to Exit";
            Size = new Size(800, 600);
            DoubleBuffered = true;
            KeyPress += (s, e) => Application.Exit();

            random = new Random();
            StartNewCircle();

            // Start the animation
            System.Windows.Forms.Timer timer = new System.Windows.Forms.Timer();
            timer.Interval = 30; // Update every 30 milliseconds
            timer.Tick += Timer_Tick;
            timer.Start();
        }

        private void StartNewCircle()
        {
```

```csharp
        // Pick a random position (keep it away from edges)
        circleX = random.Next(100, ClientSize.Width - 100);
        circleY = random.Next(100, ClientSize.Height - 100);

        // Start with a small radius and random starting color
        radius = 5;
        redValue = random.Next(100, 200);
    }

    private void Timer_Tick(object sender, EventArgs e)
    {
        // Grow the circle
        radius += 2;

        // Change the color (cycle through red values)
        redValue += 3;
        if (redValue > 255) redValue = 0;

        // If circle gets too big, start a new one
        if (radius > 150)
        {
            StartNewCircle();
        }

        // Redraw the window
        Invalidate();
    }

    protected override void OnPaint(PaintEventArgs e)
    {
        base.OnPaint(e);
        Graphics g = e.Graphics;

        // Clear the background to black
        g.Clear(Color.Black);

        // Create a semi-transparent brush with our changing color
        Color circleColor = Color.FromArgb(180, redValue, 100, 255 - redValue);

        using (Brush brush = new SolidBrush(circleColor))
        {
            // Draw the circle centered at our position
            g.FillEllipse(brush, circleX - radius, circleY - radius,
                    radius * 2, radius * 2);
        }

        // Draw an outline for extra effect
        using (Pen outline = new Pen(Color.White, 2))
        {
            g.DrawEllipse(outline, circleX - radius, circleY - radius,
                    radius * 2, radius * 2);
        }
    }
}
}
```

Expected Output:

A black window appears with a circle growing from a random point. The circle's color shifts from red-purple to purple as it grows. When it reaches about 150 pixels in radius, a new circle starts growing from a different random location. This continues until you press any key to exit.

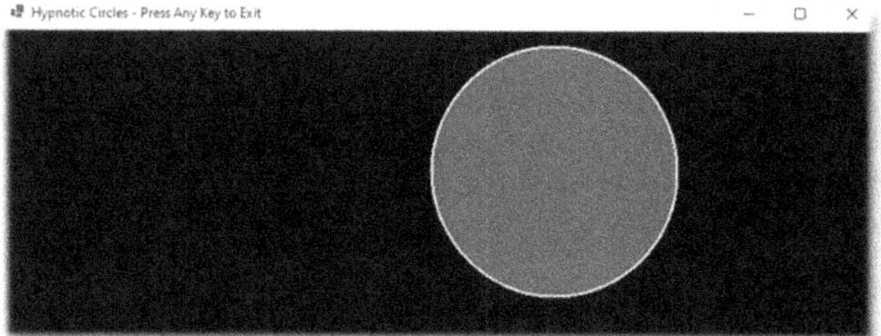

What's Happening:

1. **The Timer**: Every 30 milliseconds, `Timer_Tick` runs to simulate our "game loop".

2. **Growing and Changing**: Each tick, we increase the radius and change the color. This creates the animation effect.

3. **Random Positioning**: When a circle gets too big, `StartNewCircle()` picks a new random spot to start over.

4. **Semi-transparent Color**: We use `Alpha = 180` to make the circles slightly see-through, creating a cooler visual effect.

5. **Centering the Circle**: Notice we draw at `circleX - radius`? That's because `FillEllipse` draws from the top-left corner, but we want our circle centered at our `circleX, circleY` point.

Try These Variations:

- **Multiple Circles**: Create arrays to store multiple circles and draw them all at once
- **Different Shapes**: Try using `FillRectangle` instead of `FillEllipse`
- **Color Modes**: Cycle through different RGB values (try green or blue instead of red)
- **Speed Control**: Change the `timer.Interval` to make it faster or slower
- **Size Limits**: Try different maximum sizes for the circles

---

 **Pro Tip:**

The `Invalidate()` method only triggers a redraw – it doesn't immediately call `OnPaint()`. Windows decides when to actually redraw based on performance. This is similar to how old games had to work with the display refresh rate of the monitor!

Wrap-up: What You've Learned

Congrats! You've just leveled up from console warrior to graphics wizard.

Key Takeaways

- Understanding why Windows Forms is Windows-only
- Setting up a Windows Forms project in both Visual Studio and VS Code
- Understanding what GDI+ is and what it's used for
- Using Brushes (for filling) and Pens (for outlines)
- Understanding RGB color mixing (and alpha transparency)
- Drawing basic shapes with GDI+ (circles, rectangles, lines)
- Using the `Random` class to generate unpredictable numbers
- Creating simple animations using a timer
- Understanding the game loop concept (update and draw)
- Graphics programming follows the same pattern as classic games: initialize, update, draw, repeat
- Random numbers are essential for making games feel alive and unpredictable
- Colors are numbers (RGB values), and you can manipulate them mathematically
- Animation is just drawing slightly different things in the same spot really fast
- The coordinate system starts at (0,0) in the top-left corner
- GDI+ provides high-level commands that handle low-level pixel manipulation for you

Even though this bonus chapter is Windows-specific, the concepts you learned here apply to any graphics system - whether it's game engines like Unity, cross-platform frameworks like SDL, or even web-based graphics with HTML5 Canvas. The ideas of drawing shapes, using colors, generating random values, and creating animation loops are universal.

Chapter 5

Collections

"The whole is greater than the sum of its parts." — Aristotle

You've probably noticed by now that programming is all about managing data. Whether you're building a web browser that needs to remember all your open tabs, a music app that stores thousands of songs, or a text editor that tracks every change you make for the undo button, you need ways to organize and access information efficiently. The weapon of choice? Collections. They're the containers that hold your data, and knowing which one to use can mean the difference between software that flies and software that crawls. Think about Netflix managing millions of users, Spotify organizing billions of songs, or Google Maps keeping track of every street in the world. None of it would work without smart use of collections.

In this chapter, you'll learn how to store and manage groups of related data instead of juggling individual variables. We'll explore different types of collections, each designed for specific situations: some are great when you know exactly how much data you have, others shine when things are constantly changing, and some are built for lightning-fast searches through massive amounts of information. By the end, you'll understand not just how to use these tools, but when and why to choose one over another. A skill that separates beginners from developers who write clean, efficient code.

Core Concepts Covered

- ✓ Organizing multiple pieces of data in structured containers
- ✓ Understanding fixed versus dynamic data structures
- ✓ Choosing the right collection based on how you need to access data
- ✓ Trading off between memory usage and speed
- ✓ Managing data that changes size during program execution
- ✓ Accessing data by position versus accessing data by unique identifiers
- ✓ Processing items in specific orders (first-in-first-out, last-in-first-out)
- ✓ Ensuring uniqueness in datasets
- ✓ Building strings efficiently when combining many pieces of text

---

Organized Hoarding

 **Trivia:**

The Library of Alexandria (around 300 BCE) held perhaps 400,000 scrolls—humanity's first massive "collection" of knowledge. To grow it, every ship docking had to surrender any books aboard for copying. Its destruction over several centuries is considered one of history's greatest intellectual tragedies. Today's internet is similar—billions of items organized in collections, backed up worldwide so it can't all be lost at once.

So, you've learned about loops, and you've probably noticed something frustrating: loops are great for doing things multiple times, but what if you need to loop through a bunch of items? So far, you've been stuck with individual variables like `potion1`, `potion2`, `potion3`... and that gets old fast.

Let's say you're making a game and you need to track the player's inventory. Maybe the Prince is collecting health potions.

With what you know now, you'd probably do something like this:

```
string potion1 = "Small Health Potion";
string potion2 = "Medium Health Potion";
string potion3 = "Large Health Potion";
string potion4 = "Elixir of Life";
```

Cool. Four potions. But what happens when the Prince picks up a fifth potion? You'd have to add `string potion5` to your code and recompile the whole game. And what if he picks up 50 potions? 100? Are you going to sit there and type `potion1` through `potion100`? That's not programming, that's punishment.

This is where **collections** come to save the day. Collections let you store multiple items in a single structure without knowing ahead of time how many items you'll need. Think of them as magical bags that can hold as much stuff as you want (well almost, computers do have limits, but they're pretty generous).

In this chapter, we're going to learn about the most common collections you'll use: Arrays, Lists, Dictionaries, and a few others. By the end, you'll be managing inventories, enemies, level data, and more like a pro.

Arrays: Your First Collection

An **array** is like a row of lockers, all lined up and numbered. Each locker can hold one item, and you access items by their locker number (called an **index**). Arrays are the simplest form of collection, and they've been around since the dawn of programming.

As mentioned before in the array's sneak peek the two square brackets [ ] after the type tells you, and C# that it's an array. Then when you instantiate it you either specify the size (count of items it will hold).

Here's how you create an array in C#:

```
string[] potions = new string[5];
```

This creates an array that can hold 5 strings. Right now, all the slots are empty (well, technically they're `null`, but we'll get to that).

You can put items in specific slots like this:

```
potions[0] = "Small Health Potion";
potions[1] = "Medium Health Potion";
potions[2] = "Large Health Potion";
```

Wait, why does it start at 0?

Great question! In programming, we start counting from 0 because computers think in terms of "how far from the start." The first item is 0 steps away, the second is 1 step away, and so on. It's weird at first, but you'll get used to it. Plus, it makes you look smart at parties when you say "arrays are zero-indexed." (Okay, maybe not at parties, but definitely in coding forums.)

You can also create and fill an array at the same time:

```
string[] potions = { "Small Health Potion", "Large Health Potion" };
```

Much cleaner!

When you instantiate an array by immediately set the actual values like above, then C# will set the correct size from the count of items you assign to it automatically!

Now let's use this in an example:

```csharp
using System;

class Program
{
    static void Main()
    {
        string[] inventory = { "Sword", "Health Potion", "Key", "Torch" };

        Console.WriteLine("The Prince's inventory:");
        for (int i = 0; i < inventory.Length; i++)
        {
            Console.WriteLine($"Slot {i}: {inventory[i]}");
        }
    }
}
```

Expected Output:

```
The Prince's inventory:
Slot 0: Sword
Slot 1: Health Potion
Slot 2: Key
Slot 3: Torch
```

Notice that `inventory.Length` gives us the number of items in the array. Super handy for loops!

Real-World Use: Why Arrays Matter Everywhere

Arrays are used constantly in all kinds of software. A spreadsheet program uses arrays to store rows and columns of data. A music player uses arrays to store the playlist. Even your phone's contact list is probably stored in an array. Any time you have a fixed or predictable amount of data that needs to be accessed by position, arrays are your go-to.

In our Prince's adventure arrays could store the level layout. Each floor tile could be represented by a number: 0 for empty space, 1 for solid ground, 2 for spikes, 3 for a gate, etc. The entire level? Just an array of numbers that the game reads to know where to draw everything:

```csharp
// 0 = air, 1 = floor, 2 = spike trap, 3 = gate
int[] levelRow = { 0, 1, 1, 2, 1, 1, 3, 1, 1, 0 };
```

When the Prince moves, the game checks the array to see what's in front of him. If it's a 2 (spike), ouch! Time to lose some health.

2D and 3D Arrays: Grids and Cubes

Okay, so a regular array is like a single row of lockers. But what if you need a *grid* of lockers? Like a game level that needs rows *and* columns?

Enter the **2D array**:

```
int[,] levelGrid = new int[10, 20];
```

This creates a grid with 10 rows and 20 columns.

The comma between the two square brackets [,] basically allows you to specify the column and grid size when you instantiate the 2D array.

And when you need set the specific value you now access items using two indices:

```
levelGrid[0, 0] = 1;   // Top-left corner is a floor tile
levelGrid[0, 1] = 0;   // Next to it is air
levelGrid[5, 10] = 2;  // Somewhere in the middle is a spike trap
```

Here's a quick example of creating a small level:

```csharp
using System;

class Program
{
    static void Main()
    {
        int[,] miniLevel = {
            { 0, 0, 0, 0, 0 },
            { 0, 1, 1, 1, 0 },
            { 0, 1, 2, 1, 0 },
            { 0, 1, 1, 1, 0 },
            { 1, 1, 1, 1, 1 }
        };

        Console.WriteLine("Mini level layout:");
        for (int row = 0; row < 5; row++)
        {
            for (int col = 0; col < 5; col++)
            {
                Console.Write(miniLevel[row, col] + " ");
            }
            Console.WriteLine();
        }
    }
}
```

Expected Output:

```
Mini level layout:
0 0 0 0 0
0 1 1 1 0
0 1 2 1 0
0 1 1 1 0
1 1 1 1 1
```

3D Arrays? What Sorcery Is This?

If 2D arrays are grids, then **3D arrays** are cubes. Think of a game like Minecraft where you have width, height, *and* depth.

You now need to use three indices:

```
int[,,] worldChunk = new int[16, 16, 16];
worldChunk[8, 10, 5] = 1; // A block at coordinates (8, 10, 5)
```

Most of the time, 2D arrays are all you need. But 3D arrays are there if you ever decide to build the next Minecraft in your bedroom.

 **Pro Tip:**

2D and 3D arrays are powerful, but they can get memory-hungry fast. A 1000x1000 2D array is a million slots! Most modern games use smarter data structures (like dictionaries or spatial partitioning), but arrays are still great for fixed-size grids like board games or small levels.

The Problem with Arrays

Arrays are awesome, but they have a major limitation: **they're fixed in size**. Once you create an array with 5 slots, you're stuck with 5 slots forever. If you need a 6th slot, you have to create a whole new array, copy everything over, and toss the old one. That's a pain.

Imagine the player's inventory can hold only 5 items because that's how big you made the array. But then you decide to add a 6th item later in development. Now you're rewriting code, and your QA tester is giving you the stink-eye because you broke something.

This is where the generic **List** comes in and saves your sanity.

Generics: One Size Fits All

Before we dive into Lists, let's quickly talk about something you'll see a lot, "**Generics**". You might have noticed that some types use `<T>` syntax (T being the type) in things like `List<string>` or `List<int>`. That angle bracket notation is how C# does generics.

Sometimes you want to create a class or collection that can work with any type of data, but you don't want to lose the benefits of type safety. Imagine if there was only one kind of List, and it could hold anything, strings, numbers, objects, whatever. That would be messy because you'd never know what you were getting out of it.

Generics solve this problem. When you create a `List<string>`, you're saying "this is a List that only holds strings." When you create a `List<int>`, you're saying "this is a List that only holds integers."

The List class itself is generic (it can work with any type), but once you specify the type in the angle brackets, it becomes type-safe.

```
List<string> names = new List<string>();
names.Add("Prince");
names.Add("Guard");
// names.Add(42);  // This would cause an error because 42 isn't a string
```

Generics aren't just used in collections. Any class can be generic if it needs to work with a specific type that you want to define later. For example, you might create a `Box<T>` class that can hold any type of item, but once you specify `Box<Sword>` or `Box<Potion>`, it only works with that specific type.

The `<T>` is just a placeholder that means "some type that you'll specify later." You'll see other letters too, like `<TKey, TValue>` in dictionaries. The letters don't matter, `T` is just convention for "Type."

For now, just remember when you see angle brackets like `List<string>`, you're using generics, and it means "a collection (or class) that works specifically with strings."

Generic Lists: Arrays' Cooler Sibling

A **List** (specifically, `List<T>`) is like an array that can grow and shrink automatically. It's part of C#'s "generic collections," which means you can make a List of any type: `List<string>`, `List<int>`, `List<Enemy>`, whatever you need.

Here's how you create a List:

```
using System;
using System.Collections.Generic;

class Program
{
    static void Main()
    {
        List<string> inventory = new List<string>();

        inventory.Add("Sword");
        inventory.Add("Health Potion");
        inventory.Add("Key");

        Console.WriteLine("The Prince's inventory:");
        for (int i = 0; i < inventory.Count; i++)
        {
            Console.WriteLine($"Slot {i}: {inventory[i]}");
        }
    }
}
```

Expected Output:

```
The Prince's inventory:
Slot 0: Sword
Slot 1: Health Potion
Slot 2: Key
```

Notice a few things:

- You don't need to specify a size when creating the List.
- Use `Add()` to put items in the List.
- Use `Count` (not `Length`) to see how many items are in the List.
- You still access items with an indexer: `inventory[i]`, just like arrays.

Why Lists Are Better Than Arrays

Lists have a ton of useful methods that make your life easier

Hers is a few examples:

```csharp
List<string> items = new List<string> { "Sword", "Potion", "Key" };

items.Remove("Potion");        // Removes the first occurrence of "Potion"
items.RemoveAt(0);             // Removes the item at index 0 ("Sword")
items.Insert(1, "Torch");      // Inserts "Torch" at index 1
items.Clear();                 // Removes everything
bool hasKey = items.Contains("Key");  // Checks if "Key" exists
```

You can also initialize a List with items right away:

```csharp
List<int> scores = new List<int> { 100, 200, 150, 300 };
```

Lists Are Everywhere

Lists are probably the most commonly used collection in modern programming. Shopping cart systems use lists to store items. Email programs use lists to store messages in your inbox. Social media apps use lists to store your feed. Any time you have data that changes in size where items get added or removed then a List is usually the best choice.

For our Prince you could use a List to manage enemies in the current room. As enemies are defeated, you remove them from the List. When new enemies spawn (maybe through a trapdoor), you add them to the List.

The List grows and shrinks dynamically as the program runs:

```csharp
using System;
using System.Collections.Generic;

class Enemy
{
    public string Name { get; set; }
    public int Health { get; set; }
```

```csharp
}

class Program
{
    static void Main()
    {
        List<Enemy> enemies = new List<Enemy>
        {
            new Enemy { Name = "Guard", Health = 30 },
            new Enemy { Name = "Skeleton", Health = 20 }
        };

        Console.WriteLine("Enemies in the room:");
        foreach (Enemy enemy in enemies)
        {
            Console.WriteLine($"{enemy.Name} (HP: {enemy.Health})");
        }

        // The Prince defeats the Guard!
        enemies.RemoveAt(0);

        Console.WriteLine("\nAfter defeating the Guard:");
        foreach (Enemy enemy in enemies)
        {
            Console.WriteLine($"{enemy.Name} (HP: {enemy.Health})");
        }
    }
}
```

Expected Output:

```
Enemies in the room:
Guard (HP: 30)
Skeleton (HP: 20)

After defeating the Guard:
Skeleton (HP: 20)
```

 **Pro Tip:**

Use `foreach` loops with Lists when you don't need the index. It's cleaner and easier to read.

Collection Types: A Quick Tour

Before we dive deeper into specific collections, let's take a look at some collection types that are available. C# has a bunch of collection types, each with its own strengths.

Here's a handy table with some collection types and how they are used:

Collection	Description	When to Use It
Array	Fixed-size, indexed collection.	When you know the exact number of items ahead of time (level grids, fixed inventories).
List<T>	Dynamic array that grows/shrinks automatically.	When you need a flexible, ordered collection (enemy lists, player inventory).
Dictionary<TKey, TValue>	Key-value pairs for super-fast lookups.	When you need to find items by a unique identifier (player stats by name, items by ID).
Queue<T>	First-In-First-Out (FIFO) collection.	When you need to process items in order (task queue, animation frames).
Stack<T>	Last-In-First-Out (LIFO) collection.	When you need to undo actions or backtrack (undo system, pathfinding).
HashSet<T>	Unordered collection of unique items.	When you need to ensure no duplicates (tags, unique item IDs).
LinkedList<T>	Doubly-linked list for efficient insertions/removals.	When you need to frequently insert/remove items in the middle (less common in games).

We'll focus on the most important ones: **Dictionary**, **Queue**, **Stack**, and **HashSet**. But first, let's talk about why Lists are so popular.

Why We Love Lists

Lists are the workhorse of C# collections. They're fast, flexible, and easy to use. Under the hood, a List is actually an array that automatically resizes itself when it runs out of space. When you add items beyond its current capacity, it creates a new, bigger array, copies everything over, and dumps the old one. You never see this happening and it just works.

Here's a practical example where we manage power-ups in our game:

```csharp
using System;
using System.Collections.Generic;

class PowerUp
```

```csharp
{
    public string Name { get; set; }
    public int Duration { get; set; }
}

class Program
{
    static void Main()
    {
        List<PowerUp> activePowerUps = new List<PowerUp>();

        activePowerUps.Add(new PowerUp { Name = "Invincibility", Duration = 10 });
        activePowerUps.Add(new PowerUp { Name = "Speed Boost", Duration = 5 });

        Console.WriteLine("Active power-ups:");
        foreach (PowerUp powerUp in activePowerUps)
        {
            Console.WriteLine($"{powerUp.Name} ({powerUp.Duration} seconds left)");
        }

        // Simulate one second passing
        for (int i = activePowerUps.Count - 1; i >= 0; i--)
        {
            activePowerUps[i].Duration--;
            if (activePowerUps[i].Duration <= 0)
            {
                Console.WriteLine($"\n{activePowerUps[i].Name} has worn off!");
                activePowerUps.RemoveAt(i);
            }
        }
    }
}
```

Expected Output:

```
Active power-ups:
Invincibility (10 seconds left)
Speed Boost (5 seconds left)
```

Notice we're looping backward when removing items. That's because removing an item shifts all the items after it, which can mess up your loop if you're going forward. Looping backward avoids this issue.

Pro Tip:

When removing items from a List inside a loop, always loop backward:

```csharp
for (int i = list.Count - 1; i >= 0; i--)
```

or use RemoveAll() with a condition.

Dictionaries: Lightning-Fast Lookups

Okay, Lists are great, but what if you need to find something quickly without looping through the entire collection? Let's say you have 10,000 items in your inventory (maybe you're a hoarder in an RPG). If you use a List and search for "Golden Sword," you might have to check all 10,000 items one by one. That's slow.

Enter the **Dictionary**. A Dictionary stores data as **key-value pairs**. You give it a unique key (like an item's name or ID), and it returns the value instantly with no searching required. It's like having a magical librarian who knows exactly where every book is.

Here's how you create a Dictionary:

```csharp
using System;
using System.Collections.Generic;

class Program
{
    static void Main()
    {
        Dictionary<string, int> itemPrices = new Dictionary<string, int>();

        itemPrices.Add("Sword", 100);
        itemPrices.Add("Health Potion", 50);
        itemPrices.Add("Key", 25);

        Console.WriteLine("Price of Health Potion: " + itemPrices["Health Potion"]);
    }
}
```

Expected Output:

```
Price of Health Potion: 50
```

You can also initialize a Dictionary with values:

```csharp
Dictionary<string, int> itemPrices = new Dictionary<string, int>
{
    { "Sword", 100 },
    { "Health Potion", 50 },
    { "Key", 25 }
};
```

Why Are Dictionaries So Fast?

Dictionaries use something called a **hash table** under the hood. When you add a key-value pair, the Dictionary calculates a "hash code" from the key (basically a unique number). It uses this hash code to instantly figure out where to store the value in memory. When you look up a key later, it calculates the hash code again and jumps straight to the right spot. No looping, no searching, just instant access.

This is why Dictionaries are insanely fast, even with thousands or millions of items!

Fast Lookups Matter

Dictionaries are used whenever you need to look something up quickly by a unique identifier. Websites use dictionaries to store user sessions (the session ID is the key). Databases use dictionary-like structures (called indexes) to find records fast. Your computer's file system uses dictionaries to quickly locate files by name. Any time you need "give me the data for this specific thing," dictionaries are the answer.

For our Prince you might use a Dictionary to store tile types. Instead of looping through an array to find out what tile 47 represents, you just look it up:

```
Dictionary<int, string> tileTypes = new Dictionary<int, string>
{
    { 0, "Air" },
    { 1, "Floor" },
    { 2, "Spike Trap" },
    { 3, "Gate" }
};

Console.WriteLine("Tile 2 is: " + tileTypes[2]);
```

Expected Output:

```
Tile 2 is: Spike Trap
```

Another example is tracking player stats by name:

```
using System;
using System.Collections.Generic;

class Program
{
    static void Main()
    {
        Dictionary<string, int> playerStats = new Dictionary<string, int>
        {
            { "Health", 100 },
            { "Mana", 50 },
            { "Stamina", 80 }
        };

        Console.WriteLine("Player Health: " + playerStats["Health"]);

        // Take damage
        playerStats["Health"] -= 20;
        Console.WriteLine("Player Health after damage: " + playerStats["Health"]);
    }
}
```

Expected Output:

```
Player Health: 100
Player Health after damage: 80
```

Pro Tip:

Dictionaries don't maintain any particular order for their items. If you add items in a specific sequence, don't expect them to come out in that same order when you loop through them. If you need both fast lookups AND a guaranteed order, you'll need to use a different approach—either sort the keys before looping, or keep a separate List to track the order.

If you try to access a key that doesn't exist, you'll get an error. So, use `ContainsKey()` to check if it exists first:

```
if (playerStats.ContainsKey("Armor"))
{
    Console.WriteLine("Armor: " + playerStats["Armor"]);
}
else
{
    Console.WriteLine("Armor stat not found!");
}
```

Or use `TryGetValue()` for a cleaner approach:

```
if (playerStats.TryGetValue("Armor", out int armor))
{
    Console.WriteLine("Armor: " + armor);
}
else
{
    Console.WriteLine("Armor stat not found!");
}
```

Note: You will notice that all "TryXxx" methods usually return bool (true or false) to indicate if it worked or not and if it did then actual result will be part of the `out` argument.

Other Useful Collections

Let's take a look at some other collection types and where they are useful.

Queue: First In, First Out

A **Queue** is like a line at a theme park. The first person to get in line is the first person to get on the ride. In programming terms, it's **First-In-First-Out (FIFO)**.

Use `Enqueue()` to add items to the back of the line and `Dequeue()` to take items from the front:

```
using System;
using System.Collections.Generic;

class Program
{
```

```csharp
    static void Main()
    {
        Queue<string> taskQueue = new Queue<string>();

        taskQueue.Enqueue("Open chest");
        taskQueue.Enqueue("Defeat guard");
        taskQueue.Enqueue("Pull lever");

        Console.WriteLine("Processing tasks:");
        while (taskQueue.Count > 0)
        {
            string task = taskQueue.Dequeue();
            Console.WriteLine("- " + task);
        }
    }
}
```

Expected Output:

```
Processing tasks:
- Open chest
- Defeat guard
- Pull lever
```

Processing in Order

Queues are used in print spoolers (documents print in the order they were sent), customer service systems (tickets are handled first-come-first-served), and networking (data packets are processed in order). Any time you need to handle things in the order they arrive, queues are perfect.

For our Prince queues are great for AI behaviors or animation sequences. Maybe our Prince needs to perform a series of actions like open a door, walk through, and close it behind him. You queue up those actions and process them one at a time.

Stack: Last In, First Out

A **Stack** is like a stack of plates. The last plate you put on top is the first one you take off. In programming terms, it's **Last-In-First-Out (LIFO)**.

Use `Push()` to add items to the top and `Pop()` to take items from the top:

```csharp
using System;
using System.Collections.Generic;

class Program
{
    static void Main()
    {
        Stack<string> undoStack = new Stack<string>();

        undoStack.Push("Move forward");
        undoStack.Push("Open door");
        undoStack.Push("Pick up key");
```

```
        Console.WriteLine("Undoing actions:");
        while (undoStack.Count > 0)
        {
            string action = undoStack.Pop();
            Console.WriteLine("- Undo: " + action);
        }
    }
}
```

Expected Output:

```
Undoing actions:
- Undo: Pick up key
- Undo: Open door
- Undo: Move forward
```

Undo and Backtracking

Stacks are used in undo systems (Ctrl+Z in text editors), web browser history (the back button), and even how your computer manages function calls internally (the call stack). Any time you need to reverse or backtrack through actions, stacks are the way to go.

For our Prince stacks are perfect for undo systems or backtracking in pathfinding. If the Prince needs to remember his path through a maze, you Push each move onto a stack. If he hits a dead end, you Pop moves off the stack to retrace his steps.

HashSet: No Duplicates Allowed

A **HashSet** is like a List, but it doesn't allow duplicate values. It is also unordered, so items are not guaranteed to stay in the order you added them:

```csharp
using System;
using System.Collections.Generic;

class Program
{
    static void Main()
    {
        HashSet<string> uniqueItems = new HashSet<string>();

        uniqueItems.Add("Sword");
        uniqueItems.Add("Potion");
        uniqueItems.Add("Sword"); // This won't be added (duplicate)

        Console.WriteLine("Unique items:");
        foreach (string item in uniqueItems)
        {
            Console.WriteLine("- " + item);
        }
    }
}
```

Expected Output:

```
Unique items:
- Sword
- Potion
```

Internally, HashSets is based on a hash table (like a Dictionary) which makes it extremely fast for checking if an item exists, they're great for things like tags or unique identifiers.

Ensuring Uniqueness

HashSets can be used to track unique visitors to a website, remove duplicate entries from datasets, or manage tags and categories where duplicates don't make sense. Any time you need to ensure something appears only once, HashSets have you covered.

For our Prince you could use a HashSet to track which rooms our Prince has visited. As he explores the dungeon, you add each room ID to the HashSet. If he tries to enter a room already in the set, you know he's been there before and can show different dialogue or skip cutscenes.

Linked Lists: The Chain of Neighbors

A **LinkedList** is a collection where each item (called a "node") keeps track of both its neighbors, the item before and after it. This is called a **doubly-linked list** because each node has two links (previous and next), unlike a **singly-linked list** where nodes only know about the next item.

This structure makes LinkedLists great for frequently inserting or removing items in the middle of the collection, because you only need to update a few links rather than shifting all the items like you would in a List. However, LinkedLists are slower than Lists for random access (like `myList[42]`) because you have to walk through the chain to get to a specific position.

Honestly, you won't use LinkedLists much in everyday coding, Lists are almost always better for most situations. But if you're ever building something like a playlist where songs need to be inserted or removed in the middle frequently, or you're implementing certain algorithms that need efficient insertions, LinkedLists might come in handy.

Here's a quick example:

```csharp
using System;
using System.Collections.Generic;

class Program
{
    static void Main()
    {
        LinkedList<string> chain = new LinkedList<string>();

        chain.AddLast("First");
```

```csharp
        chain.AddLast("Second");
        chain.AddFirst("Start");

        foreach (string item in chain)
        {
            Console.WriteLine(item);
        }
    }
}
```

Expected Output:

```
Start
First
Second
```

You probably won't use this much, but it's good to know it exists.

Collection Hierarchies: Seeing the Big Picture

Now that you've learned about all these different collections, you might be wondering how they're related. Why does `List` let you use square brackets but `Queue` doesn't? Why can you use `foreach` on all of them? The answer lies in something called. Think of these interfaces as contracts that guarantee certain capabilities.

Most collections in C# inherit from one or more of these interfaces:

- **IEnumerable**: The most basic interface. It just means "you can loop through this with a `foreach` loop." Every collection we've covered implements this, which is why you could use `foreach` on all of them.
- **ICollection**: Adds the ability to count items, add items, remove items, and check if the collection contains something. It includes properties like `Count` and methods like `Add()`, `Remove()`, `Clear()`, and `Contains()`.
- **IList**: Goes further by adding the ability to access items by index (like `myList[0]`) and insert or remove items at specific positions. It includes methods like `Insert()` and `RemoveAt()`.

To follow id a table describing how the collections you just learned fit into this hierarchy.

Collection Hierarchy

Collection	IEnumerable	ICollection	IList	Key Capabilities
Array	✓	✓	✓	Can loop, count, and access by index. Fixed size.
List<T>	✓	✓	✓	Can loop, count, access by index, and grow/shrink dynamically.
Dictionary<TKey, TValue>	✓	✓	✗	Can loop and count, but accesses items by key instead of index.
Queue<T>	✓	✓	✗	Can loop and count, but only removes from the front (FIFO).
Stack<T>	✓	✓	✗	Can loop and count, but only removes from the top (LIFO).
HashSet<T>	✓	✓	✗	Can loop and count, ensures uniqueness, no index access.
LinkedList<T>	✓	✓	✗	Can loop and count, efficient insertions, but no index access.

Collections that implement `IList` give you the familiar index access with square brackets. Collections that only implement `ICollection` give you methods to add and remove items, but you access them in specific ways (keys for Dictionary, front of line for Queue, top of stack for Stack). And everything implements `IEnumerable`, which is why `foreach` always works.

You don't need to memorize this chart, but understanding this hierarchy helps explain why different collections have different capabilities. When we cover interfaces in more detail, you'll see how this system works.

StringBuilder: The Duct Tape of Text

When you're working with collections of strings, you might need to combine them into one big string. Maybe you're building a report, generating HTML, or creating a long message from multiple pieces.

Your first instinct might be to do this:

```
string result = "";
for (int i = 0; i < 1000; i++)
{
    result += "Item " + i + ", ";
}
```

This works, but there's a problem. Strings in C# are **immutable**, which means they can't be changed once they're created. Every time you use `+=` to add to a string, C# actually creates a brand-new string in memory, copies everything over, and throws away the old one. Do this in a loop 1000 times, and you're creating and destroying 1000 strings. That's slow and wasteful.

Enter **StringBuilder**. It's designed specifically for building strings efficiently. Instead of creating new strings every time, it maintains a buffer that can grow as needed.

Use `Append()` to add text to the StringBuilder, and when you're done, call `ToString()` to get the final string. StringBuilder also has methods like `AppendLine()` that adds text plus a newline and `Clear()` which will empty the buffer.

Here's how to put these together:

```csharp
using System;
using System.Text;

class Program
{
    static void Main()
    {
        StringBuilder builder = new StringBuilder();

        for (int i = 0; i < 10; i++)
        {
            builder.Append("Item ");
            builder.Append(i);
            builder.Append(", ");
        }

        string result = builder.ToString();
        Console.WriteLine(result);
    }
}
```

Expected Output:

```
Item 0, Item 1, Item 2, Item 3, Item 4, Item 5, Item 6, Item 7, Item 8, Item 9,
```

Pro Tip:

If you're only combining a few strings (like 2-5), regular string concatenation is fine. But if you're building strings in a loop or combining lots of pieces, StringBuilder is way faster and more efficient.

Fun Experiment: Managing the Prince's Inventory

Alright, hotshot, time to put your collection skills to the test!

The Prince's Journey: The Guard's Bounty

The story so far...

The Prince turns a corner and freezes. Standing between him and the passage ahead is a palace guard, one of the Vizier's loyal soldiers. Unlike the skeletal warriors animated by dark magic, this is a living opponent with skill and training. The guard spots him instantly and draws his scimitar, the blade gleaming in the torchlight. There's no avoiding this confrontation. The Prince tightens his grip on his own sword, remembering his earlier practice with the rusty blade.

Steel rings against steel as they clash, the sound echoing through the stone corridors. The fight is intense but brief. The Prince's desperation and agility overcome the guard's training. As his opponent falls, the Prince catches his breath and notices something crucial: the guard carried supplies. A small pouch at his belt contains healing potions, a ring of keys, perhaps even a torch or provisions. But the Prince's pockets are limited, and he's already carrying several items from his journey so far. He needs to make decisions on what to keep, what to leave behind, what might be vital for the trials ahead. Before he can continue deeper into the dungeon, he must take stock of everything he's collected and organize his belongings. In this deadly maze, managing his inventory well could mean the difference between life and death.

The Challenge

Create a simple inventory system for the Prince. The player should be able to:

1. Add items to the inventory (stored in a List).
2. Remove items by name.
3. Display all items in the inventory.
4. Check if a specific item exists in the inventory.

Use a loop to create a simple menu that lets the player choose what to do.

Try building this yourself first!

Example Answer

Here's one way to solve it:

```csharp
using System;
using System.Collections.Generic;

class Program
{
    static void Main()
    {
        List<string> inventory = new List<string>();
```

```csharp
while (true)
{
    Console.WriteLine("\n--- Prince's Inventory ---");
    Console.WriteLine("1. Add item");
    Console.WriteLine("2. Remove item");
    Console.WriteLine("3. Show inventory");
    Console.WriteLine("4. Check for item");
    Console.WriteLine("5. Quit");
    Console.Write("Choose an option: ");

    string choice = Console.ReadLine();

    if (choice == "1")
    {
        Console.Write("Enter item name: ");
        string item = Console.ReadLine();
        inventory.Add(item);
        Console.WriteLine($"{item} added to inventory.");
    }
    else if (choice == "2")
    {
        Console.Write("Enter item name to remove: ");
        string item = Console.ReadLine();
        if (inventory.Remove(item))
        {
            Console.WriteLine($"{item} removed from inventory.");
        }
        else
        {
            Console.WriteLine($"{item} not found in inventory.");
        }
    }
    else if (choice == "3")
    {
        Console.WriteLine("Inventory:");
        foreach (string item in inventory)
        {
            Console.WriteLine($"- {item}");
        }
    }
    else if (choice == "4")
    {
        Console.Write("Enter item name to check: ");
        string item = Console.ReadLine();
        if (inventory.Contains(item))
        {
            Console.WriteLine($"{item} is in the inventory.");
        }
        else
        {
            Console.WriteLine($"{item} is not in the inventory.");
        }
    }
    else if (choice == "5")
    {
        Console.WriteLine("Thanks for playing!");
        break;
    }
    else
    {
```

```
                Console.WriteLine("Invalid choice. Try again.");
            }
        }
    }
}
```

Expected Output:

```
--- Prince's Inventory ---
1. Add item
2. Remove item
3. Show inventory
4. Check for item
5. Quit
Choose an option: 1
Enter item name: Sword
Sword added to inventory.

--- Prince's Inventory ---
1. Add item
2. Remove item
3. Show inventory
4. Check for item
5. Quit
Choose an option: 1
Enter item name: Health Potion
Health Potion added to inventory.

--- Prince's Inventory ---
1. Add item
2. Remove item
3. Show inventory
4. Check for item
5. Quit
Choose an option: 3
Inventory:
- Sword
- Health Potion

--- Prince's Inventory ---
1. Add item
2. Remove item
3. Show inventory
4. Check for item
5. Quit
Choose an option: 4
Enter item name to check: Key
Key is not in the inventory.

--- Prince's Inventory ---
1. Add item
2. Remove item
3. Show inventory
4. Check for item
5. Quit
Choose an option: 5
Thanks for playing!
```

Wrap-up: What You've Learned

Nice work! You just leveled up your coding skills big time.

Key Takeaways

- **Arrays** are fixed-size collections perfect for storing data when you know exactly how many items you need. They're great for level grids, fixed inventories, and anything that doesn't change size.
- **2D and 3D arrays** let you create grids and cubes of data for more complex structures like game levels or 3D worlds.
- **Generics** let collections and classes work with any type while staying type-safe. When you see `List<string>`, the `<string>` part is generics in action.
- **Lists** are dynamic arrays that grow and shrink automatically. They're your go-to for most situations where you need to store multiple items like inside inventories, enemy lists, task queues, you name it.
- **Dictionaries** store key-value pairs and provide lightning-fast lookups. Use them when you need to find data by a unique identifier, like player stats, item prices, or configuration settings.
- **Queues** are First-In-First-Out (FIFO) collections, perfect for processing things that comes in order like print jobs, animation frames, or AI action queues.
- **Stacks** are Last-In-First-Out (LIFO) collections, ideal for undo systems, backtracking, or any time you need to reverse through a sequence of actions.
- **HashSets** store unique items with no duplicates, great for tracking visited locations, unique IDs, or tags.
- **StringBuilder** efficiently builds long strings by avoiding the performance cost of string immutability. Use it when combining lots of strings in loops.

Now that you know about collections, your loops suddenly become way more powerful. You can iterate through inventories, process enemy lists, manage game state, and so much more. Collections are one of the most important tools in programming, and you'll use them constantly.

Chapter 6

Methods

"Simplicity is the ultimate sophistication." — Leonardo da Vinci

Imagine you're building a massive application for example a photo editor like Photoshop, or a navigation app like Google Maps maybe a video game like Minecraft. These programs contain millions of lines of code. If all that code was written as one giant block running from top to bottom, it would be impossible to build, understand, or maintain. Methods are the solution to this chaos. They let you break down complex problems into smaller, manageable pieces that you can name, test, and reuse throughout your program. Every time you click a button, upload a file, or see something animate on screen, there's a method behind it making that happen. Methods are the fundamental building blocks that transform a messy pile of instructions into organized, professional software.

The real power of methods comes from their ability to hide complexity and create reliable tools. When you use a calculator app, you don't need to know how the square root calculation works internally and you just call that function and trust it gives you the right answer. Methods work the same way in your code. You can build a complex piece of functionality once, give it a clear name, and then use it anywhere without worrying about the details. This abstraction is what makes programming scalable. Whether you're calculating physics in a simulation, processing images, or validating user input, methods let you build layers of functionality where each piece does its job well and can be trusted by the rest of your program. Master methods, and you've mastered the core skill that separates hobbyist code from professional software.

Core Concepts Covered

- ✓ Breaking complex problems into smaller, manageable pieces
- ✓ Code reusability and avoiding repetition
- ✓ Organizing logic into single-purpose, testable units
- ✓ Passing information between different parts of your program
- ✓ Returning results from calculations and operations
- ✓ Creating abstraction layers that hide complexity
- ✓ Variable lifetime and accessibility within different contexts
- ✓ Understanding when state should be local versus shared across your program

---

The Building Blocks of Your Code Kingdom

 **Trivia:**

The QWERTY keyboard was designed in the 1870s to slow down typists—fast typing jammed mechanical typewriters. Letters were arranged so common pairs were far apart, forcing slower typing. When computers arrived, there was no reason to keep this inefficient layout, but everyone already knew QWERTY. We still use it today, a perfect example of "legacy support"—keeping old methods because too many people depend on them.

So far, you've been writing code that runs from top to bottom like our Prince running through a level. But imagine if you had to write out every single action every single time. Want the Prince to jump? Write 50 lines of code. Want him to jump again? Write those same 50 lines again. Want him to do a running jump? Better copy-paste and modify another 50 lines. Your code would look like a teenager's bedroom: everything technically exists, but nothing is where it should be. Your code would be repetitive, and impossible to navigate.

This is where **methods** come to the rescue. Think of methods as your special moves. Pressing a button combo makes our Prince do a specific action like running jump, sword attack or careful step. You don't need to remember how each muscle moves, you just press the buttons and boom, it happens. Methods work the same way in code.

A method is a named block of code that performs a specific task. Once you create it, you can use it (or "call" it) whenever you need that task done. It's like teaching your character a new move, and once they know it, they can do it anytime you ask.

The Power of Methods

Remember those games written by one or two people? Any good software really, they didn't write everything from scratch every time. They built methods that are small, reliable chunks of code that can be reused wherever they are needed.

Methods help you to:

- **Avoid repeating yourself** (we'll talk more about DRY later, but trust me, repetition is the enemy)
- **Organize your code** into logical chunks (like organizing your game into levels)
- **Test smaller pieces** separately (find bugs faster)
- **Make changes in one place** that affect your whole program (update the Prince's jump height? Change it in one method, done!)
- **Read your code like a story** instead of a giant wall of confusing text

Your First Method

Let's start simple. Here's a method that doesn't take any information and doesn't give anything back, it just does what you ask it to do:

```csharp
namespace PrinceOfProgramming
{
    class Program
    {
        static void Main(string[] args)
        {
            Console.WriteLine("The Prince awakens in the dungeon...");

            // Call our method
            DisplayHealthBar();

            Console.WriteLine("Press any key to begin your adventure...");
            Console.ReadKey();
        }

        static void DisplayHealthBar()
        {
            Console.WriteLine("====================");
            Console.WriteLine("Health: ♥♥♥");
            Console.WriteLine("====================");
        }
    }
}
```

Expected Output:

```
The Prince awakens in the dungeon...
====================
Health: ♥♥♥
====================
Press any key to begin your adventure...
```

See what happened? We **defined** a method called `DisplayHealthBar()` at the bottom. Then up in `Main`, we **called** it by writing its name with parentheses. When the program hits that line, it jumps down to the method, runs all the code inside it, then jumps back and continues where it left off.

Every app uses methods constantly. A calculator app has methods like `Add()`, `Subtract()`, and `DisplayResult()`. A banking app has `CheckBalance()`, `TransferMoney()`, and `ValidatePassword()`. Methods are how programmers break down complex tasks into manageable pieces.

Our Prince could have methods like `DrawHealthBar()`, `AnimateRunning()`, `CheckFloorCollision()`, and `PlayFootstepSound()` that get called dozens of times per second as he moves through the dungeon.

Breaking Down the Method Structure

Let's decode this method:

```
static void DisplayHealthBar()
{
    // Code goes here
}
```

We see the following items:

- `static`: Don't worry too much about this yet, it's needed because we're calling the method from `Main`, which is also static. We'll understand this better when we get to the classes chapter.
- `void`: This means the method doesn't return anything. It just does its job and finishes. Like throwing a punch, you just do it, you don't get anything back (hopefully if you punched hard enough).
- `DisplayHealthBar`: The method's name. Use descriptive names that tell you what it does. Not `DoStuff()` or `Method1()`. That's like naming your cat "Animal."
- `()`: Parentheses are where parameters go (we'll get to that in a minute). Empty parentheses mean it doesn't need any information to do its job.
- `{ }`: Curly braces contain all the code that runs when the method is called.

Method Parameters: Methods That Need Information

A method that does exactly the same thing every time is useful, but methods become *really* powerful when you can give them information. These pieces of information are called **parameters** or **arguments**. The terms are pretty much interchangeable, though technically parameters are in the definition and arguments are what you pass in, but nobody will judge you for mixing them up.

Let's take a look at methods receiving and using arguments:

```
namespace PrinceOfProgramming
{
    class Program
    {
        static void Main(string[] args)
        {
```

```csharp
        DisplayHealthBar(3);  // Prince at full health

        Console.WriteLine("\nThe Prince takes damage from spikes!");

        DisplayHealthBar(1);  // Prince badly injured

        Console.ReadKey();
    }

    static void DisplayHealthBar(int hearts)
    {
        Console.WriteLine("====================");
        Console.Write("Health: ");

        for (int i = 0; i < hearts; i++)
        {
            Console.Write("♥");
        }

        Console.WriteLine();
        Console.WriteLine("====================");
    }
  }
}
```

Expected Output:

```
====================
Health: ♥♥♥
====================

The Prince takes damage from spikes!
====================
Health: ♥
====================
```

Now `DisplayHealthBar` takes a parameter called `hearts`. When we call it, we pass in a number, and the method uses that number to decide how many hearts to draw. Same method, different results based on what you give it!

Email apps have a `SendEmail(recipient, subject, message)` method that works for any email. Shopping apps have `CalculateTotal(items, taxRate)` that works for any cart. The same code handles different data.

Our Prince will have calls like `DisplayHealthBar(playerCurrentHealth)` constantly, showing the right amount of health. Take damage? The number goes down. Drink a potion? Number goes up. One method handles all health displays.

Multiple Method Parameters

Methods can take multiple pieces of information:

```csharp
namespace PrinceOfProgramming
{
    class Program
    {
```

```csharp
static void Main(string[] args)
{
    AttackEnemy("Guard", 25, "sword slash");
    AttackEnemy("Skeleton", 15, "running jump attack");

    Console.ReadKey();
}

static void AttackEnemy(string enemyName, int damage, string attackType)
{
    Console.WriteLine($"The Prince performs a {attackType}!");
    Console.WriteLine($"Hit the {enemyName} for {damage} damage!");
    Console.WriteLine();
}
    }
}
```

Expected Output:

```
The Prince performs a sword slash!
Hit the Guard for 25 damage!

The Prince performs a running jump attack!
Hit the Skeleton for 15 damage!
```

Method Parameters are separated by commas, and you need to provide them in the same order when you call the method. The first argument goes to the first parameter, second to second, and so on.

Method Overloading: Same Name, Different Method Parameters

C# lets you create multiple methods with the same name, as long as they have different parameters.

This is called **method overloading**, and it's useful when you want to do similar things in slightly different ways:

```csharp
namespace PrinceOfProgramming
{
    class Program
    {
        static void Main(string[] args)
        {
            Attack();                  // Basic attack
            Attack(25);                // Attack with specific damage
            Attack("Guard", 30);       // Attack specific enemy with damage

            Console.ReadKey();
        }

        static void Attack()
        {
            Console.WriteLine("The Prince attacks with his sword!");
        }

        static void Attack(int damage)
        {
```

```
        Console.WriteLine($"The Prince attacks for {damage} damage!");
    }

    static void Attack(string enemy, int damage)
    {
        Console.WriteLine($"The Prince attacks {enemy} for {damage} damage!");
    }
  }
}
```

Expected Output:

```
The Prince attacks with his sword!
The Prince attacks for 25 damage!
The Prince attacks Guard for 30 damage!
```

C# figures out which version to call based on what arguments you provide. Different number of parameters? Different method. Different types of parameters? Different method. This lets you create flexible methods that work in multiple situations while keeping the same intuitive name.

Graphics libraries use overloading heavily: `DrawCircle(radius)`, `DrawCircle(x, y, radius)`, `DrawCircle(x, y, radius, color)` all do similar things with increasing detail. Console methods do this too: `Console.WriteLine()`, `Console.WriteLine(text)`, `Console.WriteLine(number)`.

For our Prince you might have `Jump()` for a normal jump, `Jump(height)` for a specific jump height, and `Jump(height, direction)` for controlled jumps in a direction.

Optional Method Parameters: Give Them a Default

Sometimes you want a parameter to be optional and if the caller doesn't provide it then the method uses a default value.

You do this by assigning a value to the parameter in the method definition:

```
namespace PrinceOfProgramming
{
    class Program
    {
        static void Main(string[] args)
        {
            OpenChest("Gold");            // Uses default message
            OpenChest("Sword", "You found the legendary blade!"); // Custom message

            Console.ReadKey();
        }

        static void OpenChest(string item, string message = "You found an item!")
        {
            Console.WriteLine(message);
            Console.WriteLine($"Obtained: {item}");
            Console.WriteLine();
        }
    }
```

```
}
```

Expected Output:

```
You found an item!
Obtained: Gold

You found the legendary blade!
Obtained: Sword
```

The `message` parameter has a default value of `"You found an item!"`. If you don't provide it when calling the method, that's what gets used. If you do provide it, your value overrides the default and gets used.

Pro Tip:

Optional parameters must come AFTER required parameters. You can't put a required parameter after an optional one—C# won't allow it.

Named Arguments: Call Method with Parameters by Name

Normally you have to pass method parameters in the exact order they're defined. But with **named arguments**, you can specify which parameter you're setting by using its name:

```csharp
namespace PrinceOfProgramming
{
    class Program
    {
        static void Main(string[] args)
        {
            // Normal way - must be in order
            SpawnEnemy("Guard", 50, 15);

            // Named arguments - can be in any order!
            SpawnEnemy(damage: 20, health: 30, enemyType: "Skeleton");

            Console.ReadKey();
        }

        static void SpawnEnemy(string enemyType, int health, int damage)
        {
            Console.WriteLine($"Spawned {enemyType}: HP={health}, DMG={damage}");
        }
    }
}
```

Expected Output:

```
Spawned Guard: HP=50, DMG=15
Spawned Skeleton: HP=30, DMG=20
```

Named arguments make your code more readable, especially when you have methods with lots of parameters. You can see exactly what each value represents without having to look up the method definition.

When configuring complex systems, named arguments shine.

Instead of:

```
CreateWindow(800, 600, true, false, "Game", true, 32);
```

you can write:

```
CreateWindow(width: 800, height: 600, resizable: true, title: "Game");
```

Much clearer! We now know what each argument is.

For our Prince a method like `SpawnEnemy(type: "Guard", position: doorX, facingLeft: true, health: 50)` is way more readable than a bunch of mystery numbers and booleans in order.

You can also mix named and positional arguments, but all positional arguments must come first:

```
SpawnEnemy("Guard", health: 50, damage: 15); // This works
// SpawnEnemy(enemyType: "Guard", 50, 15); // This won't compile!
```

Return Statement

Before we talk about methods that returns values, let's quickly cover the basic `return` statement. Even in methods that don't return anything (`void` methods), you can use `return;` to exit the method early:

```
static void CheckDoor(bool hasKey)
{
    if (!hasKey)
    {
        Console.WriteLine("Door is locked. Need a key!");
        return; // Exit the method here - don't run the code below
    }

    Console.WriteLine("Door opens!");
    Console.WriteLine("The Prince enters the next room.");
}
```

When the method hits `return;`, it immediately stops and goes back to wherever it was called from. Any code after the `return` doesn't run. This is useful for avoiding nested if statements and making your code more readable by handling a scenario early and return, then the rest of your method can assume everything is fine.

Methods That Give Something Back

Sometimes you don't just want a method to just *do* something, you want it to do something and give you the result. For example, a method doing a calculation and giving you the answer back.

That's where **return values** come in:

```csharp
namespace PrinceOfProgramming
{
    class Program
    {
        static void Main(string[] args)
        {
            int currentHealth = 2;
            int maxHealth = 3;

            bool isLowHealth = CheckLowHealth(currentHealth, maxHealth);

            if (isLowHealth)
            {
                Console.WriteLine("WARNING: Health is low! Find a potion!");
            }
            else
            {
                Console.WriteLine("Health is good. Continue exploring.");
            }

            Console.ReadKey();
        }

        static bool CheckLowHealth(int current, int max)
        {
            // Returns true if health is below 50%
            return current < (max / 2.0);
        }
    }
}
```

Expected Output:

```
WARNING: Health is low! Find a potion!
```

Notice that instead of `void` in front of the method name, we wrote `bool`. That tells C# this method will return a boolean value (true or false). Inside the method, we use the `return` keyword to send that value back to whoever called the method.

Weather apps have methods like `GetTemperature()` that return the current temp. Social media apps have `IsUserOnline()` that returns true/false. Shopping carts have `CalculateDiscount()` that returns the savings amount. Methods that return values let you use the result in decisions and calculations.

For our Prince methods like `IsPlayerDead()`, `CalculateFallDamage()`, `HasKey()`, and `CanOpenDoor()` would all return values that the game uses to decide what happens next. For example, show game over screen, subtract health, play unlock sound, etc.

Another Example with Numbers

The method takes two integers and returns an integer containing the sum of the two arguments. Simple math, reusable code:

```csharp
namespace PrinceOfProgramming
{
    class Program
    {
        static void Main(string[] args)
        {
            int level = 5;
            int baseHealth = 3;

            int maxHealth = CalculateMaxHealth(baseHealth, level);

            Console.WriteLine($"Level {level} Prince");
            Console.WriteLine($"Max Health: {maxHealth} hearts");

            Console.ReadKey();
        }

        static int CalculateMaxHealth(int baseHearts, int playerLevel)
        {
            // Each level adds one extra heart
            return baseHearts + playerLevel;
        }
    }
}
```

Expected Output:

```
Level 5 Prince
Max Health: 8 hearts
```

Pro Tip:

A method can only return ONE value. If you need to return multiple things, you have a few options: return an array (collection), a tuple, a custom class or struct (more on that later), or use `out` parameters (coming up soon).

When to Make a Method

Here's a good rule: if you're doing the same thing more than once, or if a chunk of code has a clear purpose, make it a method.

 **Don't do this:**

Repeating code that does the same thing more than once

```
// Inside Main - repetitive and messy
Console.WriteLine("Checking door...");
Console.WriteLine("Door requires a key.");
Console.WriteLine("You don't have the key!");
Console.WriteLine();

// Later in the code...
Console.WriteLine("Checking door...");
Console.WriteLine("Door requires a key.");
Console.WriteLine("You don't have the key!");
Console.WriteLine();
```

 **Do this:**

Use a method and call that whenever you need to perform the same task.

```
static void Main(string[] args)
{
    CheckDoor();

    Console.WriteLine("The Prince finds a key!");
    Console.WriteLine();

    CheckDoor();

    Console.ReadKey();
}

static void CheckDoor()
{
    Console.WriteLine("Checking door...");
    Console.WriteLine("Door requires a key.");
    Console.WriteLine("You don't have the key!");
    Console.WriteLine();
}
```

See how much cleaner that is? And if you want to change the message, you only change it in one place.

Names: Code That Doesn't Make You Cry

In games button combos are usually somewhat intuitive: up + forward = running jump. Imagine if it was punch + kick to do a running jump!? That would be confusing. Your method names should also be clear and obvious.

Method names should be verbs or start with verbs because methods *do* things. They're actions. `Jump()`, `Attack()`, `Calculate()`. You get the idea.

 **Good Names:**

- `CalculateDamage()`
- `CheckCollision()`
- `OpenTreasureChest()`
- `SaveGameProgress()`
- `IsPlayerFacingLeft()`

 **Terrible names that will haunt you at 2 AM:**

- `DoStuff()`
- `Process()`
- `HandleIt()`
- `Go()`
- `Method1()`

Single Purpose: One Method, One Job

Each method should do ONE thing and do it well. Don't create a method called
`UpdateGameAndCheckCollisionsAndPlaySoundAndDrawGraphics()`. That's like having a
button that makes our Prince jump, attack, drink a potion, and solve a puzzle all at once.
Chaos. Whenever a method requires a "And" in the method name a red flag should go up.
Ask yourself, is it still doing one thing?

 **Don't do this:**

```csharp
static void DoEverything(int health, string enemyName, bool hasKey)
{
    // Drawing health
    Console.WriteLine($"Health: {health}");

    // Attacking enemy
    Console.WriteLine($"Attacking {enemyName}");

    // Checking door
    if (hasKey)
    {
        Console.WriteLine("Opening door");
    }

    // This method does too many unrelated things!
}
```

 **Rather do this:**

```csharp
static void DisplayHealth(int health)
{
    Console.WriteLine($"Health: {health}");
}

static void AttackEnemy(string enemyName)
{
```

```csharp
    Console.WriteLine($"Attacking {enemyName}");
}

static void TryOpenDoor(bool hasKey)
{
    if (hasKey)
    {
        Console.WriteLine("Opening door");
    }
    else
    {
        Console.WriteLine("Door is locked");
    }
}
```

Now each method has a clear, single purpose. Easy to understand, easy to test, easy to reuse.

Word processors have separate methods for `SaveDocument()`, `SpellCheck()`, `CountWords()`, and `PrintDocument()`. Each does one job well. When Microsoft needs to fix the spell checker, they only touch that one method and the rest of the app keeps working.

For our Prince we could have an `Update()` method that orchestrates everything by calling smaller focused methods: `HandlePlayerInput()`, `UpdatePhysics()`, `CheckCollisions()`, `UpdateEnemyAI()`, `DrawGraphics()`. Each handle one responsibility, making the code manageable even for a solo developer.

Methods Calling Other Methods

Think about it, methods can call other methods. In fact, your entire program is just methods calling methods calling methods…

Let us look at a few methods calling each other, try and follow them beginning with the Main method:

```csharp
namespace PrinceOfProgramming
{
    class Program
    {
        static void Main(string[] args)
        {
            StartGame();
            Console.ReadKey();
        }

        static void StartGame()
        {
            ShowIntro();
            CreateCharacter();
            BeginLevel1();
        }

        static void ShowIntro()
        {
            Console.WriteLine("=== PRINCE ESCAPE ===");
            Console.WriteLine("A long time ago in a distant land...");
```

```
            Console.WriteLine();
        }

        static void CreateCharacter()
        {
            Console.WriteLine("The Prince is ready for adventure!");
            Console.WriteLine();
        }

        static void BeginLevel1()
        {
            Console.WriteLine("Level 1: The Dungeon");
            Console.WriteLine("Your quest begins...");
        }
    }
}
```

Expected Output:

```
=== PRINCE ESCAPE ===
A long time ago in a distant land...

The Prince is ready for adventure!

Level 1: The Dungeon
Your quest begins...
```

Main calls StartGame(), which calls ShowIntro(), CreateCharacter(), and BeginLevel1(). Each method has a clear job, and together they create the game's opening sequence. This is how all programs are structured with a hierarchy of methods, each handling one piece of the puzzle.

Many Arguments: Pass Structs and Classes Instead

Sometimes you need to pass a LOT of information to a method.

Look at this mess:

```
static void CreateEnemy(string name, int health, int damage, int speed,
                        string weaponType, bool canFly, int armor, string faction)
{
    // That's a lot of parameters...
}
```

That's getting too long when you call it:

```
CreateEnemy("Guard", 50, 15, 5, "sword", false, 10, "Palace");
```

What does each number mean? You'd have to constantly look back at the method definition to remember.

This is where classes and structs come in handy (we'll dive deep into those later, but here's a preview):

```csharp
namespace PrinceOfProgramming
{
    class Program
    {
        // Simple struct to hold enemy data
        struct Enemy
        {
            public string Name;
            public int Health;
            public int Damage;
            public string Weapon;
        }

        static void Main(string[] args)
        {
            Enemy guard = new Enemy
            {
                Name = "Palace Guard",
                Health = 50,
                Damage = 15,
                Weapon = "Scimitar"
            };

            DisplayEnemyInfo(guard);

            Console.ReadKey();
        }

        static void DisplayEnemyInfo(Enemy enemy)
        {
            Console.WriteLine($"Enemy: {enemy.Name}");
            Console.WriteLine($"Health: {enemy.Health}");
            Console.WriteLine($"Damage: {enemy.Damage}");
            Console.WriteLine($"Weapon: {enemy.Weapon}");
        }
    }
}
```

Expected Output:

```
Enemy: Palace Guard
Health: 50
Damage: 15
Weapon: Scimitar
```

Much cleaner! Instead of eight separate parameters, we pass one Enemy struct that contains all the information. The method receives the whole package.

Shopping carts pass an Order object instead of separate price, quantity, tax, shipping, discount, and customer info parameters. Medical software passes a Patient object instead of dozens of individual fields. It keeps code clean and prevents mistakes.

For our Prince instead of passing playerX, playerY, playerHealth, playerDirection, playerIsJumping, playerIsFalling to every method, the game passes a single Player object containing all player data. Methods can access whatever they need: `player.X`, `player.Health`, etc.

> **Pro Tip:**
>
> Use structs for small, simple data containers (like positions, colors, or stats). Use classes for more complex objects that have behavior. We'll get into the nitty-gritty differences later.

The `ref` Keyword: Changing the Original

Normally, when you pass a variable to a method, the method gets a *copy* of that value. Changes inside the method don't affect the original:

```csharp
namespace PrinceOfProgramming
{
    class Program
    {
        static void Main(string[] args)
        {
            int health = 3;

            Console.WriteLine($"Health before: {health}");
            TakeDamage(health, 1);
            Console.WriteLine($"Health after: {health}");
            // Health is still 3! The method didn't change the original.

            Console.ReadKey();
        }

        static void TakeDamage(int currentHealth, int damage)
        {
            currentHealth = currentHealth - damage;
            Console.WriteLine($"Inside method: {currentHealth}");
        }
    }
}
```

Expected Output:

```
Health before: 3
Inside method: 2
Health after: 3
```

The method changed `currentHealth`, but that was just a copy. The original `health` in `Main` wasn't touched.

But what if you *want* to change the original? Then we can uUse the `ref` keyword:

```csharp
namespace PrinceOfProgramming
{
    class Program
```

```csharp
{
    static void Main(string[] args)
    {
        int health = 3;

        Console.WriteLine($"Health before: {health}");
        TakeDamage(ref health, 1);
        Console.WriteLine($"Health after: {health}");
        // Now health is 2! The method changed the original.

        Console.ReadKey();
    }

    static void TakeDamage(ref int currentHealth, int damage)
    {
        currentHealth = currentHealth - damage;
        Console.WriteLine($"Inside method: {currentHealth}");
    }
}
}
```

Expected Output:

```
Health before: 3
Inside method: 2
Health after: 2
```

Notice both the method definition AND the method call need the `ref` keyword. This is like saying "I'm not giving you a copy, I'm giving you direct access to the original."

Graphics programs use `ref` when applying filters: `AdjustBrightness(ref image, 20)` modifies the image directly instead of creating a copy. Physics simulations use `ref` to update object positions efficiently.

For our Prince a `MovePlayer(ref position, direction, speed)` method could directly update the player's position in memory. When handling thousands of game objects, avoiding copies saves memory and can improve performance.

 **Pro Tip:**

Use `ref` sparingly. It can make code harder to follow because you're modifying things outside the method's scope. Most of the time, returning a value is clearer.

The `out` Keyword: More Return Values (Sort Of)

Remember earlier when I said methods can only return one value? The `out` keyword is a sneaky way around that limitation:

```csharp
namespace PrinceOfProgramming
{
```

```csharp
class Program
{
    static void Main(string[] args)
    {
        int health;
        int maxHealth;

        GetPlayerStats(out health, out maxHealth);

        Console.WriteLine($"Current Health: {health}");
        Console.WriteLine($"Max Health: {maxHealth}");

        Console.ReadKey();
    }

    static void GetPlayerStats(out int health, out int maxHealth)
    {
        health = 5;
        maxHealth = 10;
    }
}
```

Expected Output:

```
Current Health: 5
Max Health: 10
```

With `out`, you can "return" multiple values by modifying the parameters.

The main difference from `ref` is:

- `ref` requires the variable to be initialized before passing it in
- `out` doesn't care what the initial value is, the method MUST assign it a value before finishing

Dictionary lookups use this pattern: `if (dictionary.TryGetValue(key, out value))` returns true/false for success and puts the found value in the `out` parameter. File readers use `TryParseInt(text, out number)` to convert strings safely.

For our Prince a method like `TryPickUpItem(playerPosition, out item)` could return true if an item was found nearby and use `out` to provide which item it was. The game checks the bool to decide whether to play the pickup sound and updates inventory with the item.

 **Pro Tip:**

These days, C# has better ways to return multiple values (like tuples), but `out` is still used in older code and some built-in C# methods, so it's good to know about it.

Variable Scope: Where Variables Live and Die

It's a good time now to talk about something that trips up a lot of beginners: **scope**. Don't worry, it's not as scary as it sounds. Scope is just a fancy word for "where can I use this variable?"

Think of it like rooms in the dungeon. Our Prince can use items he's carrying anywhere he goes, but items sitting in a specific room? Those only exist in that room. Leave the room, and poof, you can't access them anymore. Variables work the same way.

Local Scope: Variables That Live Inside Methods

When you create a variable inside a method, it only exists inside that method. It's born when the method starts, and it dies when the method ends.

Other methods can't see it or use it:

```csharp
namespace PrinceOfProgramming
{
    class Program
    {
        static void Main(string[] args)
        {
            EnterRoom1();
            EnterRoom2();
            Console.ReadKey();
        }

        static void EnterRoom1()
        {
            string sword = "Golden Scimitar";
            Console.WriteLine($"Room 1: Found {sword}");
        }

        static void EnterRoom2()
        {
            string sword = "Ancient Blade";
            Console.WriteLine($"Room 2: Found {sword}");
            // The sword from Room1? Can't access it here!
        }
    }
}
```

Expected Output:

```
Room 1: Found Golden Scimitar
Room 2: Found Ancient Blade
```

Each method has its own `sword` variable. They're completely separate like being in different rooms, different swords. If you try to use Room1's sword in `EnterRoom2()`, C# will yell at you with an error.

Banking apps have methods like `ProcessTransaction()` where temporary variables like `feeAmount` or `exchangeRate` only exist during that transaction. Once done, those variables vanish with no risk of accidentally using old data in the next transaction.

For our Prince each time `AttackEnemy()` runs, it creates fresh local variables for `damageDealt` and `hitSound`. When the attack finishes, those variables disappear. The next attack gets new ones with no leftover data from previous attacks.

Block Scope: Even Smaller Rooms

Variables can live in even smaller spaces than methods for example inside loops, if statements, or other similar code wrapped in curly braces { }.

Once the program leaves those braces, the variable no longer exists:

```csharp
namespace PrinceOfProgramming
{
    class Program
    {
        static void Main(string[] args)
        {
            int health = 3;

            if (health < 5)
            {
                string message = "Health is low!";
                Console.WriteLine(message);
            }

            // message doesn't exist here - would cause an error!

            for (int i = 0; i < 3; i++)
            {
                Console.WriteLine($"Step {i + 1}");
            }

            // i doesn't exist here either!
            Console.WriteLine($"Health: {health}"); // But health does!

            Console.ReadKey();
        }
    }
}
```

Expected Output:

```
Health is low!
Step 1
Step 2
Step 3
Health: 3
```

The variable `message` only lives inside the if statement. The variable `i` only lives inside the for loop. Step outside those curly braces, and they're gone. But `health` was declared at the method level, so it's accessible throughout the entire method.

>  **Pro Tip:**
>
> This is actually a good thing! It prevents variables from accidentally getting reused or changed in ways you didn't intend. It's like putting the sword back in its room when you're done—keeps things organized.

Why Variables Disappear

When a block of code or method finishes executing, all its local variables are cleaned up by C#. This is called "going out of scope." The memory they used gets freed up for other things.

It's automatic and you don't have to worry about it:

```csharp
static void CheckTrap()
{
    int trapDamage = 10;
    Console.WriteLine($"Trap deals {trapDamage} damage!");
    // trapDamage dies here when the method ends
}
```

Each time `CheckTrap()` is called, a brand new `trapDamage` variable is created, used, and then destroyed. The next call gets a fresh one. They're not the same variable, they just have the same name.

Lifetime vs. Visibility

A variable has two important qualities:

- **Lifetime:** How long the variable exists in memory
- **Visibility:** Where in the code you can actually use it

Usually these are the same. Once a variable goes out of scope (becomes invisible), its lifetime ends and it gets cleaned up:

```csharp
int health = 3; // Lifetime & visibility: entire method

if (health < 5)
{
    int potionPower = 2; // Lifetime & visibility: only this block
    health += potionPower;
}

Console.WriteLine($"Health: {health}"); // health still visible
// potionPower? Gone. Not visible anymore.
```

Global Scope: Variables Everyone Can See

So far, all our variables have been local to methods or blocks. But you can also create variables at the **class level** that every method in that class can access.

These are called **fields** (or sometimes "global variables" or "class variables").

```csharp
namespace PrinceOfProgramming
{
    class Program
    {
        static int playerHealth = 3; // Class-level variable
        static string playerName = "Prince";

        static void Main(string[] args)
        {
            Console.WriteLine($"{playerName} starts with {playerHealth} health");
            TakeDamage();
            DrinkPotion();
            Console.ReadKey();
        }

        static void TakeDamage()
        {
            playerHealth -= 1;
            Console.WriteLine($"{playerName} takes damage! Health: {playerHealth}");
        }

        static void DrinkPotion()
        {
            playerHealth += 2;
            Console.WriteLine($"{playerName} drinks potion! Health: {playerHealth}");
        }
    }
}
```

Expected Output:

```
Prince starts with 3 health
Prince takes damage! Health: 2
Prince drinks potion! Health: 4
```

Both `playerHealth` and `playerName` are declared outside any method, at the class level. Every method in the `Program` class can see and modify them. They're like items in our Prince's inventory where he carries them everywhere with him.

 **When Global Scope is Good**

Global variables are useful for:

- **Shared state** that many methods need to access (like player health, score, or game settings)
- **Configuration values** that don't change often (like max health, game title)
- **Avoiding passing the same parameters** to every single method

Web servers use global config variables like `MaxConnections` or `DatabaseURL` that every method needs. Desktop apps store user preferences globally, for example a theme, language or font size so that any part of the app can access them without passing them around.

For our Prince we could have class-level variables like `playerX`, `playerY`, `playerHealth`, `currentLevel`, and `gameScore` that need to be accessed by rendering methods, collision methods, save/load methods, and UI methods. Passing all these to every method would be a nightmare.

 ## When Global Scope is Bad

When ANY method can change a global variable, it becomes really hard to track down bugs. If `playerHealth` is suddenly wrong, which of your 50 methods changed it? Good luck finding out!

Global variables create these problems:

- **Hard to debug**: Any method could have changed it
- **Unexpected side effects**: Method A changes a global variable, breaking Method B
- **Tightly coupled code**: Methods become dependent on specific global variables existing
- **Testing nightmares**: You can't test methods in isolation anymore

Look at this example where everything depends on a global variable:

```csharp
// BAD: Everything depends on global state
static int enemyCount = 10;

static void SpawnEnemy()
{
    enemyCount++; // Modifying global state
}

static void CheckWinCondition()
{
    if (enemyCount == 0) // Depends on global state
    {
        Console.WriteLine("Victory!");
    }
}
```

If `enemyCount` get messed up anywhere, everything breaks!

A better approach is to pass values as parameters and return results:

```csharp
// BETTER: Methods receive what they need and return results
static int SpawnEnemy(int currentCount)
{
    return currentCount + 1; // Returns new count
}

static bool CheckWinCondition(int enemyCount)
{
    return enemyCount == 0; // Just checks, doesn't modify anything
```

```
}
```

 **Pro Tip:**

Use global variables sparingly. If you find yourself creating lots of them, that's a sign your code structure might need improvement. When in doubt, pass parameters and return values instead.

The Golden Rule of Scope

Variables can see "outward" but not "inward":

- Code inside a method can see class-level variables AND variables declared in that method
- Code inside a loop can see variables declared in the loop, the method, AND the class
- Code in a method CANNOT see variables declared inside its loops or if statements (those are "further in")

It's like standing in a room looking out through doorways where you can see the hallway from the room, but you can't see into other rooms from the hallway:

```csharp
static int level = 1; // Visible everywhere in the class

static void PlayGame()
{
    string playerName = "Prince"; // Visible in this method and blocks inside it

    for (int room = 1; room <= 3; room++)
    {
        Console.WriteLine($"{playerName} - Level {level}, Room {room}");
        // Can see level, playerName, AND room here
    }

    // room doesn't exist here anymore
}
```

Understanding scope helps you figure out where variables can live and prevents confusing errors where C# says "that variable doesn't exist!" when you're sure it does. It exists but just not where you're trying to use it.

Scope prevents chaos in large programs. In a 100,000-line application, you don't want every variable visible everywhere, that's asking for trouble. Methods keep their temporary calculations private, exposing only what others need.

For our Prince temporary animation frame numbers, collision detection calculations, and pathfinding distances stay local to their methods. Only important state like player position, health, and inventory exists at the class level where multiple systems need it.

Recursion: Methods Calling Itself (Danger Zone!)

This is going to sound weird, but a method can call *itself*. This is called **recursion**, and it's both powerful and dangerous. It's like finding the sword for our Prince. You're excited to have it, but you can definitely hurt yourself if you're not careful.

Here's a simple example with a countdown:

```csharp
namespace PrinceOfProgramming
{
    class Program
    {
        static void Main(string[] args)
        {
            Console.WriteLine("Countdown to gate closing:");
            Countdown(5);
            Console.WriteLine("Gate closed!");

            Console.ReadKey();
        }

        static void Countdown(int number)
        {
            if (number <= 0)
            {
                return; // Stop the recursion!
            }

            Console.WriteLine(number);
            Countdown(number - 1); // Method calls itself with a smaller number
        }
    }
}
```

Expected Output:

```
Countdown to gate closing:
5
4
3
2
1
Gate closed!
```

Here's what happens:

- `Countdown(5)` prints 5, then calls `Countdown(4)`
- `Countdown(4)` prints 4, then calls `Countdown(3)`
- `Countdown(3)` prints 3, then calls `Countdown(2)`
- `Countdown(2)` prints 2, then calls `Countdown(1)`
- `Countdown(1)` prints 1, then calls `Countdown(0)`
- `Countdown(0)` sees the number is 0 and stops (returns)

The method keeps calling itself until it hits the **base case** (when `number <= 0`). This is crucial. Without a way to stop, the method would call itself forever until your program crashes with a "stack overflow" error (not the coding help website, a real stack overflow).

The Dark Side of Recursion

Recursion is cool, but dangerous:

1. **Easy to crash**

```
// DON'T RUN THIS - IT WILL CRASH!
static void BadRecursion(int number)
{
    Console.WriteLine(number);
    BadRecursion(number + 1); // No way to stop!
}
```

This method has no base case. It'll keep calling itself, adding numbers, until the program runs out of memory and crashes. It's like the Prince falling into an infinite pit.

2. **Performance issues**

Recursion uses memory for each call. Deep recursion (calling itself many times) can be slow and memory-hungry. A loop is almost always more efficient.

3. **Hard to debug**

When things go wrong with recursion, it's tough to figure out what happened because the method is calling itself over and over.

When to Use Recursion (Rarely)

Recursion is elegant for certain problems:

- **Tree structures** (like file folders within folders)
- **Mathematical sequences** (Fibonacci numbers, factorials)
- **Pathfinding** in some algorithms

But for most application code, loops are simpler, safer, and faster.

 **Pro Tip:**

If you're ever thinking "should I use recursion?", the answer is usually "nope, use a loop instead." Recursion is like that spinning blade trap in the dungeon—looks cool, but you probably want to avoid it.

Here's the countdown example as a loop (much safer):

```
static void CountdownWithLoop(int number)
{
    for (int i = number; i > 0; i--)
    {
        Console.WriteLine(i);
    }
}
```

Same result, less risk, easier to understand.

Fun Experiment: Navigating the Blade Traps

Let's start using what we learned in this chapter and build some methods!

The Prince's Journey: The Slicing Chamber

The story continues...

The Prince emerges into a wide chamber and stops dead in his tracks. Before him looms the Vizier's most diabolical trap yet, a massive guillotine mechanism with enormous blades, one descending from above and another rising from below, meeting in the middle with a thunderous crash that echoes through the stone halls. The blades move in a relentless rhythm: open, slam shut, open, slam shut. Beyond the deadly mechanism, he can see multiple passages, each one potentially leading deeper into the dungeon or perhaps toward freedom. But there's no way around, he must pass through this killing corridor.

The Prince's heart pounds as he watches the blades' pattern, but panic won't save him here. He realizes that surviving this trap isn't about one desperate dash. He needs to break the problem down into smaller pieces: when does the blade open? How long does he have? Which passage should he check first? Can he test each path safely without getting trapped? He takes a steadying breath and begins to think methodically. Each trap ahead is a separate challenge that requires its own solution. If he can approach this systematically, checking one trap at a time, testing each passage carefully, building his understanding piece by piece he might just make it through alive.

The Challenge

Create a method called `CheckTrapAhead()` that takes two parameters: `trapType` (a string like "spikes", "chomper", "falling platform") and `hasPotion` (a Boolean).

The method should:

4. Display a message about the trap type
5. Return a Boolean indicating if the Prince survives:
    - If there's a potion, the Prince survives any trap

- Without a potion, the Prince only survives "falling platform" (he can jump over it)
- Other traps without a potion are deadly

6. Then create a second method called `NavigateDungeon()` that calls `CheckTrapAhead()` three times with different traps and displays whether the Prince made it through the dungeon alive.

Give it a try before looking at the solution!

Example Solution

Here's one way to solve it:

```csharp
using System;

namespace PrinceOfProgramming
{
    class Program
    {
        static void Main(string[] args)
        {
            Console.WriteLine("=== THE PRINCE ENTERS THE DUNGEON ===");
            Console.WriteLine();

            NavigateDungeon();

            Console.ReadKey();
        }

        static bool CheckTrapAhead(string trapType, bool hasPotion)
        {
            Console.WriteLine($"The Prince encounters: {trapType}!");

            if (hasPotion)
            {
                Console.WriteLine("The Prince drinks a healing potion!");
                Console.WriteLine("The Prince survives the trap!");
                return true;
            }

            if (trapType == "falling platform")
            {
                Console.WriteLine("The Prince jumps across just in time!");
                return true;
            }

            Console.WriteLine("The Prince is defeated!");
            return false;
        }

        static void NavigateDungeon()
        {
            bool survived;

            // First trap - no potion, but it's a falling platform
            survived = CheckTrapAhead("falling platform", false);
            Console.WriteLine();
```

```csharp
                if (!survived)
                {
                    Console.WriteLine("GAME OVER");
                    return;
                }

                // Second trap - spikes with no potion
                survived = CheckTrapAhead("spikes", false);
                Console.WriteLine();

                if (!survived)
                {
                    Console.WriteLine("GAME OVER");
                    return;
                }

                // If we made it here, the Prince is defeated
                // But let's give them another chance with a potion!
                Console.WriteLine("Wait! The Prince finds a health potion!");
                Console.WriteLine();

                // Third trap - chomper but now we have a potion
                survived = CheckTrapAhead("chomper", true);
                Console.WriteLine();

                if (survived)
                {
                    Console.WriteLine("The Prince has escaped the dungeon!");
                    Console.WriteLine("VICTORY!");
                }
            }
        }
}
```

Expected Output:

```
=== THE PRINCE ENTERS THE DUNGEON ===

The Prince encounters: falling platform!
The Prince jumps across just in time!

The Prince encounters: spikes!
The Prince is defeated!

GAME OVER
```

Note: The output will differ based on the trap sequence and potion availability in your implementation!

This solution demonstrates:

- Methods with parameters and return values
- Methods calling other methods
- Using boolean returns to make decisions
- Clear, descriptive method names
- Single-purpose methods

Ways to improve it: You could add a `ref` parameter to track our Prince's health across multiple traps, or create an `Enemy` struct and pass that instead of just strings. You could even add a loop to navigate multiple rooms. The possibilities are endless!

Wrap-up: What You've Learned

You've just learned the building blocks that make programs actually work!

Key Takeaways

- **Methods are reusable chunks of code** that perform specific tasks like our Prince's special moves
- **Method names should be descriptive verbs** that tell you exactly what they do
- **Each method should have a single and clear purpose,** don't make a method that does everything
- **Parameters (arguments) let you pass information** into methods so they can work with different data
- **Return values let methods give information back** to the code that called them
- **The `ref` keyword lets methods modify** the original variable, not just a copy
- **The `out` keyword forces a method to assign a value** and is useful for returning multiple values
- **Passing structs or classes instead of many individual parameters** keeps your code cleaner and more organized
- **Methods can call other methods**, creating a hierarchy that breaks complex tasks into simple steps
- **Variable scope determines where variables can be accessed**, local variables live inside methods or blocks, while class-level variables are accessible everywhere
- **Variables have both lifetime and visibility**; they exist in memory for a certain period and can only be accessed from certain places in your code
- **Global (class-level) variables are powerful but dangerous**, use them sparingly to avoid bugs and keep code maintainable
- **Recursion is when a method calls itself**, its powerful but risky, usually a loop is better

Methods transform your code from a long scroll of repeated instructions into an organized toolbox of reusable parts. Good applications are not written as one 10,000-line file's, it is broken up into single purpose methods that can do everything that needs to be done.

Async & Await

"He who hurries cannot walk with dignity." — Confucius

Imagine you're streaming your favorite show on Netflix while downloading a game update in the background, and your computer is still responsive enough to let you browse the web or check your email. That's async programming in action. Without it, you'd have to wait for each task to completely finish before starting the next one. Without multitasking there will be no smooth experiences. Modern software relies heavily on async programming to stay responsive. Your web browser loads images while you're already reading the article, your music app streams songs while building your playlist, and chat applications send messages without freezing your ability to type the next one. It's the difference between software that feels fluid and natural versus software that makes you sit and wait.

In this bonus chapter, you'll learn about a programming pattern that allows your code to juggle multiple tasks without blocking or freezing. While this might seem advanced for beginners, understanding the basics now will help you recognize these patterns in real code and prepare you for building responsive applications later. Think of it like ABS brakes in a car. You don't need to understand the hydraulics or sensors to drive safely, but knowing the system exists and why it matters will make you a better, more confident driver. If this chapter feels challenging, remember you can always skip it and return when you're more comfortable with the fundamentals.

Core Concepts Covered

✓   How programs can perform multiple operations simultaneously without freezing
✓   The difference between blocking operations and non-blocking operations
✓   Managing tasks that take time to complete (like file operations or network requests)
✓   Keeping applications responsive while waiting for slow operations
✓   Understanding how code execution can pause and resume
✓   When to use concurrent programming patterns versus traditional sequential code

"I'll Be Back" Programming

 **Trivia:**

In 2003, a power company's alarm system had a bug that processed events one-at-a-time instead of simultaneously. When power lines failed in Ohio, alarms froze for over an hour instead of alerting operators. The problem cascaded into the Northeast Blackout—50 million people lost power for up to two days, costing $6 billion. Modern grids use asynchronous systems that handle thousands of events at once without freezing.

Up until now, all the methods you've learned about run from start to finish in one go, straightforward and predictable. Async methods are different. They're a special type of method that can pause, let other code run, and then resume later. This is a more advanced concept that you don't technically need right away as a beginner programmer.

So why are we covering it now?

First, you're going to see async code everywhere in real-world programming. If you look at tutorials, download sample code, or explore game engines, you'll constantly run into words like `async`, `await`, and `Task`. This bonus chapter gives you a heads-up so you're not completely lost when you encounter them.

Second, as soon as you start building anything with a user interface, whether that's a game, desktop app, or a web application, you will need to understand async programming to keep your programs responsive. It's better to get a basic introduction now than to struggle with frozen, unresponsive applications later.

Third, some of the coolest programming projects involve reading files, downloading data, or doing things that take time. Async programming is what makes these operations work smoothly without freezing your entire program.

If you find this chapter confusing or overwhelming, that's completely okay! You can skip it for now and come back later when you're more comfortable with regular methods, classes, and the other fundamentals. This is a "bonus" chapter for a reason, it's here when you need it, but it's not going to break your learning journey if you decide to move past it.

Think of it like learning about power slides in a racing game before you've mastered other basics. It's cool to know they exist, and some players pick them up right away, but you can always come back and learn them when you're ready.

"I feel the need… the need for speed!" — Top Gun (1986)

What Does "Async" Actually Mean?

Imagine you're playing the graphical version of our Prince's adventure, and our Prince needs to pull a lever that slowly opens a gate across the level. Now, what if the entire game froze, music stopped, enemies froze mid-swing, you couldn't move until that gate finished opening? That would be awful, right?

That's basically what happens when you write "synchronous" code that does something slow (like downloading a file, reading from a database, or waiting for user input). Your whole program just... stops. Sits there. Waits. Like a guard who fell asleep at his post.

Async (short for asynchronous) programming let your code say: "Hey, I'm going to start this slow task, but don't wait for me, go ahead and do other stuff, and I'll let you know when I'm done."

In game terms the gate starts opening, enemies keep patrolling, music keeps playing, and you can still move around. When the gate finishes opening, the game gets a little notification and can trigger whatever needs to happen next.

Think about any program that need to save something. When you hit "Save" you don't want the entire program to freeze for 5 seconds while it writes to your hard drive. With async code, the save starts in the background, and you can keep working. When it's done, maybe you see a little "Saved" notification pop up.

Why Should You Care?

If you're writing a simple console program that just asks for your name and prints "Hello," async isn't important. But as soon as you start building:

- **Application with graphics** (you need to update the screen while loading assets)
- **Web applications** (downloading data from the internet)
- **Apps with file operations** (reading/writing big save files)
- **Anything with a user interface** (so clicking a button doesn't freeze the whole window)

...then async becomes your new best buddy. Without it, your programs feel clunky and frozen, like trying to play a game at 2 frames per second.

>  **Pro Tip:**
>
> Even experienced programmers sometimes avoid async when they shouldn't. If you're doing anything that takes longer than a few milliseconds (reading files, network calls, database queries), seriously consider making it async. Your users will thank you!

Async Methods

An async method is just a regular method with a special power. It can pause itself, let other code run, and then resume when it's ready.

Here's how you make a method async:

```csharp
async Task DoSomethingSlowAsync()
{
    // This method can now use "await" inside it
    Console.WriteLine("Starting slow task...");
    await Task.Delay(2000); // Wait 2 seconds without freezing
    Console.WriteLine("Slow task completed!");
}
```

Notice three things:
1. The `async` keyword before the return type
2. The return type is `Task` (we'll explain this in a sec)
3. The method name ends with "Async" (this is a convention, not required, but it's helpful)

Imagine a method called `OpenGateAsync()` that starts opening a gate, waits for the animation to finish, and then triggers the next event. The "async" means the rest of your game keeps running while the gate opens.

The Await Keyword

`await` is where the magic happens. When you put `await` before an async operation, you're telling your program:

"Okay, this is going to take a while. Go ahead and do other stuff, and come back to this line when it's done.":

```csharp
async Task LoadLevelAsync()
{
    Console.WriteLine("Loading level assets...");
    await Task.Delay(3000); // Pretend this is loading textures
    Console.WriteLine("Level loaded! Ready to play!");
}
```

Without `await`, your program would just skip past the slow operation and keep going, which would cause all kinds of problems (like trying to display textures before they're loaded).

Pro Tip:

You can only use `await` inside an `async` method. It's like a special tool that only works in async territory.

Task: Because Waiting Is Blocking

When you make a method async, it doesn't return a regular value right away, it returns a `Task`. Think of a `Task` as a promise: "I promise I'll finish this work eventually."

There are two flavors:

Task - For methods that don't return a value (like a void method):

```
async Task PrintDelayedMessageAsync(string message)
{
    await Task.Delay(1000);
    Console.WriteLine(message);
}
```

Task<T> - Generic Task for methods that DO return a value.

Remember our short introduction into Generics? The "T" in "Task<T>" means "the type of value the task will give you back when it's done."

So, `Task<int>` returns an int, `Task<string>` returns a string, and so on:

```
async Task<int> CalculateDamageAsync(int swordStrength)
{
    await Task.Delay(100); // Simulate complex calculation
    return swordStrength * 2;
}
```

When you call an async method, you get back a Task immediately (the promise), and you can `await` it to get the actual result:

```
int damage = await CalculateDamageAsync(10);
Console.WriteLine($"You dealt {damage} damage!");
```

When our Prince starts climbing a ledge, the game could get a `Task` that represents "climbing in progress." When the task completes, our Prince is safely on the ledge, and the game can continue.

Task.Delay vs. Thread.Sleep

Wait a minute! (pun intended) What if we actually want our code to pause for a while, how do I do that if async methods don't wait?

In synchronous code the most common way to pause execution for a period of time is by calling the `Thread.Sleep()` method. This will stop everything running on the current thread for the specified number of milliseconds and continue after. In async code we can use the `Task.Delay()` to wait without stopping everything else. Both these methods take a single argument of type int which is basically the number of milliseconds it need to wait. Let's take a look at these two methods.

Thread.Sleep(milliseconds)

```
void DoSomethingSlow()
{
    Console.WriteLine("Starting...");
    Thread.Sleep(2000); // Blocks completely
    Console.WriteLine("Done!");
}
```

As mentioned, `Thread.Sleep` literally puts your entire thread to sleep. Nothing else can run on that thread until the sleep is over. It's like the guard at the castle gate taking a nap, nobody gets through until he wakes up.

Use "Thread.Sleep" when:

- You're in synchronous code and truly need to pause everything
- You're doing really simple console programs where async isn't worth it
- You're intentionally trying to simulate a CPU-bound delay in testing

Task.Delay(milliseconds)

```
async Task DoSomethingSlowAsync()
{
    Console.WriteLine("Starting...");
    await Task.Delay(2000); // Yields control to other code
    Console.WriteLine("Done!");
}
```

Here our `Task.Delay` creates a timer that completes after the specified time, but it doesn't block anything. Other code can run while you're waiting. It's like setting an alarm and going to do other stuff and then getting notified when time's up.

Use "Task.Delay" when:

- You're in async code (with the await keyword)
- You want to simulate a delay without blocking
- You're creating animations, cooldowns, or timed events in games

```
// Synchronous version - BLOCKS
void SimulateTrapSync()
{
    Console.WriteLine("Spikes shoot out!");
    Thread.Sleep(1000);
    Console.WriteLine("Spikes retract!");
}

// Async version - DOESN'T BLOCK
async Task SimulateTrapAsync()
{
    Console.WriteLine("Spikes shoot out!");
    await Task.Delay(1000);
    Console.WriteLine("Spikes retract!");
}
```

The async version would let animations keep running, music keeps playing, and the player keep seeing updates. The sync version would freeze everything.

 **Pro Tip:**

In a game, when you press a floor switch and spikes emerge from the walls, it uses precise timing. With `Task.Delay`, you could recreate that by starting the spike animation, delay for the animation duration, then check if the player got hit. All while the rest of the game keeps running!

Why Async Prevents "Frozen Apps"

Now that you understand the difference between blocking and non-blocking delays, let's see why this matters for real applications. Here's synchronous code (the not so responsive way):

```
void LoadGameSync()
{
    Console.WriteLine("Loading game...");
    Thread.Sleep(3000); // FREEZES EVERYTHING for 3 seconds
    Console.WriteLine("Game loaded!");
}
```

If you called this in a game, your entire window would freeze. No animations, no music, no input. Just... frozen. Players would think the game crashed!

Now the async version (the more responsive way):

```
async Task LoadGameAsync()
{
    Console.WriteLine("Loading game...");
    await Task.Delay(3000); // Allows other code to run
    Console.WriteLine("Game loaded!");
}
```

With this version, the game can keep showing a loading animation, play background music, and even let you click a "Cancel" button if you want. The program stays responsive.

Calling Async Methods from Sync Methods

Something that trips up a lot of beginners is **you can't properly await an async method from a regular (synchronous) method.**

Let's say you have this async method:

```csharp
async Task LoadPlayerDataAsync()
{
    Console.WriteLine("Loading player data...");
    await Task.Delay(2000);
    Console.WriteLine("Player data loaded!");
}
```

And you try to call it from a regular method like this:

```csharp
void StartGame()
{
    // This won't work the way you think!
    LoadPlayerDataAsync(); // No await here - this is a problem!
    Console.WriteLine("Game started!");
}
```

Expected Output:

```
Game started!
Loading player data...
(2 second pause)
Player data loaded!
```

Wait, what? "Game started!" appears BEFORE the player data loads? That's because without `await`, the method just kicks off the task and immediately continues. It's like telling someone to go buy groceries and not waiting for them to come back before baking a cake that needs those groceries, you might only get the eggs after the cake was baked, not good!

The wrong solutions:

```csharp
void StartGame()
{
    // BAD: Using .Result (blocks and can cause deadlocks)
    LoadPlayerDataAsync().Result;

    // BAD: Using .Wait() (same problem)
    LoadPlayerDataAsync().Wait();

    // BAD: Using .GetAwaiter().GetResult() (still blocking)
    LoadPlayerDataAsync().GetAwaiter().GetResult();
}
```

These all BLOCK the thread, which defeats the entire purpose of async! It's like using Thread.Sleep where you're back to freezing your program.

 **The RIGHT solution:**

```
async Task StartGameAsync()
{
    await LoadPlayerDataAsync();
    Console.WriteLine("Game started!");
}
```

Expected Output:

```
Loading player data...
(2 second pause)
Player data loaded!
Game started!
```

Make the calling method async too! Now it works properly! The async "spreads" up through your code. If method A calls async method B, then method A should also be async.

But what about our applications Main method? In C# 7.1 and later, you can make Main async:

```
static async Task Main(string[] args)
{
    await StartGameAsync();
}
```

Now everything is async starting with our very first method!

 **Pro Tip:**

This "async all the way" pattern is important. Once you introduce async into your code, it tends to bubble up to the top. Don't fight it, embrace it! If you find yourself wanting to call an async method, make your method async too.

What Happens If You Forget to Await?

This is a sneaky bug that can cause all sorts of weird problems.

Look at this code:

```
async Task SaveAndLoadAsync()
{
    Console.WriteLine("Starting operations...");

    SaveGameAsync(); // Oops! Forgot to await
    LoadGameAsync(); // Forgot here too!
```

```
    Console.WriteLine("Operations complete!");
}

async Task SaveGameAsync()
{
    Console.WriteLine("Saving...");
    await Task.Delay(2000);
    Console.WriteLine("Save complete!");
}

async Task LoadGameAsync()
{
    Console.WriteLine("Loading...");
    await Task.Delay(1500);
    Console.WriteLine("Load complete!");
}
```

Expected Output:

```
Starting operations...
Saving...
Loading...
Operations complete!
(1.5 second pause)
Load complete!
(0.5 second pause)
Save complete!
```

Whoa! "Operations complete!" printed before the save and load actually finished! That's because without `await`, you're just starting the tasks and moving on immediately. It's like a chef who starts cooking three dishes but doesn't wait to see if they're done before plating everything.

Imagine you save the game and immediately try to load a different level. Without awaiting, you might start loading before the save finishes, potentially corrupting your save file!

Here's the fix:

```
async Task SaveAndLoadAsync()
{
    Console.WriteLine("Starting operations...");

    await SaveGameAsync(); // Wait for save to finish
    await LoadGameAsync(); // Then wait for load to finish

    Console.WriteLine("Operations complete!");
}
```

Expected Output:

```
Starting operations...
Saving...
(2 second pause)
Save complete!
Loading...
(1.5 second pause)
```

```
Load complete!
Operations complete!
```

Much better! Now everything happens in the right order.

Pro Tip:

Most modern IDEs will warn you if you forget to await an async method. Look for warnings like "This async method lacks 'await' operators" or "Because this call is not awaited, execution continues before the call is completed." Don't ignore these warnings!

Other Useful Task Methods

As you get more comfortable with async programming, you'll encounter some other helpful Task methods. You don't need to understand these fully right now, but it's good to know they exist:

Task.WhenAll(): Waits for multiple async operations to complete. Useful when you want to load textures, sounds, and level data all at the same time instead of one after another. This can make your loading screens much faster!

Task.WhenAny(): Waits for the FIRST async operation to complete out of several. Perfect for implementing timeouts (like "answer within 10 seconds or lose a life") or race conditions in games.

Task.Run(): Runs code on a background thread. This is useful for heavy calculations that would otherwise slow down your game, like generating a large procedural dungeon or calculating complex AI pathfinding.

We'll not go in too much detail here since were only focusing on learning to program. For now, it's good enough to just know what `async`, `await` is all about.

Pro Tip:

Some games give you a few minutes to complete the level before the bomb explodes, or for our Prince his Princess got married to the Evil Vizier. You could implement a similar countdown timer using `async` methods—have one task counting down time while another task runs the rest of the program!

To Async or not to Async, that is the question

 **When NOT to Use Async**

Okay, async isn't always the answer. Here's when you should probably skip it:

1. **Super-fast operations** - If something takes less than a millisecond, async adds unnecessary complexity
2. **Simple console programs** - If you're just asking for input and printing output, sync is fine
3. **When you're learning the basics** - Don't stress about async until you're comfortable with regular methods

This is overkill so don't do this:

```csharp
async Task<int> AddNumbersAsync(int a, int b)
{
    return await Task.FromResult(a + b); // Pointless
}

// Just do this instead:
int AddNumbers(int a, int b)
{
    return a + b;
}
```

 **When you SHOULD use async:**

- File operations (reading/writing)
- Network calls (downloading, API requests)
- Database queries
- Anything that takes more than ~50-100 milliseconds
- UI operations where you want to keep the interface responsive

 **Pro Tip:**

If you're working on a program and you're loading files, textures, levels, etc. make those methods are async. If you're just checking if the player pressed the jump button, regular synchronous code is perfectly fine.

A More Complete Example

Let's build a simple "dungeon trap" system that can work for our Prince:

```csharp
class DungeonTrap
{
    static async Task Main(string[] args)
    {
        Console.WriteLine("You enter a dark corridor...");
        Console.WriteLine();

        // Start the trap sequence
        await TriggerTrapSequenceAsync();

        Console.WriteLine();
        Console.WriteLine("You've survived the trap!");
    }

    static async Task TriggerTrapSequenceAsync()
    {
        Console.WriteLine("You step on a pressure plate...");
        await Task.Delay(1000);

        Console.WriteLine("Spikes shoot out from the walls!");
        await Task.Delay(1500);

        Console.WriteLine("You roll forward just in time!");
        await Task.Delay(1000);

        Console.WriteLine("The spikes retract with a grinding sound.");
    }
}
```

Expected Output:

```
You enter a dark corridor...

You step on a pressure plate...
(1 second pause)
Spikes shoot out from the walls!
(1.5 second pause)
You roll forward just in time!
(1 second pause)
The spikes retract with a grinding sound.

You've survived the trap!
```

Notice how each step has a natural pause, making it feel dramatic… just like those tense moments in a game when you trigger a trap and have to react quickly!

If this was a game, and you did not use `Task.Delay`, then all your animations and sound will stop and you would need to wait for all your calculations to finish.

Understanding Thread Context and Synchronization

When you use async/await, your code might resume on a different thread than it started on. This usually isn't a problem in console applications, but it can be when you're working with user interfaces.

What's the problem?

In UI applications and games, there's usually a "main thread" (sometimes called the UI thread) that's responsible for drawing things on the screen and handling user input. If you try to update the screen from a different thread, your program will crash or do weird things.

Imagine the Prince is controlled by the main animator, but suddenly a background worker tries to move our Prince at the same time. You'd get a jumbled mess of conflicting animations!

The Synchronization Context

C# has a smart solution called a "synchronization context." When you use await in a UI application, C# automatically tries to resume your code on the same thread it started on.

This is usually exactly what you want:

```csharp
async Task UpdatePlayerHealthAsync()
{
    // This runs on the main/UI thread
    Console.WriteLine("Calculating damage...");

    await Task.Delay(1000); // Simulate complex calculation

    // This ALSO runs on the main/UI thread (automatically!)
    Console.WriteLine("Health updated on screen!");
}
```

In console applications, this all happens automatically behind the scenes, so you don't need to worry about it. But when you start building applications with windows and buttons, threading becomes important.

When You Need Explicit Thread Control

Sometimes you need to explicitly tell code to run on the UI thread, especially if you're working with background threads or older threading patterns. Different UI frameworks handle this differently:

Windows Forms uses Invoke:

```csharp
// Inside a Windows Forms application
Task.Run(() =>
{
    // This runs on a background thread
    Thread.Sleep(2000); // Heavy processing

    // Switch to UI thread to update a label
    myLabel.Invoke((Action)(() =>
    {
        myLabel.Text = "Boss loaded!";
    }));
});
```

WPF uses the Dispatcher:

```csharp
// Inside a WPF application
Task.Run(() =>
{
    // This runs on a background thread
    Thread.Sleep(2000); // Heavy processing

    // Switch to UI thread to update a label
    Dispatcher.Invoke(() =>
    {
        myLabel.Content = "Boss loaded!";
    });
});
```

For Your Console Programs

The good news? For all the console examples in this tutorial, you don't need to worry about any of this! Console applications don't have a UI thread, so threading is much simpler. But now you know what's coming when you start building applications with graphics and windows.

When you get to that point, just remember to use `await` properly, and C# will usually handle the threading for you. If you see errors about "cross-thread operations," that's when you need to think about `Invoke` (Windows Forms) or `Dispatcher` (WPF).

Pro Tip:

The synchronization context handles most threading automatically when you use `await`. You only need `Invoke` or `Dispatcher` in special cases where you're explicitly creating background threads with `Task.Run` or older threading APIs. In modern async code with proper `await` usage, you rarely need these.

Fun Experiment: The Checkpoint Spell

Let us use what we have learned and simulate some async operations!

The Prince's Journey: A Message from Above

Meanwhile...

Far above the dungeon, in her palace chambers, the Princess has not been idle. She knows the Prince is trapped below, and she's been desperately seeking a way to help him. Among her loyal companions is a small mouse, once a palace scribe, transformed by the Vizier's cruel magic. This enchanted creature can slip through cracks and passages no human could navigate, moving between the upper palace and the depths of the dungeon. The Princess has given the mouse a vital mission: find the Prince and help him preserve his progress.

She's discovered that the Vizier has placed magical checkpoints throughout the dungeon, ancient mechanisms that can record a prisoner's location and status, then restore them if needed. If the Prince can learn to use these checkpoints, he could save his progress as he explores, and if he falls to a trap or guard, the magic might restore him to his last saved position instead of forcing him to start over. The mouse scurries down through the palace walls, carrying the Princess's instructions, ready to teach the Prince how to work with these magical save points. But there's a catch, the magic takes time to work, and the Prince must learn to let it complete without interruption, or risk losing everything!

The Challenge

Create an async method called `SaveGameAsync()` that simulates saving a game to disk. It should:

1. Print "Saving game..."
2. Wait 2 seconds (simulating disk write time using `Task.Delay`)
3. Print "Save complete!" with a timestamp using `DateTime.Now`
4. Return a `bool` indicating success (just return `true` for now)

Then create another async method called `LoadGameAsync()` that:

1. Prints "Loading game..."
2. Waits 1.5 seconds
3. Prints "Game loaded!"
4. Returns the player's name as a string (just return "The Prince" for now)

In your Main method:

- Call both methods in sequence (save first, then load)
- Print the loaded player name
- Make sure everything is properly awaited!

Bonus challenge:

- Create a third method called `SaveAndLoadAsync()` that calls both save and load, and times how long the whole operation takes using `DateTime.Now` before and after. (Hint: Use `TimeSpan` to calculate the difference!)

Try building this yourself first!

Example Solution

Here's one way to solve it:

```csharp
using System;
using System.Threading.Tasks;

class SaveLoadSystem
{
    static async Task Main(string[] args)
    {
        Console.WriteLine("=== Prince of Programming Save System ===");
        Console.WriteLine();

        await SaveAndLoadAsync();
    }

    static async Task SaveAndLoadAsync()
    {
        DateTime startTime = DateTime.Now;

        bool saveSuccess = await SaveGameAsync();
        Console.WriteLine($"Save result: {saveSuccess}");
        Console.WriteLine();

        string playerName = await LoadGameAsync();
        Console.WriteLine($"Welcome back, {playerName}!");

        DateTime endTime = DateTime.Now;
        TimeSpan duration = endTime - startTime;
        Console.WriteLine();
        Console.WriteLine($"Total operation time: {duration.TotalSeconds:F1} seconds");
    }

    static async Task<bool> SaveGameAsync()
    {
        Console.WriteLine("Saving game...");
        await Task.Delay(2000); // Simulate disk write

        string timestamp = DateTime.Now.ToString("yyyy-MM-dd HH:mm:ss");
        Console.WriteLine($"Save complete! [{timestamp}]");
        return true;
    }

    static async Task<string> LoadGameAsync()
    {
        Console.WriteLine("Loading game...");
        await Task.Delay(1500); // Simulate disk read
        Console.WriteLine("Game loaded!");
        return "The Prince";
    }
```

```
}
```

Expected Output:

```
=== Prince of Programming Save System ===

Saving game...
(2 second pause)
Save complete! [2025-11-29 14:32:15]
Save result: True

Loading game...
(1.5 second pause)
Game loaded!
Welcome back, The Prince!

Total operation time: 3.5 seconds
```

Notice how the total time is about 3.5 seconds (2 + 1.5), because we're waiting for each operation to complete before starting the next one. In an application or game, you might want to do these simultaneously if they don't depend on each other!

 **Pro Tip:**

Modern game engines like Unity and Godot have their own async patterns, but the core concept is the same: keep your game responsive by not blocking on slow operations. Once you understand async/await in C#, you'll recognize these patterns everywhere in other languages as well.

Wrap-up: What You've Learned

Async and await are some of the most powerful tools in modern programming. They let you write code that stays responsive even when doing slow operations. Just like open world games today that keeps running smoothly even when loading new terrain and areas while you cross it.

Key Takeaways

- **Async methods** can pause and resume, letting other code run in between
- **Await** tells your program to wait for an async operation without freezing
- **Task** represents ongoing work that will complete eventually
- **Task<T>** represents ongoing work that will return a value
- **Task.Delay** is async-friendly and doesn't block; **Thread.Sleep** blocks everything
- You **can't properly await from sync methods**, so you have to make your method async instead!
- **Forgetting to await** causes your code to continue before the work is done (major bug!)

- Synchronization context automatically returns you to the UI thread after await in UI applications
- **Console apps don't have UI thread restrictions**, making them perfect for learning async basics
- **Windows Forms uses Invoke** and **WPF uses Dispatcher** when you need explicit thread control
- Other Task methods like **Task.WhenAll** and **Task.WhenAny** exist for more advanced scenarios
- Not every method needs to be async, only use it when you're doing genuinely slow operations

Think of async programming as giving your game multiple "attention threads." Our Prince can climb a ledge while a gate is opening while music is playing while enemies are patrolling. Nothing has to wait for anything else to finish, that's the magic of async!

Classes

"Everything should be made as simple as possible, but not simpler." — Albert Einstein

Imagine you're building any piece of software, maybe a music player, a photo editor, a social media app, or maybe a real game. You quickly realize that your program needs to juggle dozens, hundreds, or even thousands of "things" at once. A music player tracks songs, playlists, artists, and albums. A photo editor manages images, layers, filters, and brushes. Without a way to organize all this, your code becomes an impossible tangle of variables where you can't tell what belongs to what. You'd spend more time hunting for bugs than actually building features.

This is where classes come in. Classes are the fundamental building blocks that let you organize complex programs into manageable pieces. Classes let you create custom types that bundle related data and behavior together, turning chaos into structure. Every major application you've ever used be it web browsers, video editors or operating systems, they all are built using thousands of classes working together. Understanding classes unlocks the ability to write real, professional software. Once you grasp this concept, you'll see how programmers take massive, complicated problems and break them down into understandable, maintainable pieces.

Core Concepts Covered

- ✓ Creating custom data types that model real-world entities
- ✓ Bundling related data and behavior into cohesive units
- ✓ Controlling access to data to prevent errors and maintain consistency
- ✓ Reusing code through blueprints that can create multiple instances
- ✓ Organizing large programs into manageable, single-purpose components
- ✓ Difference between lightweight data containers and complex objects
- ✓ Minimizing dependencies between classes for flexible, maintainable code
- ✓ Organizing code into separate files and accessing classes across namespaces

Making Your Own Types

 **Trivia:**

The "Save" icon (floppy disk) represents technology obsolete for 20+ years, yet everyone recognizes it means "save." This is abstraction—the icon represents the concept of saving, not the specific technology. We still "dial" phones, "cc" emails (carbon copy from typewriters), and "film" videos even though we don't use dials, carbon paper, or film anymore. The symbol survives because it represents an idea, not a thing.

So far, you've been writing code that runs from top to bottom, maybe with some methods to organize things. But imagine you're building a game and you need to track the Prince health, position, whether he's got his sword or how many health potions he's carrying. Then you need guards, doors, spikes, floor tiles, potions, and pressure plates.

If you tried to handle all of that with separate variables, you'd end up with something like:

```
int princeHealth = 100;
int princeX = 50;
int princeY = 100;
bool princeSwordDrawn = false;

int guard1Health = 50;
int guard1X = 200;
int guard1Y = 100;
bool guard1Alert = false;

int guard2Health = 50;
int guard2X = 350;
int guard2Y = 100;
bool guard2Alert = true;

// And this is just TWO guards... imagine having 20 enemies!
```

This is a nightmare. If you wanted to make the Prince jump, you'd have to remember which variables belonged to him. If you wanted a guard to chase the Prince, you'd need to remember which X and Y belonged to which guard. One typo and Guard 2 might teleport into the ceiling.

Classes solve this chaos. A class is basically a blueprint or a template that describes what something IS and what it can DO.

Build One, Make Many

Think of a class like a cookie cutter. The cookie cutter itself isn't a cookie, it's the shape that MAKES cookies. Once you have the cutter, you can make dozens of identical cookies (or close enough, depending on your baking skills).

In programming terms:

- The **class** is the cookie cutter (the blueprint)
- An **object** or **instance** is the actual cookie (the thing you create from the blueprint)

Here's a simple class representing our Prince:

```
public class Prince
{
    public int Health;
    public int X;
    public int Y;
    public bool HasSword;
}
```

Now instead of tracking four separate variables, we have ONE thing, a `Prince` object that contains all the information about the Prince.

Here's how you create and use it:

```
Prince player = new Prince();
player.Health = 100;
player.X = 50;
player.Y = 100;
player.HasSword = true;

Console.WriteLine($"Prince is at position ({player.X}, {player.Y}) " +
    $"with {player.Health} health.");
```

Expected Output:

```
Prince is at position (50, 100) with 100 health.
```

See how much cleaner that is? Everything about the Prince is bundled together. You don't have to remember variable names anymore. You just type `player.` and a good code editor will show you everything our Prince has.

In applications, classes represent real-world things for example a `Customer` class in a shopping app, a `BankAccount` class in banking software, or a `Document` class in a word processor.

For our Prince game every entity, the Prince, guards, doors, spikes, potions etc. would be its own class. When the Prince drinks a potion, the game creates a `Potion` object, checks if it overlaps with the `Prince` object, and if so, increases `player.Health`.

Constructors: Setting Up Your Objects

When you create a new object using: `new Prince()`, you're calling something called a **constructor**. A constructor is a special method that runs automatically when an object is created. It's where you set up the initial state of your object.

The `new` **Keyword:**

When you use: `new Prince()`, two things happen:

1.   C# allocates memory for a new Prince object
2.   C# calls the constructor to initialize that object

Without `new`, you don't get an object. You just have a blueprint sitting there doing nothing.

Right now, when we create a Prince object, we have to set everything manually:

```
Prince player = new Prince();
player.Health = 100;
player.X = 50;
player.Y = 100;
player.HasSword = true;
```

That's tedious. Let's add a constructor that does this for us:

```
public class Prince
{
    public int Health;
    public int X;
    public int Y;
    public bool HasSword;

    // Constructor - same name as the class, no return type
    public Prince()
    {
        Health = 100;
        X = 0;
        Y = 0;
        HasSword = false;
    }
}
```

A constructor uses the same name as the class but unlike a normal method do not have a return type.

Now when you create a Prince, it starts with sensible defaults:

```
Prince player = new Prince();
Console.WriteLine($"Health: {player.Health}, Position: ({player.X}, {player.Y})");
```

Expected Output:

```
Health: 100, Position: (0, 0)
```

But what if you want to start our Prince at different positions than the defaults?

You can add **parameters** to your constructor:

```
public class Prince
{
    public int Health;
    public int X;
    public int Y;
    public bool HasSword;

    // Constructor with parameters
    public Prince(int startX, int startY)
    {
        Health = 100;
        X = startX;
        Y = startY;
        HasSword = false;
    }
}
```

Now you can create princes start at different locations:

```
Prince player1 = new Prince(50, 100);
Prince player2 = new Prince(200, 150);

Console.WriteLine($"Player 1: ({player1.X}, {player1.Y})");
Console.WriteLine($"Player 2: ({player2.X}, {player2.Y})");
```

Expected Output:

```
Player 1: (50, 100)
Player 2: (200, 150)
```

Remember method overloading? You can also have **multiple constructors.**

Let's take a look at constructor overloading:

```
public class Prince
{
    public int Health;
    public int X;
    public int Y;
    public bool HasSword;

    // Default constructor
    public Prince()
    {
```

```csharp
        Health = 100;
        X = 0;
        Y = 0;
        HasSword = false;
    }

    // Constructor with position
    public Prince(int startX, int startY)
    {
        Health = 100;
        X = startX;
        Y = startY;
        HasSword = false;
    }

    // Constructor with everything
    public Prince(int startX, int startY, int startHealth, bool hasSword)
    {
        Health = startHealth;
        X = startX;
        Y = startY;
        HasSword = hasSword;
    }
}
```

Now you have some options:

```csharp
Prince player1 = new Prince();                    // Default
Prince player2 = new Prince(50, 100);             // Set position
Prince player3 = new Prince(50, 100, 75, true);   // Set everything
```

Three calls that creates the same Prince object but each having its own values set up differently.

In a shopping app, a `Product` constructor might set default values like `InStock = true` and `Rating = 0.0`.

For our Prince when a level starts, we create a new `Prince` object with `new Prince(startX, startY)` to place the player at the level's entrance. When a guard spawns, it could be: `new Guard(guardX, guardY, patrolPath)`. Constructors are how you bring objects to life with the right starting values.

Pro Tip:

If you don't write any constructor, C# gives you a free default constructor that does nothing. But as soon as you write ONE constructor, the free one goes away. So, if you want both a default that don't need any arguments and a custom constructor, you have to write both.

Building a More Realistic Class

Let's make our Prince class more useful. At the moment it's just a container for variables. But classes can also have **methods,** functions that belong to the class and operate on its data:

```
public class Prince
{
    public int Health;
    public int X;
    public int Y;
    public bool HasSword;

    public Prince(int startX, int startY)
    {
        Health = 100;
        X = startX;
        Y = startY;
        HasSword = false;
    }

    public void TakeDamage(int damage)
    {
        Health -= damage;
        if (Health < 0)
        {
            Health = 0;
        }
        Console.WriteLine($"Prince took {damage} damage! Health: {Health}");
    }

    public void Move(int deltaX, int deltaY)
    {
        X += deltaX;
        Y += deltaY;
        Console.WriteLine($"Prince moved to ({X}, {Y})");
    }
}
```

Now the Prince can DO things:

```
Prince player = new Prince(50, 100);
player.Move(10, 0);       // Move right
player.TakeDamage(25);    // Get hit by a guard
```

Expected Output:

```
Prince moved to (60, 100)
Prince took 25 damage! Health: 75
```

Instead of scattering damage calculation and movement code all over your program, it's RIGHT HERE in the Prince class. If you need to change how damage works, you know exactly where to look. That's the power of **encapsulation** where we keep all related data and behavior together.

Purpose: Single Responsibility

Each class should have ONE main job. The `Prince` class handles everything about the Prince. It shouldn't also handle other stuff like enemy AI, sound effects or menu navigation.

 **Good class design:**

```
public class Prince { /* Player stuff */ }
public class Guard { /* Enemy stuff */ }
public class Door { /* Door stuff */ }
public class Level { /* Level layout stuff */ }
```

 **Bad class design:**

```
public class Game
{
    /*

    Everything...

    10,000 lines of chaos

    */
}
```

When a program or game is made, developers don't just throw everything into one file. They separated the player movement code, the enemy AI, the level loading, the graphics rendering. Same idea with classes, keep them focused.

In an email application, you'd have separate classes like `EmailMessage`, `Inbox`, `AttachmentHandler`, and `SpamFilter`, each doing one thing well.

In Undertale (the game made by Toby Fox), there are classes for the player, for enemies, for bullets in bullet-hell sequences, for dialogue boxes, for menu items. Each has one job. When Toby wanted to add a new attack pattern, he created a new bullet class. He didn't shove it into some giant "GameManager" class.

Access Modifiers (Encapsulation)

Access modifiers control who can see and use your class members.

The main ones are:

- `public` - Anyone can access it, even code in other assemblies
- `private` - Only this class can access it (default for fields)
- `internal` - Only code in the same assembly can access it (default for classes)
- `protected` - This class and its children can access it (we'll cover this in inheritance)

Let's take a look at a class that is using access modifiers:

```csharp
public class Prince
{
    public int Health;     // Anyone can read/write, even other assemblies
    internal int Score;    // Only our assembly can see this
    private int _secretScore; // Only Prince class can see this

    public void AddSecret()
    {
        _secretScore++;    // Only this class knows about secrets
    }

    internal void UpdateScore(int points)
    {
        Score += points;   // Only our assembly can call this
    }
}
```

Access modifiers let you decide which parts of your code are **public and accessible**, and which parts are **private and protected** so they can't be misused or accidentally changed. It helps you control what other developers can see and use in your code. It let you expose only the parts meant to be used; while hiding everything else so nobody accidentally relies on internal details.

When to use each:

- `public`: APIs and features that other programmers (or other projects) are meant to use.
    - Example: A method that returns our Prince's health so the UI knows what health bar to draw.
- `private`: Internal implementation details that only this class itself should access.
    - Example: A hidden variable that tracks how many times our Prince has been hit in the last second.
- `internal`: Helpers and utilities that are shared inside your own project or assembly, but hidden from outside users.
    - Example: A score calculation helper used by multiple game screens inside your project.
- `protected`: Members meant for this class and for classes that inherit from it, but not for general outside use.
    - Example: A base Enemy class exposing its attack logic only to specific enemy types like different guards.

Imagine you're playing a multiplayer version of our Prince game. If health was always public and writable, a hacker could just do `player.Health = 99999` and become invincible. By making the actual health field private and only exposing it through controlled methods, you can add a bit of validation and security.

As you can see our `Health` is public, which means ANY code can do this:

```csharp
player.Health = -500;   // Uh oh...
player.Health = 9999;   // Cheater!
```

That's not great. We want to control HOW health can be changed.

We can make the field private and add methods to change it safely:

```csharp
public class Prince
{
    private int _health;
    private int _maxHealth;

    public Prince(int startX, int startY)
    {
        _health = 100;
        _maxHealth = 100;
        X = startX;
        Y = startY;
    }

    public int X;
    public int Y;

    public int GetHealth()
    {
        return _health;
    }

    public void SetHealth(int value)
    {
        if (value < 0)
        {
            _health = 0;
        }
        else if (value > _maxHealth)
        {
            _health = _maxHealth;
        }
        else
        {
            _health = value;
        }
    }
}
```

Now health is protected:

```csharp
Prince player = new Prince(50, 100);
player.SetHealth(-50);  // Gets clamped to 0
Console.WriteLine($"Health: {player.GetHealth()}");
```

Expected Output:

```
Health: 0
```

In a banking app, the account balance would be `private` with methods like `Deposit()` and `Withdraw()` to control it, you can't let anyone directly set `balance = 1000000`. The `internal` modifier might be used for debug functions that the development team needs across different files in their assembly, but don't want exposed if someone else uses their code as a library.

Our Prince's actual `_health` field is private so someone can't accidentally (or maliciously) set it to invalid values, but we still provide safe ways to change it through methods or properties.

> **Pro Tip:**
>
> Make things private by default. Only make them public if other classes NEED to access them. Use `internal` when you need to share something across your assembly but want to keep it hidden from anyone else who might use your code. This is called the **Principle of Least Privilege**, don't give out access you don't have to.

Naming Conventions

Good naming makes your code readable. Now that you know more about access modifiers, here's the style we'll use (also what most C# developers use):

For public, internal and protected members (things other classes can see):
- **PascalCase** (first letter of each word capitalized)
- Example: `Health`, `TakeDamage`, `MaxJumpHeight`

For private fields (things only THIS class should see):
- **_camelCase** (first letter lowercase, rest of words capitalized with underscore prefix)
- Example: `_health`, `_position`, `_isAlive`

For local variables and parameters: (things inside a method or block scope)
- **camelCase** (first letter lowercase, rest of words capitalized)
- Example: `damage`, `newPosition`, `isJumping`

Let's update our class to follow these conventions:

```csharp
public class Prince
{
    // Private fields - underscore + camelCase
    private int _health;
    private int _maxHealth;
    private bool _hasSecretPower;

    // Public fields/properties - PascalCase
    public int X;
    public int Y;
```

```csharp
    public Prince(int startX, int startY)
    {
        _health = 100;
        _maxHealth = 100;
        _hasSecretPower = false;
        X = startX;
        Y = startY;
    }

    public void TakeDamage(int damage)  // parameter is camelCase
    {
        _health -= damage;
        if (_health < 0)
        {
            _health = 0;
        }
    }
}
```

The underscore prefix on private fields makes it instantly clear: "This is local class data, not something from outside."

Properties: A Better Way

Having `GetHealth()` and `SetHealth()` methods works, but it's clunky. C# has a better solution called **properties**.

Properties are a powerful feature that let you control how data is accessed while looking like simple fields to the code using them. They act as "smart fields" - from the outside they look and feel like variables, but internally they can run validation, trigger events, calculate values on-the-fly, or do anything else you need. This gives you the best of both worlds: the convenience of direct field access with the safety and flexibility of methods.

Think of properties like a store clerk. When you ask for an item, the clerk doesn't just hand you whatever you want - they might check if it's in stock, verify you're old enough to buy it, update the inventory system, or even fetch it from the back room. But from your perspective, you just asked for something and got it (or didn't). Properties work the same way in that they look simple on the outside but can also some work behind the scenes.

If we had a `Health` that was public, then ANY code can do this:

```csharp
player.Health = -500;   // Uh oh...
player.Health = 9999;   // Cheater!
```

That's not great. We want to control HOW health can be changed. We can make the field private and use a property to provide controlled access:

```csharp
public class Prince
{
    private int _health;
    private int _maxHealth = 100;

    public int Health
    {
        get { return _health; }
        set
        {
            if (value < 0)
            {
                _health = 0;
            }
            else if (value > _maxHealth)
            {
                _health = _maxHealth;
            }
            else
            {
                _health = value;
            }
        }
    }

    public int X { get; set; }  // Simple auto-property
    public int Y { get; set; }

    public Prince(int startX, int startY)
    {
        _health = 100;
        X = startX;
        Y = startY;
    }
}
```

Now you can use it like a field, but the validation still happens:

```csharp
Prince player = new Prince(50, 100);
player.Health = -50;  // Gets clamped to 0
Console.WriteLine($"Health: {player.Health}");

player.Health = 200;  // Gets clamped to max (100)
Console.WriteLine($"Health: {player.Health}");
```

Expected Output:

```
Health: 0
Health: 100
```

Notice how clean the usage is: `player.Health = 50` and `player.Health` look like simple field access, but the property provides all the validation logic hidden inside.

Property Styles

There are several ways to create properties depending on your needs.

Normal properties use explicit `get` and `set` blocks with your own code and/or backing field when you need validation or custom logic:

```
private int _health;
public int Health
{
    get { return _health; }
    set { _health = value < 0 ? 0 : value; }
}
```

Auto-properties like `public int X { get; set; }` are shorthand where the compiler creates a hidden backing field automatically.

You can't add your own logic to how they're accessed or modified, but they're perfect for simple data that doesn't need validation:

```
public int X { get; set; }
public string Name { get; set; }
```

Expression-bodied properties use the `=>` arrow syntax for read-only properties that calculate their value on-the-fly.

These are perfect for computed values that don't need to be stored:

```
public bool IsAlive => _health > 0;
public string Status => _health > 50 ? "Healthy" : "Wounded";
```

Expression-bodied properties are always read-only when using just the `=>` arrow - they calculate a value but you can't assign to them.

However, you can also use expression syntax for properties with a backing field that ARE writable:

```
private int _health;

// Expression-bodied getter only (read-only)
public int Health => _health;

// Expression-bodied getter with normal setter (read-write)
public int Health
{
    get => _health;
    set => _health = value < 0 ? 0 : value;
}

// You can even make the setter expression-bodied if it's simple
public int X
{
    get => _x;
    set => _x = value;
}
```

 **Pro Tip:**

Use expression-bodied properties (=>) when you can write the entire logic in one line. If you need multiple statements or complex logic, use the block syntax with get { } and set { } instead.

Property Variations

You can also control property access with different modifiers:

Read-only properties only have a get block, preventing anyone from changing them from outside the class.

These are useful for calculated values or data that should never be modified externally:

```csharp
public int Health { get; }  // Can only be set in constructor
public bool IsAlive => _health > 0;  // Calculated, always read-only
```

Write-only properties only have a set block (rarely used).

These are uncommon but occasionally useful for things like passwords or sensitive data you want to accept but never reveal:

```csharp
private string _password;
public string Password
{
    set { _password = HashPassword(value); }  // Can set but never get
}
```

Mixed access modifiers let you have different access levels for get and set.

The most common pattern is public get; private set where anyone can read the value, but only the class itself can change it:

```csharp
public int Score { get; private set; }  // Public read, private write

public void AddPoints(int points)
{
    Score += points;  // Only methods in this class can modify Score
}
```

You can also combine this with normal properties:

```csharp
private int _score;
public int Score
{
    get { return _score; }
    private set { _score = value; }  // Public get, private set
}
```

When to Use Properties

Properties are ideal in these situations:

 **For data that needs validation or constraints:**

```csharp
private int _health;
public int Health
{
    get => _health;
    set => _health = value < 0 ? 0 : (value > 100 ? 100 : value);
}
```

 **For calculated or derived values:**

```csharp
public bool IsAlive => Health > 0;
public int HealthPercent => (Health * 100) / MaxHealth;
public string FullName => $"{FirstName} {LastName}";
```

 **For data you want to expose but control:**

```csharp
public int Score { get; private set; }  // Others can see it, only you can change it
```

 **For triggering side effects when data changes:**

```csharp
private int _health;
public int Health
{
    get => _health;
    set
    {
        _health = value;
        if (_health <= 0)
        {
            OnDeath();  // Trigger event when health reaches zero
        }
    }
}
```

When NOT to Use Properties

Avoid properties in these situations:

 **For expensive operations that don't look expensive:**

Properties should feel lightweight.

If getting or setting a value does a lot of work, use a method instead to make that clear:

```csharp
// BAD - looks simple but does heavy work
public List<Enemy> NearbyEnemies
{
    get
    {
        // Searches through thousands of enemies every time!
        return AllEnemies.Where(e => DistanceTo(e) < 100).ToList();
    }
}

// GOOD - method name makes it clear this does work
public List<Enemy> FindNearbyEnemies()
{
    return AllEnemies.Where(e => DistanceTo(e) < 100).ToList();
}
```

 **For operations with side effects that aren't obvious:**

Getting a property value shouldn't have surprising consequences:

```csharp
// BAD - reading a property modifies the game state!
public int NextRandomNumber
{
    get { return _random.Next(); }  // Changes internal random state
}

// GOOD - method makes it clear something is happening
public int GetNextRandomNumber()
{
    return _random.Next();
}
```

For operations that can fail or throw exceptions:

Properties should generally succeed. If an operation might fail, use a method:

```csharp
// BAD - might throw exception when accessing
public FileData CurrentFile
{
    get { return LoadFileFromDisk(_filename); }  // Might fail!
}

// GOOD - method signals this might fail
public FileData LoadCurrentFile()
{
    return LoadFileFromDisk(_filename);
}
```

 **For returning arrays that can be modified:**

If you return an array or collection from a property, callers can modify it, potentially breaking your class's internal state:

```csharp
// BAD - caller can modify internal array
private int[] _scores = new int[10];
public int[] Scores { get { return _scores; } }

// Someone can do: player.Scores[0] = 999999;

// BETTER - return a copy or read-only version
public int[] GetScores() { return (int[])_scores.Clone(); }
public IReadOnlyList<int> Scores => _scores;
```

In a music player app, `CurrentSong` would be a property (simple data), but `LoadNextSong()` would be a method (does work). `Volume` would be a property with validation (0-100), but `ApplyEqualizer()` would be a method (expensive operation). In our game, `Prince.Health` is a property (simple data with validation), `Prince.IsAlive` is a calculated property, but `Prince.Attack()` is a method (performs an action with side effects).

 **Pro Tip:**

If you're not sure whether to use a property or method, ask yourself: "Does this represent a characteristic of the object (property) or an action the object performs (method)?" Health is a characteristic. Attacking is an action.

Static Classes and Members

Sometimes you don't want multiple instances of something. You just want ONE.

That's what `static` is for:

```csharp
public static class GameSettings
{
    public static int ScreenWidth = 800;
    public static int ScreenHeight = 600;
    public static bool SoundEnabled = true;
}

// You use it WITHOUT creating an instance
Console.WriteLine($"Screen size:" +
    $" {GameSettings.ScreenWidth}x{GameSettings.ScreenHeight}");
```

You don't do `GameSettings settings = new GameSettings()`. You just use `GameSettings.ScreenWidth` directly. There's only ONE set of game settings for the entire program. In fact, you CAN'T create an instance of a static class, it doesn't make sense to.

 **When to use static:**

- Utility classes (like `Math.Sqrt()`, `Console.WriteLine()`)
- Game-wide settings or managers (like a `GameManager` singleton)
- Helper functions that don't need object data

 **When NOT to use static:**

- Things you want multiple of (players, enemies, items)
- Anything that needs different instances with different data

Here's a static helper class for our game:

```csharp
public static class GameMath
{
    public static int Distance(int x1, int y1, int x2, int y2)
    {
        int dx = x2 - x1;
        int dy = y2 - y1;
        return (int)Math.Sqrt(dx * dx + dy * dy);
    }
}


// Usage:
Prince player = new Prince(50, 100);
Guard enemy = new Guard(200, 100);

int distance = GameMath.Distance(player.X, player.Y, enemy.X, enemy.Y);
Console.WriteLine($"Guard is {distance} pixels away!");
```

Expected Output:

```
Guard is 150 pixels away!
```

In most applications, utility functions like string formatting, date calculations, or math helpers are static. You don't need a "Math object" to calculate square roots. Configuration classes that hold app-wide settings are also static.

Our Prince might include a static `GameSettings` class that store screen resolution, difficulty level, and sound volume, all the things that should be the same everywhere.

You can also have static members in non-static classes. For example, you might have a `Prince` class where each instance has its own health, but you want to track the total number of princes created:

```csharp
public class Prince
{
    public static int TotalCreated = 0;   // Shared by all princes

    private int _health;
    public int Health { get { return _health; } }

    public Prince()
    {
        _health = 100;
```

```csharp
        TotalCreated++;   // Increment the shared counter
    }
}

// Usage:
Prince p1 = new Prince();
Prince p2 = new Prince();
Console.WriteLine($"Created {Prince.TotalCreated} princes");
```

Expected Output:

```
Created 2 princes
```

Structs: "Lightweight Classes"

A `struct` is like a class, but simpler and more efficient for small, simple types:

- **Classes** are *reference types* (passed by reference, stored on the heap)
- **Structs** are *value types* (passed by copy, stored on the stack)

Translation: Structs are faster for small, simple data like coordinates or colors.

```csharp
public struct Point
{
    public int X;
    public int Y;

    public Point(int x, int y)
    {
        X = x;
        Y = y;
    }
}

// Usage:
Point princePos = new Point(50, 100);
Point guardPos = new Point(200, 100);

Console.WriteLine($"Prince: ({princePos.X}, {princePos.Y})");
```

Expected Output:

```
Prince: (50, 100)
```

When to use structs:

- Small, simple data (coordinates, colors, dates)
- You won't have thousands of them
- You don't need inheritance

When to use classes:

- Complex objects with behavior (players, enemies)
- Things that need inheritance
- Large objects

In most applications, structs are used for lightweight data like `Point`, `Rectangle`, `Color`, or `DateTime` that get passed around a lot. In 3D graphics programs, a `Vector3` struct (with X, Y, Z coordinates) is used millions of times per frame and using structs makes this faster.

Our Prince might use a `Point` struct for tile coordinates or a `Velocity` struct for movement speed, but the Prince himself is a class because he's complex and has behavior.

Pro Tip:

If you're not sure, use a class. Structs have quirks (especially when mutating them) that can confuse beginners. They're great once you understand them, but classes are safer to start with.

Records: Easy Comparisons

Records (introduced in C# 9.0) are like classes, but they make it easy to compare objects by VALUE instead of by reference:

```
public record HighScore(string PlayerName, int Score);

// Usage:
HighScore score1 = new HighScore("Player1", 1000);
HighScore score2 = new HighScore("Player1", 1000);

Console.WriteLine(score1 == score2);  // True! (same values)
```

Expected Output:

```
True
```

With normal classes, `score1 == score2` would be `False` because they're different objects. But records compare VALUES, which is perfect for things like high scores, save game states, or configuration data.

When to use records:

- Data that should be compared by value
- Immutable data (things that don't change)
- DTOs (Data Transfer Objects) for saving/loading

In business applications, records are perfect for data you're loading from databases or APIs like `CustomerInfo`, `OrderDetails`, or `ProductData`. In configuration files, a `GameSettings` record would let you easily check if two configurations are identical.

For our Prince when saving high scores, each score could be a record. When checking if a new score already exists in the leaderboard, the record's built-in comparison makes it easy. We might also use records for save game data: `new SaveData(Level, Health, Position)` can be compared to see if two saves are identical.

Classes That Mind Their Own Business

One of the most important principles in class design is keeping your classes **loosely coupled** which mean they don't rely too heavily on each other's internal details. When classes are tightly coupled, changing one class can break several others, making your code fragile and hard to maintain.

What is coupling?

Great Question! In short, it's how much one class knows about and depends on another class.

Here's an example of tight coupling:

```
public class Prince
{
    public int Health;
    public int X;
    public int Y;
}

public class HealthBar
{
    public void Draw(Prince prince)
    {
        // This class knows TOO MUCH about Prince's internals
        int barWidth = prince.Health * 2;
        Console.WriteLine($"Health: [{new string('=', barWidth)}]");

        // What if we later change how Prince stores health?
        // Or what if we want to use HealthBar for enemies too?
    }
}
```

The problem here is that `HealthBar` is tightly coupled to `Prince`. It can only work with Prince objects, and it directly accesses Prince's internal structure.

Here's a better approach:

```
// Usage:
Prince player = new Prince(50, 100);
Guard enemy = new Guard(200, 100);

HealthBar bar = new HealthBar();
bar.Draw(player.Health, 100);  // Works for Prince
```

```csharp
bar.Draw(enemy.Health, 50);      // Works for Guard too!

public class HealthBar
{
    public void Draw(int currentHealth, int maxHealth)
    {
        // Now it works with ANY object - just give it the numbers
        int barWidth = (int)((double)currentHealth / maxHealth * 20);
        Console.WriteLine($"Health: [{new string('=', barWidth)}]");
    }
}
```

Why loose coupling matters:

- **Flexibility** - Classes can be reused in different contexts
- **Maintainability** - Changes to one class won't cascade through your codebase
- **Testability** - Loosely coupled classes are easier to test in isolation
- **Collaboration** - Different programmers can work on different classes without conflicts

How to reduce dependencies:

1. **Pass only what you need** - Don't pass entire objects if you only need one or two values
2. **Use interfaces** - We'll cover interfaces a bit later, but they let classes work together without knowing each other's details
3. **Avoid reaching into objects** - If you find yourself writing `player.Inventory.Items[0].Stats.Damage`, you're probably too coupled
4. **Think about responsibilities** - Each class should focus on its own job, not manage other classes' jobs

A practical example:

```csharp
// Tightly coupled - Guard knows too much about Prince
public class Guard
{
    public void Chase(Prince target)
    {
        if (X < target.X)
            X += 5;
        // What if we later want guards to chase other things?
        // Or what if Prince's position system changes?
    }
}

// Loosely coupled - Guard works with any position
public class Guard
{
    public void ChasePosition(int targetX, int targetY)
    {
        if (X < targetX)
            X += 5;
        // Now guards can chase anything with a position!
    }
}
```

```
// Usage:
guard.ChasePosition(player.X, player.Y);    // Chase the Prince
guard.ChasePosition(treasure.X, treasure.Y);    // Or run to the treasure
guard.ChasePosition(exitDoor.X, exitDoor.Y);    // Or run to the exit
```

In a music player app, the `Playlist` class shouldn't directly manage the audio output, that's the `AudioPlayer` class's job. Instead, `Playlist` just provides the next song's file path, and `AudioPlayer` handles playback. This way, you can swap out the audio engine without touching the playlist logic. Four our Prince, a loosely coupled design means we can add new enemy types, new hazards, or new game mechanics without rewriting half our codebase.

Class Sizes and Separate Files

In a real project, each class, struct, and record gets its own file. The file name should match the type name exactly. If you have a `Prince` class, you'd have a file named `Prince.cs`. If you have a `Guard` class, you'd have `Guard.cs`. A `Point` struct goes in `Point.cs`, and a `HighScore` record goes in `HighScore.cs`.

Why separate files?

Imagine scrolling through a 5,000-line file trying to find where `Guard` is defined, then scrolling past `Door`, `Spike`, `Potion`, and a dozen other types. Separate files make life easier:

```
Project/
    ├── Prince.cs
    ├── Guard.cs
    ├── Door.cs
    ├── Spike.cs
    ├── Point.cs
    └── HighScore.cs
```

Modern C# conventions - one type per file

- **Classes** - Always in their own files
- **Structs** - In their own files (unless they're tiny helpers)
- **Records** - In their own files
- **Enums** - In their own files

Why this matters in real projects

- **Version control** - When using Git, different developers can work on different types without conflicts
- **Navigation** - You know exactly where to find `Prince.cs` - no searching through massive files
- **Code reviews** - Changes to one class don't clutter up unrelated code
- **IDE features** - Search, refactoring, and navigation all work better

When it's okay to group things together
- Very small, tightly related helper structs (like `Point` and `Size` if both are tiny)
- Private nested classes that only exist inside another class
- Multiple related records that are just simple data containers

How big should a class be?

There's no hard rule, but if your class has more than a few hundred lines, it's probably doing too much. Ask yourself: "Is this class doing more than one thing?"

A `Prince` class that ALSO handles rendering graphics, playing sound effects, managing UI, and saving files should probably be split into:

- `Prince` - Player state and behavior
- `PrinceRenderer` - Drawing the prince
- `PrinceSoundManager` - Prince sound effects
- `PrinceSaveData` - Saving/loading prince data

In any professional application—whether it's a music player, photo editor, or game—you'll find hundreds or thousands of files, each containing one type. Visual Studio's solution for Microsoft Word probably has files like `Document.cs`, `Paragraph.cs`, `SpellChecker.cs`, `Formatter.cs`, and so on. In our game, as we add more features, we'd create `Potion.cs`, `Trap.cs`, `Level.cs`, keeping everything organized and maintainable.

 **Pro Tip:**

Most IDEs make this easy. In Visual Studio or VS Code, you can right-click your project and select "Add New Class" which will create a new `.cs` file with the basic class structure already set up for you. Name the file, and you're ready to code.

Bringing Classes Together

Now that you know each class should be in its own file, you need to know how to use those classes together. When classes are in different namespaces, you need to tell C# where to find them.

The `using` directive

If you create a `Guard` class in one file inside the `PrinceOfProgramming.Enemies` namespace, you can use it in another file by adding a `using` directive at the top.

File: Guard.cs

```
namespace PrinceOfProgramming.Enemies
```

```csharp
{
    public class Guard
    {
        public int Health { get; set; }
        public int X { get; set; }
        public int Y { get; set; }
    }
}
```

File: Program.cs

```csharp
using PrinceOfProgramming.Enemies;   // Now I can use the Guard class!

public class Game
{
    public static void Main()
    {
        Guard enemy = new Guard();   // Works because of the using directive
        enemy.Health = 50;
    }
}
```

Without the **using** directive, you'd have to type the full namespace every time:

```csharp
PrinceOfProgramming.Enemies.Guard enemy = new PrinceOfProgramming.Enemies.Guard();
```

That will get annoying fast!

The using **directive can reference:**

- **Built-in .NET libraries** like System (comes with C#)
- **External packages** you download through NuGet (a package manager for C# - like an app store for code libraries)
- **Your own namespaces** from other parts of your project

Example with multiple namespaces:

```csharp
using System;
using PrinceOfProgramming.Characters;
using PrinceOfProgramming.Items;
using PrinceOfProgramming.Traps;

public class Game
{
    public static void Main()
    {
        Prince player = new Prince(50, 100);      // From Characters namespace
        Guard enemy = new Guard(200, 100);        // From Characters namespace
        Potion healthPotion = new Potion();       // From Items namespace
        Spike trap = new Spike(150, 100);         // From Traps namespace
    }
}
```

Pro Tip:

When you create a new class file in Visual Studio or VS Code, the IDE usually automatically adds the appropriate namespace declaration based on your project name and folder structure. You just need to add the corresponding `using` directive in files where you want to use that class.

Putting It All Together

Let's build a small example using some custom types:

```csharp
using System;

public class Prince
{
    private int _health;
    private int _maxHealth = 100;

    public int Health
    {
        get { return _health; }
        set { _health = value < 0 ? 0 : (value > _maxHealth ? _maxHealth : value); }
    }

    public int X { get; set; }
    public int Y { get; set; }

    public Prince(int startX, int startY)
    {
        _health = 100;
        X = startX;
        Y = startY;
    }

    public void TakeDamage(int damage)
    {
        Health -= damage;
        Console.WriteLine($"Prince took {damage} damage! Health: {Health}");
    }
}

public struct Point
{
    public int X;
    public int Y;

    public Point(int x, int y)
    {
        X = x;
        Y = y;
    }
}

public static class GameMath
{
```

```csharp
    public static int Distance(int x1, int y1, int x2, int y2)
    {
        int dx = x2 - x1;
        int dy = y2 - y1;
        return (int)Math.Sqrt(dx * dx + dy * dy);
    }
}

public static class Game
{
    public static void Main()
    {
        Prince player = new Prince(50, 100);
        Point guardPosition = new Point(200, 100);

        Console.WriteLine($"Prince is at ({player.X}, {player.Y})");
        Console.WriteLine($"Guard is at ({guardPosition.X}, {guardPosition.Y})");

        int distance = GameMath.Distance(player.X, player.Y, guardPosition.X,
            guardPosition.Y);
        Console.WriteLine($"Distance between them: {distance}");

        player.TakeDamage(30);
    }
}
```

Expected Output:

```
Prince is at (50, 100)
Guard is at (200, 100)
Distance between them: 150
Prince took 30 damage! Health: 70
```

Fun Experiment: The Mirror's Guardian

Let's use what we learned and create some cool custom types for our Prince's adventure!

The Prince's Journey: Reflections of the Enemy

The story continues...

The Prince enters a chamber and stops, transfixed by what stands before him, an enormous ornate mirror, its gilded frame covered in ancient runes that pulse with an eerie green light. His reflection stares back at him, but something is wrong. The eyes in the mirror glow with the same unnatural luminescence he's seen in the Vizier's skeletal warriors. As he watches, horrified, his reflection begins to move independently, drawing a spectral sword and stepping forward through the glass as if it were water. The mirror-Prince materializes fully in the chamber, a perfect copy created by the Vizier's dark magic, designed to guard this passage using the real Prince's own abilities against him.

The doppelganger begins to circle, tracking his movements with unsettling precision, its glowing eyes locked onto him with predatory focus. The Prince realizes this guardian will chase him relentlessly, attacking the moment he comes within range. To escape this chamber, he must understand how his magical twin operates, how it tracks him, how it moves, how it attacks. Only by studying this dark reflection of himself can he hope to outmaneuver it and continue his journey toward freedom and his beloved Princess.

The Challenge

Create a `Guard` class and a `Combat` helper class. The Guard should have:

- A health property with a max of 50
- X and Y positions
- A `bool IsAlert` property
- A constructor that takes starting X, Y positions
- A `MoveToward(int targetX, int targetY)` method that moves the guard 5 pixels toward the target position
- A `TakeDamage(int damage)` method similar to Prince

Create a static `Combat` class with:

- An `Attack(int attackerX, int attackerY, object target, int damage)` method that checks if the target is a Prince or Guard, and if so, deals damage to it

Then create a simple scenario where a guard chases the Prince, and they can both take damage.

Example Answer

Here's one way to solve it:

```csharp
public class Prince
{
    private int _health;
    private int _maxHealth = 100;

    public int Health
    {
        get { return _health; }
        set { _health = value < 0 ? 0 : (value > _maxHealth ? _maxHealth : value); }
    }

    public int X { get; set; }
    public int Y { get; set; }

    public Prince(int startX, int startY)
    {
        _health = 100;
        X = startX;
        Y = startY;
    }

    public void TakeDamage(int damage)
    {
        Health -= damage;
        Console.WriteLine($"Prince took {damage} damage! Health: {Health}");
    }
```

```csharp
}

public class Guard
{
    private int _health;
    private int _maxHealth = 50;

    public int Health
    {
        get { return _health; }
        set { _health = value < 0 ? 0 : (value > _maxHealth ? _maxHealth : value); }
    }

    public int X { get; set; }
    public int Y { get; set; }
    public bool IsAlert { get; set; }

    public Guard(int startX, int startY)
    {
        _health = 50;
        X = startX;
        Y = startY;
        IsAlert = true;
    }

    public void MoveToward(int targetX, int targetY)
    {
        if (X < targetX)
        {
            X += 5;
        }
        else if (X > targetX)
        {
            X -= 5;
        }

        if (Y < targetY)
        {
            Y += 5;
        }
        else if (Y > targetY)
        {
            Y -= 5;
        }

        Console.WriteLine($"Guard moves to ({X}, {Y})");
    }

    public void TakeDamage(int damage)
    {
        Health -= damage;
        Console.WriteLine($"Guard took {damage} damage! Health: {Health}");
    }
}

public static class Combat
{
    public static void Attack(int attackerX, int attackerY, object target, int damage)
    {
        if (target.GetType() == typeof(Prince))
        {
```

```csharp
                Prince prince = (Prince)target;
                Console.WriteLine($"Attack from ({attackerX}, {attackerY})!");
                prince.TakeDamage(damage);
            }
            else if (target.GetType() == typeof(Guard))
            {
                Guard guard = (Guard)target;
                Console.WriteLine($"Attack from ({attackerX}, {attackerY})!");
                guard.TakeDamage(damage);
            }
        }
    }
}

public static class GameMath
{
    public static int Distance(int x1, int y1, int x2, int y2)
    {
        int dx = x2 - x1;
        int dy = y2 - y1;
        return (int)Math.Sqrt(dx * dx + dy * dy);
    }
}

public static class Game
{
    public static void Main()
    {
        Prince player = new Prince(50, 100);
        Guard enemy = new Guard(200, 100);

        Console.WriteLine("A guard spots the Prince!");

        // Guard chases until close
        while (GameMath.Distance(enemy.X, enemy.Y, player.X, player.Y) > 20)
        {
            enemy.MoveToward(player.X, player.Y);
        }

        Console.WriteLine("The guard is close enough to attack!");
        Combat.Attack(enemy.X, enemy.Y, player, 10);

        Console.WriteLine("The Prince fights back!");
        Combat.Attack(player.X, player.Y, enemy, 15);
    }
}
```

Expected Output:

```
A guard spots the Prince!
Guard moves to (195, 100)
Guard moves to (190, 100)
Guard moves to (185, 100)
Guard moves to (180, 100)
Guard moves to (175, 100)
Guard moves to (170, 100)
Guard moves to (165, 100)
Guard moves to (160, 100)
Guard moves to (155, 100)
Guard moves to (150, 100)
Guard moves to (145, 100)
Guard moves to (140, 100)
```

```
Guard moves to (135, 100)
Guard moves to (130, 100)
Guard moves to (125, 100)
Guard moves to (120, 100)
Guard moves to (115, 100)
Guard moves to (110, 100)
Guard moves to (105, 100)
Guard moves to (100, 100)
Guard moves to (95, 100)
Guard moves to (90, 100)
Guard moves to (85, 100)
Guard moves to (80, 100)
Guard moves to (75, 100)
Guard moves to (70, 100)
The guard is close enough to attack!
Attack from (70, 100)!
Prince took 10 damage! Health: 90
The Prince fights back!
Attack from (50, 100)!
Guard took 15 damage! Health: 35
```

Wrap-up: What You've Learned

Classes are the building blocks of organized code. They bundle data and behavior into reusable blueprints.

Key Takeaways

- Classes are blueprints; objects are instances made from those blueprints
- Constructors initialize objects when you use the `new` keyword
- Each class should have a single responsibility
- Access modifiers (`public`, `private`, `internal`, `protected`) protect your data and control what other code can see
- Naming conventions help make code readable (PascalCase for public, _camelCase for private)
- Property variations control how data is accessed (read-only, write-only, mixed access)
- Static classes/members are for things you only want one of
- Structs are for small, simple value types
- Records make comparing data easy
- Keeping classes loosely coupled makes code more flexible and maintainable
- Each class, struct, and record should be in its own separate file for better organization
- Use `using` directives to access classes from other namespaces

Every entity in a game, players, enemies, items, UI elements are all typically a class. Classes keep your code organized so you don't end up with a 10,000-line mess.

Chapter 8

Inheritance

"We stand on the shoulders of giants." — Isaac Newton

Imagine you're building your own software and you notice patterns everywhere. Your music app has songs, albums, and playlists that all need to be saved and loaded. Your photo editor has layers, filters, and brushes that all need undo/redo functionality. Even your web browser has tabs, bookmarks, and history entries that all need to be stored and retrieved. Writing the same save and load code for each would be mind-numbing. This is where inheritance becomes your best friend. It's one of the fundamental pillars of object-oriented programming that lets you say "these things are similar, so let's write the common stuff once and let everything else build on top of it." It's how modern software stays organized and manageable as it grows from hundreds to millions of lines of code.

Inheritance isn't just about saving time typing, it's about modeling how we naturally think about the world. When you learn about mammals in biology, you don't re-learn that they breathe oxygen, have a heartbeat, and regulate body temperature for each species. You learn those traits once for mammals, then learn what makes a dolphin different from a bat. Software works the same way. Whether you're building the Spotify app where every audio item shares playback controls, or Photoshop where every tool has common keyboard shortcuts, or even the operating system on your phone where every app inherits notification capabilities. Inheritance is the pattern that makes complex software possible. Once you understand it, you'll start seeing it everywhere, and more importantly, you'll know exactly when and how to use it in your own code.

Core Concepts Covered

- ✓ Organizing code by modeling relationships between similar things
- ✓ Sharing common functionality across multiple types without duplication
- ✓ Creating hierarchies that match how we naturally categorize objects
- ✓ Making code that's easy to extend with new types without breaking existing code
- ✓ Understanding when similarity means "is-a" versus "has-a" relationships
- ✓ Defining contracts that guarantee certain capabilities exist across different types
- ✓ Overriding default behavior to create specialized variations
- ✓ Treating different types uniformly while maintaining their unique characteristics

Family Traits in Code

 **Trivia:**

Your DNA contains about 3 billion base pairs of information—roughly 750 megabytes of data compressed into something microscopic. Every cell in your body contains a complete copy of this entire instruction manual. If you printed out your DNA code as letters, it would fill 200 phone books of 1,000 pages each. Scientists are now experimenting with using synthetic DNA to store digital data because it's incredibly dense and stable—one gram of DNA could theoretically store 215 million gigabytes of information.

So, you've learned about classes and how they're like blueprints for creating objects. But sometimes you have classes that are really similar to each other. Imagine you're making a game and you have Guards, Archers, and our Prince. They all move around, take damage, and can attack. Do you really want to write the same `TakeDamage()` and `Move()` methods three times?

Nope! That's where **inheritance** comes to save the day. All three characters are basically "Characters" right? They share a bunch of stuff. Inheritance lets you create a base "Character" class with all the common stuff, and then your Guard, Archer, and Prince classes can **inherit** from it, meaning they automatically get all that shared code. Then you just add the special stuff that makes each one unique.

It's like how in most games all enemies have basic movement and combat, but the Fat Guards are slow and tough, while the Skeleton Warriors are quick and creepy. They all inherit "enemy-ness" but add their own flavor.

Leveling Up Your Classes

Inheritance is when one class (called a **child class** or **derived class**) takes on all the properties and methods of another class (called a **parent class** or **base class**). The child class gets everything the parent has, plus it can add its own special features or change how some things work.

Why is this useful?

1. **Less Repeated Code**: Write common stuff once in the parent class, use it everywhere.
2. **Easier to Maintain**: If you need to fix or change something common, you only change it in one place.
3. **Organized Code**: Your code structure matches how you think about your program. All characters are characters, all enemies are enemies, etc.
4. **Flexibility**: You can treat different types of objects the same way when they share a parent. (We'll see this in action soon!)

Inheritance is everywhere. Think about a document editor like Microsoft Word where every document type (Word Doc, PDF, Text File) shares common features like saving, printing, and spell-checking. They'd all inherit from a base `Document` class, then add their own special features.

For our Prince every enemy can inherit from a base Enemy class. Every weapon can inherit from a base Weapon class. UI button? You guessed it, a base Button class.

How to Use Inheritance

Let's start with a basic example. We'll create a `Character` class that has health and can take damage. Then we'll make a `Guard` class and a `Prince` class that both inherit from `Character`.

Notice the use of the `:` (colon) after the class name with the parent class name it inherits from:

```csharp
using System;

namespace PrinceOfProgramming
{
    // Base class - the parent
    class Character
    {
        public string Name;
        public int Health;
        public int XPosition;
        public int YPosition;

        public Character(string name, int health, int x, int y)
        {
            Name = name;
            Health = health;
            XPosition = x;
            YPosition = y;
        }

        public void TakeDamage(int damage)
        {
            Health -= damage;
            Console.WriteLine($"{Name} takes {damage} damage! Health: {Health}");
```

```csharp
        if (Health <= 0)
        {
            Console.WriteLine($"{Name} has been defeated!");
        }
    }

    public void Move(int xChange, int yChange)
    {
        XPosition += xChange;
        YPosition += yChange;
        Console.WriteLine($"{Name} moves to ({XPosition}, {YPosition})");
    }
}

// Child class - inherits from Character
class Guard : Character
{
    public string WeaponType;

    // Call the parent constructor using "base"
    public Guard(string name, int health, int x, int y, string weapon)
        : base(name, health, x, y)
    {
        WeaponType = weapon;
    }

    public void Patrol()
    {
        Console.WriteLine($"{Name} the guard patrols with a {WeaponType}.");
    }
}

// Another child class
class Prince : Character
{
    public int PotionsRemaining;

    public Prince(string name, int health, int x, int y, int potions)
        : base(name, health, x, y)
    {
        PotionsRemaining = potions;
    }

    public void DrinkPotion()
    {
        if (PotionsRemaining > 0)
        {
            Health += 10;
            PotionsRemaining--;
            Console.WriteLine($"{Name} drinks a potion! Health: {Health}, " +
                $"Potions left: {PotionsRemaining}");
        }
        else
        {
            Console.WriteLine($"{Name} has no potions left!");
        }
    }
}

class Program
{
```

```csharp
static void Main()
{
    Guard guard1 = new Guard("Guard", 30, 10, 5, "Scimitar");
    Prince player = new Prince("The Prince", 100, 0, 0, 3);

    // Both can use methods from Character class
    guard1.Move(2, 0);
    player.Move(5, 3);

    // Both can take damage
    guard1.TakeDamage(15);
    player.TakeDamage(25);

    // Each has their own special methods
    guard1.Patrol();
    player.DrinkPotion();

    // Prince gets in a fight!
    player.TakeDamage(50);
    player.DrinkPotion();
    player.TakeDamage(30);
    }
  }
}
```

Expected Output:

```
Guard moves to (12, 5)
The Prince moves to (5, 3)
Guard takes 15 damage! Health: 15
The Prince takes 25 damage! Health: 75
Guard the guard patrols with a Scimitar.
The Prince drinks a potion! Health: 85, Potions left: 2
The Prince takes 50 damage! Health: 35
The Prince drinks a potion! Health: 45, Potions left: 1
The Prince takes 30 damage! Health: 15
```

See what happened? Both `Guard` and `Prince` can use `Move()` and `TakeDamage()` even though we never wrote those methods in their classes. They inherited them from `Character`! But each class also has its own special abilities, guards can patrol, and the Prince can drink potions.

 **Pro Tip:**

Notice the `: base(name, health, x, y)` part? That's calling the parent class's constructor. Since the parent class needs those values to set up the character, the child class passes them along. Think of it like the child saying, "Hey parent, here's the info you need. Handle your stuff, then I'll handle mine."

Designing Good Inheritance

Just because you *can* inherit doesn't mean you *should*. You need to think about the relationship between classes.

Inheritance should represent an "**is-a**" relationship:

- A Guard **is a** Character ✓
- A Prince **is a** Character ✓
- A Sword **is a** Character ✗ (That makes no sense!)
- A Sword **is a** Weapon ✓

If you can't say "is-a" naturally, inheritance probably isn't the right tool. Maybe you want **composition** instead (having one class contain another class as a property), but that's a topic for another day.

Keep Your Base Class General

Your base class should only have stuff that *all* child classes will share. Don't put specific stuff in the base class just because one or two children need it.

 **Don't do this:**

```csharp
class Character
{
    public string Name;
    public int Health;
    public int ArrowCount;  // Wait, not all characters use arrows!
    public bool CanOpenGates; // Only the Prince should open gates!
}
```

Do this instead:

```csharp
class Character
{
    public string Name;
    public int Health;
    // Only the common stuff
}

class Archer : Character
{
    public int ArrowCount; // Specific to archers
}

class Prince : Character
{
    public bool CanOpenGates; // Specific to the prince
}
```

Don't Go Too Deep

Inheritance hierarchies can get messy if you go too many levels deep. If you have `Character` → `Enemy` → `Guard` → `SwordGuard` → `EliteSwordGuard` → `ImmortalEliteSwordGuard`, you're probably overdoing it. Keep it simple, usually 2-3 levels are plenty.

Think about it like this: you don't need a separate class for every single variation of guard. You could have a `Guard` class and just give them different properties like `ArmorLevel` or `Speed` to make them different.

Interface vs. Abstract Class vs. Regular Class

Okay, so you know about regular classes. But C# gives you two more tools for inheritance situations: **interfaces** and **abstract classes**. Let's break down when to use each.

Interface: The Contract

An **interface** is like a contract that says "any class that signs this contract *must* implement these methods." Interfaces don't have any code in them, just method signatures.

They define *what* a class can do, but not *how* it does it:

```csharp
interface IDamageable
{
    void TakeDamage(int damage);
    int GetHealth();
}

class Character : IDamageable
{
    public int Health = 100;

    public void TakeDamage(int damage)
    {
        Health -= damage;
    }

    public int GetHealth()
    {
        return Health;
    }
}

class Pot : IDamageable
{
    private bool isBroken = false;

    public void TakeDamage(int damage)
    {
        isBroken = true;
        Console.WriteLine("The pot shatters!");
    }

    public int GetHealth()
```

```
    {
        return isBroken ? 0 : 1;
    }
}
```

See? Both `Character` and `Pot` are totally different things, but they both implement `IDamageable`. Now you could have a method that takes any `IDamageable` object and damages it, whether it's a character or a pot!

When to use interfaces:
- When unrelated classes need to do the same thing in different ways
- When you want to allow a class to "be" multiple things (C# only allows inheriting from one class, but you can implement multiple interfaces!)
- When you want to define a capability, not a type of thing

Interfaces are everywhere. `ISaveable`, `IPrintable`, `IComparable` let you treat different objects the same way based on what they can *do*.

For out Prince we also need interfaces to make things easy. `ICollidable`, `IDrawable`, `ISaveable` will allow us to treat different objects the same way based on what they can *do*, not what they *are*.

> ### Pro Tip:
>
> By convention, interface names begin with the letter "**I**". Names like `IDamageable`, `IMovable`, and `IClickable` make interfaces instantly recognizable in your code.

Abstract Class: The In-Between

An **abstract class** is like a regular base class, but with a twist, you can't create instances of it directly. It's meant to be inherited from.

Abstract classes can have regular methods with code, but they can also have **abstract methods** that have no code and child classes *must* implement those:

```
abstract class Enemy
{
    public string Name;
    public int Health;

    public Enemy(string name, int health)
    {
        Name = name;
        Health = health;
    }

    // Regular method - all enemies can use this
    public void TakeDamage(int damage)
    {
```

```csharp
        Health -= damage;
        if (Health <= 0)
        {
            OnDeath();
        }
    }

    // Abstract method - each enemy type must define this
    public abstract void Attack();

    // Abstract method - each enemy has unique death behavior
    protected abstract void OnDeath();
}

class Guard : Enemy
{
    public Guard() : base("Guard", 30) { }

    public override void Attack()
    {
        Console.WriteLine($"{Name} swings his sword!");
    }

    protected override void OnDeath()
    {
        Console.WriteLine($"{Name} collapses to the ground.");
    }
}

class SkeletonWarrior : Enemy
{
    public SkeletonWarrior() : base("Skeleton", 20) { }

    public override void Attack()
    {
        Console.WriteLine($"{Name} lunges with supernatural speed!");
    }

    protected override void OnDeath()
    {
        Console.WriteLine($"{Name} crumbles into a pile of bones.");
    }
}
```

When to use abstract classes:
- When you have a base class that should never be created on its own
- When you have some shared code, but some methods need to be different for each child
- When child classes have a clear "is-a" relationship with the parent

In a game, you'd never just create a generic "Enemy", it's always a specific type of enemy. That's perfect for an abstract class!

Quick Comparison Table

Feature	Regular Class	Abstract Class	Interface
Can be instantiated?	Yes	No	No
Can have method implementations?	Yes	Yes	No (mostly)*
Can have methods and properties?	Yes	Yes	Yes
Can have fields?	Yes	Yes	No
Child must implement abstract methods?	N/A	Yes	Yes
Can inherit from multiple?	No	No	Yes

***Note:** Modern C# > 8.0 actually allows interfaces to have default implementations, but as a beginner, just think of interfaces as pure contracts with no code.

Pattern Matching: Checking Types

Sometimes you have a base class reference but you need to know what specific type it really is. Earlier we showed how you can use `GetType()` and `typeof()` to check an object's type and then cast it. That works, but it's verbose and you need separate lines for checking the type and converting it. **Pattern matching** gives you a cleaner, more efficient way to do both at once. If you have a `Character` but need to know whether it's actually a `Guard` or a `Prince`, pattern matching lets you check the type and get a properly-typed variable in a single step, making your code more readable and less error-prone.

The `is` Keyword

The `is` keyword checks if an object is a certain type:

```
using System;

Character someCharacter = new Guard("Bob", 30, 5, 5, "Sword");

if (someCharacter is Guard)
{
    Console.WriteLine("This is a guard!");
}

if (someCharacter is Prince)
{
    Console.WriteLine("This is the prince!");
}
```

Expected Output:

```
This is a guard!
```

Even better, you can check the type *and* create a variable of that type in one line:

```
Character someCharacter = new Prince("The Prince", 100, 0, 0, 3);

if (someCharacter is Prince p)
{
    // p is now a Prince variable, so we can use Prince-specific stuff
    p.DrinkPotion();
}
```

This is super handy! You check the type and get a properly-typed variable to work with immediately.

The `as` Keyword

The `as` keyword tries to convert an object to a type. If it can't, it returns `null` instead of crashing:

```
Character someCharacter = new Guard("Bob", 30, 5, 5, "Sword");

Prince maybePrince = someCharacter as Prince;

if (maybePrince != null)
{
    maybePrince.DrinkPotion();
}
else
{
    Console.WriteLine("Not a prince, can't drink potions!");
}
```

Expected Output:

```
Not a prince, can't drink potions!
```

Pro Tip:

Use `is` when you want to check the type and immediately work with it (most common). Use `as` when you're not sure what type something is and want to safely attempt a conversion without your program crashing. If the conversion fails, you get null instead of an error. Think of `is` as "check and use" and `as` as "try and see."

Switch Statements with Pattern Matching

Modern C# > 7.0 lets you use pattern matching in switch statements, which is really cool for handling different types:

```csharp
void HandleCharacter(Character character)
{
    switch (character)
    {
        case Prince p:
            Console.WriteLine($"The Prince has {p.PotionsRemaining} potions!");
            break;
        case Guard g:
            Console.WriteLine($"A guard with a {g.WeaponType} approaches!");
            break;
        default:
            Console.WriteLine("Unknown character type!");
            break;
    }
}

// Test it
HandleCharacter(new Prince("Hero", 100, 0, 0, 5));
HandleCharacter(new Guard("Enemy", 30, 10, 5, "Spear"));
```

Expected Output:

```
The Prince has 5 potions!
A guard with a Spear approaches!
```

This is fantastic for both business and game code! In business apps, imagine you're processing different types of documents or handling different employee types.

In games, imagine you're checking collisions where you can handle different types of objects differently:

```csharp
void OnCollision(Character other)
{
    switch (other)
    {
        case Guard g:
            Console.WriteLine("Fight the guard!");
            break;
        case Prince p:
            Console.WriteLine("Wait, you can't fight yourself!");
            break;
    }
}
```

Controlling Behavior: Letting Children Decide

Imagine you've got a base `Character` class with a `TakeDamage()` method. It works fine for most characters, it subtracts health, check if dead etc. But then you add a `ShieldedGuard` who should block some damage, and a `Ghost` enemy who should take half damage from physical attacks. Do you write completely separate damage methods for each? That defeats the whole point of inheritance! What you need is a way to say "here's the default behavior, but child classes can change it if they want." That's exactly what `virtual` and `override` do. Mark a method as `virtual` in the base class, and child classes can `override` it with their own version. This lets you keep the same method name and interface while changing what actually happens when you call it.

Using `virtual` and `override`

Mark a method as `virtual` in the base class to say "child classes can change this if they want." Then use `override` in the child class to actually change it:

```csharp
class Character
{
    public string Name;
    public int Health;

    public Character(string name, int health)
    {
        Name = name;
        Health = health;
    }

    // Virtual method - can be overridden
    public virtual void Speak()
    {
        Console.WriteLine($"{Name}: ...");
    }
}

class Prince : Character
{
    public Prince() : base("The Prince", 100) { }

    // Override the base class method
    public override void Speak()
    {
        Console.WriteLine($"{Name}: I must save the Princess!");
    }
}

class Guard : Character
{
    public Guard() : base("Guard", 30) { }

    public override void Speak()
    {
        Console.WriteLine($"{Name}: Stop right there!");
    }
}

class SilentEnemy : Character
{
    public SilentEnemy() : base("Skeleton", 20) { }

    // Don't override Speak - just use the base class version
```

```
}
```

Let's test it:

```
Character prince = new Prince();
Character guard = new Guard();
Character skeleton = new SilentEnemy();

prince.Speak();
guard.Speak();
skeleton.Speak();
```

Expected Output:

```
The Prince: I must save the Princess!
Guard: Stop right there!
Skeleton: ...
```

See how each type can have its own behavior? This is called **polymorphism** where we treat different types the same way, but they act differently. It's like pressing the attack button and the animation is different if you're doing a running attack versus a standing attack, but you're still pressing the same button.

 **Pro Tip:**

If you override a method, you can still call the original base class version using `base.MethodName()`. This is useful when you want to add to the base behavior, not replace it entirely:

Let's look at an example of making a call to the base method to execute that logic and then adding our own logic:

```
public override void TakeDamage(int damage)
{
    base.TakeDamage(damage); // Do the normal damage logic
    Console.WriteLine("Ouch! That hurt!"); // Add extra behavior
}
```

Sealed: No More Changes

Sometimes you want to say "this is the final version, no more overriding allowed." That's what `sealed` does.

You can seal a whole class so it can't be inherited from, or seal a single method so it can't be overridden anymore:

```
// Can't inherit from this class
sealed class FinalBoss : Enemy
{
```

```csharp
    // ...
}

// This would cause an error:
// class UltraFinalBoss : FinalBoss { } // Error!

// Or seal just a method
class Enemy
{
    public virtual void Attack() { }
}

class Guard : Enemy
{
    // Override and seal it
    public sealed override void Attack()
    {
        Console.WriteLine("Guard attacks!");
    }
}

class EliteGuard : Guard
{
    // Can't override Attack anymore - it's sealed!
    // public override void Attack() { } // Error!
}
```

You don't use `sealed` a lot as a beginner, but it's good to know it exists. It's mainly for when you're designing a library and want to control how people extend your classes.

Traps of Inheritance

Let's talk about common mistakes. Inheritance is powerful, but it's easy to mess up.

Don't Use Inheritance Just to Reuse Code

Inheritance should model a real relationship, not just be a way to copy-paste code. If two classes need the same method but aren't related, use composition or helper classes instead.

 **Bad:**

```csharp
// Door and Chest both need an "IsLocked" property
class Door : Chest  // Makes no sense! A door is not a chest!
{
}
```

 **Good:**

```csharp
class Lockable
{
    public bool IsLocked;
    public void Lock() { IsLocked = true; }
    public void Unlock() { IsLocked = false; }
}
```

```csharp
class Door
{
    private Lockable lockable = new Lockable();
    public void Lock() { lockable.Lock(); }
}

class Chest
{
    private Lockable lockable = new Lockable();
    public void Lock() { lockable.Lock(); }
}
```

Don't Make Everything Inherit from One Giant Base Class

It's tempting to make a `GameObject` class and have literally everything in your program inherit from it. But then you end up with weird things like your Menu button having a `Health` property or your Background having a `TakeDamage()` method.

Keep your base classes focused. It's okay to have multiple base classes for different categories of things.

Don't Inherit When Composition Makes More Sense

If the relationship is more like "has-a" than "is-a," use composition:

- A car **has an** engine (composition) ✓
- A car **is an** engine (inheritance) ✗

In games:

- A character **has a** weapon (composition) ✓
- A character **is a** weapon (inheritance) ✗

Don't Forget About Interfaces

Sometimes you don't need inheritance at all! If you just need unrelated things to do something similar, use an interface:

```csharp
// Everything that can be clicked implements this
interface IClickable
{
    void OnClick();
}

class Button : IClickable
{
    public void OnClick()
    {
        Console.WriteLine("Button clicked!");
    }
}
```

```csharp
// Can inherit from one class and multiple interfaces
class Enemy : Character, IClickable
{
    public void OnClick()
    {
        Console.WriteLine("Enemy selected!");
    }
}
```

Inheritance in Action

Let's put it all together with a more complete example that shows how inheritance helps organize our code.

This is a bit lengthy but try and follow the code and guess the output before trying it yourself:

```csharp
using System;
using System.Collections.Generic;

namespace PrinceOfProgramming
{
    // Base class for anything that can take damage
    abstract class Character
    {
        public string Name { get; protected set; }
        public int Health { get; protected set; }
        public int MaxHealth { get; protected set; }
        public int XPosition { get; set; }
        public int YPosition { get; set; }
        public bool IsAlive => Health > 0;

        protected Character(string name, int maxHealth, int x, int y)
        {
            Name = name;
            MaxHealth = maxHealth;
            Health = maxHealth;
            XPosition = x;
            YPosition = y;
        }

        public virtual void TakeDamage(int damage)
        {
            Health -= damage;
            if (Health < 0) Health = 0;

            Console.WriteLine($"{Name} takes {damage} damage! Health: {Health}/{MaxHealth}");

            if (!IsAlive)
            {
                OnDeath();
            }
        }

        public void Move(int xChange, int yChange)
        {
            XPosition += xChange;
            YPosition += yChange;
            Console.WriteLine($"{Name} moves to ({XPosition}, {YPosition})");
```

```csharp
    }

    protected virtual void OnDeath()
    {
        Console.WriteLine($"{Name} has been defeated!");
    }

    public abstract void PerformAction();
}

class Prince : Character
{
    public int PotionsRemaining { get; private set; }
    public int SwordDamage { get; private set; }

    public Prince(int x, int y) : base("The Prince", 100, x, y)
    {
        PotionsRemaining = 3;
        SwordDamage = 20;
    }

    public void DrinkPotion()
    {
        if (PotionsRemaining > 0 && Health < MaxHealth)
        {
            int healAmount = Math.Min(10, MaxHealth - Health);
            Health += healAmount;
            PotionsRemaining--;
            Console.WriteLine($"{Name} drinks a potion! " +
                $"Health: {Health}/{MaxHealth}, Potions left: {PotionsRemaining}");
        }
        else if (PotionsRemaining == 0)
        {
            Console.WriteLine($"{Name} has no potions left!");
        }
        else
        {
            Console.WriteLine($"{Name} is already at full health!");
        }
    }

    public void Attack(Character target)
    {
        Console.WriteLine($"{Name} strikes with his sword!");
        target.TakeDamage(SwordDamage);
    }

    public override void PerformAction()
    {
        Console.WriteLine($"{Name} can: [M]ove, [A]ttack, [D]rink Potion");
    }

    protected override void OnDeath()
    {
        Console.WriteLine($"{Name} falls to the ground. The kingdom is lost...");
    }
}

class Guard : Character
{
    public string WeaponType { get; private set; }
```

```csharp
    private int attackDamage;

    public Guard(string name, int x, int y, string weapon, int damage)
        : base(name, 30, x, y)
    {
        WeaponType = weapon;
        attackDamage = damage;
    }

    public void Attack(Character target)
    {
        Console.WriteLine($"{Name} attacks with their {WeaponType}!");
        target.TakeDamage(attackDamage);
    }

    public override void PerformAction()
    {
        Console.WriteLine($"{Name} patrols the palace halls with a {WeaponType}.");
    }

    protected override void OnDeath()
    {
        Console.WriteLine($"{Name} collapses. His weapon clatters to the ground.");
    }
}

class SkeletonWarrior : Character
{
    private int attackDamage = 25;

    public SkeletonWarrior(int x, int y) : base("Skeleton Warrior", 20, x, y)
    {
    }

    public void Attack(Character target)
    {
        Console.WriteLine($"{Name} lunges with supernatural speed!");
        target.TakeDamage(attackDamage);
    }

    public override void PerformAction()
    {
        Console.WriteLine($"{Name} rattles menacingly.");
    }

    protected override void OnDeath()
    {
        Console.WriteLine($"{Name} crumbles into a pile of bones.");
    }

    // Skeletons are spooky and take less damage
    public override void TakeDamage(int damage)
    {
        int reducedDamage = damage - 5;
        if (reducedDamage < 1) reducedDamage = 1;
        Console.WriteLine($"{Name}'s bones absorb some damage!");
        base.TakeDamage(reducedDamage);
    }
}

class Game
```

```csharp
{
    private Prince player;
    private List<Character> enemies;

    public Game()
    {
        player = new Prince(0, 0);
        enemies = new List<Character>
        {
            new Guard("Elite Guard", 10, 5, "Scimitar", 15),
            new Guard("Palace Guard", 15, 8, "Spear", 12),
            new SkeletonWarrior(20, 10)
        };
    }

    public void Run()
    {
        Console.WriteLine("=== INHERITANCE QUEST ===\n");

        player.PerformAction();
        Console.WriteLine();

        foreach (var enemy in enemies)
        {
            if (enemy.IsAlive)
            {
                enemy.PerformAction();
            }
        }

        Console.WriteLine("\n--- Combat begins! ---\n");

        // Prince fights the first guard
        player.Move(5, 3);
        Guard firstGuard = enemies[0] as Guard;
        player.Attack(firstGuard);

        if (firstGuard.IsAlive)
        {
            firstGuard.Attack(player);
        }

        player.Attack(firstGuard);
        Console.WriteLine();

        // Prince takes a potion break
        player.DrinkPotion();
        Console.WriteLine();

        // Fight the skeleton
        SkeletonWarrior skeleton = enemies[2] as SkeletonWarrior;
        Console.WriteLine("--- A Skeleton Warrior appears! ---");
        skeleton.Attack(player);
        player.Attack(skeleton);
        player.Attack(skeleton);
        Console.WriteLine();

        // Check final status
        Console.WriteLine("--- Battle Summary ---");
        Console.WriteLine($"Prince Health: {player.Health}/{player.MaxHealth}");
        Console.WriteLine($"Potions Remaining: {player.PotionsRemaining}");
```

```csharp
            Console.WriteLine($"Enemies Defeated: {enemies.FindAll(e => !e.IsAlive).Count}");
        }
    }

    class Program
    {
        static void Main()
        {
            Game game = new Game();
            game.Run();
        }
    }
}
```

Expected Output:

```
=== INHERITANCE QUEST ===

The Prince can: [M]ove, [A]ttack, [D]rink Potion

Elite Guard patrols the palace halls with a Scimitar.
Palace Guard patrols the palace halls with a Spear.
Skeleton Warrior rattles menacingly.

--- Combat begins! ---

The Prince moves to (5, 3)
The Prince strikes with his sword!
Elite Guard takes 20 damage! Health: 10/30
Elite Guard attacks with their Scimitar!
The Prince takes 15 damage! Health: 85/100
The Prince strikes with his sword!
Elite Guard takes 20 damage! Health: 0/30
Elite Guard collapses. His weapon clatters to the ground.

The Prince drinks a potion! Health: 95/100, Potions left: 2

--- A Skeleton Warrior appears! ---
Skeleton Warrior lunges with supernatural speed!
The Prince takes 25 damage! Health: 70/100
The Prince strikes with his sword!
Skeleton Warrior's bones absorb some damage!
Skeleton Warrior takes 15 damage! Health: 5/20
The Prince strikes with his sword!
Skeleton Warrior's bones absorb some damage!
Skeleton Warrior takes 15 damage! Health: 0/20
Skeleton Warrior crumbles into a pile of bones.

--- Battle Summary ---
Prince Health: 70/100
Potions Remaining: 2
Enemies Defeated: 2
```

Look at how clean this is! Each character type has its own behavior, but they all share common functionality. The Game class doesn't need to know the details of each character type, it just calls methods on the Character base class. That's the power of inheritance and polymorphism!

Notice how:

- All characters can move and take damage (from base class)
- Each has unique attack messages (overridden behavior)
- The Skeleton has special defense (overridden TakeDamage)
- The Prince has special abilities (potions)
- We can treat all enemies the same way in the list, even though they're different types underneath!

Fun Experiment: The Gauntlet of Traps

Time to put your inheritance skills to the test! Let's create a trap system that fits into our Prince's adventure!

The Prince's Journey: Hierarchy of Danger

The story continues...

The Prince barely escapes his mirror-self, slipping through a narrow archway just as the spectral blade slashes where his head had been moments before. The passage seals behind him with a grinding of stone, trapping his doppelganger on the other side. He catches his breath in the new corridor, then freezes. Blocking the path ahead stands another palace guard, but this one is different from those he's fought before. The man's belly protrudes noticeably, his breathing labored, yet he grips his scimitar with surprising confidence. The Prince realizes the Vizier employs many types of guards. Some quick and agile, others slower but more resilient. They share the same basic training, the same fundamental abilities, but each brings unique strengths to combat.

Beyond this guard, the Prince spots a corridor lined with deadly traps, each mechanism glowing with the Vizier's magic. If he can defeat this guard and navigate the trap-filled gauntlet beyond, he might finally find a path toward freedom. He steadies his sword and prepares to face yet another variation of the dangers the Vizier has systematically placed throughout this cursed dungeon.

The Challenge

Create an inheritance hierarchy for different trap types in the palace.

Here's what you need to do:

1. Create an abstract base class called `Trap` with:
   - Properties: `IsActive` (bool), `XPosition` (int), `YPosition` (int), `Damage` (int)
   - An abstract method `Trigger(Character target)` that each trap type will implement differently
   - A regular method `Activate()` that sets `IsActive` to true and prints a message
   - A regular method `Deactivate()` that sets `IsActive` to false

2. Create three trap types that inherit from `Trap`:
    - `SpikeTrap`: Does 50 damage instantly. When triggered, prints a message about spikes shooting up.
    - `PoisonGasTrap`: Does 10 damage per second (just print that it does ongoing damage). When triggered, prints about green gas filling the room.
    - `FallingFloorTrap`: Does 100 damage (it's a long fall!). When triggered, prints about the floor giving way.
3. Create a `Prince` class (or reuse the one from earlier) with Health and a `TakeDamage()` method.
4. In your `Main()` method:
    - Create a Prince with 100 health
    - Create one of each trap type at different positions
    - Have the Prince walk into each trap (check if it's active, then trigger it)
    - Show the Prince's remaining health after each trap

Bonus Challenge:

- Add a `TimedTrap` that inherits from `Trap` and automatically activates and deactivates on a timer. Give it an `IsOnCycle` property and override `Trigger()` to only work if the trap is currently in its "on" phase of the cycle.

Give it a shot! Remember, inheritance is all about avoiding code repetition while keeping things organized. Don't peek at the answer too quickly, sometimes the best learning comes from struggling a bit and then having that "aha!" moment.

Example Answer

Here's one way to solve it:

```csharp
using System;

namespace PrinceOfProgramming
{
    // Base trap class
    abstract class Trap
    {
        public bool IsActive { get; protected set; }
        public int XPosition { get; set; }
        public int YPosition { get; set; }
        public int Damage { get; protected set; }

        protected Trap(int x, int y, int damage)
        {
            XPosition = x;
            YPosition = y;
            Damage = damage;
            IsActive = true; // Traps start active by default
        }

        public void Activate()
        {
```

```csharp
            IsActive = true;
            Console.WriteLine($"Trap at ({XPosition}, {YPosition}) is now ACTIVE!");
        }

        public void Deactivate()
        {
            IsActive = false;
            Console.WriteLine($"Trap at ({XPosition}, {YPosition}) is now deactivated.");
        }

        // Each trap type implements this differently
        public abstract void Trigger(Character target);
    }

    class SpikeTrap : Trap
    {
        public SpikeTrap(int x, int y) : base(x, y, 50)
        {
        }

        public override void Trigger(Character target)
        {
            if (!IsActive)
            {
                Console.WriteLine("The spike trap is dormant. Safe to pass.");
                return;
            }

            Console.WriteLine($"SSHHING! Deadly spikes shoot up from the floor at " +
                $"({XPosition}, {YPosition})!");
            target.TakeDamage(Damage);
        }
    }

    class PoisonGasTrap : Trap
    {
        public PoisonGasTrap(int x, int y) : base(x, y, 10)
        {
        }

        public override void Trigger(Character target)
        {
            if (!IsActive)
            {
                Console.WriteLine("The gas trap is dormant. The air is clear.");
                return;
            }

            Console.WriteLine($"HISSSS! Green poisonous gas fills the room at " +
                $"({XPosition}, {YPosition})!");
            Console.WriteLine($"The gas deals {Damage} damage per second! " +
                $"Get out quickly!");
            target.TakeDamage(Damage);
        }
    }

    class FallingFloorTrap : Trap
    {
        public FallingFloorTrap(int x, int y) : base(x, y, 100)
        {
        }
```

```csharp
    public override void Trigger(Character target)
    {
        if (!IsActive)
        {
            Console.WriteLine("The floor is stable here.");
            return;
        }

        Console.WriteLine($"CRACK! The floor crumbles away at ({XPosition}, " +
            $"{YPosition})!");
        Console.WriteLine("You're falling into darkness!");
        target.TakeDamage(Damage);
    }
}

// Bonus: Timed trap
class TimedTrap : Trap
{
    public bool IsOnCycle { get; private set; }
    private int currentTick = 0;
    private int onDuration = 3;  // On for 3 ticks
    private int offDuration = 2; // Off for 2 ticks

    public TimedTrap(int x, int y, int damage) : base(x, y, damage)
    {
        IsOnCycle = true;
    }

    public void UpdateCycle()
    {
        currentTick++;
        int totalCycle = onDuration + offDuration;
        int cyclePosition = currentTick % totalCycle;

        IsOnCycle = cyclePosition < onDuration;

        Console.WriteLine($"[Timed Trap at ({XPosition}, {YPosition}) - " +
            $"Cycle: {(IsOnCycle ? "ON" : "OFF")}]");
    }

    public override void Trigger(Character target)
    {
        if (!IsActive)
        {
            Console.WriteLine("The timed trap has been permanently disabled.");
            return;
        }

        if (!IsOnCycle)
        {
            Console.WriteLine($"The trap at ({XPosition}, {YPosition}) " +
                $"is in its OFF cycle. Safe!");
            return;
        }

        Console.WriteLine($"WHOOSH! The timed trap activates at ({XPosition}," +
            $" {YPosition})!");
        target.TakeDamage(Damage);
    }
}
```

```csharp
// Character class for the Prince
class Character
{
    public string Name { get; private set; }
    public int Health { get; private set; }
    public int MaxHealth { get; private set; }
    public int XPosition { get; set; }
    public int YPosition { get; set; }

    public Character(string name, int maxHealth, int x, int y)
    {
        Name = name;
        MaxHealth = maxHealth;
        Health = maxHealth;
        XPosition = x;
        YPosition = y;
    }

    public void TakeDamage(int damage)
    {
        Health -= damage;
        if (Health < 0) Health = 0;

        Console.WriteLine($"{Name} takes {damage} damage! Health:" +
            $" {Health}/{MaxHealth}");

        if (Health == 0)
        {
            Console.WriteLine($"{Name} has fallen! Game Over.");
        }
    }

    public void MoveTo(int x, int y)
    {
        XPosition = x;
        YPosition = y;
        Console.WriteLine($"\n{Name} carefully moves to position " +
            $"({XPosition}, {YPosition})...");
    }
}

class Program
{
    static void Main()
    {
        Console.WriteLine("=== THE GAUNTLET OF TRAPS ===\n");

        // Create our hero
        Character prince = new Character("The Prince", 100, 0, 0);
        Console.WriteLine($"{prince.Name} enters the palace dungeon with" +
            $" {prince.Health} health.\n");

        // Create the deadly traps
        SpikeTrap spikeTrap = new SpikeTrap(5, 0);
        PoisonGasTrap gasTrap = new PoisonGasTrap(10, 0);
        FallingFloorTrap floorTrap = new FallingFloorTrap(15, 0);
        TimedTrap timedTrap = new TimedTrap(20, 0, 30);

        Console.WriteLine("The dungeon is filled with deadly traps!\n");
```

```csharp
        // Trap 1: Spike Trap
        prince.MoveTo(5, 0);
        spikeTrap.Trigger(prince);

        // Trap 2: Poison Gas (but we deactivate it first!)
        Console.WriteLine("\n*The Prince pulls a lever on the wall*");
        gasTrap.Deactivate();
        prince.MoveTo(10, 0);
        gasTrap.Trigger(prince);

        // Trap 3: Falling Floor
        prince.MoveTo(15, 0);
        floorTrap.Trigger(prince);

        // Check if Prince survives
        if (prince.Health <= 0)
        {
            Console.WriteLine("\nThe traps were too much. The quest ends here...");
            return;
        }

        // Bonus: Timed Trap - show a few cycles
        Console.WriteLine("\n--- The Prince approaches a mysterious timed trap ---");
        prince.MoveTo(20, 0);

        for (int i = 0; i < 6; i++)
        {
            timedTrap.UpdateCycle();
            timedTrap.Trigger(prince);
            Console.WriteLine();

            if (prince.Health <= 0)
            {
                break;
            }
        }

        // Final status
        Console.WriteLine("\n=== GAUNTLET COMPLETE ===");
        if (prince.Health > 0)
        {
            Console.WriteLine($"{prince.Name} survived! Final Health:" +
                $" {prince.Health}/{prince.MaxHealth}");
            Console.WriteLine("But many more dangers await in the palace...");
        }
    }
  }
}
```

Expected Output:

```
=== THE GAUNTLET OF TRAPS ===

The Prince enters the palace dungeon with 100 health.

The dungeon is filled with deadly traps!

The Prince carefully moves to position (5, 0)...
SSHHING! Deadly spikes shoot up from the floor at (5, 0)!
The Prince takes 50 damage! Health: 50/100
```

```
*The Prince pulls a lever on the wall*
Trap at (10, 0) is now deactivated.

The Prince carefully moves to position (10, 0)...
The gas trap is dormant. The air is clear.

The Prince carefully moves to position (15, 0)...
CRACK! The floor crumbles away at (15, 0)!
You're falling into darkness!
The Prince takes 100 damage! Health: 0/100
The Prince has fallen! Game Over.

The gauntlet was too much. The quest ends here...
```

Or if you had deactivated more traps or had more health, you'd see the timed trap section:

```
[Timed Trap at (20, 0) - Cycle: ON]
WHOOSH! The timed trap activates at (20, 0)!
The Prince takes 30 damage! Health: 20/100

[Timed Trap at (20, 0) - Cycle: ON]
WHOOSH! The timed trap activates at (20, 0)!
The Prince takes 30 damage! Health: 0/100
The Prince has fallen! Game Over.
```

See how inheritance helped organize this? All traps share the basic trap properties and activation logic, but each has its own unique triggering behavior. You could easily add more trap types (arrow traps, crushing ceiling, etc.) without changing any existing code!

Pro Tip:

Notice how the `Trigger()` method checks `IsActive` at the start? That's a common pattern to check conditions before doing the main logic. It keeps your code clean and avoids deep nesting.

Wrap-up: What You've Learned

Wow, you made it through inheritance!

Key Takeaways

- **Inheritance** lets child classes get all the properties and methods from a parent class, plus add their own special features
- Use inheritance for **"is-a"** relationships (a Guard IS-A Character)
- Child classes can **override** methods to change how they work
- **Abstract classes** can't be instantiated directly and can force child classes to implement certain methods

- **Interfaces** define contracts that classes must follow, and a class can implement multiple interfaces
- Use `is` to check if an object is a certain type (and optionally create a typed variable)
- Use `as` to safely try converting to a type (returns null if it fails)
- Use pattern matching in `switch` statements to handle different types cleanly
- `virtual`: Marks a method as overridable in child classes
- `override`: Replaces a virtual method from the parent class
- `sealed`: Prevents further overriding or inheritance
- `abstract`: Forces child classes to implement a method
- Keep base classes general and only include what ALL children will share
- Don't go too deep with inheritance (2-3 levels max usually)
- Use interfaces when classes need to share capabilities but aren't related
- Use composition (has-a) when inheritance (is-a) doesn't make sense
- Make methods virtual only if you actually expect them to be overridden

Inheritance is everywhere in software development. In business applications, you'll see it with documents, employees, transactions, and reports. In game development, it's used for game objects, enemies, weapons, and UI elements. Almost every major framework and game engine uses it:

- All business reports inherit from a base Report class
- All database records inherit from a base Model class
- All UI controls inherit from a base Control class
- And in games: all GameObjects inherit from a base GameObject class, all enemies from Enemy, all weapons from Weapon

It keeps your code organized, reduces duplication, and makes it easy to add new types of things to your game. Plus, it makes your code more maintainable. If you need to fix a bug or add a feature that affects all characters, you just change the base Character class and bam, all children get the fix automatically!

Now you're ready to build proper class hierarchies! You've got the foundation now and you're thinking in objects, and that's huge!

Chapter 9

Events

"All action results from thought." — Ralph Waldo Emerson

Events are one of the most powerful patterns in modern software development. They allow different parts of your application to communicate without being directly connected. Imagine a doorbell that rings in your house. The button outside doesn't need to know who's inside or what they'll do when they hear it; it just sends a signal. The same principal powers everything from clicking buttons in web browsers to receiving notifications on your phone, from stock trading platforms that react to market changes in real-time to smart home systems where your lights turn on when motion is detected. Events let you build software that's responsive, flexible, and easy to modify because each component can focus on its own job while still reacting to what happens elsewhere.

Understanding events transforms how you think about program flow. Instead of writing rigid, top-to-bottom code where everything is tightly connected, you'll learn to create systems where objects broadcast what's happening and other objects choose to listen and respond. This pattern is called "publish and subscribe" or "observer pattern" and is fundamental to building maintainable software that can grow and change over time. When you master events, you're not just learning a C# feature; you're learning a design philosophy that will make you a better programmer in any language, whether you're building desktop applications, web services, mobile apps, or interactive systems.

Core Concepts Covered

- ✓ Decoupling components so they can work independently
- ✓ The publish/subscribe (observer) pattern for communication between objects
- ✓ Passing behavior (methods) as values to create flexible, reusable code
- ✓ Writing inline anonymous functions for quick, focused operations
- ✓ Handling asynchronous operations and background tasks
- ✓ Designing systems where objects react to changes without tight dependencies

When Your Code Rings a Bell

 **Trivia:**

Mathematician Edward Lorenz discovered the "butterfly effect" by accident in 1961. Running a weather simulation, he entered 0.506 instead of 0.506127 to save time. That tiny 0.000127 difference created completely different weather predictions. This proved some systems are so sensitive that small changes cascade into huge effects—like events triggering other events. Its why weather forecasts can't be accurate beyond 10 days.

When our Prince steps on a pressure plate. Suddenly, a gate slams shut behind you, spikes shoot up from the floor, and a timer starts counting down. How does the pressure plate "tell" all these other objects what to do?

You *could* write code like this:

```
// BAD APPROACH - Don't do this!
if (prince.IsOnPressurePlate)
{
    gate.Close();
    spikes.Activate();
    timer.Start();
    soundEffect.Play("doom_sound.wav");
}
```

But this is terrible! Why? Because now your pressure plate code needs to *know* about gates, spikes, timers, and sound effects. What if you want to add a new trap? You'd have to dig into the pressure plate code and modify it. What if you have 50 different pressure plates that do different things? Your code becomes a tangled mess faster than our Prince can say "I need a health potion."

This is where **events** come to the rescue! Events let objects send out a signal saying "Hey, something happened!" without caring who's listening or what they do about it. It's like the Prince shouting "Guards!" when he's spotted, he doesn't need to know how many guards will show up or what they'll do, he just alerts everyone.

Think about it in terms of the game, when you drink a health potion, multiple things happen, your health bar updates, a sound plays, the potion disappears from inventory, maybe an achievement counter gets incremented. Instead of the potion code directly calling all these systems, it just fires a "HealthPotionUsed" event, and everyone interested reacts.

Pro Tip:

Events are the backbone of modern game engines like Unity and Unreal. When you click a button in a game menu, that's an event. When an enemy dies, that's an event. When you level up, that's an event. Learning events now will make game development (and all programming) much easier later!

Delegates: Method's Phone Number

Before we can use events, we need to understand **delegates**. Think of a delegate as a fancy way to pass around methods like they're variables. It's like giving someone a phone number. You're not making the call; you're just giving them the ability to call when they need to.

Creating a Delegate

Here's the basic syntax:

```csharp
// This creates a "delegate type" - a blueprint for methods
public delegate void PressurePlateHandler(string trapName);
```

This says: "Any method that matches this signature (takes a string, returns void) can be used with this delegate." Now you can create variables of this type and assign methods to them:

```csharp
public class TrapSystem
{
    public void ActivateSpikes(string trapName)
    {
        Console.WriteLine($"Spikes activated: {trapName}");
    }

    public void CloseGate(string trapName)
    {
        Console.WriteLine($"Gate closed: {trapName}");
    }
}

class Program
{
    static void Main()
    {
        TrapSystem traps = new TrapSystem();

        // Assign a method to the delegate
```

```csharp
        PressurePlateHandler handler = traps.ActivateSpikes;

        // Call it like a regular method
        handler("spike_trap_01");

        // You can reassign to a different method
        handler = traps.CloseGate;
        handler("main_gate");
    }
}
```

Expected Output:

```
Spikes activated: spike_trap_01
Gate closed: main_gate
```

But here's the nice about them, you can chain multiple methods together:

```csharp
class Program
{
    static void Main()
    {
        TrapSystem traps = new TrapSystem();

        // Start with one method
        PressurePlateHandler handler = traps.ActivateSpikes;

        // Add another method using +=
        handler += traps.CloseGate;

        // Now calling it will execute BOTH methods!
        handler("deadly_trap");
    }
}
```

Expected Output:

```
Spikes activated: deadly_trap
Gate closed: deadly_trap
```

Publish And Subscribe

Now let's turn this delegate into an event. This is where the "publish and subscribe" pattern comes in:

```csharp
public class PressurePlate
{
    // The "event" keyword makes this a proper event
    public event PressurePlateHandler OnPlateActivated;

    public void StepOn()
    {
        Console.WriteLine("*CLICK* The pressure plate sinks into the floor...");

        // This is "publishing" or "firing" the event
        // The question mark checks if anyone is listening (null-safe)
        OnPlateActivated?.Invoke("deadly_spike_trap");
```

```
        }
}
```

Now let's create some objects that want to listen to this event:

```csharp
public class SpikeTraps
{
    public void ActivateSpikes(string trapName)
    {
        Console.WriteLine($">>> SPIKES SHOOT UP FROM THE FLOOR! ({trapName})");
    }
}

public class Gate
{
    public void CloseGate(string trapName)
    {
        Console.WriteLine($">>> IRON GATE SLAMS SHUT! ({trapName})");
    }
}

public class Timer
{
    public void StartCountdown(string trapName)
    {
        Console.WriteLine($">>> COUNTDOWN BEGINS: 60 SECONDS! ({trapName})");
    }
}
```

Now here's the magic, let's wire everything together:

```csharp
class Program
{
    static void Main()
    {
        PressurePlate plate = new PressurePlate();
        SpikeTraps spikes = new SpikeTraps();
        Gate gate = new Gate();
        Timer timer = new Timer();

        // SUBSCRIBING to the event - this is where the magic happens!
        plate.OnPlateActivated += spikes.ActivateSpikes;
        plate.OnPlateActivated += gate.CloseGate;
        plate.OnPlateActivated += timer.StartCountdown;

        Console.WriteLine("The Prince cautiously enters the chamber...");
        Console.WriteLine();

        // When the Prince steps on the plate, ALL subscribed methods get called!
        plate.StepOn();

        Console.WriteLine();
        Console.WriteLine("Later, the spikes mechanism breaks...");

        // You can unsubscribe too!
        plate.OnPlateActivated -= spikes.ActivateSpikes;

        plate.StepOn();
    }
}
```

Expected Output:

```
The Prince cautiously enters the chamber...

*CLICK* The pressure plate sinks into the floor...
>>> SPIKES SHOOT UP FROM THE FLOOR! (deadly_spike_trap)
>>> IRON GATE SLAMS SHUT! (deadly_spike_trap)
>>> COUNTDOWN BEGINS: 60 SECONDS! (deadly_spike_trap)

Later, the spikes mechanism breaks...
*CLICK* The pressure plate sinks into the floor...
>>> IRON GATE SLAMS SHUT! (deadly_spike_trap)
>>> COUNTDOWN BEGINS: 60 SECONDS! (deadly_spike_trap)
```

See what happened? The `PressurePlate` doesn't know anything about spikes, gates, or timers. It just fires its event, and everyone who's listening reacts. You can add or remove listeners without ever touching the `PressurePlate` code. That's the beauty of events!

The Standard Pattern with EventHandler

There's a standard pattern that professional C# developers use for events. Instead of creating your own delegate, you can use the built-in `EventHandler<T>`:

```csharp
// Step 1: Create an EventArgs class to hold event data
public class TrapEventArgs : EventArgs
{
    public string TrapName { get; set; }
    public int DamageAmount { get; set; }
    public bool IsFatal { get; set; }
}

// Step 2: Create your class with a proper event
public class PressurePlate
{
    // Use EventHandler<T> instead of creating your own delegate
    public event EventHandler<TrapEventArgs> OnPlateActivated;

    public void StepOn()
    {
        Console.WriteLine("*CLICK* The pressure plate sinks into the floor...");

        // Create the event data
        TrapEventArgs args = new TrapEventArgs
        {
            TrapName = "deadly_spike_trap",
            DamageAmount = 50,
            IsFatal = true
        };

        // Fire the event with proper null-check
        OnPlateActivated?.Invoke(this, args);
    }
}
```

Now our listeners look like this:

```csharp
public class HealthSystem
```

```csharp
{
    private int playerHealth = 100;

    public void OnTrapActivated(object sender, TrapEventArgs e)
    {
        playerHealth -= e.DamageAmount;
        Console.WriteLine($">>> Player took {e.DamageAmount} damage! " +
            $"Health: {playerHealth}");

        if (e.IsFatal && playerHealth <= 0)
        {
            Console.WriteLine(">>> GAME OVER!");
        }
    }
}
```

Why this pattern?

- `EventHandler<T>` is a built-in delegate that everyone recognizes
- `EventArgs` lets you pass detailed information about what happened
- The `sender` parameter tells you *who* fired the event (useful when multiple objects share the same event handler)
- It's consistent with how all of .NET's events work, so other programmers will instantly understand your code

Pro Tip:

You'll see `sender` typed as `object` in event handlers. That's because events can be fired by any type of object. If you need to know specifically that it was a PressurePlate, you can cast it: `PressurePlate plate = sender as PressurePlate;`. But usually, you don't need to care who sent it, you just react to the event data in the EventArgs.

Delegates on Easy Mode

Creating custom delegates every time gets tedious. That's why C# includes two super handy built-in delegate types: `Action` and `Func`. They're like pre-made delegate templates that cover 99% of what you'll ever need.

Action Delegate: Just Do the Thing

`Action` is a delegate that doesn't return anything (void).

You can have up to 16 parameters!

```csharp
// These are all valid Actions:
Action simpleAction;                    // No parameters, returns nothing
Action<string> oneParam;                // One string parameter
Action<string, int> twoParams;          // Two parameters
```

```csharp
Action<string, int, bool> threeParams;  // Three parameters
// ... and so on
```

Let's see it in action (pun intended):

```csharp
public class GuardAI
{
    public void Patrol()
    {
        Console.WriteLine("Guard is patrolling...");
    }

    public void ChasePlayer(string direction)
    {
        Console.WriteLine($"Guard is chasing towards the {direction}!");
    }

    public void Attack(string weapon, int damage)
    {
        Console.WriteLine($"Guard attacks with {weapon} for {damage} damage!");
    }
}

class Program
{
    static void Main()
    {
        GuardAI guard = new GuardAI();

        // Action with no parameters
        Action patrolAction = guard.Patrol;
        patrolAction();

        // Action with one parameter
        Action<string> chaseAction = guard.ChasePlayer;
        chaseAction("east");

        // Action with two parameters
        Action<string, int> attackAction = guard.Attack;
        attackAction("sword", 25);
    }
}
```

Expected Output:

```
Guard is patrolling...
Guard is chasing towards the east!
Guard attacks with sword for 25 damage!
```

Here's where **Action** really shines, you can use it for events without creating custom delegates:

```csharp
public class GameEvents
{
    // No need to create custom delegates!
    public event Action OnGameStart;
    public event Action<int> OnScoreChanged;
    public event Action<string, int> OnPlayerDamaged;
```

```csharp
    public void StartGame()
    {
        Console.WriteLine("Game starting...");
        OnGameStart?.Invoke();
    }

    public void AddScore(int points)
    {
        Console.WriteLine($"Score +{points}");
        OnScoreChanged?.Invoke(points);
    }

    public void DamagePlayer(string damageType, int amount)
    {
        Console.WriteLine($"Player hit by {damageType}!");
        OnPlayerDamaged?.Invoke(damageType, amount);
    }
}

class Program
{
    static void Main()
    {
        GameEvents events = new GameEvents();

        // Subscribe with simple methods or lambdas
        events.OnGameStart += () => Console.WriteLine("  → Music starts playing");
        events.OnGameStart += () => Console.WriteLine("  → Level loads");

        events.OnScoreChanged += (points) =>
            Console.WriteLine($"  → Total score updated by {points}");

        events.OnPlayerDamaged += (type, amount) =>
            Console.WriteLine($"  → Health reduced by {amount} ({type})");

        // Trigger the events
        events.StartGame();
        Console.WriteLine();
        events.AddScore(100);
        Console.WriteLine();
        events.DamagePlayer("spike trap", 25);
    }
}
```

Expected Output:

```
Game starting...
  → Music starts playing
  → Level loads

Score +100
  → Total score updated by 100

Player hit by spike trap!
  → Health reduced by 25 (spike trap)
```

When we call the methods on the GameEvents instance it triggers the events that was set up earlier.

You probably noticed the brackets, equals sign, and "arrow" `() =>`. This is called a **lambda**. A lambda is an **anonymous method**, or a method with no name that runs the code written after the arrow.

The parameters inside the brackets must **match the delegate used by the event**. For example, `OnGameStart` has no parameters, so the lambda only uses `()`. `OnPlayerDamaged` has two parameters, so the lambda must include two arguments `(type, amount)`. We'll cover lambdas in more detail soon!

Func Delegate: Do Stuff and Get Something Back

`Func` is like `Action`, but it *returns* a value.

The last type parameter is always the return type:

```
Func<int> noParamsReturnsInt;            // No parameters, returns int
Func<string, int> stringToInt;           // Takes string, returns int
Func<int, int, bool> compareTwoInts;     // Takes two ints, returns bool
Func<string, int, double, string> complex; // Takes string, int, double; returns string
```

Using Func with Events

While `Action` is most common for events, `Func` can be useful when you need subscribers to return values like checking permissions, validating conditions, or allowing subscribers to "vote" on whether something should happen:

```csharp
public class Door
{
    public string Name { get; set; }

    // Func event that returns bool - subscribers can veto entry
    public event Func<bool> CanEnter;

    public bool TryEnter()
    {
        Console.WriteLine($"Trying to enter {Name}...");

        // If no subscribers, allow entry
        if (CanEnter == null)
        {
            Console.WriteLine("  → Door is unlocked!");
            return true;
        }

        // Check each subscriber - if ANY returns false, deny entry
        foreach (Func<bool> handler in CanEnter.GetInvocationList())
        {
            if (!handler())
            {
                Console.WriteLine("  → Entry denied!");
                return false;
            }
        }
```

```csharp
            Console.WriteLine("  → All checks passed, entering!");
            return true;
        }
    }

public class KeyChecker
{
    private bool hasKey;

    public KeyChecker(bool hasKey)
    {
        this.hasKey = hasKey;
    }

    public bool CheckHasKey()
    {
        if (hasKey)
        {
            Console.WriteLine("    ✓ Key check passed");
            return true;
        }
        else
        {
            Console.WriteLine("    ✗ Missing key!");
            return false;
        }
    }
}

public class HealthChecker
{
    private int health;

    public HealthChecker(int health)
    {
        this.health = health;
    }

    public bool CheckHealth()
    {
        if (health >= 50)
        {
            Console.WriteLine("    ✓ Health check passed");
            return true;
        }
        else
        {
            Console.WriteLine("    ✗ Not enough health!");
            return false;
        }
    }
}

class Program
{
    static void Main()
    {
        Door secretDoor = new Door { Name = "Secret Door" };

        KeyChecker keyCheck = new KeyChecker(hasKey: true);
        HealthChecker healthCheck = new HealthChecker(health: 75);
```

```csharp
        // Subscribe multiple checks - ALL must return true
        secretDoor.CanEnter += keyCheck.CheckHasKey;
        secretDoor.CanEnter += healthCheck.CheckHealth;

        bool entered = secretDoor.TryEnter();
        Console.WriteLine($"Result: {(entered ? "ENTERED" : "BLOCKED")}\n");

        // Try again without key
        Console.WriteLine("==============================");
        Console.WriteLine();

        Door lockedDoor = new Door { Name = "Locked Door" };
        KeyChecker noKey = new KeyChecker(hasKey: false);

        lockedDoor.CanEnter += noKey.CheckHasKey;
        lockedDoor.CanEnter += healthCheck.CheckHealth;

        bool entered2 = lockedDoor.TryEnter();
        Console.WriteLine($"Result: {(entered2 ? "ENTERED" : "BLOCKED")}");
    }
}
```

Expected Output:

```
Trying to enter Secret Door...
   V Key check passed
   V Health check passed
 → All checks passed, entering!
Result: ENTERED


==============================


Trying to enter Locked Door...
   ? Missing key!
 → Entry denied!
Result: BLOCKED
```

When to use Func for events:

- When subscribers need to validate or approve an action
- When you want a "veto" system where any subscriber can block something
- When collecting responses from multiple systems (like checking if player can afford something)
- For permission checks, validation rules, or conditional logic

Important: When using `Func` events, you need to handle the return values explicitly (like in the `GetInvocationList()` loop above). With `Action` events, all subscribers just execute. With `Func` events, you decide how to combine the return values. Do you need ALL to return true? Just ONE? The first one? That's up to your program logic.

Using Action and Func Outside of Events

While we've focused on using `Action` delegate and `Func` delegate with events, they're useful anywhere you need to pass methods around:

```csharp
public class CombatSystem
{
    // Using Func for damage calculation
    public int CalculateDamage(int baseDamage, Func<int, int> modifier)
    {
        return modifier(baseDamage);
    }

    // Using Action for effects
    public void ApplyEffect(string effectName, Action effect)
    {
        Console.WriteLine($"Applying {effectName}...");
        effect();
    }
}

class Program
{
    static void Main()
    {
        CombatSystem combat = new CombatSystem();

        // Pass different damage modifiers as Func
        int normalDamage = combat.CalculateDamage(50, (damage) => damage);
        int criticalDamage = combat.CalculateDamage(50, (damage) => damage * 2);
        int reducedDamage = combat.CalculateDamage(50, (damage) => damage / 2);

        Console.WriteLine($"Normal: {normalDamage}, Critical: {criticalDamage}," +
            $" Reduced: {reducedDamage}");

        Console.WriteLine();

        // Pass different effects as Action
        combat.ApplyEffect("Poison", () =>
            Console.WriteLine("  → Player takes 5 poison damage"));
        combat.ApplyEffect("Heal", () =>
            Console.WriteLine("  → Player heals 20 HP"));
    }
}
```

Expected Output:

```
Normal: 50, Critical: 100, Reduced: 25

Applying Poison...
  → Player takes 5 poison damage
Applying Heal...
  → Player heals 20 HP
```

When to use Action vs Func:

- Use `Action` when you want to *do* something (side effects, no return value)
- Use `Func` when you want to *calculate, check,* or *get* something (returns a value)

- In events, `Action` is most common, but `Func` can be useful for validation and approval systems
- Outside events, use them anytime you need to pass behavior as a parameter

 **Pro Tip:**

While you *can* use `Func` for events, it's unusual because you'd be returning values from event handlers, which gets messy when you have multiple subscribers. Stick with `Action` or `EventHandler<T>` for events, but use `Func` for conditions and calculations that work *with* your events.

Lambdas: Functions in Disguise

Remember how we've been creating separate methods for everything? Sometimes you want to do something quick and simple without creating a whole method for it. That's where **lambdas** come in. A lambda is a quick, anonymous method you can write inline.

Basic Lambda Syntax

The basic syntax is: `(parameters) => expression` or `(parameters) => { statements }`

Let's start simple:

```csharp
class Program
{
    static void Main()
    {
        // Regular method way
        Action sayHello = SayHelloMethod;
        sayHello();

        // Lambda way - much shorter!
        Action sayHelloLambda = () => Console.WriteLine("Hello from lambda!");
        sayHelloLambda();
    }

    static void SayHelloMethod()
    {
        Console.WriteLine("Hello from method!");
    }
}
```

Expected Output:

```
Hello from method!
Hello from lambda!
```

Now let's add some parameters:

```csharp
class Program
{
    static void Main()
    {
        // Lambda with one parameter (parentheses optional for single param)
        Action<string> greet = name => Console.WriteLine($"Hello, {name}!");
        greet("Prince");

        // Lambda with multiple parameters (parentheses required)
        Action<string, int> showDamage = (enemy, damage) =>
            Console.WriteLine($"{enemy} takes {damage} damage!");
        showDamage("Guard", 25);

        // Lambda with return value (using Func)
        Func<int, int, int> add = (a, b) => a + b;
        int sum = add(10, 15);
        Console.WriteLine($"Sum: {sum}");

        // Multi-line lambda (needs curly braces)
        Func<int, int, int> calculateDamage = (attack, defense) =>
        {
            int baseDamage = attack - defense;
            int finalDamage = Math.Max(1, baseDamage); // At least 1 damage
            Console.WriteLine($"  Calculating: {attack} - {defense} = {finalDamage}");
            return finalDamage;
        };

        int damage = calculateDamage(30, 10);
        Console.WriteLine($"Final damage: {damage}");
    }
}
```

Expected Output:

```
Hello, Prince!
Guard takes 25 damage!
Sum: 25
  Calculating: 30 - 10 = 20
Final damage: 20
```

Lambdas with Events

Lambdas are perfect for quick event subscriptions. Let us take a look at another example now that you know what a lambda is:

```csharp
public class Door
{
    public event Action<string> OnDoorOpened;

    public void Open(string keyType)
    {
        Console.WriteLine($"Using {keyType} to open door...");
        OnDoorOpened?.Invoke(keyType);
    }
}
```

```csharp
class Program
{
    static void Main()
    {
        Door door = new Door();

        // Subscribe multiple lambdas
        door.OnDoorOpened += (key) => Console.WriteLine($"  → Door creaks open");
        door.OnDoorOpened += (key) => Console.WriteLine($"  → Light pours in");
        door.OnDoorOpened += (key) =>
        {
            if (key == "golden_key")
                Console.WriteLine($"  → Secret treasure room revealed!");
        };

        door.Open("golden_key");
        Console.WriteLine();
        door.Open("iron_key");
    }
}
```

Expected Output:

```
Using golden_key to open door...
  → Door creaks open
  → Light pours in
  → Secret treasure room revealed!

Using iron_key to open door...
  → Door creaks open
  → Light pours in
```

Capturing Variables (Closures)

Lambdas can "capture" variables from the surrounding code. This is super powerful but can be confusing:

```csharp
class Program
{
    static void Main()
    {
        int score = 0;

        // This lambda can access and modify the 'score' variable!
        Action<int> addPoints = (points) =>
        {
            score += points;
            Console.WriteLine($"Score: {score}");
        };

        addPoints(10);
        addPoints(25);
        addPoints(5);

        Console.WriteLine($"Final score: {score}");
    }
}
```

Expected Output:

```
Score: 10
Score: 35
Score: 40
Final score: 40
```

You will notice that when we call the `addPoints` lambda method and pass in a value, the `score` variable outside of the lambda gets updated.

When to use lambdas vs. regular methods:
- Use lambdas for simple, one-off operations
- Use regular methods when the logic gets complex
- Use regular methods when you need to unsubscribe from events later (lambdas are hard to unsubscribe)
- Lambdas are great for quick experiments and prototypes

 **Pro Tip:**

You can't easily unsubscribe a lambda from an event because it's anonymous. If you need to unsubscribe later, store the lambda in a variable first, or use a named method instead.

Lambdas with Async Code

Remember our bonus **"Async & Await"** chapter from earlier? If you skipped it, you may want to go back and read it first to learn more about asynchronous programming. Otherwise, here's how we can use it with lambdas!

Lambdas work great with asynchronous programming. The `Task.Run()` method, which runs code on a background thread, uses lambdas to define what work should happen in the background.

Here's a quick preview:

```csharp
using System;
using System.Threading.Tasks;

public class GameLoader
{
    public event Action<int> OnLoadProgress;
    public event Action OnLoadComplete;

    public async Task LoadGameDataAsync()
    {
        Console.WriteLine("Starting game load...");

        // Task.Run uses a lambda to run code in the background
        await Task.Run(async () =>
        {
```

```csharp
        // Simulate loading different assets
        for (int i = 1; i <= 5; i++)
        {
            await Task.Delay(500); // Simulate work
            OnLoadProgress?.Invoke(i * 20); // Fire progress event
        }
    });

    OnLoadComplete?.Invoke();
    Console.WriteLine("Game load complete!");
    }
}

class Program
{
    static async Task Main()
    {
        GameLoader loader = new GameLoader();

        // Subscribe with lambdas
        loader.OnLoadProgress += (progress) =>
            Console.WriteLine($"  Loading... {progress}%");

        loader.OnLoadComplete += () =>
            Console.WriteLine("  All assets loaded!");

        await loader.LoadGameDataAsync();

        Console.WriteLine("\nGame is ready to play!");
    }
}
```

Expected Output:

```
Starting game load...
  Loading... 20%
  Loading... 40%
  Loading... 60%
  Loading... 80%
  Loading... 100%
  All assets loaded!
Game load complete!

Game is ready to play!
```

Notice you can also add `async` in front of the lambda: `async () =>` this way we can now also `await` the inner `Task.Delay` method.

Why lambdas and async work well together:
- `Task.Run()` needs a delegate (a piece of code to run), and lambdas provide a clean way to write that inline
- You can capture variables in the lambda, making it easy to access state from background threads
- Events and lambdas together create a clean pattern for progress updates and completion notifications

This pattern is everywhere in modern development, loading assets, saving games, downloading content, and running AI calculations all use this combination of async code, lambdas, and events.

 **Pro Tip:**

When using `Task.Run()` with lambdas that fire events, be careful about thread safety. Game engines like Unity require UI updates to happen on the main thread, so you might need to use a dispatcher or synchronization context.

Fun Experiment: The Dungeon Event System

Let us use what we've learned about events in our own code!

The Prince's Journey: The Pressure Plate's Secret

The story continues...

The Prince stands before a massive iron gate, its surface covered in ancient mechanisms and gears that seem to shift and click on their own. There's no lever, no obvious lock, just intricate patterns of metal that suggest this barrier responds to something more complex than brute force. As he examines the floor, the light from a fire torch reveals a suspicious stone tile slightly lower than the others, maybe a pressure plate? He's seen these before in the Vizier's dungeon, but this one feels different. When he cautiously steps on it, nothing happens immediately. Instead, he hears a series of metallic sounds echoing through nearby chambers: grinding stone, the rattle of chains, distant impacts. The gate remains closed, but the dungeon has clearly awakened around him.

The Prince realizes this isn't a simple trap, it's a signal system. The pressure plate doesn't directly control the gate; instead, it sends a message to various mechanisms throughout this section of the dungeon, each responding in its own way. Some might be opening doors, others activating traps, and somewhere in this chain of reactions, the gate before him will finally yield. But he can't see all the connections from where he stands. He needs to understand how these distant mechanisms communicate with each other and how one event triggers another, how the entire system coordinates without any direct connections. Only by mapping out these invisible relationships can he hope to navigate this chamber safely and open the path to freedom.

The Challenge

Create a simple dungeon system where our Prince explores rooms and triggers events. You need:

1. A `Room` class with events for entering and pulling a lever

2. At least two different objects that react to room events (e.g., `Monster`, `Door`)
3. Use `Action` delegates for at least one event type
4. Use lambdas for at least one event subscription
5. Use `Func<bool>` to determine if our Prince can enter a room (like needing a key)

Bonus Challenges:
- Add a scoring system using lambdas
- Make rooms have a "danger level" and warn the player with a lambda
- Create a treasure chest that only opens when all monsters are defeated

Try building this yourself first!

Example Answer

Here's one way to solve it:

```csharp
using System;
using System.Collections.Generic;

public class Room
{
    public string Name { get; set; }
    public int DangerLevel { get; set; }
    public event Action<string> OnRoomEntered;
    public event Action<string> OnLeverPulled;
    public Func<bool> CanEnter { get; set; }

    public void Enter()
    {
        if (CanEnter != null && !CanEnter())
        {
            Console.WriteLine($">>> The door to {Name} is locked!");
            return;
        }

        Console.WriteLine($"\n>>> The Prince enters {Name}");
        OnRoomEntered?.Invoke(Name);
    }

    public void PullLever()
    {
        Console.WriteLine($"\n>>> The Prince pulls a lever in {Name}!");
        OnLeverPulled?.Invoke(Name);
    }
}

public class Monster
{
    public string Type { get; set; }
    public bool IsAlive { get; set; } = true;

    public void OnLeverPulled(string roomName)
    {
        if (IsAlive)
            Console.WriteLine($"    !!! {Type} awakens!");
    }
}
```

```csharp
    public void Defeat()
    {
        IsAlive = false;
        Console.WriteLine($"    >>> {Type} defeated!");
    }
}

public class Door
{
    public string LeadsTo { get; set; }

    public void OnLeverPulled(string roomName)
    {
        Console.WriteLine($"    >>> Door to {LeadsTo} opens!");
    }
}

public class Prince
{
    public bool HasKey { get; set; } = false;
    public int Score { get; set; } = 0;
}

class Program
{
    static void Main()
    {
        Prince prince = new Prince();

        Room entrance = new Room
        {
            Name = "Entrance",
            DangerLevel = 1,
            CanEnter = () => true
        };

        Room treasury = new Room
        {
            Name = "Treasury",
            DangerLevel = 2,
            CanEnter = () => prince.HasKey // Using Func!
        };

        Monster skeleton = new Monster { Type = "Skeleton" };
        Door exitDoor = new Door { LeadsTo = "Exit" };

        // Subscribe to events
        entrance.OnRoomEntered += (name) =>
            Console.WriteLine("    → Torches light up");

        entrance.OnRoomEntered += (name) =>
            prince.Score += 10;

        treasury.OnRoomEntered += (name) =>
        {
            if (treasury.DangerLevel >= 2)
                Console.WriteLine($"    ⚠ Danger level {treasury.DangerLevel}!");
        };

        entrance.OnLeverPulled += skeleton.OnLeverPulled;
```

```csharp
        entrance.OnLeverPulled += exitDoor.OnLeverPulled;

        Console.WriteLine("=== THE PRINCE'S QUEST ===");

        entrance.Enter();
        entrance.PullLever();

        skeleton.Defeat();

        treasury.Enter(); // Locked!

        Console.WriteLine("\n[The Prince finds a key...]");
        prince.HasKey = true;

        treasury.Enter(); // Works now!

        Console.WriteLine($"\n=== QUEST COMPLETE ===");
        Console.WriteLine($"Final Score: {prince.Score}");
    }
}
```

Expected Output:

```
=== THE PRINCE'S QUEST ===

>>> The Prince enters Entrance
    → Torches light up

>>> The Prince pulls a lever in Entrance!
    !!! Skeleton awakens!
    >>> Door to Exit opens!
    >>> Skeleton defeated!
>>> The door to Treasury is locked!

[The Prince finds a key...]

>>> The Prince enters Treasury
    ??  Danger level 2!

=== QUEST COMPLETE ===
Final Score: 10
```

Notice how this solution:
- Uses both `Action` delegates and `Func` delegates
- Multiple lambda expressions for different purposes
- Events properly decouple objects
- `CanEnter` Func controls room access based on game state
- Simple, focused example that demonstrates all key concepts

>  **Pro Tip:**
>
> As you write more code, you'll develop an intuition for when to use events vs. when to use direct method calls. Generally, you should use events when multiple systems might care about something happening. Use direct calls when you have a clear one-to-one relationship. When in doubt, start with direct calls and refactor to events when you notice tight coupling becoming a problem.

Wrap-Up: What You've Learned

You just learned one of the most powerful concepts in programming!

Key Takeaways

- **Events** let different parts of your code communicate without being tightly coupled. The object that fires the event doesn't need to know who's listening or what they'll do, it just sends out a signal.
- **Delegates** are types that represent methods. They're the foundation that events are built on, letting you pass around methods like variables. Instead of creating custom delegates every time, C# gives you two versatile built-in types:
    - `Action` delegate for methods that do something (no return value)
    - `Func` delegate for methods that calculate or return something
- Subscribe to events with `+=` and unsubscribe with `-=`. When the event fires, all subscribed methods get called automatically. This is the publish/subscribe pattern that's everywhere in modern software.
- Lambdas are quick, anonymous methods you can write inline using the `=>` syntax. They're perfect for simple event handlers or one-off operations. They can capture variables from the surrounding code (closures), which is powerful but something to use carefully. Lambdas work especially well with async code and `Task.Run()` for background operations.
- The key principle: loose coupling through events. Objects should do their job well without needing to know intimate details about other objects. Events are one of the best tools to achieve this.

In desktop applications, button clicks are events. In web applications, form submissions and API responses trigger events. Mobile apps use events for touch gestures and notifications. Database systems fire events when data changes. Operating systems use events extensively for file system changes, network connections, user logins etc. Whether you're building a game, a business application, a website, or a mobile app, events are one of the core patterns that keep your code organized and maintainable.

LINQ

"The greatest ideas are the simplest." — William Golding

Working with collections of data is one of the most common tasks in programming. Whether you're filtering a list of search results, sorting user profiles by activity, calculating statistics from sensor readings, or finding patterns in large datasets, you need efficient ways to query and transform collections. Traditional approaches using loops and conditionals work, but they're verbose and the logic gets buried in implementation details. LINQ (Language Integrated Query) changes this by letting you express *what* you want rather than *how* to get it. It's like asking a librarian "show me all science fiction books published after 2010" instead of walking through every aisle yourself checking each book's genre and publication date.

This declarative approach to data manipulation isn't just convenient, it fundamentally changes how you think about solving problems. LINQ is used everywhere in modern software: streaming services use it to recommend content based on your viewing history, e-commerce sites filter products by price and rating, social media platforms sort and group your timeline, data analysis tools process millions of records to find trends, and search engines rank results based on relevance. Learning LINQ teaches you to think in terms of data transformations and queries, a skill that translates directly to database queries (SQL), data processing pipelines, and functional programming concepts that are increasingly important across all programming languages.

Core Concepts Covered

- ✓ Querying and filtering collections based on conditions
- ✓ Transforming data from one shape to another
- ✓ Chaining operations together for complex data manipulation
- ✓ Aggregating data to calculate summaries and statistics
- ✓ Grouping and organizing data by common properties
- ✓ Thinking declaratively about data rather than imperatively about loops
- ✓ Understanding deferred vs. immediate execution of queries

Finding Stuff Like a Boss

Trivia:

In 1854, Dr. John Snow mapped every cholera death in London on a street map. By analyzing this data—essentially querying "where are deaths clustered?"—he discovered they surrounded one water pump. This proved cholera spread through water, not air as everyone believed. Removing that pump handle ended the outbreak. His data analysis technique saved thousands of lives and founded modern epidemiology.

The truth is, you can write every program without ever using LINQ. You can filter lists with `foreach` loops and `if` statements. You can sort with manual algorithms. You can calculate sums and averages with loops and counters. Programmers did all of this for decades before LINQ existed.

But just like how classes help you organize code better than using only primitive types, and just like how collections like `List<T>` and `Dictionary<T>` make working with data easier than managing arrays manually, LINQ helps you write shorter, clearer, and more precise code.

Imagine for our Prince you need to find all guards within attacking distance.

Without LINQ, you'd write something like this:

```csharp
using System;

List<Guard> nearbyGuards = new List<Guard>();

foreach (Guard guard in allGuards)
{
    if (guard.DistanceFromPrince <= 10 && guard.IsAlive)
    {
        nearbyGuards.Add(guard);
    }
}

// Now sort them by distance
```

```
nearbyGuards.Sort((a, b) => a.DistanceFromPrince.CompareTo(b.DistanceFromPrince));

// Get just their names
List<string> guardNames = new List<string>();
foreach (Guard guard in nearbyGuards)
{
    guardNames.Add(guard.Name);
}
```

That's a lot of code just to filter, sort, and transform a list!

With LINQ, you can do all of that in one clean, readable statement:

```
var guardNames = allGuards
    .Where(g => g.DistanceFromPrince <= 10 && g.IsAlive)
    .OrderBy(g => g.DistanceFromPrince)
    .Select(g => g.Name);
```

If you really want you could have the entire statement in a single line. But for readability it's better to put each LINQ operation on its own line.

LINQ (Language Integrated Query) is like having SQL for your collections. It lets you query, filter, transform, and aggregate data using a clean, readable syntax. Instead of writing loops and conditionals scattered throughout your code, you express *what* you want, not *how* to get it.

Think about an inventory system for our Prince. You might need to:
- Find all weapons with damage above 50
- Sort potions by healing amount
- Count how many quest items the player has
- Group equipment by type (armor, weapons, accessories)
- Calculate the total value of all items

Without LINQ, each of these requires loops, conditionals, and temporary variables. With LINQ, each becomes a single, easy to read statement.

LINQ is used everywhere in C# development. Web applications, desktop software, mobile apps, data analysis tools, they can all use LINQ to work with data efficiently. Learning to use LINQ efficiently will make you a better programmer!

Basic LINQ Operations

Let's start with a collection of guards for our Prince and explore the most common LINQ operations.

Setting Up Our Data

First, we need some data to work with:

```csharp
using System;
using System.Collections.Generic;
using System.Linq; // Don't forget this!

class Program
{
    public class Guard
    {
        public string Name { get; set; }
        public int Health { get; set; }
        public int DistanceFromPrince { get; set; }
        public bool IsAlerted { get; set; }
        public string WeaponType { get; set; }
        public int AttackPower { get; set; }
    }

    private static List<Guard> CreateGuards()
    {
        return new List<Guard>
        {
            new Guard { Name = "Guard A", Health = 100, DistanceFromPrince = 5,
                IsAlerted = false, WeaponType = "sword", AttackPower = 25 },
            new Guard { Name = "Guard B", Health = 75, DistanceFromPrince = 15,
                IsAlerted = false, WeaponType = "spear", AttackPower = 30 },
            new Guard { Name = "Guard C", Health = 50, DistanceFromPrince = 8,
                IsAlerted = true, WeaponType = "sword", AttackPower = 25 },
            new Guard { Name = "Guard D", Health = 100, DistanceFromPrince = 3,
                IsAlerted = false, WeaponType = "axe", AttackPower = 35 },
            new Guard { Name = "Guard E", Health = 25, DistanceFromPrince = 20,
                IsAlerted = true, WeaponType = "sword", AttackPower = 20 }
        };
    }

    static void Main()
    {
        List<Guard> guards = CreateGuards();

        // Example code will start here...
    }
}
```

Note: Upcoming examples will be using this setup for the data. So, if you try to recreate the examples locally make sure you have the `Guard` class and the `CreateGuards()` method. Below examples may start with the same `Main` but do different LINQ operations.

Before we dive into examples, let's take a quick look at some of the most useful LINQ methods you'll encounter and what they do.

Most Used LINQ methods

Method	What It Does	Returns
`.Where()`	Filters items based on a condition	Filtered collection
`.Select()`	Transforms each item into something else	Transformed collection
`.OrderBy()`	Sorts items in ascending order	Sorted collection
`.OrderByDescending()`	Sorts items in descending order	Sorted collection
`.ThenBy()`	Secondary sort (ascending) after OrderBy	Sorted collection
`.ThenByDescending()`	Secondary sort (descending) after OrderBy	Sorted collection
`.GroupBy()`	Groups items by a key	Collection of groups

Now let's see these methods in action!

Where - Filtering Data

The `.Where()` method filters items based on a condition.

It's like asking "give me only the items that match this rule.":

```
static void Main()
{
    List<Guard> guards = CreateGuards();

    // Find guards within 10 units
    var nearbyGuards = guards.Where(g => g.DistanceFromPrince <= 10);

    Console.WriteLine("Nearby guards (distance <= 10):");
    foreach (var guard in nearbyGuards)
    {
        Console.WriteLine($" {guard.Name} at distance {guard.DistanceFromPrince}");
    }

    Console.WriteLine();

    // Find healthy guards (health >= 75)
    var healthyGuards = guards.Where(g => g.Health >= 75);

    Console.WriteLine("Healthy guards (health >= 75):");
    foreach (var guard in healthyGuards)
    {
        Console.WriteLine($" {guard.Name} with {guard.Health} HP");
    }

    Console.WriteLine();

    // Multiple conditions
    var dangerousNearbyGuards = guards
        .Where(g => g.DistanceFromPrince <= 10 && g.Health > 50);
```

```
        Console.WriteLine("Dangerous nearby guards:");
        foreach (var guard in dangerousNearbyGuards)
        {
            Console.WriteLine($" {guard.Name} - " +
                $"Distance: {guard.DistanceFromPrince}, HP: {guard.Health}");
        }
}
```

Expected Output:

```
Nearby guards (distance <= 10):
 Guard A at distance 5
 Guard C at distance 8
 Guard D at distance 3

Healthy guards (health >= 75):
 Guard A with 100 HP
 Guard B with 75 HP
 Guard D with 100 HP

Dangerous nearby guards:
 Guard A - Distance: 5, HP: 100
 Guard D - Distance: 3, HP: 100
```

Select - Transforming Data

The `.Select()` method transforms each item in a collection.

It's like saying "for each item, give me this specific part" or "turn each item into something else.":

```
static void Main()
{
    List<Guard> guards = CreateGuards();

    // Get just the names
    var guardNames = guards.Select(g => g.Name);
    Console.WriteLine($"All guard names: {string.Join(", ", guardNames)}");

    Console.WriteLine();

    // Get just the distances
    var distances = guards.Select(g => g.DistanceFromPrince);
    Console.WriteLine($"All distances: {string.Join(", ", distances)}");

    Console.WriteLine();

    // Create new objects with selected properties
    var guardSummaries = guards.Select(g => new
    {
        g.Name,
        Status = g.IsAlerted ? "ALERT" : "Patrol",
        ThreatLevel = g.AttackPower > 30 ? "High" : "Normal"
    });

    Console.WriteLine("Guard summaries:");
    foreach (var summary in guardSummaries)
```

```
    {
        Console.WriteLine($"  {summary.Name}: {summary.Status} - " +
            $"Threat: {summary.ThreatLevel}");
    }
}
```

Expected Output:

```
All guard names: Guard A, Guard B, Guard C, Guard D, Guard E

All distances: 5, 15, 8, 3, 20

Guard summaries:
  Guard A: Patrol - Threat: Normal
  Guard B: Patrol - Threat: Normal
  Guard C: ALERT - Threat: Normal
  Guard D: Patrol - Threat: High
  Guard E: ALERT - Threat: Normal
```

OrderBy and OrderByDescending - Sorting Data

These methods sort your collection based on a property or value:

```
static void Main()
{
    List<Guard> guards = CreateGuards();

    // Sort by distance (ascending)
    var byDistance = guards.OrderBy(g => g.DistanceFromPrince);

    Console.WriteLine("Guards sorted by distance (closest first):");
    foreach (var guard in byDistance)
    {
        Console.WriteLine($"  {guard.Name} at distance" +
            $" {guard.DistanceFromPrince}");
    }

    Console.WriteLine();

    // Sort by health (descending)
    var byHealth = guards.OrderByDescending(g => g.Health);

    Console.WriteLine("Guards sorted by health (strongest first):");
    foreach (var guard in byHealth)
    {
        Console.WriteLine($"  {guard.Name} with {guard.Health} HP");
    }

    Console.WriteLine();

    // Multiple sorting criteria
    var sorted = guards
        .OrderBy(g => g.WeaponType)            // First by weapon
        .ThenByDescending(g => g.AttackPower); // Then by attack power

    Console.WriteLine("Guards sorted by weapon, then attack power:");
    foreach (var guard in sorted)
    {
        Console.WriteLine($"  {guard.Name} - {guard.WeaponType} " +
```

```
                $"({guard.AttackPower} damage)");
    }
}
```

Expected Output:

```
Guards sorted by distance (closest first):
  Guard D at distance 3
  Guard A at distance 5
  Guard C at distance 8
  Guard B at distance 15
  Guard E at distance 20

Guards sorted by health (strongest first):
  Guard A with 100 HP
  Guard D with 100 HP
  Guard B with 75 HP
  Guard C with 50 HP
  Guard E with 25 HP

Guards sorted by weapon, then attack power:
  Guard D - axe (35 damage)
  Guard B - spear (30 damage)
  Guard A - sword (25 damage)
  Guard C - sword (25 damage)
  Guard E - sword (20 damage)
```

GroupBy - Organizing Data

`GroupBy` is one of the most powerful LINQ methods.

It organizes items into groups based on a key:

```csharp
static void Main()
{
    List<Guard> guards = CreateGuards();

    // Group guards by weapon type
    var guardsByWeapon = guards.GroupBy(g => g.WeaponType);

    Console.WriteLine("Guards grouped by weapon:");
    foreach (var group in guardsByWeapon)
    {
        Console.WriteLine($"\n{group.Key}:");
        foreach (var guard in group)
        {
            Console.WriteLine($"  - {guard.Name} (Attack: {guard.AttackPower})");
        }
    }

    Console.WriteLine();
    Console.WriteLine("═══════════════════════════════════");
    Console.WriteLine();

    // Group and calculate statistics
    var weaponStats = guards
        .GroupBy(g => g.WeaponType)
        .Select(group => new
```

```csharp
            {
                Weapon = group.Key,
                Count = group.Count(),
                TotalHealth = group.Sum(g => g.Health),
                AvgAttack = group.Average(g => g.AttackPower)
            });

    Console.WriteLine("Weapon statistics:");
    foreach (var stat in weaponStats)
    {
        Console.WriteLine($"{stat.Weapon}:");
        Console.WriteLine($"  Count: {stat.Count}");
        Console.WriteLine($"  Total HP: {stat.TotalHealth}");
        Console.WriteLine($"  Avg Attack: {stat.AvgAttack:F1}");
    }

    Console.WriteLine();
    Console.WriteLine("===================================");
    Console.WriteLine();

    // Group by alert status
    var guardsByStatus = guards
        .GroupBy(g => g.IsAlerted ? "Alerted" : "Patrolling")
        .Select(group => new
        {
            Status = group.Key,
            Guards = group.Select(g => g.Name).ToList()
        });

    Console.WriteLine("Guards by status:");
    foreach (var statusGroup in guardsByStatus)
    {
        Console.WriteLine($"{statusGroup.Status}: {string.Join(", ",
            statusGroup.Guards)}");
    }
}
```

Expected Output:

```
Guards grouped by weapon:

sword:
  - Guard A (Attack: 25)
  - Guard C (Attack: 25)
  - Guard E (Attack: 20)

spear:
  - Guard B (Attack: 30)

axe:
  - Guard D (Attack: 35)


===================================


Weapon statistics:
sword:
  Count: 3
  Total HP: 175
  Avg Attack: 23.3

spear:
```

```
  Count: 1
  Total HP: 75
  Avg Attack: 30.0

axe:
  Count: 1
  Total HP: 100
  Avg Attack: 35.0


Guards by status:
Patrolling: Guard A, Guard B, Guard D
Alerted: Guard C, Guard E
```

Common LINQ Methods

Method	What It Does	Returns
`.First()`	Gets the first item (throws error if empty)	Single item
`.FirstOrDefault()`	Gets the first item or null if empty	Single item or null
`.Last()`	Gets the last item (throws error if empty)	Single item
`.LastOrDefault()`	Gets the last item or null if empty	Single item or null
`.Count()`	Counts items (optionally with a condition)	Integer
`.Any()`	Checks if any items match a condition	Boolean
`.All()`	Checks if all items match a condition	Boolean
`.Sum()`	Adds up values	Number
`.Average()`	Calculates average of values	Number
`.Max()`	Finds highest value	Number
`.Min()`	Finds lowest value	Number

Let's look at these LINQ methods in action:

```csharp
static void Main()
{
    List<Guard> guards = CreateGuards();

    // First - Get the first item (throws error if empty)
    var firstGuard = guards.First();
    Console.WriteLine($"First guard: {firstGuard.Name}");
```

```csharp
    // FirstOrDefault - Get the first item or null if empty (safer)
    var firstAlerted = guards.FirstOrDefault(g => g.IsAlerted);
    Console.WriteLine($"First alerted guard: " +
        $"{firstAlerted?.Name ?? "None"}");

    // Last and LastOrDefault work the same way
    var lastGuard = guards.Last();
    Console.WriteLine($"Last guard: {lastGuard.Name}");

    Console.WriteLine();

    // Count - Count all items or items matching a condition
    int totalGuards = guards.Count();
    int alertedGuards = guards.Count(g => g.IsAlerted);
    int swordGuards = guards.Count(g => g.WeaponType == "sword");

    Console.WriteLine($"Total guards: {totalGuards}");
    Console.WriteLine($"Alerted guards: {alertedGuards}");
    Console.WriteLine($"Guards with swords: {swordGuards}");

    Console.WriteLine();

    // Any - Check if any items match a condition
    bool anyNearby = guards.Any(g => g.DistanceFromPrince < 5);
    bool anyWithBow = guards.Any(g => g.WeaponType == "bow");

    Console.WriteLine($"Any guards very close (< 5)? {anyNearby}");
    Console.WriteLine($"Any guards with bows? {anyWithBow}");

    Console.WriteLine();

    // All - Check if all items match a condition
    bool allAlive = guards.All(g => g.Health > 0);
    bool allNearby = guards.All(g => g.DistanceFromPrince < 10);

    Console.WriteLine($"All guards alive? {allAlive}");
    Console.WriteLine($"All guards nearby? {allNearby}");

    Console.WriteLine();

    // Sum, Average, Max, Min - Aggregate functions
    int totalHealth = guards.Sum(g => g.Health);
    double avgHealth = guards.Average(g => g.Health);
    int maxHealth = guards.Max(g => g.Health);
    int minHealth = guards.Min(g => g.Health);
    int maxAttack = guards.Max(g => g.AttackPower);

    Console.WriteLine("Statistics:");
    Console.WriteLine($"  Total health: {totalHealth}");
    Console.WriteLine($"  Average health: {avgHealth}");
    Console.WriteLine($"  Max health: {maxHealth}");
    Console.WriteLine($"  Min health: {minHealth}");
    Console.WriteLine($"  Highest attack: {maxAttack}");
}
```

Expected Output:

```
First guard: Guard A
First alerted guard: Guard C
Last guard: Guard E

Total guards: 5
Alerted guards: 2
Guards with swords: 3

Any guards very close (< 5)? True
Any guards with bows? False

All guards alive? True
All guards nearby? False

Statistics:
  Total health: 350
  Average health: 70
  Max health: 100
  Min health: 25
  Highest attack: 35
```

Chaining LINQ Operations

The real power of LINQ comes from chaining operations together.

Each LINQ method returns a new collection that you can immediately query further:

```csharp
static void Main()
{
    List<Guard> guards = CreateGuards();
    // Complex query: Find nearby, healthy, unalerted guards and get their names
    var priorityTargets = guards
        .Where(g => g.DistanceFromPrince <= 10)     // Nearby
        .Where(g => g.Health >= 75)                 // Healthy
        .Where(g => !g.IsAlerted)                   // Not alerted
        .OrderBy(g => g.DistanceFromPrince)         // Closest first
        .Select(g => g.Name);                       // Just the names

    Console.WriteLine("Priority targets (nearby, healthy, unalerted):");
    foreach (var name in priorityTargets)
    {
        Console.WriteLine($"  → {name}");
    }

    Console.WriteLine();

    // Another complex query: Find the strongest nearby threat
    var strongestNearbyThreat = guards
        .Where(g => g.DistanceFromPrince <= 10)
        .OrderByDescending(g => g.AttackPower)
        .ThenBy(g => g.DistanceFromPrince)
        .FirstOrDefault();

    if (strongestNearbyThreat != null)
    {
        Console.WriteLine("Strongest nearby threat:");
```

```
            Console.WriteLine($"  {strongestNearbyThreat.Name}");
            Console.WriteLine($"  Attack: " +
                $"{strongestNearbyThreat.AttackPower}");
            Console.WriteLine($"  Distance: " +
                $"{strongestNearbyThreat.DistanceFromPrince}");
    }

    Console.WriteLine();

    // Calculate average attack power of sword users
    double avgSwordAttack = guards
        .Where(g => g.WeaponType == "sword")
        .Average(g => g.AttackPower);

    Console.WriteLine($"Average attack power of sword users: " +
        $"{avgSwordAttack:F1}");
}
```

Expected Output:

```
Priority targets (nearby, healthy, unalerted):
  → Guard D
  → Guard A

Strongest nearby threat:
  Guard D
  Attack: 35
  Distance: 3

Average attack power of sword users: 23.3
```

 **Pro Tip:**

When chaining LINQ operations, think about the order. Put `.Where()` operations early to reduce the number of items being processed by later operations. For example, filtering before sorting is more efficient than sorting everything and then filtering.

Using LINQ to Build New Collections

LINQ is perfect for transforming one collection into another:

```
class Enemy
{
    public string Type { get; set; }
    public int Health { get; set; }
    public bool IsBoss { get; set; }
}

public class Treasure
{
    public string Name { get; set; }
    public int Value { get; set; }
    public string Rarity { get; set; }
```

```csharp
}

class Program
{
    static void Main()
    {
        List<Enemy> enemies = new List<Enemy>
        {
            new Enemy { Type = "Guard", Health = 0, IsBoss = false },
            new Enemy { Type = "Skeleton", Health = 0, IsBoss = false },
            new Enemy { Type = "Elite Guard", Health = 0, IsBoss = false },
            new Enemy { Type = "Boss Guard", Health = 0, IsBoss = true }
        };

        // Build a new collection of treasures from defeated enemies
        List<Treasure> loot = enemies
            .Where(e => e.Health == 0)  // Only defeated enemies
            .Select(e => new Treasure
            {
                Name = $"{e.Type} Treasure",
                Value = e.IsBoss ? 100 : 25,
                Rarity = e.IsBoss ? "Legendary" : "Common"
            })
            .ToList(); // Convert the result back to a List

        Console.WriteLine("Loot collected:");
        foreach (var treasure in loot)
        {
            Console.WriteLine($"  {treasure.Name}: {treasure.Value} " +
                $"gold ({treasure.Rarity})");
        }

        int totalGold = loot.Sum(t => t.Value);
        Console.WriteLine($"\nTotal gold: {totalGold}");

        Console.WriteLine();
        Console.WriteLine("=================================");
        Console.WriteLine();

        // Create a summary report
        var report = enemies
            .GroupBy(e => e.IsBoss ? "Boss" : "Regular")
            .Select(group => new
            {
                Type = group.Key,
                Count = group.Count(),
                TotalValue = group.Sum(e => e.IsBoss ? 100 : 25)
            });

        Console.WriteLine("Enemy loot summary:");
        foreach (var item in report)
        {
            Console.WriteLine($"{item.Type} enemies: {item.Count}x = " +
                $"{item.TotalValue} gold total");
        }
    }
}
```

Expected Output:

```
Loot collected:
  Guard Treasure: 25 gold (Common)
  Skeleton Treasure: 25 gold (Common)
  Elite Guard Treasure: 25 gold (Common)
  Boss Guard Treasure: 100 gold (Legendary)

Total gold: 175

═══════════════════════════════════════

Enemy loot summary:
Regular enemies: 3x = 75 gold total
Boss enemies: 1x = 100 gold total
```

Here's another batch of useful LINQ methods that you can explore in your own time:

Method	What It Does	Returns
.SelectMany()	Flattens nested collections	Flattened collection
.Distinct()	Removes duplicate items	Collection without duplicates
.Take()	Takes first N items	Collection with N items
.Skip()	Skips first N items	Collection without first N items
.ToList()	Converts to List (executes query immediately)	List<T>
.ToArray()	Converts to Array (executes query immediately)	T[]

Fun Experiment: The Vizier's Intelligence

Let's see what's left of the evil Vizier guards to protect his treasures!

The Prince's Journey: The Vizier's Concern

Meanwhile...

High above in the Sultan's throne room, the Evil Vizier sits upon the ornate seat that should belong to another, his fingers drumming impatiently on the golden armrest. Two of his most loyal guards stand at attention below the throne steps, awaiting orders. The Vizier's eyes glow with the same unnatural green light that powers his magical creations in the dungeon below. He has been watching, always watching. Through scrying pools and enchanted mirrors, he has tracked the Prince's every move through his elaborate prison. What concerns him now is not whether the Prince will escape. The boy has proven far more resourceful than expected, but when and how prepared he will be when he does.

The Vizier gestures, and magical energy swirls before him, coalescing into shimmering lists of data hovering in the air. Each line represents a room in his dungeon: which chambers the Prince has cleared, which guards have fallen, what treasures have been claimed, which traps have been overcome. The sorcerer wants answers, and he want them quickly. Which rooms posed the greatest threat? Where did his defenses fail? What pattern of progression did the Prince follow? Most importantly, how much strength, how many resources, how much knowledge will the Prince possess when he finally emerges?

The Vizier must analyze this vast collection of information, filter through the chaos of battle reports and trap triggers, sort the data by danger and value, and identify exactly what awaits him when the Prince breaks free. Only by understanding the complete picture of his enemy's journey can he prepare his final defenses. He waves his hand, and the magical data begins to reorganize itself at his command, ready to reveal the truths hidden within the numbers.

The Challenge

Create a dungeon statistics system that tracks rooms, enemies, and treasures. You need:

1. Create classes for Room, Enemy, and Treasure with appropriate properties
2. Populate a dungeon with at least 5 rooms containing enemies and treasures
3. Use LINQ to answer these questions:
    - Which room has the most enemies?
    - What's the total treasure value in the entire dungeon?
    - Which room has the highest average enemy health?
    - How many rooms have been cleared (all enemies defeated)?
    - What's the most common enemy type?

Bonus Challenges:
- Find all rooms where total treasure value exceeds total enemy health
- Calculate a "difficulty rating" for each room
- Find the optimal room to explore (high treasure, low danger)

Try building this yourself first!

Example Answer

Here's one way to solve it:

```csharp
using System;
using System.Collections.Generic;
using System.Linq;

public class Enemy
{
    public string Type { get; set; }
    public int Health { get; set; }
    public bool IsDefeated { get; set; }
}

public class Treasure
{
    public string Name { get; set; }
```

```csharp
    public int Value { get; set; }
}

public class Room
{
    public string Name { get; set; }
    public List<Enemy> Enemies { get; set; } = new List<Enemy>();
    public List<Treasure> Treasures { get; set; } = new List<Treasure>();
}

class Program
{
    static void Main()
    {
        List<Room> dungeon = new List<Room>
        {
            new Room
            {
                Name = "Entrance Hall",
                Enemies = new List<Enemy>
                {
                    new Enemy { Type = "Skeleton", Health = 30, IsDefeated = true },
                    new Enemy { Type = "Skeleton", Health = 30, IsDefeated = true }
                },
                Treasures = new List<Treasure>
                {
                    new Treasure { Name = "Health Potion", Value = 50 },
                    new Treasure { Name = "Silver Coin", Value = 10 }
                }
            },
            new Room
            {
                Name = "Armory",
                Enemies = new List<Enemy>
                {
                    new Enemy { Type = "Guard", Health = 50, IsDefeated = false },
                    new Enemy { Type = "Guard", Health = 50, IsDefeated = false },
                    new Enemy { Type = "Elite Guard", Health = 75, IsDefeated = false }
                },
                Treasures = new List<Treasure>
                {
                    new Treasure { Name = "Steel Sword", Value = 200 },
                    new Treasure { Name = "Leather Armor", Value = 150 }
                }
            },
            new Room
            {
                Name = "Treasury",
                Enemies = new List<Enemy>
                {
                    new Enemy { Type = "Skeleton", Health = 30, IsDefeated = false }
                },
                Treasures = new List<Treasure>
                {
                    new Treasure { Name = "Gold Coins", Value = 500 },
                    new Treasure { Name = "Ruby", Value = 300 }
                }
            },
            new Room
            {
                Name = "Torture Chamber",
```

```csharp
            Enemies = new List<Enemy>
            {
                new Enemy { Type = "Zombie", Health = 40, IsDefeated = true },
                new Enemy { Type = "Zombie", Health = 40, IsDefeated = true },
                new Enemy { Type = "Skeleton", Health = 30, IsDefeated = true }
            },
            Treasures = new List<Treasure>
            {
                new Treasure { Name = "Ancient Key", Value = 0 }
            }
        },
        new Room
        {
            Name = "Throne Room",
            Enemies = new List<Enemy>
            {
                new Enemy { Type = "Boss Guard", Health = 150, IsDefeated = false },
                new Enemy { Type = "Elite Guard", Health = 75, IsDefeated = false }
            },
            Treasures = new List<Treasure>
            {
                new Treasure { Name = "Royal Crown", Value = 1000 }
            }
        }
    }
};

Console.WriteLine("=== DUNGEON ANALYTICS ===\n");

// 1. Room with most enemies
var mostEnemies = dungeon.OrderByDescending(r => r.Enemies.Count).First();
Console.WriteLine($"Most enemies: {mostEnemies.Name} " +
    $"({mostEnemies.Enemies.Count} enemies)");

// 2. Total treasure value
int totalTreasure = dungeon.SelectMany(r => r.Treasures).Sum(t => t.Value);
Console.WriteLine($"Total treasure: {totalTreasure} gold");

// 3. Room with highest avg enemy health
var strongestRoom = dungeon
    .Where(r => r.Enemies.Any())
    .Select(r => new { r.Name, AvgHealth = r.Enemies.Average(e => e.Health) })
    .OrderByDescending(x => x.AvgHealth)
    .First();
Console.WriteLine($"Strongest enemies: {strongestRoom.Name} " +
    $"({strongestRoom.AvgHealth:F1} HP avg)");

// 4. Cleared rooms
int cleared = dungeon.Count(r => r.Enemies.All(e => e.IsDefeated));
var clearedNames = dungeon.Where(r => r.Enemies.All(e => e.IsDefeated))
    .Select(r => r.Name);
Console.WriteLine($"Cleared rooms: {cleared}/{dungeon.Count}" +
    $" ({string.Join(", ", clearedNames)})");

// 5. Most common enemy
var commonEnemy = dungeon
    .SelectMany(r => r.Enemies)
    .GroupBy(e => e.Type)
    .OrderByDescending(g => g.Count())
    .First();
Console.WriteLine($"Most common enemy: {commonEnemy.Key} ({commonEnemy.Count()}x)");
```

```csharp
        Console.WriteLine("\n=== BONUS ANALYTICS ===\n");

        // Bonus: Rooms where treasure > danger
        var goodRooms = dungeon
            .Select(r => new
            {
                r.Name,
                Treasure = r.Treasures.Sum(t => t.Value),
                Danger = r.Enemies.Where(e => !e.IsDefeated).Sum(e => e.Health)
            })
            .Where(x => x.Treasure > x.Danger && x.Danger > 0);

        Console.WriteLine("High reward rooms (treasure > danger):");
        foreach (var room in goodRooms)
            Console.WriteLine($"  {room.Name}: {room.Treasure} gold vs {room.Danger} HP");

        // Bonus: Difficulty rating
        var difficulty = dungeon
            .Select(r => new
            {
                r.Name,
                Rating = r.Enemies.Count(e => !e.IsDefeated) * 10 +
                        r.Enemies.Where(e => !e.IsDefeated).Sum(e => e.Health)
            })
            .Where(x => x.Rating > 0)
            .OrderByDescending(x => x.Rating);

        Console.WriteLine("\nDifficulty ratings:");
        foreach (var room in difficulty)
            Console.WriteLine($"  {room.Name}: {room.Rating}");

        // Bonus: Optimal room
        var optimal = dungeon
            .Where(r => r.Enemies.Any(e => !e.IsDefeated))
            .Select(r => new
            {
                r.Name,
                Treasure = r.Treasures.Sum(t => t.Value),
                Danger = r.Enemies.Where(e => !e.IsDefeated).Sum(e => e.Health),
                Ratio = r.Treasures.Sum(t => t.Value) /
                        (double)r.Enemies.Where(e => !e.IsDefeated).Sum(e => e.Health)
            })
            .OrderByDescending(x => x.Ratio)
            .First();

        Console.WriteLine($"\nOptimal room: {optimal.Name}");
        Console.WriteLine($"  Ratio: {optimal.Ratio:F2} ({optimal.Treasure} gold / " +
            $"{optimal.Danger} HP)");
    }
}
```

Expected Output:

```
=== DUNGEON ANALYTICS ===

Most enemies: Torture Chamber (3 enemies)
Total treasure: 2210 gold
Strongest enemies: Throne Room (112.5 HP avg)
Cleared rooms: 2/5 (Entrance Hall, Torture Chamber)
Most common enemy: Skeleton (4x)
```

```
=== BONUS ANALYTICS ===

High reward rooms (treasure > danger):
  Treasury: 800 gold vs 30 HP

Difficulty ratings:
  Throne Room: 245
  Armory: 205
  Treasury: 40

Optimal room: Treasury
  Ratio: 26.67 (800 gold / 30 HP)
```

Notice how this solution:

- Uses diverse LINQ methods (`.Where()`, `.Select()`, `.SelectMany()`, `.OrderBy()`, `.GroupBy()`, `.Sum()`, `.Average()`, `.Count()`, `.All()`, `.Any()`)
- Complex method chaining for multi-step queries
- Anonymous types for temporary result objects
- Practical game analytics useful in real development
- Concise, readable code that clearly expresses intent

 **Pro Tip:**

LINQ is powerful and makes code more readable, but remember it can be slower than hand-written loops for huge collections. For most code, LINQ is perfect and the readability is worth it. In performance-critical sections (like processing thousands of objects every frame), consider traditional loops. Always measure performance before optimizing — premature optimization is the enemy of good code!

Wrap-Up: What You've Learned

Congratulations! You've just learned one of C# most elegant and powerful features.

Key Takeaways

LINQ (Language Integrated Query) transforms how you work with collections. Instead of writing loops and if-statements scattered throughout your code, you can express what you want in a clear, readable chain of operations.

The most common LINQ methods you'll use are:

- `.Where()`: Filter items based on conditions
- `.Select()`: Transform items into a different shape
- `.OrderBy()` / `.OrderByDescending()`: Sort your data
- `.First()` / `.FirstOrDefault()`: Get the first matching item
- `.Count()`: Count items (with or without conditions)

- `.Any()` / `.All()`: Check if items match conditions
- `.Sum()` / `.Average()` / `.Max()` / `.Min()`: Calculate values
- `.GroupBy()`: Organize items into groups
- `.SelectMany()`: Flatten nested collections

Method chaining is where LINQ really shines. You can filter, transform, sort, and aggregate data in one smooth, readable flow. Each operation feeds into the next, making complex data manipulation feel natural.

The beauty of LINQ is that it makes your intent clear. When you read `.Where(enemy => enemy.Health > 0).OrderBy(enemy => enemy.Distance)`, you immediately understand what's happening, there's no need to parse through nested loops and conditionals.

 **Important:**
- Put `.Where()` operations early in the chain to reduce items processed later
- Use `.FirstOrDefault()` instead of `.First()` when the collection might be empty
- `.ToList()` or `.ToArray()` executes the query immediately (otherwise LINQ uses deferred execution)
- LINQ creates new collections without modifying the original

LINQ gives you a data-driven programming style that scales beautifully as your projects grow. You're now equipped to handle complex data manipulation with elegance and clarity. Whether you're building the next indie hit or working on enterprise software, LINQ will be one of your most-used tools.

Exception Handling

"Failure is simply the opportunity to begin again, this time more intelligently."

— Henry Ford

Have you ever wondered why your favorite apps don't just crash and disappear when something goes wrong? When Spotify can't connect to the internet, it doesn't explode, it shows you a friendly message and lets you listen to downloaded music. When your web browser encounters a broken image, it displays a placeholder instead of destroying the entire page. This graceful handling of problems is what separates professional software from amateur projects. Exception handling is the safety net that catches errors before they become catastrophes, allowing programs to recover, inform users, and continue operating even when the unexpected happens.

Every piece of software faces uncertainty. Files get deleted, networks go down, users type unexpected input, and hardware fails in creative ways. Writing code that only works when everything goes perfectly is like building a house that only stands up on sunny days. Exception handling teaches you to anticipate failure, plan for it, and build systems that remain stable and reliable even when things go wrong. It's one of the most important skills separating hobbyist programmers from professionals who ship software that millions of people depend on every day. Whether you're building mobile apps, web services, desktop applications, or games, knowing how to handle errors properly is absolutely essential.

Core Concepts Covered

✓ Detecting and responding to runtime errors without crashing
✓ Separating error-handling code from normal program logic
✓ When problems should stop execution versus when they should be handled gracefully
✓ Building resilient systems that recover from failures automatically
✓ Communicating errors effectively across different parts of a program
✓ Creating meaningful error messages that help diagnose problems
✓ Handling errors in asynchronous operations that run in the background
✓ Designing robust validation systems for user input and external data

Catching Your Mistakes Gracefully

 **Trivia:**

In 1859, the Carrington Event—the largest solar storm ever recorded—made telegraph systems worldwide burst into flames and shock operators. Some telegraphs kept working for hours powered only by the aurora. If this happened today, it could fry power grids and satellites, causing trillions in damage. Modern systems have "exception handling" to detect surges and shut down safely before being destroyed.

Imagine you're playing and you make the Prince jump across a chasm. You time it perfectly, hit the jump button... and the game crashes with "ERROR: PRINCESS NOT FOUND." That would be terrible, right?

That's basically what happens when your code runs into a problem it doesn't know how to handle. Maybe you tried to open a file that doesn't exist. Maybe you asked the player to enter a number and they typed "banana" instead. Maybe you tried to divide by zero (which, as we all know from math class, causes the universe to implode... or calculators very upset).

Exception handling is your code's way of saying, "Okay, something went wrong, but I'm not going to freak out and crash. Let me handle this like a professional."

What Are Exceptions?

An **exception** is an unexpected event that occurs during program execution. Think of it like this: you're the Prince running through the dungeon, and suddenly a floor tile collapses. That was not expected! So, let's assume this is our exception.

You have three choices:

1. **Do nothing** and fall to your death (program crashes)
2. **Catch yourself** on the ledge and climb back up (handle the exception)

3. **Yell for help** and let someone else deal with it (throw the exception to another part of your code)

In C#, when something goes wrong, the system creates an exception object and "throws" it. If you don't "catch" it, your program crashes and shows the player (or user) a scary error message. Not cool.

Try-Catch: Your Safety Net

The `try-catch` block is like putting a safety mat under the Prince when he's jumping across dangerous gaps.

Here's how it works:

```
try
{
    // This is the dangerous stuff you want to try
    // If something goes wrong here, jump to the catch block
}
catch (Exception ex)
{
    // This is your backup plan when things go wrong
    // Handle the error gracefully
}
```

Let's see a real example for our Prince. Imagine we're asking the player how much health potion they want to drink:

```
using System;

namespace PrinceOfProgramming
{
    class HealthPotionSystem
    {
        static void Main(string[] args)
        {
            int playerHealth = 50;
            int maxHealth = 100;

            Console.WriteLine($"The Prince's health: {playerHealth}/{maxHealth}");
            Console.WriteLine("You found a health potion! " +
                "How much do you want to drink? (1-50)");

            try
            {
                string input = Console.ReadLine();
                int potionAmount = int.Parse(input);

                playerHealth = playerHealth + potionAmount;
                Console.WriteLine($"The Prince drinks {potionAmount} " +
                    $"health points worth of potion.");
                Console.WriteLine($"New health: {playerHealth}/{maxHealth}");
            }
            catch (Exception ex)
            {
```

```
            Console.WriteLine("The Prince accidentally knocked over " +
                "the potion bottle!");
            Console.WriteLine("(You need to enter a valid number, friend.)");
        }

        Console.WriteLine("Press any key to continue your journey...");
        Console.ReadKey();
    }
  }
}
```

Expected Output (if player types "25"):

```
The Prince's health: 50/100
You found a health potion! How much do you want to drink? (1-50)
25
The Prince drinks 25 health points worth of potion.
New health: 75/100
Press any key to continue your journey...
```

However, what if the user did something unexpected?

Expected Output (if player types "banana"):

```
The Prince's health: 50/100
You found a health potion! How much do you want to drink? (1-50)
banana
The Prince accidentally knocked over the potion bottle!
(You need to enter a valid number, friend.)
Press any key to continue your journey...
```

See how the game doesn't crash when the player types something silly? That's the magic of exception handling! Instead of your program dying dramatically, it catches the problem and handles it gracefully.

Catching Specific Exceptions

But here's the twist, not all exceptions are created equal. Using `catch (Exception ex)` is like putting a giant net under the entire dungeon that catches *everything*. But sometimes you want to be more specific. It's like having different strategies for different problems like if you need to handle spike traps differently than collapsing floors.

Here are some common exception types you'll encounter:

```
using System;

namespace PrinceOfProgramming
{
    class TrapSystem
    {
        static void Main(string[] args)
        {
            int[] treasureRooms = { 100, 250, 500, 750, 1000 };
```

```csharp
        Console.WriteLine("Which treasure room do you want to enter? (0-4)");

        try
        {
            string input = Console.ReadLine();
            int roomNumber = int.Parse(input);

            int treasureAmount = treasureRooms[roomNumber];
            Console.WriteLine($"You found {treasureAmount} gold coins in room " +
                $"{roomNumber}!");
        }
        catch (FormatException)
        {
            Console.WriteLine("That's not a valid room number! " +
                "The Prince stands confused.");
        }
        catch (IndexOutOfRangeException)
        {
            Console.WriteLine("That room doesn't exist! " +
                "The Prince walks into a wall.");
        }
        catch (Exception ex)
        {
            Console.WriteLine("Something unexpected happened! " +
                "The Prince is bewildered.");
            Console.WriteLine($"Technical details: {ex.Message}");
        }

        Console.ReadKey();
    }
  }
}
```

Expected Output *(if player types "2"):*

```
Which treasure room do you want to enter? (0-4)
2
You found 500 gold coins in room 2!
```

Expected Output *(if player types "sword"):*

```
Which treasure room do you want to enter? (0-4)
sword
That's not a valid room number! The Prince stands confused.
```

Expected Output *(if player types "99"):*

```
Which treasure room do you want to enter? (0-4)
99
That room doesn't exist! The Prince walks into a wall.
```

Notice how we have multiple `catch` blocks? They work from most specific to least specific (that's why the general `Exception` is at the bottom). It's like having different responses for different problems.

>  **Pro Tip:**
>
> Always put more specific exceptions before general ones. If you put `catch (Exception ex)` first, it'll catch everything, and your other catch blocks will never run. The compiler will even yell at you about it!

The Finally Block: No Matter What

Sometimes you need code that runs whether an exception happened or not. That's where `finally` comes in. It's like the end-of-level checkpoint; no matter if you made it through perfectly or barely survived, you're going to reach that checkpoint.

Think about opening a door in the dungeon. Whether the Prince gets through successfully or gets attacked by a guard, you still want to close and lock the door behind you so enemies can't follow. That's what `finally` is for!

```csharp
using System;

namespace PrinceOfProgramming
{
    class DoorSystem
    {
        static void Main(string[] args)
        {
            Console.WriteLine("The Prince approaches a mysterious door...");
            Console.WriteLine("Enter the password to open it:");

            bool doorIsOpen = false;

            try
            {
                doorIsOpen = true;
                Console.WriteLine("*CREAK* The door opens...");

                string password = Console.ReadLine();

                if (password != "POODLE")
                {
                    throw new Exception("Wrong password! Guards are alerted!");
                }

                Console.WriteLine("Success! The Prince slips through the door.");
            }
            catch (Exception ex)
            {
                Console.WriteLine(ex.Message);
                Console.WriteLine("The Prince quickly retreats!");
            }
            finally
            {
                if (doorIsOpen)
                {
                    Console.WriteLine("*SLAM* The door closes and " +
                        "locks behind the Prince.");
```

```
                }
            }

            Console.ReadKey();
        }
    }
}
```

Expected Output (*correct password*):

```
The Prince approaches a mysterious door...
Enter the password to open it:
*CREAK* The door opens...
POODLE
Success! The Prince slips through the door.
*SLAM* The door closes and locks behind the Prince.
```

Expected Output (*wrong password*):

```
The Prince approaches a mysterious door...
Enter the password to open it:
*CREAK* The door opens...
BANANA
Wrong password! Guards are alerted!
The Prince quickly retreats!
*SLAM* The door closes and locks behind the Prince.
```

See how "The door closes and locks behind the Prince" happens no matter what? That's the power of `finally`! This is super useful for cleaning up resources like closing files, disconnecting from databases, or making sure game assets get unloaded properly.

When to Throw Exceptions

Now here's where it gets interesting. You don't just *catch* exceptions, sometimes you need to *throw* them yourself. Think of it like this, if the Prince steps on a pressure plate trap, someone needs to trigger the spikes. That someone is you, the programmer!

You throw an exception when your code encounters a situation that it can't or shouldn't handle locally. It's like the Prince yelling "TRAP!" to warn other parts of the game system.

Here's when you should throw exceptions:

 **Throw When:** Your Method Can't Do What It's Supposed To

```
using System;

namespace PrinceOfProgramming
{
    class SwordFight
    {
        static void AttackEnemy(string enemyType, int princeHealth)
        {
            if (princeHealth <= 0)
            {
```

```csharp
                throw new Exception("The Prince is too weak to fight!");
            }

            if (string.IsNullOrEmpty(enemyType))
            {
                throw new ArgumentException("Enemy type cannot be empty!");
            }

            Console.WriteLine($"The Prince attacks the {enemyType}!");
            Console.WriteLine("*CLANG* *SLASH*");
        }

        static void Main(string[] args)
        {
            try
            {
                AttackEnemy("Guard", 10);
                AttackEnemy("", 10);   // This will cause an exception!
            }
            catch (ArgumentException ex)
            {
                Console.WriteLine($"Combat Error: {ex.Message}");
            }
            catch (Exception ex)
            {
                Console.WriteLine($"Something went wrong: {ex.Message}");
            }

            Console.ReadKey();
        }
    }
}
```

Expected Output:

```
The Prince attacks the Guard!
*CLANG* *SLASH*
Combat Error: Enemy type cannot be empty!
```

Throw When: Someone Passes Invalid Data to Your Method

```csharp
using System;

namespace PrinceOfProgramming
{
    class PotionMixer
    {
        static string MixPotion(int ingredient1, int ingredient2, int ingredient3)
        {
            if (ingredient1 < 0 || ingredient2 < 0 || ingredient3 < 0)
            {
                throw new ArgumentException("You can't use negative " +
                    "amounts of ingredients! That's not how alchemy works!");
            }

            if (ingredient1 > 100 || ingredient2 > 100 || ingredient3 > 100)
            {
                throw new ArgumentException("Too much ingredient! " +
                    "The potion explodes!");
```

```
            }

            return "A shimmering health potion appears!";
        }

        static void Main(string[] args)
        {
            try
            {
                Console.WriteLine(MixPotion(10, 20, 30));
                Console.WriteLine(MixPotion(50, -5, 20));   // This will throw!
            }
            catch (ArgumentException ex)
            {
                Console.WriteLine($"Potion Mixing Failed: {ex.Message}");
            }

            Console.ReadKey();
        }
    }
}
```

Expected Output:

```
A shimmering health potion appears!
Potion Mixing Failed: You can't use negative amounts of ingredients! That's not how alchemy
works!
```

When NOT to Throw Exceptions

 **Important:** Here's the golden rule: **Don't use exceptions for normal program flow.**
Exceptions are for *exceptional* circumstances (hence the name). They're relatively slow
compared to normal code, and they're meant for situations you didn't expect.

DON'T Throw For: Things You Can Check with Regular Code

```
// BAD - Using exceptions for normal logic
static void CheckHealth(int health)
{
    try
    {
        if (health <= 0)
        {
            throw new Exception("Dead");
        }
    }
    catch (Exception)
    {
        Console.WriteLine("Game Over");
    }
}

// GOOD - Using regular if statements
static void CheckHealth(int health)
{
    if (health <= 0)
```

```
    {
        Console.WriteLine("Game Over");
    }
}
```

Think about when you jump, the game doesn't throw an exception if you're too far from the ledge. It just checks if the distance is valid and says "nope, not jumping." That's normal game logic, not an exception.

 **DON'T Throw For:** Expected User Input Mistakes

```csharp
using System;

namespace PrinceOfProgramming
{
    class UserInputExample
    {
        // BAD - Throwing for every invalid input
        static int GetPlayerChoice_Bad()
        {
            string input = Console.ReadLine();
            int choice = int.Parse(input);  // Will throw if not a number!

            if (choice < 1 || choice > 3)
            {
                throw new Exception("Invalid choice!");
            }

            return choice;
        }

        // GOOD - Handling expected problems with validation
        static int GetPlayerChoice_Good()
        {
            string input = Console.ReadLine();

            if (!int.TryParse(input, out int choice))
            {
                Console.WriteLine("That's not a number! Try again.");
                return -1;
            }

            if (choice < 1 || choice > 3)
            {
                Console.WriteLine("Please choose 1, 2, or 3.");
                return -1;
            }

            return choice;
        }

        static void Main(string[] args)
        {
            Console.WriteLine("The Prince stands at a crossroads:");
            Console.WriteLine("1. Go left");
            Console.WriteLine("2. Go right");
            Console.WriteLine("3. Go back");
            Console.WriteLine("Choose your path:");
```

```
        int choice = GetPlayerChoice_Good();

        if (choice > 0)
        {
            Console.WriteLine($"The Prince takes path {choice}!");
        }

        Console.ReadKey();
    }
    }
}
```

Expected Output (*valid input*):

```
The Prince stands at a crossroads:
1. Go left
2. Go right
3. Go back
Choose your path:
2
The Prince takes path 2!
```

Expected Output (*invalid input*):

```
The Prince stands at a crossroads:
1. Go left
2. Go right
3. Go back
Choose your path:
banana
That's not a number! Try again.
```

See the difference? In the good example, we expect that players might type nonsense, so we check for it with normal code. We only throw exceptions when something truly unexpected and wrong happens.

 **Pro Tip:**

Use `TryParse` methods (like `int.TryParse`) when you expect the user might give you bad input. They return `true` or `false` instead of throwing exceptions, making your code faster and cleaner!

Useful Exception Types

C# comes with a bunch of built-in exception types.

Here are a few that you will use often:

```
// ArgumentException - Someone passed a bad argument to your method
throw new ArgumentException("Player name cannot be empty!");
```

```csharp
// ArgumentNullException - Someone passed null when they shouldn't have
throw new ArgumentNullException(nameof(playerName), "Player name is required!");

// InvalidOperationException - The operation isn't allowed right now
throw new InvalidOperationException("Cannot attack while the Prince is jumping!");

// FileNotFoundException - Can't find a file
throw new FileNotFoundException("Save game not found!");

// NotImplementedException - You haven't finished this part yet
throw new NotImplementedException("Time travel feature coming in version 2.0!");
```

The `nameof` Keyword

See that `nameof(playerName)` in the example above? That's a super handy keyword that gives you the actual name of a variable as a string.

It's amazing for exceptions because if you ever rename the variable, `nameof` automatically updates!

```csharp
static void SaveGame(string saveFileName)
{
    if (string.IsNullOrEmpty(saveFileName))
    {
        // This will say "saveFileName cannot be empty"
        throw new ArgumentException($"{nameof(saveFileName)} cannot be empty!");
    }

    Console.WriteLine($"Saving game to {saveFileName}...");
}
```

If you later rename `saveFileName` to `fileName`, the exception message automatically changes too. It's like having auto-correct for your error messages!

Custom Exceptions: Making Your Own

Sometimes the built-in exceptions just don't cut it. Maybe you're making a specific system and want specific error types. That's where custom exceptions come in!

Creating a custom exception is like designing a custom trap for our Prince. You inherit from the `Exception` class and add whatever special properties or behaviors you need:

```csharp
using System;
using System.Reflection.Emit;
using System.Runtime.Intrinsics.Arm;

namespace PrinceOfProgramming
{
    // Custom exception for save game corruption
    class SaveGameCorruptedException : Exception
    {
        public string SaveFilePath { get; set; }
        public string CorruptionReason { get; set; }
```

```csharp
    public SaveGameCorruptedException(string filePath, string reason)
        : base($"Save game corrupted: {reason}")
    {
        SaveFilePath = filePath;
        CorruptionReason = reason;
    }
}

class SaveGameSystem
{
    static void LoadSaveGame(string saveData, string filePath)
    {
        // Validate save file format
        if (!saveData.StartsWith("PRINCE_SAVE"))
        {
            throw new SaveGameCorruptedException(filePath,
                "Invalid save file header");
        }

        // Try to parse level number
        string[] parts = saveData.Split('|');
        if (parts.Length < 3)
        {
            throw new SaveGameCorruptedException(filePath,
                "Missing required data");
        }

        string levelValue = parts[2].Split(':')[1];
        if (!int.TryParse(levelValue, out int level))
        {
            throw new SaveGameCorruptedException(filePath,
                $"Level '{levelValue}' is not a valid number");
        }

        Console.WriteLine($"Save loaded: Level {level}");
    }

    static void Main(string[] args)
    {
        Console.WriteLine("=== Save Game System ===\n");

        try
        {
            // This save file has corrupted level data
            LoadSaveGame("PRINCE_SAVE|HEALTH:50|LEVEL:abc",
                "save1.dat");
        }
        catch (SaveGameCorruptedException ex)
        {
            Console.WriteLine($"ERROR: {ex.Message}");
            Console.WriteLine($"File: {ex.SaveFilePath}");
            Console.WriteLine($"Reason: {ex.CorruptionReason}");
            Console.WriteLine("Starting new game instead...");
        }

        Console.ReadKey();
    }
}
}
```

Expected Output:

```
=== Save Game System ===

ERROR: Save game corrupted: Level 'abc' is not a valid number
File: save1.dat
Reason: Level 'abc' is not a valid number
Starting new game instead...
```

Custom exceptions are fantastic when you're building a complex system. In a real game, you might have `SaveGameException`, `MultiplayerConnectionException`, `AssetLoadingException`, and so on. Each one can carry specific information about what went wrong and where.

To Throw or not to Throw, that is another question

Let me break down the decision-making process for you:

 **Throw an exception when:**

- Your method absolutely can't do what it's supposed to do
- Someone is using your method wrong (bad arguments)
- A critical resource is unavailable (file missing, database down)
- Something happens that should never happen in normal operation
- You need to signal an error across multiple layers of code

 **Don't throw an exception when:**

- The problem is expected and you can handle it with normal logic
- You're using exceptions to control program flow
- Checking for the problem is simple (like checking if a number is negative)
- Performance matters and exceptions would slow things down
- The user is expected to make mistakes (input validation)

Think about Undertale, that quirky indie game. The battle system lets you choose to fight or spare enemies. If the player chooses an invalid action, the game doesn't crash, it just says "That won't work!" and lets you try again. That's handling expected input, not an exception.

But if the program tries to load a file and it's corrupted? That's an exception! The program can't continue without valid save data, so it needs to throw an exception and let the user know something serious went wrong.

Async Exceptions: When Errors Strike in the Background

Remember when we learned about async and await? Well, exceptions in async code can work a bit differently. Think of it this way, imagine you send the Prince to scout ahead while you're doing something else. If the Prince encounters a trap while scouting, you need to know about it when you check back on him!

When an async method throws an exception, that exception gets wrapped up and delivered to you when you `await` the task. It's like the Prince sending a messenger pigeon back to say "Hey, I ran into trouble!"

Basic Async Exception Handling

Here's how exceptions work with async methods:

```csharp
using System;
using System.Threading.Tasks;

namespace PrinceOfProgramming
{
    class AsyncDungeonExplorer
    {
        static async Task<int> SearchRoomForTreasureAsync(int roomNumber)
        {
            Console.WriteLine($"Searching room {roomNumber}...");
            await Task.Delay(1000);

            if (roomNumber == 13)
            {
                throw new Exception("Cursed room! The treasure is trapped!");
            }

            int treasureFound = roomNumber * 10;
            Console.WriteLine($"Found {treasureFound} gold in room {roomNumber}!");
            return treasureFound;
        }

        static async Task Main(string[] args)
        {
            int totalTreasure = 0;

            try
            {
                totalTreasure += await SearchRoomForTreasureAsync(5);
                // Next Line will throw!
                totalTreasure += await SearchRoomForTreasureAsync(13);
                totalTreasure += await SearchRoomForTreasureAsync(8);
            }
            catch (Exception ex)
            {
                Console.WriteLine($"Search Failed: {ex.Message}");
            }

            Console.WriteLine($"Total treasure: {totalTreasure} gold");
            Console.ReadKey();
        }
    }
}
```

Expected Output:

```
Searching room 5...
Found 50 gold in room 5!
Searching room 13...
Search Failed: Cursed room! The treasure is trapped!
Total treasure: 50 gold
```

See how the exception is caught just like with regular code? The magic happens when you `await` the task and that's when any exceptions get thrown.

Pro Tip:

If you forget to `await` a task and just call the async method without waiting for it, exceptions might get lost! Always await your async methods unless you have a very specific reason not to.

Handling Multiple Async Operations with `WhenAll`

Now here's where things get interesting. What if you want the Prince to search multiple rooms *at the same time*? You can use `Task.WhenAll` to wait for several async operations to complete.

But what happens if multiple rooms have traps?

```csharp
using System;
using System.Collections.Generic;
using System.Linq;
using System.Threading.Tasks;

namespace PrinceOfProgramming
{
    class MultiRoomExplorer
    {
        static async Task<string> ExploreRoomAsync(int roomNumber)
        {
            await Task.Delay(500);

            if (roomNumber == 3 || roomNumber == 7)
            {
                throw new Exception($"Room {roomNumber} has a trap!");
            }

            return $"Room {roomNumber} is clear!";
        }

        static async Task Main(string[] args)
        {
            Console.WriteLine("=== Exploring Multiple Rooms ===\n");

            var tasks = new List<Task<string>>
            {
```

```csharp
            ExploreRoomAsync(1),
            ExploreRoomAsync(3),    // Has trap!
            ExploreRoomAsync(5),
            ExploreRoomAsync(7)     // Has trap!
        };

        try
        {
            string[] results = await Task.WhenAll(tasks);
            foreach (string result in results)
            {
                Console.WriteLine(result);
            }
        }
        catch (Exception ex)
        {
            // With await, you only get the FIRST exception
            Console.WriteLine($"Danger! {ex.Message}");
            Console.WriteLine("\n--- Checking all tasks ---");

            // To see ALL errors, check each task individually
            foreach (var task in tasks)
            {
                if (task.IsFaulted)
                {
                    Console.WriteLine($"Failed: {task.Exception?
                        .InnerException?.Message}");
                }
                else if (task.IsCompletedSuccessfully)
                {
                    Console.WriteLine($"Success: {task.Result}");
                }
            }
        }

        Console.ReadKey();
    }
  }
}
```

Expected Output:

```
=== Exploring Multiple Rooms ===

Danger! Room 3 has a trap!

--- Checking all tasks ---
Success: Room 1 is clear!
Failed: Room 3 has a trap!
Success: Room 5 is clear!
Failed: Room 7 has a trap!
```

Notice something important, when you catch the exception from `Task.WhenAll`, you only get the *first* exception by default. But all the tasks still ran, and some of them might have failed too! To see all the errors, you need to check each task's status individually using the `task.IsFaulted` property.

Understanding `AggregateException` (What's Really Happening)

What happens when multiple async tasks fail? .NET actually wraps all those exceptions into something called an `AggregateException`. But when you use `await`, it automatically unwraps that and gives you just the first exception. It's like the Prince's scouts all coming back with bad news, but the messenger only tells you about the first problem.

If you want to see *all* the exceptions at once, you can catch the `AggregateException` directly:

```csharp
namespace PrinceOfProgramming
{
    class AggregateExceptionExample
    {
        static async Task<string> ExploreRoomAsync(int roomNumber)
        {
            await Task.Delay(300);

            if (roomNumber == 3 || roomNumber == 7 || roomNumber == 13)
            {
                throw new Exception($"Room {roomNumber}: Trap!");
            }

            return $"Room {roomNumber} clear!";
        }

        static async Task Main(string[] args)
        {
            var tasks = new List<Task<string>>
            {
                ExploreRoomAsync(1),
                ExploreRoomAsync(3),    // Will fail
                ExploreRoomAsync(7),    // Will fail
                ExploreRoomAsync(13)    // Will fail
            };

            Task<string[]> allTasks = Task.WhenAll(tasks);

            // Using Wait() instead of await gives us AggregateException
            try
            {
                allTasks.Wait();  // Blocks and throws AggregateException
            }
            catch (Exception ex)
            {
                Console.WriteLine("=== Using await (only first exception) ===");
                Console.WriteLine($"Exception type: {ex.GetType().Name}");
                Console.WriteLine($"Message: {ex.Message}\n");
            }

            // Now catch the AggregateException by checking the task directly
            try
            {
                allTasks.Wait();  // This throws AggregateException (not await!)
            }
            catch (AggregateException aggEx)
            {
                Console.WriteLine("=== Catching AggregateException ===");
                Console.WriteLine($"Exception type: {aggEx.GetType().Name}");
                Console.WriteLine($"Inner exception count: {aggEx.InnerExceptions.Count}\n");
```

```
                Console.WriteLine("All exceptions:");
                foreach (var innerEx in aggEx.InnerExceptions)
                {
                    Console.WriteLine($"  - {innerEx.Message}");
                }
            }

            Console.ReadKey();
        }
    }
}
```

Expected Output:

```
=== Using await (only first exception) ===
Exception type: Exception
Message: Room 3: Trap!

=== Catching AggregateException ===
Exception type: AggregateException
Inner exception count: 3

All exceptions:
  - Room 3: Trap!
  - Room 7: Trap!
  - Room 13: Trap!
```

So when should you actually catch `AggregateException`?

Catch AggregateException when:
- You're using `Task.Wait()` or `Task.Result` instead of `await`
- You need to see ALL exceptions from multiple failed operations at once
- You're working with parallel operations using `Parallel.ForEach` or similar constructs

Use individual task checking when:
- You're using modern async/await (which is almost always)
- You want more control over how each failure is handled
- You're building a system that should be resilient to individual failures

 **Pro Tip:**

The `Flatten()` method on `AggregateException` is useful if you have tasks that themselves start other tasks, creating nested `AggregateExceptions`. Think of it like opening a chest that contains other chests—`Flatten()` dumps all the treasure into one pile!

Handling Each Task Separately (The Recommended Pattern)

For most real-world scenarios, you want to handle each task's errors individually rather than stopping everything when one fails:

```csharp
namespace PrinceOfProgramming
{
    class SafeMultiRoomExplorer
    {
        static async Task<(int room, int treasure, string error)> SearchRoomAsync(int room)
        {
            try
            {
                Console.WriteLine($"Exploring room {room}...");
                await Task.Delay(500);

                if (room == 3 || room == 7)
                {
                    throw new Exception($"Trap in room {room}!");
                }

                int treasure = room * 25;
                Console.WriteLine($"Room {room} is safe!");
                return (room, treasure, error: null);
            }
            catch (Exception ex)
            {
                Console.WriteLine($"Room {room}: DANGER!");
                return (room, treasure: 0, error: ex.Message);
            }
        }

        static async Task Main(string[] args)
        {
            Console.WriteLine("=== Safe Multi-Room Search ===\n");

            var tasks = new List<Task<(int room, int treasure, string error)>>
            {
                SearchRoomAsync(1),
                SearchRoomAsync(3),
                SearchRoomAsync(5),
                SearchRoomAsync(7)
            };

            var results = await Task.WhenAll(tasks);

            int totalTreasure = results.Where(r => r.error == null).Sum(r => r.treasure);

            Console.WriteLine("\n=== Results ===");
            foreach (var result in results)
            {
                if (result.error == null)
                {
                    Console.WriteLine($"Room {result.room}: Found {result.treasure} gold!");
                }
                else
                {
                    Console.WriteLine($"Room {result.room}: {result.error}");
                }
            }
```

```csharp
            Console.WriteLine($"\nTotal treasure: {totalTreasure} gold");
            Console.ReadKey();
        }
    }
}
```

Expected Output:

```
=== Safe Multi-Room Search ===

Exploring room 1...
Exploring room 3...
Exploring room 5...
Exploring room 7...
Room 1 is safe!
Room 5 is safe!
Room 7: DANGER!
Room 3: DANGER!

=== Results ===
Room 1: Found 25 gold!
Room 3: Trap in room 3!
Room 5: Found 125 gold!
Room 7: Trap in room 7!

Total treasure: 150 gold
```

This pattern is useful in many types of applications. Imagine loading multiple resources at once like files, data, images, or configuration settings. If one item fails to load, you don't want the entire application to crash. Instead, you want to know which ones failed so you can use a fallback option, retry the operation, or handle the error gracefully.

In Hollow Knight, the game loads tons of rooms, enemies, and assets asynchronously. If they handled async errors poorly, one corrupted file could crash the entire game. Instead, they probably catch errors for each asset individually and fall back to safe defaults.

Important: Remember the golden rule? Some examples above were throwing exceptions and writing messages to the console (like "a trap was found") to indicate that something went wrong. This was done for demonstration purposes only. **Exceptions should not be used as normal program flow**, only for unexpected error situations.

Fun Experiment: The Architect's Blueprint

Okay, time to put your new exception-handling skills to the test!

The Prince's Journey: Testing the Architect's Plans

The story continues...

The Prince discovers a hidden alcove containing dusty scrolls, the original blueprints of this very dungeon. As he unrolls the parchment, he recognizes the architect's notations, room names, danger ratings and treasure locations. But many entries have been corrupted by time and moisture, the ink smeared and numbers illegible. Ahead of him stretches a terrifying gap between two stone platforms, and beyond it, multiple passages branch into darkness. He realizes the Vizier's dungeon was built with specific rules. Maximum danger levels for each room type, limits on treasure amounts to prevent vault collapses, strict naming conventions for the magical wards.

Before he attempts that deadly leap across the chasm, before he commits to any passage beyond, he needs to verify these blueprints. Which room configurations are valid? Which have been corrupted beyond use? If he trusts a flawed blueprint and leaps toward a passage that doesn't match the specifications, he'll plunge into the abyss below. He must validate each room's data carefully, separating the reliable information from the dangerous corruption. Only then can he make the jump with confidence, knowing exactly what awaits him on the other side.

The Challenge

Create a dungeon configuration validator where:

1. The player enters data for 5 dungeon rooms (room name, danger level 1-10, treasure amount)
2. Validate each input and throw appropriate exceptions for invalid data
3. Use custom exceptions for dungeon-specific validation errors
4. Use try-catch to handle user input errors gracefully
5. Keep track of successfully configured rooms and failed attempts
6. Display a final report of valid rooms and total treasure

Try it yourself before looking at the solution!

Example Solution

Here's one way to solve it:

```csharp
using System;
using System.Collections.Generic;

namespace PrinceOfProgramming
{
    class InvalidDungeonDataException : Exception
    {
        public string RoomName { get; set; }
        public string ValidationError { get; set; }

        public InvalidDungeonDataException(string roomName, string error)
            : base($"Room '{roomName}' validation failed: {error}")
        {
```

```csharp
            RoomName = roomName;
            ValidationError = error;
        }
    }

    class DungeonRoom
    {
        public string Name { get; set; }
        public int DangerLevel { get; set; }
        public int Treasure { get; set; }

        public DungeonRoom(string name, int danger, int treasure)
        {
            if (string.IsNullOrWhiteSpace(name))
            {
                throw new ArgumentException("Room name cannot be empty");
            }

            if (danger < 1 || danger > 10)
            {
                throw new InvalidDungeonDataException(name,
                    $"Danger level must be 1-10, got {danger}");
            }

            if (treasure < 0)
            {
                throw new InvalidDungeonDataException(name,
                    $"Treasure cannot be negative, got {treasure}");
            }

            if (treasure > 10000)
            {
                throw new InvalidDungeonDataException(name,
                    "Treasure exceeds maximum vault capacity (10000)");
            }

            Name = name;
            DangerLevel = danger;
            Treasure = treasure;
        }
    }

    class DungeonValidator
    {
        static void Main(string[] args)
        {
            Console.WriteLine("=== DUNGEON CONFIGURATION VALIDATOR ===");
            Console.WriteLine("Configure 5 dungeon rooms\n");

            List<DungeonRoom> validRooms = new List<DungeonRoom>();
            int failedAttempts = 0;

            string[] defaultNames = { "Entrance Hall", "Armory", "Treasury",
                                      "Throne Room", "Secret Chamber" };

            for (int i = 0; i < 5; i++)
            {
                Console.WriteLine($"\n--- Room {i + 1}: {defaultNames[i]} ---");

                try
                {
```

```csharp
                Console.Write("Danger level (1-10): ");
                int danger = int.Parse(Console.ReadLine());

                Console.Write("Treasure amount (0-10000): ");
                int treasure = int.Parse(Console.ReadLine());

                DungeonRoom room = new DungeonRoom(defaultNames[i], danger, treasure);
                validRooms.Add(room);
                Console.WriteLine($"✓ {room.Name} configured successfully!");
            }
            catch (FormatException)
            {
                Console.WriteLine("ERROR: Input must be a valid number");
                failedAttempts++;
            }
            catch (InvalidDungeonDataException ex)
            {
                Console.WriteLine($"ERROR: {ex.Message}");
                failedAttempts++;
            }
            catch (ArgumentException ex)
            {
                Console.WriteLine($"ERROR: {ex.Message}");
                failedAttempts++;
            }
        }

        Console.WriteLine("\n" + new string('=', 50));
        Console.WriteLine("CONFIGURATION REPORT");
        Console.WriteLine(new string('=', 50));

        Console.WriteLine($"\nValid Rooms: {validRooms.Count}");
        int totalTreasure = 0;
        foreach (var room in validRooms)
        {
            Console.WriteLine($"  {room.Name}: Danger {room.DangerLevel}, " +
                            $"Treasure {room.Treasure}");
            totalTreasure += room.Treasure;
        }

        Console.WriteLine($"\nFailed Attempts: {failedAttempts}");
        Console.WriteLine($"Total Treasure: {totalTreasure} gold");

        if (validRooms.Count == 5)
        {
            Console.WriteLine("\nDungeon fully configured and ready!");
        }
        else
        {
            Console.WriteLine("\nWarning: Dungeon incomplete - " +
                "using defaults for missing rooms");
        }

        Console.ReadKey();
    }
  }
}
```

Expected Output (with some invalid inputs):

```
=== DUNGEON CONFIGURATION VALIDATOR ===
Configure 5 dungeon rooms


--- Room 1: Entrance Hall ---
Danger level (1-10): 5
Treasure amount (0-10000): 100
V Entrance Hall configured successfully!

--- Room 2: Armory ---
Danger level (1-10): 15
Treasure amount (0-10000): 100
ERROR: Room 'Armory' validation failed: Danger level must be 1-10, got 15

--- Room 3: Treasury ---
Danger level (1-10): 8
Treasure amount (0-10000): banana
ERROR: Input must be a valid number

--- Room 4: Throne Room ---
Danger level (1-10): 3
Treasure amount (0-10000): 500
V Throne Room configured successfully!

--- Room 5: Secret Chamber ---
Danger level (1-10): 7
Treasure amount (0-10000): 15000
ERROR: Room 'Secret Chamber' validation failed: Treasure exceeds maximum vault capacity
(10000)


==================================================
CONFIGURATION REPORT
==================================================

Valid Rooms: 2
  Entrance Hall: Danger 5, Treasure 100
  Throne Room: Danger 3, Treasure 500

Failed Attempts: 3
Total Treasure: 600 gold

Warning: Dungeon incomplete - using defaults for missing rooms
```

Notice how this solution:

- Uses exceptions for **real validation errors** (out of range values, invalid data)
- Doesn't use exceptions for normal game logic
- Handles expected user input errors (format exceptions) gracefully
- Uses a custom exception for domain-specific validation rules
- Validates data in the constructor where it belongs
- Provides clear error messages for debugging
- Continues processing even when some inputs fail

This is a realistic example of how you'd validate configuration data in a real program!

Wrap-Up: What You've Learned

Congrats, you've conquered exception handling!

Key Takeaways

- **Understand what exceptions are**: Unexpected events that occur during program execution
- **Use `try-catch` blocks**: Catch exceptions and handle them gracefully instead of crashing
- **Catch specific exceptions**: Handle different problems in different ways
- **Use `finally` blocks**: Run cleanup code that executes no matter what
- **Know when to throw**: When your code encounters an unrecoverable situation
- **Know when NOT to throw**: When you can handle problems with normal logic
- **Create custom exceptions**: Make your own exception types for game-specific errors
- **Use `nameof()`**: Get variable names as strings for better error messages
- **Handle async exceptions**: Catch errors from async methods using try-catch with await
- **Work with `Task.WhenAll`**: Handle multiple async operations and their exceptions properly
- **Understand `AggregateException`**: Know what happens under the hood with multiple failures
- **Handle multiple errors**: Check individual task results when multiple async operations fail
- **Use proper async patterns**: Wrap async operations with error handling to build robust systems

Exception handling is like being the dungeon designer. You set up situations where things might go wrong, but you also provide ways to handle those problems gracefully. A good program doesn't punish users for every little mistake, it gives them chances to recover and learn.

Exceptions are for exceptional circumstances. Don't use them for normal logic or expected user behavior. Use them when something truly goes wrong and needs special attention. And when working with async code, always remember that exceptions are delivered when you await the task. So, make sure you're catching them at the right place!

Now your code can handle mistakes, unexpected situations, even for asynchronous operations like a pro. Whether you're loading game assets, processing network requests, or running background calculations, you know how to keep your program running smoothly even when things go wrong. The Prince would be proud!

Chapter 11

Data Storage

"The faintest ink is better than the best memory." — Chinese Proverb

Every program you've ever used from your web browser to your favorite mobile app, they all need to remember things. When you close Spotify and open it again, it remembers your playlists. When you restart your computer, your desktop icons are still in the same place. When you return to Netflix, it knows exactly where you left off in that series you're binge-watching. None of this happens by magic. Behind the scenes, these programs are constantly saving and loading data, turning the information in memory into something permanent that survives beyond a single session. Without data storage, every time you closed a program, it would be like meeting it for the first time all over again. No settings, no history, no progress saved.

But it's not just about remembering your preferences or game progress. Modern software needs to handle all kinds of data in all kinds of formats. A photo editing app needs to save your images. A note-taking app needs to organize your thoughts into files you can sync across devices. A music player needs to read metadata from thousands of songs. A code editor needs to remember your recently opened files and where you left your cursor. Each of these scenarios requires different approaches to storing data. Some need human-readable formats for debugging and transparency, others need compact formats for efficiency, and some need structures that other programs can understand and share. Learning how to store and retrieve data effectively is one of the most practical skills in programming, because almost every useful program needs to persist information between sessions.

Core Concepts Covered

- ✓ Reading from and writing to files on disk
- ✓ Understanding where files are stored and how to control their location
- ✓ Converting complex objects into storable formats and back again
- ✓ Choosing appropriate data formats based on your program's needs
- ✓ Handling errors gracefully when file operations fail
- ✓ Balancing between human-readable and compact data storage
- ✓ Organizing data in ways that make it easy to save, load, and maintain

Saving Things So They Don't Vanish

 **Trivia:**

The Rosetta Stone (196 BCE) stored the same decree in three languages: hieroglyphics, Demotic script, and ancient Greek. When archaeologists found it in 1799, hieroglyphics had been unreadable for 1,400 years—but scholars could read ancient Greek, so they used it to decrypt the others. This is like storing backups in multiple formats. NASA has old mission data on tapes they can't read anymore because the tape readers are extinct.

So, you've learned how to create variables, write logic, build classes, and make your code do back flips. But when your program closes, POOF, everything disappears like the Prince falling through a trapdoor. All your hard work, gone.

What if you want to save the Prince's progress? His health, which level he's on, how many potions he's collected? Or maybe you're building a high score system, or saving game settings so players don't have to reconfigure everything each time they start up?

That's where **data storage** comes in. This is how we make our programs remember things between sessions.

Basic File I/O (Input/Output)

Think of files like save game slots. When you save your Prince's progress, you're writing data to a file on your disk. When you load that save, you're reading data back from that file.

In C#, the `System.IO` namespace gives us the tools to work with files. Let's start simple by just saving some basic text to a file:

```csharp
using System;
using System.IO;

namespace PrinceOfProgramming
{
```

```csharp
    class Program
    {
        static void Main(string[] args)
        {
            // Writing to a file
            string savePath = "prince_save.txt";
            string saveData = "Level: 1, Health: 100, Potions: 3";

            File.WriteAllText(savePath, saveData);
            Console.WriteLine("Game saved!");

            // Reading from a file
            string loadedData = File.ReadAllText(savePath);
            Console.WriteLine("Loaded data: " + loadedData);
        }
    }
}
```

Expected Output:

```
Game saved!
Loaded data: Level: 1, Health: 100, Potions: 3
```

Just like that, you've created a file and read it back! The `File` class has some handy methods:

- `File.WriteAllText()`: Writes text to a file (creates it if it doesn't exist, overwrites if it does)
- `File.ReadAllText()`: Reads all text from a file into a string
- `File.Exists()`: Checks if a file exists (important before trying to load!)
- `File.Delete()`: Deletes a file

Here's a more game-like example:

```csharp
using System;
using System.IO;

namespace PrinceOfProgramming
{
    class Program
    {
        static void Main(string[] args)
        {
            string savePath = "prince_save.txt";

            // Check if a save file exists
            if (File.Exists(savePath))
            {
                Console.WriteLine("Continue from last save? (y/n)");
                string choice = Console.ReadLine();

                if (choice.ToLower() == "y")
                {
                    string savedGame = File.ReadAllText(savePath);
                    Console.WriteLine("Loading: " + savedGame);
                }
                else
                {
                    Console.WriteLine("Starting new game...");
```

```
            }
        }
        else
        {
            Console.WriteLine("No save file found. Starting new game...");
        }

        // Later in your game, save progress
        File.WriteAllText(savePath, "Level: 3, Health: 75, Potions: 1");
        Console.WriteLine("Progress saved!");
        }
    }
}
```

Expected Output *(if no save exists):*

```
No save file found. Starting new game...
Progress saved!
```

Expected Output *(if save exists and player chooses 'y'):*

```
Continue from last save? (y/n)
y
Loading: Level: 3, Health: 75, Potions: 1
Progress saved!
```

Pro Tip:

Always check if a file exists before trying to read it with `File.Exists()`. Trying to read a non-existent file will crash your program with a `FileNotFoundException`. Nobody wants their program to crash when players try to load their save!

Here's how to work with multiple lines:

```
using System;
using System.IO;

namespace PrinceOfProgramming
{
    class Program
    {
        static void Main(string[] args)
        {
            string[] highScores =
            {
                "Player1: 15000",
                "Player2: 12500",
                "Player3: 10000"
            };

            // Write all lines at once
            File.WriteAllLines("highscores.txt", highScores);

            // Read all lines back
```

```
        string[] loadedScores = File.ReadAllLines("highscores.txt");

        Console.WriteLine("High Scores:");
        foreach (string score in loadedScores)
        {
            Console.WriteLine(score);
        }
        }
    }
}
```

Expected Output:

```
High Scores:
Player1: 15000
Player2: 12500
Player3: 10000
```

Where Do These Files Actually Go?

When you just write `"prince_save.txt"` without specifying a full path, where does that file end up?

When running from VS Code or Visual Studio: The file gets created in your project's output directory. Usually something like `bin/Debug/net10.0/` or similar. That's where your compiled executable lives when you're developing.

When running the compiled .exe directly: The file gets created in the same folder as the .exe file itself.

But there's a problem with both of these approaches. Your users might not have permission to write files there, especially if your program is installed in the "Program Files" folder on Windows. Plus, it's messy to have save files mixed in with your program files.

Let's look at alternative ways to handle file locations:

```csharp
using System;
using System.IO;

namespace PrinceOfProgramming
{
    class Program
    {
        static void Main(string[] args)
        {
            // Option 1: Get the current directory (where the .exe is)
            string currentDir = Directory.GetCurrentDirectory();
            Console.WriteLine("Current directory: " + currentDir);

            // Option 2: Create a "Saves" folder next to your executable
            string savesFolder = Path.Combine(currentDir, "Saves");
            Directory.CreateDirectory(savesFolder); // Creates it if it doesn't exist
            string savePath = Path.Combine(savesFolder, "game_save.txt");

            File.WriteAllText(savePath, "Level: 5, Health: 80");
            Console.WriteLine("Saved to: " + savePath);
```

```csharp
            // Option 3: Use AppData folder (recommended for Windows)
            string appDataFolder = Environment.GetFolderPath(
                Environment.SpecialFolder.ApplicationData);
            string gameDataFolder = Path.Combine(appDataFolder, "MyAwesomeGame");
            Directory.CreateDirectory(gameDataFolder);
            string appDataSavePath = Path.Combine(gameDataFolder, "save.txt");

            File.WriteAllText(appDataSavePath, "Level: 5, Health: 80");
            Console.WriteLine("Saved to AppData: " + appDataSavePath);
        }
    }
}
```

Expected Output (*paths will vary on your computer*):

```
Current directory: C:\Users\YourName\Projects\PrinceOfProgramming\bin\Debug\net10.0
Saved to: C:\Users\YourName\Projects\PrinceOfProgramming\bin\Debug\net10.0\Saves\game_save.txt
Saved to AppData: C:\Users\YourName\AppData\Roaming\MyAwesomeGame\save.txt
```

You will notice that the third example is storing it in a folder named "AppData".

But where's the AppData folder?

On Windows, you can get there quickly:

1. Press `Windows Key + R`
2. Type `%appdata%` and hit Enter
3. Look for your game's folder (like "MyAwesomeGame" in the example)

Most professional software uses the AppData folder because:

- Users always have permission to write there
- It keeps save files separate from the program installation
- Each Windows user on the same computer gets their own saves
- It's the standard location Windows users expect

 **Pro Tip:**

Use `Path.Combine()` instead of manually building paths with `"folder/subfolder/file.txt"`. It automatically uses the correct slash direction for the operating system (\ on Windows, / on Mac/Linux) and prevents path errors.

To view your files in Windows Explorer:

1. Run your program to create the files
2. Look at the console output to see where the file was saved
3. Open Windows Explorer
4. Copy the folder path from your console
5. Paste it into the Explorer address bar and press Enter

6. Double-click the .txt, .csv, or .json files to view them in Notepad or your default text editor

Writing Different File Formats

Now that you know where to save files, let's look at different formats you can use. Each format has its strengths depending on what you're storing.

(Keep in mind that expected output paths would vary on your computer for the examples.)

1. Plain Text Files

The simplest format, just raw text. Great for logs, simple notes, or human-readable data:

```csharp
using System;
using System.IO;

namespace PrinceOfProgramming
{
    class Program
    {
        static void Main(string[] args)
        {
            string logPath = "game_log.txt";
            string logEntry = "Player entered the dungeon at " + DateTime.Now;

            // Append to file (adds to the end, doesn't overwrite)
            File.AppendAllText(logPath, logEntry + Environment.NewLine);

            Console.WriteLine("Log entry added!");
            Console.WriteLine("Check the file at: " + Path.GetFullPath(logPath));
        }
    }
}
```

Expected Output:

```
Log entry added!
Check the file at: C:\Users\YourName\Projects\PrinceGame\bin\Debug\net10.0\game_log.txt
```

File contents (game_log.txt):

```
Player entered the dungeon at 12/14/2025 3:45:23 PM
```

2. CSV (Comma-Separated Values)

Perfect for tabular data like high scores, inventory lists, or statistics. Think of it like a simple spreadsheet:

```csharp
using System;
using System.IO;
```

```
namespace PrinceOfProgramming
{
    class Program
    {
        static void Main(string[] args)
        {
            // Create high scores table
            string[] csvLines =
            {
                "Player,Score,Level,Date",
                "Prince,15000,12,2025-12-14",
                "Warrior,12500,10,2025-12-13",
                "Thief,10000,8,2025-12-12"
            };

            File.WriteAllLines("highscores.csv", csvLines);
            Console.WriteLine("High scores saved!");
            Console.WriteLine("File location: " + Path.GetFullPath("highscores.csv"));
        }
    }
}
```

Expected Output:

```
High scores saved!
File location: C:\Users\YourName\Projects\PrinceGame\bin\Debug\net10.0\highscores.csv
```

File contents (highscores.csv):

```
Player,Score,Level,Date
Prince,15000,12,2025-12-14
Warrior,12500,10,2025-12-13
Thief,10000,8,2025-12-12
```

You can open CSV files in Excel, Google Sheets, or any text editor. They're great for data you might want to analyze in a spreadsheet.

Serialization: Turning Objects into Data

Okay, you've got a nice `Player` class with health, position, inventory, and all sorts of properties. Manually writing each property to a CSV or text file can become a lot of work. What if you add new properties? What if you have a list of items? What about objects inside objects?

Serialization is the process of converting objects into a format that can be stored or transmitted. **Deserialization** is converting that data back into objects. Think of it like turning our Prince into a save file and then reconstructing him later!

JSON Serialization (Recommended)

JSON is the most popular serialization format today. It's human-readable, flexible, and works everywhere. In C#, we use the `System.Text.Json` namespace:

```csharp
using System;
using System.IO;
using System.Text.Json;

namespace PrinceOfProgramming
{
    class Player
    {
        public string Name { get; set; }
        public int Health { get; set; }
        public int Level { get; set; }
        public string[] Inventory { get; set; }
    }

    class Program
    {
        static void Main(string[] args)
        {
            Player prince = new Player
            {
                Name = "Prince ",
                Health = 85,
                Level = 5,
                Inventory = new[] { "Sword", "Health Potion", "Key" }
            };

            // Serialize to JSON with nice formatting
            var options = new JsonSerializerOptions { WriteIndented = true };
            string jsonString = JsonSerializer.Serialize(prince, options);

            // Save to file
            File.WriteAllText("player.json", jsonString);
            Console.WriteLine("Player saved to JSON!");
            Console.WriteLine("File location: " + Path.GetFullPath("player.json"));

            // Load from JSON
            string loadedJson = File.ReadAllText("player.json");
            Player loadedPrince = JsonSerializer.Deserialize<Player>(loadedJson);

            Console.WriteLine($"\nLoaded: {loadedPrince.Name}");
            Console.WriteLine($"Health: {loadedPrince.Health}");
            Console.WriteLine("Inventory: " + string.Join(", ",
                loadedPrince.Inventory));
        }
    }
}
```

Expected Output:

```
Player saved to JSON!
File location: C:\Users\YourName\Projects\PrinceGame\bin\Debug\net10.0\player.json

Loaded: Prince
Health: 85
```

```
Inventory: Sword, Health Potion, Key
```

File contents (player.json):

```json
json
{
  "Name": "Prince ",
  "Health": 85,
  "Level": 5,
  "Inventory": [
    "Sword",
    "Health Potion",
    "Key"
  ]
}
```

Beautiful! JSON handles complex objects, arrays, nested objects, basically everything. Most modern software use JSON for configuration files and save data.

Pro Tip:

Use `WriteIndented = true` during development so you can easily read and debug your JSON files. For release builds, you can remove it to save disk space (though modern storage is so cheap, readable files are usually worth it).

XML Serialization

XML is older than JSON and more verbose, but it's still used in many systems (especially older applications and Windows applications).

Here's how to use it:

```csharp
using System;
using System.IO;
using System.Xml.Serialization;

namespace PrinceOfProgramming
{
    public class Player
    {
        public string Name { get; set; }
        public int Health { get; set; }
        public int Level { get; set; }
        public string[] Inventory { get; set; }
    }

    class Program
    {
        static void Main(string[] args)
        {
            Player prince = new Player
            {
```

```csharp
            Name = "Prince",
            Health = 100,
            Level = 1,
            Inventory = new[] { "Sword", "Shield" }
        };

        // Serialize to XML
        XmlSerializer serializer = new XmlSerializer(typeof(Player));
        using (FileStream fs = new FileStream("player.xml", FileMode.Create))
        {
            serializer.Serialize(fs, prince);
        }
        Console.WriteLine("Player saved to XML!");
        Console.WriteLine("File location: " + Path.GetFullPath("player.xml"));

        // Deserialize from XML
        using (FileStream fs = new FileStream("player.xml", FileMode.Open))
        {
            Player loadedPrince = (Player)serializer.Deserialize(fs);
            Console.WriteLine($"\nLoaded: {loadedPrince.Name}");
            Console.WriteLine($"Health: {loadedPrince.Health}");
            Console.WriteLine("Inventory: " + string.Join(", ",
                loadedPrince.Inventory));
        }
    }
  }
}
```

Expected Output:

```
Player saved to XML!
File location: C:\Users\YourName\Projects\PrinceGame\bin\Debug\net10.0\player.xml

Loaded: Prince
Health: 100
Inventory: Sword, Shield
```

File contents (player.xml):

```xml
<?xml version="1.0"?>
<Player xmlns:xsi="http://www.w3.org/2001/XMLSchema-instance"
xmlns:xsd="http://www.w3.org/2001/XMLSchema">
  <Name>Prince</Name>
  <Health>100</Health>
  <Level>1</Level>
  <Inventory>
    <string>Sword</string>
    <string>Shield</string>
  </Inventory>
</Player>
```

Important: For XML serialization to work, your class needs to be `public` (notice the `public class Player` in this example). Also, notice that `using` statement? It automatically closes the FileStream when we're done with it.

Binary vs. Readable Formats

So far, we've looked at text-based formats (JSON, XML, CSV, plain text). These are all **human-readable**. You can open them in Notepad and see what's inside. But there's another option: **binary files**.

What's a Binary File?

A binary file stores data in the raw format computers use internally like ones and zeros. If you open a binary file in Notepad, you'll see gibberish or weird characters. Think of it like the difference between reading a book (text file) and looking at a computer's memory chip under a microscope (binary file).

Here's an example of saving data as binary:

```csharp
using System;
using System.IO;
using System.Runtime.Serialization.Formatters.Binary;

namespace PrinceOfProgramming
{
    [Serializable]
    class GameData
    {
        public int Level { get; set; }
        public int Health { get; set; }
        public string[] Items { get; set; }
    }

    class Program
    {
        static void Main(string[] args)
        {
            GameData data = new GameData
            {
                Level = 10,
                Health = 75,
                Items = new[] { "Sword", "Potion", "Key" }
            };

            // Save as binary
            BinaryFormatter formatter = new BinaryFormatter();
            using (FileStream fs = new FileStream("save.dat", FileMode.Create))
            {
                formatter.Serialize(fs, data);
            }

            Console.WriteLine("Data saved as binary!");
            Console.WriteLine("File location: " + Path.GetFullPath("save.dat"));
            Console.WriteLine("Try opening save.dat in Notepad - " +
                "you'll see gibberish!");

            // Load from binary
            using (FileStream fs = new FileStream("save.dat", FileMode.Open))
            {
                GameData loaded = (GameData)formatter.Deserialize(fs);
```

```
            Console.WriteLine($"\nLoaded - Level: {loaded.Level}, " +
                $"Health: {loaded.Health}");
        }
    }
  }
}
```

Expected Output:

```
Data saved as binary!
File location: C:\Users\YourName\Projects\PrinceGame\bin\Debug\net10.0\save.dat
Try opening save.dat in Notepad - you'll see gibberish!

Loaded - Level: 10, Health: 75
```

File contents (save.dat) if opened in Notepad:

```
☺♥♦♣ ☼■§♫♪ BGameData...items...
```

(Actual binary gibberish that is not readable!)

🖐 **Important:** `BinaryFormatter` is considered obsolete in modern C# because it has security issues. For new projects, use JSON even if you want to obfuscate data. I'm showing you binary serialization so you understand the concept, but in practice, stick with JSON for most projects.

When Should You Use Each Format?

Let's break it down:

Use Readable Text Formats (JSON, XML, CSV) when:
- **You need to debug** - Being able to open the file and see what's wrong is invaluable
- **Users might edit files** - Some software let users tweak config files manually
- **You want cross-platform compatibility** - Text files work the same on Windows, Mac, Linux
- **File size doesn't matter much** - Save files are usually tiny compared to for example images or game assets
- **You're working with other developers** - Human-readable files are easier to review

JSON specifically is perfect for:
- Configuration files (graphics settings, key bindings)
- Game save files (like Undertale, Hollow Knight, Stardew Valley)
- Level data and game content
- Anything you might want to read, debug, or modify

CSV is great for:
- Large datasets (enemy stats, item databases)
- High score tables
- Data you might want to open in Excel

Binary formats make sense when:
- **File size is critical** - Binary is more compact (but compression can help text files too)
- **You want to discourage cheating** - It's harder (but not impossible!) to edit binary files
- **Performance matters** - Reading/writing binary can be faster for huge datasets

However, even for anti-cheat purposes, binary isn't that secure. Determined players will figure it out. Many modern games use JSON and just accept that some players will tinker with their save files, it's their game, after all!

Pro Tip:

Start with JSON for everything. It's the industry standard, it's easy to debug, and it works great. Only switch to binary if you have a specific reason (like processing millions of records where the speed difference matters). Remember: readable files save you hours of debugging time!

Saving and Loading: Putting It All Together

Let's create a proper save system like you'd find in a real game:

```csharp
using System;
using System.IO;
using System.Text.Json;
using System.Collections.Generic;

namespace PrinceOfProgramming
{
    class PlayerData
    {
        public string Name { get; set; }
        public int Health { get; set; }
        public int MaxHealth { get; set; }
        public int CurrentLevel { get; set; }
        public List<string> Inventory { get; set; }
        public Dictionary<string, bool> UnlockedAchievements { get; set; }
    }

    class SaveManager
    {
        private static readonly string SaveFolder = Path.Combine(
            Environment.GetFolderPath(Environment.SpecialFolder.ApplicationData),
            "PrinceOfProgramming"
        );
        private static readonly string SavePath = Path.Combine(SaveFolder,
            "gamesave.json");

        public static void SaveGame(PlayerData player)
        {
            try
            {
```

```csharp
            // Create save folder if it doesn't exist
            Directory.CreateDirectory(SaveFolder);

            var options = new JsonSerializerOptions { WriteIndented = true };
            string jsonData = JsonSerializer.Serialize(player, options);
            File.WriteAllText(SavePath, jsonData);

            Console.WriteLine("✓ Game saved successfully!");
            Console.WriteLine($"  Location: {SavePath}");
        }
        catch (Exception ex)
        {
            Console.WriteLine($"✗ Failed to save game: {ex.Message}");
        }
    }
}

public static PlayerData LoadGame()
{
    try
    {
        if (!File.Exists(SavePath))
        {
            Console.WriteLine("No save file found. Starting new game...");
            return CreateNewPlayer();
        }

        string jsonData = File.ReadAllText(SavePath);
        PlayerData player = JsonSerializer.Deserialize<PlayerData>(jsonData);
        Console.WriteLine("✓ Game loaded successfully!");
        return player;
    }
    catch (Exception ex)
    {
        Console.WriteLine($"✗ Failed to load game: {ex.Message}");
        Console.WriteLine("Starting new game...");
        return CreateNewPlayer();
    }
}

private static PlayerData CreateNewPlayer()
{
    return new PlayerData
    {
        Name = "Prince",
        Health = 100,
        MaxHealth = 100,
        CurrentLevel = 1,
        Inventory = new List<string> { "Sword" },
        UnlockedAchievements = new Dictionary<string, bool>()
    };
}

public static void ShowSaveLocation()
{
    Console.WriteLine($"\nYour save file is stored at:");
    Console.WriteLine(SavePath);
    Console.WriteLine("\nTo view it:");
    Console.WriteLine("1. Press Windows Key + R");
    Console.WriteLine("2. Type: %appdata%\\PrinceOfProgramming");
    Console.WriteLine("3. Press Enter");
    Console.WriteLine("4. Open gamesave.json in Notepad\n");
```

```csharp
        }
    }

    class Program
    {
        static void Main(string[] args)
        {
            // Load existing save or create new player
            PlayerData prince = SaveManager.LoadGame();

            // Show player info
            Console.WriteLine($"\n=== Welcome back, {prince.Name}! ===");
            Console.WriteLine($"Level {prince.CurrentLevel} - " +
                $"Health: {prince.Health}/{prince.MaxHealth}");
            Console.WriteLine($"Inventory: {string.Join(", ", prince.Inventory)}");

            // Simulate gameplay progress
            Console.WriteLine("\n--- Simulating adventure... ---");
            prince.CurrentLevel = 3;
            prince.Health = 75;
            prince.Inventory.Add("Health Potion");
            prince.Inventory.Add("Ancient Key");
            prince.UnlockedAchievements["FirstVictory"] = true;
            prince.UnlockedAchievements["TreasureHunter"] = true;

            Console.WriteLine($"Reached Level {prince.CurrentLevel}!");
            Console.WriteLine($"New items: Health Potion, Ancient Key");
            Console.WriteLine($"Unlocked " +
                $"{prince.UnlockedAchievements.Count} achievements!");

            // Save the game
            SaveManager.SaveGame(prince);
            SaveManager.ShowSaveLocation();

            Console.WriteLine("Restart the program to see your save loaded!");
        }
    }
}
```

Expected Output (first run):

```
No save file found. Starting new game...

=== Welcome back, Prince! ===
Level 1 - Health: 100/100
Inventory: Sword

--- Simulating adventure... ---
Reached Level 3!
New items: Health Potion, Ancient Key
Unlocked 2 achievements!
V Game saved successfully!
  Location: C:\Users\YourName\AppData\Roaming\PrinceOfProgramming\gamesave.json

Your save file is stored at:
C:\Users\YourName\AppData\Roaming\PrinceOfProgramming\gamesave.json

To view it:
1. Press Windows Key + R
2. Type: %appdata%\PrinceOfProgramming
3. Press Enter
```

```
4. Open gamesave.json in Notepad

Restart the program to see your save loaded!
```

Expected Output *(second run)*:

```
V Game loaded successfully!

=== Welcome back, Prince! ===
Level 3 - Health: 75/100
Inventory: Sword, Health Potion, Ancient Key

--- Simulating adventure... ---
Reached Level 3!
New items: Health Potion, Ancient Key
Unlocked 2 achievements!
V Game saved successfully!
  Location: C:\Users\YourName\AppData\Roaming\PrinceOfProgramming\gamesave.json

Your save file is stored at:
C:\Users\YourName\AppData\Roaming\PrinceOfProgramming\gamesave.json

To view it:
1. Press Windows Key + R
2. Type: %appdata%\PrinceOfProgramming
3. Press Enter
4. Open gamesave.json in Notepad

Restart the program to see your save loaded!
```

Note: You might notice that the nice checkmark character you used in the code (✓) doesn't always appear the same in the console. That's because the console uses a different font and won't always display special or extended ASCII characters correctly.

File contents (gamesave.json):

```
{
  "Name": "Prince",
  "Health": 75,
  "MaxHealth": 100,
  "CurrentLevel": 3,
  "Inventory": [
    "Sword",
    "Health Potion",
    "Ancient Key"
  ],
  "UnlockedAchievements": {
    "FirstVictory": true,
    "TreasureHunter": true
  }
}
```

Notice how we wrapped our file operations in `try-catch` blocks? When dealing with files, lots of things can go wrong:

- The disk might be full
- The file might be corrupted

- Another program might be using the file
- The player might delete the save file while the game is running

Always handle these errors gracefully! Nobody likes a program that crashes when loading a file.

 **Pro Tip:**

Many programs create backup save files. When saving, they write to "save_temp.json" first, then if that succeeds, rename it to "save.json". That way, if something goes wrong during saving, you don't lose the player's last good save. The prince would approve of this cautious approach!

Fun Experiment: The Vizier's Magical Archive

Time to build your own save/load system!

The Prince's Journey: Breaking the Vizier's Hold

The story continues...

The Prince climbs the final spiral staircase, his heart pounding with equal parts exhaustion and determination. Stone gives way to marble as he emerges from the dungeon depths into the palace proper. He pushes open the grand doors to the throne room and there sits the Evil Vizier upon the Sultan's seat, those glowing green eyes fixed upon him with ancient malice. The sorcerer rises slowly, a cruel smile spreading across his face. "So, the little prince has finally crawled out of a hole" the Vizier taunts. "But you're too late. While you've been playing in my dungeon, I've woven my magic throughout this entire palace. Every room, every guard, every trap are all under my power, all bound to my will. Even if you strike me down, my enchantments will persist, keeping the Princess imprisoned forever."

The Prince's grip tightens on his sword, but he knows brute force won't win this battle. The Vizier's magic isn't just in the air, it's stored in hidden crystals throughout the throne room, each one preserving a piece of his dark power. If the Prince can identify these magical storage points, if he can systematically save the palace's true state and purge the Vizier's corrupted enchantments, he might break the sorcerer's hold permanently. The Princess's freedom and the entire kingdom's future depends on the Prince's ability to manage not just the battle before him, but the very data of the Vizier's magical network itself.

The Challenge

Create a simple dungeon crawler where you can:

1. Create a `GameState` class that tracks:
   - Player name
   - Player health
   - Current room number
   - Items collected (use a List)
   - Number of enemies defeated
2. Create a menu system where players can:
   - Start a new game
   - Continue from a save
   - Play (simulate moving rooms, collecting items)
   - Save and quit
3. Use JSON serialization to save and load the game state to the AppData folder
4. Add some basic gameplay:
   - Moving to different rooms (increases room number)
   - Finding items (adds to inventory)
   - Defeating enemies (increases count, reduces health a bit)

Bonus challenge:

- Add a feature to export your save as CSV for viewing in Excel

Try to make it work without peeking at the answer below!

Example Answer

Here's one way to solve it:

```csharp
using System;
using System.IO;
using System.Text.Json;
using System.Collections.Generic;

namespace PrinceOfProgramming
{
    class GameState
    {
        public string PlayerName { get; set; }
        public int Health { get; set; }
        public int MaxHealth { get; set; }
        public int CurrentRoom { get; set; }
        public List<string> Inventory { get; set; }
        public int EnemiesDefeated { get; set; }

        public GameState()
        {
            Inventory = new List<string>();
        }
    }
```

```csharp
class DungeonGame
{
    private static readonly string SaveFolder = Path.Combine(
        Environment.GetFolderPath(Environment.SpecialFolder.ApplicationData),
        "DungeonCrawler"
    );
    private static readonly string SaveFile =
        Path.Combine(SaveFolder, "dungeon_save.json");
    private GameState state;

    public void Run()
    {
        Directory.CreateDirectory(SaveFolder); // Make sure folder exists

        while (true)
        {
            ShowMainMenu();
            string choice = Console.ReadLine();

            switch (choice)
            {
                case "1":
                    StartNewGame();
                    break;
                case "2":
                    LoadGame();
                    break;
                case "3":
                    if (state != null)
                        PlayGame();
                    else
                        Console.WriteLine("Start or load a game first!");
                    break;
                case "4":
                    SaveGame();
                    break;
                case "5":
                    ExportToCSV();
                    break;
                case "6":
                    ShowSaveLocation();
                    break;
                case "7":
                    Console.WriteLine("Thanks for playing!");
                    return;
                default:
                    Console.WriteLine("Invalid choice!");
                    break;
            }

            Console.WriteLine("\nPress any key to continue...");
            Console.ReadKey();
            Console.Clear();
        }
    }

    private void ShowMainMenu()
    {
        Console.WriteLine("=== DUNGEON CRAWLER ===");
        Console.WriteLine("1. New Game");
```

```csharp
        Console.WriteLine("2. Load Game");
        Console.WriteLine("3. Play");
        Console.WriteLine("4. Save Game");
        Console.WriteLine("5. Export Stats to CSV");
        Console.WriteLine("6. Show Save Location");
        Console.WriteLine("7. Quit");
        Console.Write("\nChoice: ");
    }

    private void StartNewGame()
    {
        Console.Write("Enter your name, brave adventurer: ");
        string name = Console.ReadLine();

        state = new GameState
        {
            PlayerName = name,
            Health = 100,
            MaxHealth = 100,
            CurrentRoom = 1,
            Inventory = new List<string> { "Rusty Sword" },
            EnemiesDefeated = 0
        };

        Console.WriteLine($"\nWelcome, {name}! Your adventure begins...");
    }

    private void LoadGame()
    {
        if (!File.Exists(SaveFile))
        {
            Console.WriteLine("No save file found!");
            return;
        }

        try
        {
            string json = File.ReadAllText(SaveFile);
            state = JsonSerializer.Deserialize<GameState>(json);
            Console.WriteLine($"Welcome back, {state.PlayerName}!");
        }
        catch (Exception ex)
        {
            Console.WriteLine($"Error loading game: {ex.Message}");
        }
    }

    private void SaveGame()
    {
        if (state == null)
        {
            Console.WriteLine("No game to save!");
            return;
        }

        try
        {
            var options = new JsonSerializerOptions { WriteIndented = true };
            string json = JsonSerializer.Serialize(state, options);
            File.WriteAllText(SaveFile, json);
            Console.WriteLine("✓ Game saved successfully!");
```

```csharp
        }
        catch (Exception ex)
        {
            Console.WriteLine($"✗ Error saving game: {ex.Message}");
        }
    }

    private void ExportToCSV()
    {
        if (state == null)
        {
            Console.WriteLine("No game data to export!");
            return;
        }

        try
        {
            string csvPath = Path.Combine(SaveFolder, "game_stats.csv");
            string[] lines =
            {
                "Stat,Value",
                $"Player Name,{state.PlayerName}",
                $"Health,{state.Health}/{state.MaxHealth}",
                $"Current Room,{state.CurrentRoom}",
                $"Enemies Defeated,{state.EnemiesDefeated}",
                $"Items Collected,{state.Inventory.Count}"
            };

            File.WriteAllLines(csvPath, lines);
            Console.WriteLine("✓ Stats exported to CSV!");
            Console.WriteLine($"  Location: {csvPath}");
            Console.WriteLine("  You can open this in Excel!");
        }
        catch (Exception ex)
        {
            Console.WriteLine($"✗ Error exporting: {ex.Message}");
        }
    }

    private void ShowSaveLocation()
    {
        Console.WriteLine($"\nSave folder: {SaveFolder}");
        Console.WriteLine("\nTo view your files:");
        Console.WriteLine("1. Press Windows Key + R");
        Console.WriteLine("2. Type: %appdata%\\DungeonCrawler");
        Console.WriteLine("3. Press Enter");
    }

    private void PlayGame()
    {
        Console.Clear();
        Console.WriteLine($"=== {state.PlayerName}'s Adventure ===");
        Console.WriteLine($"Health: {state.Health}/{state.MaxHealth}");
        Console.WriteLine($"Room: {state.CurrentRoom}");
        Console.WriteLine($"Enemies Defeated: {state.EnemiesDefeated}");
        Console.WriteLine($"Inventory: {string.Join(", ",
            state.Inventory)}");
        Console.WriteLine();

        Console.WriteLine("1. Move to next room");
        Console.WriteLine("2. Search for items");
```

```csharp
                Console.WriteLine("3. Fight enemy");
                Console.WriteLine("4. Return to menu");
                Console.Write("\nChoice: ");

                string choice = Console.ReadLine();

                switch (choice)
                {
                    case "1":
                        state.CurrentRoom++;
                        Console.WriteLine($"You moved to room {state.CurrentRoom}!");
                        break;
                    case "2":
                        string[] items = { "Health Potion", "Ancient Key", "Gold Coin",
                            "Magic Scroll", "Steel Sword" };
                        Random rand = new Random();
                        string foundItem = items[rand.Next(items.Length)];
                        state.Inventory.Add(foundItem);
                        Console.WriteLine($"You found: {foundItem}!");
                        break;
                    case "3":
                        int damage = new Random().Next(10, 20);
                        state.Health -= damage;
                        state.EnemiesDefeated++;
                        Console.WriteLine($"You defeated an enemy! (Lost {damage} health)");
                        if (state.Health <= 0)
                        {
                            Console.WriteLine("\n💀 You have been defeated! Game Over!");
                            Console.WriteLine("Starting a new game...");
                            state = null;
                        }
                        break;
                    case "4":
                        return;
                }
            }
        }
    }

    class Program
    {
        static void Main(string[] args)
        {
            DungeonGame game = new DungeonGame();
            game.Run();
        }
    }
}
```

Expected Output (*example gameplay*):

```
=== DUNGEON CRAWLER ===
1. New Game
2. Load Game
3. Play
4. Save Game
5. Export Stats to CSV
6. Show Save Location
7. Quit

Choice: 1
```

```
Enter your name, brave adventurer: Hero

Welcome, Hero! Your adventure begins...

Press any key to continue...

=== DUNGEON CRAWLER ===
1. New Game
2. Load Game
3. Play
4. Save Game
5. Export Stats to CSV
6. Show Save Location
7. Quit

Choice: 3

=== Hero's Adventure ===
Health: 100/100
Room: 1
Enemies Defeated: 0
Inventory: Rusty Sword

1. Move to next room
2. Search for items
3. Fight enemy
4. Return to menu

Choice: 2
You found: Magic Scroll!

Press any key to continue...

=== DUNGEON CRAWLER ===
1. New Game
2. Load Game
3. Play
4. Save Game
5. Export Stats to CSV
6. Show Save Location
7. Quit

Choice: 4
V Game saved successfully!

Press any key to continue...

=== DUNGEON CRAWLER ===
1. New Game
2. Load Game
3. Play
4. Save Game
5. Export Stats to CSV
6. Show Save Location
7. Quit

Choice: 5
V Stats exported to CSV!
  Location: C:\Users\YourName\AppData\Roaming\DungeonCrawler\game_stats.csv
  You can open this in Excel!
```

File contents (dungeon_save.json):

```json
json
{
  "PlayerName": "Hero",
  "Health": 100,
  "MaxHealth": 100,
  "CurrentRoom": 1,
  "Inventory": [
    "Rusty Sword",
    "Magic Scroll"
  ],
  "EnemiesDefeated": 0
}
```

File contents (game_stats.csv):

```
Stat,Value
Player Name,Hero
Health,100/100
Current Room,1
Enemies Defeated,0
Items Collected,2
```

Wrap-up: What You've Learned

You've just learned how to make your programs remember things!

Key Takeaways

- **File locations matter.** Don't just save files anywhere, use the AppData folder on Windows so your saves are in the right place and users have permission to write there. Use `Path.Combine()` to build paths correctly across different operating systems.
- **Basic File I/O** lets you quickly save and load text files using the `File` class. Methods like `WriteAllText()`, `ReadAllText()`, `Exists()`, and `WriteAllLines()` handle simple file operations with ease.
- **Different formats serve different purposes.** Plain text for logs, CSV for tabular data, JSON for structured objects, and XML when you need it for legacy systems. Each has its place.
- **Serialization** is how you turn objects into savable data and back again. Instead of manually converting each property to text, serialization handles it automatically. JSON is your best friend here. It's flexible, readable, and used by most modern games.
- **Binary vs readable formats** are a choice between convenience and obscurity. Readable formats (especially JSON) make debugging easier, allow manual edits, and are the modern standard. Binary formats are more compact but harder to work with and debug. Start with JSON unless you have a specific reason not to.

- **Error handling** is crucial with files. Always use `try-catch` blocks and check if files exist before loading them. Disk full errors, permission issues, and corrupted files can all happen. Handle them gracefully so your program doesn't crash!

Next time you save something in any program, you'll know exactly what's happening behind the scenes, objects being serialized, JSON being formatted, files being written and all those details being preserved for your next session!

Chapter 12

Principals

"Simplicity is the ultimate sophistication." — Leonardo da Vinci

You've been coding for a while now, and you can probably build some pretty cool stuff. But, knowing *how* to code and knowing how to code *well* are two very different beasts. It's like the difference between being able to draw stick figures and being able to create art that people actually want to look at. Every experienced programmer has horror stories about coming back to their own code six months later and wondering what possessed them to write it that way. The principles in this chapter are the accumulated wisdom of programmers who learned the hard way, so you don't have to. These aren't abstract academic concepts, they're practical guidelines that companies like Spotify, Netflix, and even NASA use to keep their massive codebases from turning into unmaintainable nightmares.

Think about the apps you use every day like Discord, YouTube and TikTok. Behind the scenes, thousands of programmers work on these simultaneously, changing and improving code constantly. If everyone just wrote code however they felt like, the whole thing would collapse into chaos within weeks. The principles you're about to learn are what allow teams to collaborate effectively, make changes without breaking everything, and keep software maintainable over years or even decades. Master these, and you'll write code that your future self will actually thank you for. Ignore them, and you'll be that programmer debugging their own mess at 2 AM, wondering where it all went wrong.

Core Concepts Covered

- ✓ Writing reusable code that can be used in multiple places without duplication
- ✓ Keeping code simple and understandable rather than overly complex
- ✓ Focusing on current needs instead of building for hypothetical future requirements
- ✓ Organizing code so different responsibilities are handled by different parts
- ✓ Making informed decisions about when and how to optimize performance
- ✓ Objects that interact cleanly without depending on each other's internal details

The Laws of Not Regretting Your Code

 **Trivia:**

The "80/20 rule" states that roughly 80% of effects come from 20% of causes. Economist Vilfredo Pareto discovered this in 1896 noticing 80% of Italy's land belonged to 20% of the population. Microsoft found that fixing the top 20% of most-reported bugs eliminated 80% of complaints. In programming focus on the 20% of features that provide 80% of value, not perfecting everything equally.

Okay, we've learned a TON so far. You can create variables, write loops, build classes, handle events, you're basically a coding wizard at this point! But, yes there's a "but", just because you *can* write code doesn't mean you should write it like a caffeinated squirrel on a keyboard.

This chapter contains a few of my favorite **coding principles**, the ancient wisdom passed down from programmers who learned the hard way (by staying up until 3 AM trying to fix bugs in their spaghetti code). These aren't strict rules that'll blow up your computer if you break them. They're more like guidelines that'll save you from future headaches and make your code actually enjoyable to work with.

Think of them as the difference between a well-organized level for our Prince where you can see the traps and plan your moves, versus a chaotic mess where spikes pop out randomly and you die for no reason. Let's learn how to build the good kind!

DRY (Don't Repeat Yourself)

What it means: If you're copying and pasting the same code in multiple places, you're doing it wrong. That's what DRY is all about, write it once, use it everywhere.

Why it matters: Imagine you're coding the Prince's sword attack. You write the damage calculation in 5 different places throughout your game. Then you realize the damage is too high and needs to be reduced. Now you have to find and change ALL 5 places. Miss one?

Congrats, your game now has inconsistent damage that'll confuse players and drive you nuts during testing.

How to use it: When you notice you're writing similar code multiple times, stop! Create a method or a class that does that thing, then call it whenever you need it.

 **Bad Code** (WET - Write Everything Twice... or more):

```csharp
// In enemy fight scene
int damage = playerStrength * 2 + weaponBonus;
enemyHealth -= damage;
Console.WriteLine($"You dealt {damage} damage!");

// In boss fight scene
int damage = playerStrength * 2 + weaponBonus;
bossHealth -= damage;
Console.WriteLine($"You dealt {damage} damage!");

// In training room scene
int damage = playerStrength * 2 + weaponBonus;
dummyHealth -= damage;
Console.WriteLine($"You dealt {damage} damage!");
```

See how we wrote the same damage calculation three times? Now if we want to change the formula, we need to change it in three places. Yuck.

 **Good Code** (DRY):

```csharp
public class Combat
{
    public static int CalculateDamage(int strength, int weaponBonus)
    {
        return strength * 2 + weaponBonus;
    }

    public static void DealDamage(ref int targetHealth, int damage)
    {
        targetHealth -= damage;
        Console.WriteLine($"You dealt {damage} damage!");
    }
}

// In enemy fight scene
int damage = Combat.CalculateDamage(playerStrength, weaponBonus);
Combat.DealDamage(ref enemyHealth, damage);

// In boss fight scene
int damage = Combat.CalculateDamage(playerStrength, weaponBonus);
Combat.DealDamage(ref bossHealth, damage);

// In training room scene
int damage = Combat.CalculateDamage(playerStrength, weaponBonus);
Combat.DealDamage(ref dummyHealth, damage);
```

Now if we need to change the damage formula, we change it in ONE place and it updates everywhere. Beautiful!

> **Pro Tip:**
>
> The opposite of DRY is sometimes jokingly called WET (Write Everything Twice, or We Enjoy Typing, or Waste Everyone's Time). Avoid being WET, it's not as fun as it sounds

KISS (Keep It Simple, Stupid)

What it means: Don't overcomplicate things. If there's a simple solution and a complex solution, pick the simple one. Your future self (and anyone else reading your code) will thank you.

Why it matters: In our Prince adventure when you need to jump across a gap, you just... jump. You do not want the game to ask the wind speed, adjust for your character's mood, and perform a triple back flip. Simple is better. The same goes for code, complexity should only exist when it's absolutely necessary.

How to use it: Before writing complicated code, ask yourself: "Is there a simpler way to do this?" If you're writing a method that's 200 lines long with nested loops inside nested if statements inside a switch statement... you've probably lost the plot.

Bad Code (Way too complex):

```csharp
public class DoorController
{
    public void ProcessDoorInteraction(bool hasKey, bool isDoorLocked,
        bool isDoorOpen, int playerLevel, string playerClass,
        bool isNightTime, double doorDurability, bool isBossDoor)
    {
        if (!isDoorOpen)
        {
            if (isDoorLocked)
            {
                if (hasKey)
                {
                    if (playerLevel >= 5 || playerClass == "Thief")
                    {
                        if (!isBossDoor || (isBossDoor && playerLevel >= 10))
                        {
                            if (isNightTime)
                            {
                                if (doorDurability > 50)
                                {
                                    Console.WriteLine(
                                        "The door creaks open in the darkness...");
                                    isDoorOpen = true;
                                }
                                else
                                {
                                    Console.WriteLine(
                                        "The old door falls apart as you unlock it.");
```

```
                        isDoorOpen = true;
                    }
                }
                else
                {
                    Console.WriteLine("The door opens.");
                    isDoorOpen = true;
                }
            }
            else
            {
                Console.WriteLine(
                    "You need to be level 10 to open this boss door!");
            }
        }
        else
        {
            Console.WriteLine(
                "You're not skilled enough to use this key.");
        }
    }
    else
    {
        Console.WriteLine("The door is locked. You need a key!");
    }
}
else
{
    Console.WriteLine("The door swings open easily.");
    isDoorOpen = true;
}
    }
    else
    {
        Console.WriteLine("The door is already open.");
    }
    }
}
```

This is a nightmare! Good luck figuring out what's happening here when you need to fix a bug at 11 PM.

🧹 Good Code (KISS):

```
public class DoorController
{
    public void OpenDoor(Door door, Player player)
    {
        if (door.IsOpen)
        {
            Console.WriteLine("The door is already open.");
            return;
        }

        if (!door.CanBeOpenedBy(player))
        {
            Console.WriteLine(door.GetLockMessage());
            return;
        }
```

```
        door.Open();
        Console.WriteLine(door.GetOpenMessage());
    }
}
```

Much simpler! We moved the complex logic into the `Door` and `Player` classes where it belongs, and this method just coordinates the interaction. Easy to read, easy to understand, easy to fix if something breaks.

> **Pro Tip:**
>
> Complexity should be a last resort, not your first choice. Start simple, and only add complexity when you absolutely need it. You can always make something more complex later, simplifying complex code is WAY harder.

YAGNI (You Aren't Gonna Need It)

What it means: Don't write code for features you *might* need someday. Write code for what you need *right now*. Future-you can handle future problems.

Why it matters: When Jordan Mechner was making Prince of Persia, he didn't add a multiplayer mode, a crafting system, and a pet dragon just because they *might* be cool someday. He focused on making a tight single-player experience. That focus made the game great. Same with code, every extra feature you add is more code to maintain, more bugs to fix, and more complexity to navigate.

How to use it: When you're tempted to add "just in case" features, ask yourself: "Do I need this RIGHT NOW for what I'm building?" If the answer is no, **don't add it**. You can always add it later if you actually need it.

Bad Code (Over-engineering):

```
public class Player
{
    public string Name { get; set; }
    public int Health { get; set; }
    public int Mana { get; set; }  // We don't have magic yet, but maybe someday?
    public int Stamina { get; set; }  // Not using this, but it might be cool?
    public int Hunger { get; set; }  // Survival mode? Who knows!
    public int Thirst { get; set; }  // Gotta drink water, right?
    public int Reputation { get; set; }  // For the dialogue system we haven't built
    public List<Pet> Pets { get; set; }  // Pets would be awesome eventually!
    public Dictionary<string, int> RelationshipValues { get; set; }  // Romance system?
    public int CraftingLevel { get; set; }  // Maybe we'll add crafting?

    // ... 50 more properties for features that don't exist yet
}
```

This is YAGNI violation central. You're building a simple game where the Prince runs and jumps, but your player class is ready for a full-blown RPG with dating sim elements. All this extra code is just baggage that makes your project harder to understand and maintain.

 **Good Code** (Just what we need):

```
public class Player
{
    public string Name { get; set; }
    public int Health { get; set; }
    public int X { get; set; }  // Position
    public int Y { get; set; }

    public void TakeDamage(int amount)
    {
        Health -= amount;
    }

    public void Move(int deltaX, int deltaY)
    {
        X += deltaX;
        Y += deltaY;
    }
}
```

Clean, simple, and it does exactly what we need for our game right now. If we decide to add magic later, we can add a Mana property then. But for now? We don't need it.

Why not using YAGNI is bad: Every line of unused code is a liability. It makes your codebase bigger and harder to understand. Worse, you might end up maintaining and refactoring code that you never even use! It's like carrying around a backpack full of "just in case" items on a hike, you'll just get tired.

 **Pro Tip:**

In Undertale, Toby Fox famously cut features constantly during development, keeping only what made the game better. He even removed entire battle mechanics that weren't fun. That ruthless focus made the game incredible. Be like Toby, cut what you don't need.

SoC (Separation of Concerns)

What it means: Different parts of your code should handle different things. Keep your logic separate from your graphics code. Keep your combat system separate from your inventory system. Don't mix everything together into one big tangled mess.

Why it matters: In Wolfenstein 3D, the game separated the maze logic from the enemy AI from the graphics rendering? This made it possible to work on each part independently. If everything was mixed together, fixing a bug in enemy AI might accidentally break the walls. That's what happens when you don't separate concerns, chaos.

How to use it: Organize your code so that each class or method has ONE job and does it well. If a class is handling player input, graphics rendering, sound effects, game logic, and saving to files all at once... you've got a problem.

 **Bad Code** (Everything mixed together):

```csharp
public class Game
{
    public void PlayLevel()
    {
        int playerHealth = 100;
        int enemyHealth = 50;

        while (playerHealth > 0 && enemyHealth > 0)
        {
            // Input, logic, display, and sound all mixed together
            Console.Write("(A)ttack or (H)eal? ");
            string input = Console.ReadLine();

            if (input == "A")
            {
                enemyHealth -= 10;
                Console.WriteLine($"You attack! Enemy health: {enemyHealth}");
                Console.Beep(880, 200);

                // Enemy counter-attack mixed in
                playerHealth -= 5;
                Console.WriteLine($"Enemy hits back! Your health: {playerHealth}");

                // Save game mixed in
                System.IO.File.WriteAllText("save.txt", $"{playerHealth}," +
                    $"{enemyHealth}");
            }
            else if (input == "H")
            {
                playerHealth += 20;
                Console.WriteLine($"You heal! Your health: {playerHealth}");
            }
        }

        Console.WriteLine(playerHealth > 0 ? "YOU WIN!" : "GAME OVER");
    }
}
```

This is a nightmare. Input handling, game logic, graphics, sound, saving it's all jumbled together. If you want to change how combat works, you have to wade through display code and input handling. If you want to improve the graphics, you might accidentally break the combat logic. No bueno.

 **Good Code** (Separated concerns):

```csharp
public class Combat
{
```

```csharp
    public static void PerformAttack(Player attacker, Enemy target, int damage)
    {
        target.TakeDamage(damage);
        Console.WriteLine($"You attack! Enemy health: {target.Health}");
    }

    public static void PerformCounterAttack(Enemy attacker, Player target, int damage)
    {
        target.TakeDamage(damage);
        Console.WriteLine($"Enemy hits back! Your health: {target.Health}");
    }
}

public class Player
{
    public int Health { get; set; }

    public void Heal(int amount)
    {
        Health += amount;
        Console.WriteLine($"You heal! Your health: {Health}");
    }

    public void TakeDamage(int amount)
    {
        Health -= amount;
    }
}

public class Enemy
{
    public int Health { get; set; }

    public void TakeDamage(int amount)
    {
        Health -= amount;
    }
}

public class GameDisplay
{
    public static void ShowVictory()
    {
        Console.WriteLine("YOU WIN!");
    }

    public static void ShowDefeat()
    {
        Console.WriteLine("GAME OVER");
    }
}

public class Game
{
    private Player player = new Player { Health = 100 };
    private Enemy enemy = new Enemy { Health = 50 };

    public void PlayLevel()
    {
        while (player.Health > 0 && enemy.Health > 0)
        {
```

```csharp
            Console.Write("(A)ttack or (H)eal? ");
            string input = Console.ReadLine()?.ToUpper();

            if (input == "A")
            {
                Combat.PerformAttack(player, enemy, 10);

                if (enemy.Health > 0)
                {
                    Combat.PerformCounterAttack(enemy, player, 5);
                }
            }
            else if (input == "H")
            {
                player.Heal(20);
            }
        }

        if (player.Health > 0)
            GameDisplay.ShowVictory();
        else
            GameDisplay.ShowDefeat();
    }

    static void Main()
    {
        Game game = new Game();
        game.PlayLevel();
    }
}
```

Expected Output:

```
(A)ttack or (H)eal? a
You attack! Enemy health: 40
Enemy hits back! Your health: 95
(A)ttack or (H)eal? a
You attack! Enemy health: 30
Enemy hits back! Your health: 90
(A)ttack or (H)eal? h
You heal! Your health: 110
(A)ttack or (H)eal? a
You attack! Enemy health: 20
Enemy hits back! Your health: 105
(A)ttack or (H)eal? a
You attack! Enemy health: 10
Enemy hits back! Your health: 100
(A)ttack or (H)eal? a
You attack! Enemy health: 0
YOU WIN!
```

Now each class has ONE job:

- **Player** manages player state and actions
- **Enemy** manages enemy state and actions
- **Combat** handles combat calculations
- **GameDisplay** handles showing things on screen
- **Game** coordinates everything

Want to change how combat works? Look at `Combat` or the character classes. Want to improve the graphics? Look at `GameDisplay`. Everything has its place!

 **Pro Tip:**

In Star Control II, the developers separated the space exploration, ship combat, and dialogue systems into distinct parts. This made it easier to improve each system independently without breaking the others. Good separation of concerns is like good city planning in SimCity where each zone handles its own business.

Premature Optimization

What it means: "Premature optimization is the root of all evil" is a famous quote by Donald Knuth. It means: don't spend hours optimizing code to be super-fast before you even know if it's slow. Make it work first, THEN make it fast (if needed).

Why it matters: When writing any application or game the developer starts by getting the UI or animation working first, then optimized it. Don't start by trying to optimize UI or animation code that don't exist yet. That would be bonkers. Same with your code, write it clearly first, measure performance, then optimize the parts that are actually slow.

How to use it: Write clear, working code first. If it's too slow (and you've actually tested this, not just guessed), THEN optimize. Most of the time, your code will be fast enough. And when it isn't, you'll know exactly where the bottleneck is.

 **Bad Code** (Premature optimization):

```csharp
// Trying to be "clever" and fast before we even know if this is slow
public class GameMap
{
    // Using a complex data structure to optimize lookups
    private Dictionary<long, Tile> tileMap = new Dictionary<long, Tile>();

    public void SetTile(int x, int y, Tile tile)
    {
        // Encoding x and y into a single long for "faster lookups"
        long key = ((long)x << 32) | (long)y;
        tileMap[key] = tile;
    }

    public Tile GetTile(int x, int y)
    {
        // Decoding the key
        long key = ((long)x << 32) | (long)y;
        return tileMap.ContainsKey(key) ? tileMap[key] : null;
    }
}
```

This code is trying to be clever with bit-shifting and encoding coordinates into a single key. But for a small game map, this complexity is pointless! A simple 2D array would be clearer and probably just as fast (or even faster).

 **Good Code** (Clear first):

```csharp
public class GameMap
{
    private Tile[,] tiles;

    public GameMap(int width, int height)
    {
        tiles = new Tile[width, height];
    }

    public void SetTile(int x, int y, Tile tile)
    {
        tiles[x, y] = tile;
    }

    public Tile GetTile(int x, int y)
    {
        return tiles[x, y];
    }
}
```

Simple, clear, and easy to understand. If you later discover that this is too slow (which is unlikely), THEN you can optimize. But chances are, this will be plenty fast for your needs.

Why not using this principle is bad: You waste time making code complex for no reason. Worse, the "optimized" code is often harder to read and maintain. And sometimes your "optimization" doesn't even make things faster, it just makes them more confusing. Profile first, optimize second.

 **Pro Tip:**

Modern C# is already really fast. Unless you're processing millions of items or running complex physics calculations, your code is probably fine. Don't stress about micro-optimizations until you've actually measured and found a problem. Your time is better spent making your program work!

Principle of Least Knowledge (Law of Demeter)

What it means: Objects should only talk to their immediate friends, not friends of friends. Or in less weird terms, a method should only call methods on objects it directly knows about, not dig through chains of objects.

Why it matters: Think about ordering a pizza. You call the pizza place and tell them what you want. You don't call the pizza place, ask to speak to the chef, ask the chef for the number of the flour supplier, call the flour supplier to verify they have flour, then call the cheese supplier to check their inventory, and so on. That would be insane! You just tell the pizza place your order and trust them to handle all the details internally. Same with code, objects should handle their own internal business and only expose what others actually need to know.

How to use it: If you find yourself writing code like `game.World.Level.Player.Inventory.Items[0].Stats.Durability`, you're violating this principle. That's a chain of calls going through multiple objects, which means your code depends on the internal structure of all those objects. If any part of that chain changes, your code breaks.

 **Bad Code** (Digging through objects):

```csharp
public class Game
{
    public World World { get; set; }
}

public class World
{
    public Level CurrentLevel { get; set; }
}

public class Level
{
    public Player Player { get; set; }
}

public class Player
{
    public Inventory Inventory { get; set; }
    public int X { get; set; }
    public int Y { get; set; }
}

public class Inventory
{
    public List<Item> Items { get; set; }
}

// Meanwhile, somewhere else in the code...
public class EnemyAI
{
    public void ChasePlayer(Game game)
    {
        // Digging through multiple objects - BAD!
        int playerX = game.World.CurrentLevel.Player.X;
        int playerY = game.World.CurrentLevel.Player.Y;

        // Also checking player's items - BAD!
        if (game.World.CurrentLevel.Player.Inventory.Items.Count > 5)
        {
            Console.WriteLine("Player has lots of items! Attack!");
        }
```

```
        Console.WriteLine($"Chasing player at ({playerX}, {playerY})");
    }
}
```

This is a mess. The EnemyAI needs to know about Game, World, Level, Player, and Inventory just to get the player's position. If any of these change, the enemy AI breaks. Plus, the enemy AI shouldn't care about how the game is structured, it should just know about the player directly.

 **Good Code** (Direct communication):

```
public class Player
{
    public int X { get; set; }
    public int Y { get; set; }
    private Inventory inventory;

    public int GetItemCount()
    {
        return inventory.Items.Count;
    }

    public (int x, int y) GetPosition()
    {
        return (X, Y);
    }
}

public class EnemyAI
{
    private Player targetPlayer;

    public EnemyAI(Player player)
    {
        targetPlayer = player;
    }

    public void ChasePlayer()
    {
        // Direct access to what we need
        var (x, y) = targetPlayer.GetPosition();

        if (targetPlayer.GetItemCount() > 5)
        {
            Console.WriteLine("Player has lots of items! Attack!");
        }

        Console.WriteLine($"Chasing player at ({x}, {y})");
    }
}
```

Now the EnemyAI only knows about the Player object directly. It doesn't need to know about Game, World, or Level. The Player provides methods to get the information needed, hiding its internal structure. Much cleaner!

Why not using this principle is bad: Your code becomes fragile and tightly coupled. When you change one part, you might break things in completely unrelated parts because they were digging through your objects. It's like a house of cards, touch one, and the whole thing collapses.

 **Pro Tip:**

If you're using more than one or two dots in a chain (like `object.property.property.method()`), you're probably violating this principle. Ask yourself: "Should this code really know about all these intermediate objects?" Usually the answer is no.

Fun Experiment: Refactoring the Vizier's Spell

Time to put these principles into practice! You're going to refactor some messy code.

The Prince's Journey: Wisdom from the Journey

And now the conclusion…

The Prince's sword clatters to the marble floor as the final magical crystal shatters, its green light fading to nothing. The Vizier, stripped of his power, stumbles backward with a howl of rage before being pulled into a swirling vortex, banished to the very dungeon he created, perhaps to face his own deadly traps for eternity. The throne room falls silent except for the crackling of torches. The Prince stands there, breathing hard, realizing that what defeated the Vizier wasn't just courage or swordplay. It was understanding. Understanding how the magic worked, how the systems connected, how to break down an overwhelming problem into manageable pieces. Every principle he learned in that dungeon, keeping solutions simple, avoiding unnecessary complexity, separating concerns had been essential to unraveling the Vizier's intricate web of enchantments.

The Prince finally enters the Princess's chambers, the warm glow of torchlight dancing across the ornate walls. The kingdom is saved. The Princess embraces him, her eyes shining with relief and joy. But as the Prince holds her close, he finds himself reflecting on everything that brought him to this moment. It wasn't just his physical skills that saved them, it was the wisdom he gained along the way. In the dungeon's darkness, he discovered that rushing ahead without thinking led to deadly mistakes. He learned that complex solutions often failed where simple, clear thinking succeeded. He realized that preparing for every possible future trap only weighed him down, while focusing on the immediate challenge kept him alive. The Princess pulls back slightly, studying his face. "You've changed," she says softly. "You're wiser now." The Prince smiles and nods, understanding that before they can truly move forward together, before they can rebuild what the Vizier nearly destroyed, he must organize these hard-won lessons. Not just for himself, but for anyone who might one day face similar trials. Perhaps even for the guards and architects who will redesign the dungeon's defenses to protect the kingdom.

Later that night he reaches for parchment and ink, ready to document the principles that guided him from despair to victory, the wisdom that turned a trapped prince into a survivor, and a survivor into a hero. But as he begins to write, a distant rumble echoes from somewhere deep beneath the palace. The Princess's hand tightens on his arm, and they exchange a knowing glance. The Vizier's dungeon still exists, and who knows what other secrets or threats might be lurking in its depths? For now, though, they are together and safe. The Prince smiles and returns to his writing. Whatever challenges tomorrow might bring, he'll be ready. After all, he's learned the most important principle of all: the journey of learning never truly ends.

The Challenge

Below is a piece of code that violates multiple principles we've learned. Identify which principles are being violated and rewrite it to be better. The code simulates a simple treasure chest system.

Messy Code:

```csharp
public class Game
{
    public void OpenChest(int chestX, int chestY, int playerX, int playerY,
        bool hasKey, int playerGold, int playerLevel)
    {
        // Check if player is close enough
        if (Math.Abs(chestX - playerX) <= 1 && Math.Abs(chestY - playerY) <= 1)
        {
            // Calculate treasure value
            int treasureGold = playerLevel * 10;
            int treasureSilver = playerLevel * 5;
            int treasureTotal = treasureGold + treasureSilver;

            // Calculate bonus for having key
            if (hasKey)
            {
                int keyBonus = treasureTotal / 2;
                treasureTotal += keyBonus;
            }

            // Add treasure to player
            playerGold += treasureTotal;

            // Display results
            Console.WriteLine("You open the chest!");
            Console.WriteLine($"You found {treasureGold} gold and " +
                $"{treasureSilver} silver!");
            if (hasKey)
            {
                Console.WriteLine("Your key gave you a bonus!");
            }
            Console.WriteLine($"Total value: {treasureTotal}");
            Console.WriteLine($"Your gold: {playerGold}");

            // Maybe add more treasure types later?
            int treasureDiamonds = 0;
            int treasureRubies = 0;
            int treasureEmeralds = 0;
```

```
            // Save the game
            System.IO.File.WriteAllText("save.txt", $"Gold:{playerGold}");
        }
        else
        {
            Console.WriteLine("You're too far from the chest!");
        }
    }
}
```

Questions:

1. Which principles does this code violate?
2. How would you refactor it to be better?

Try finding the problems yourself first!

Example Answer:

This code violates several principles:

1. **KISS** - The method is too complex and does too many things
2. **SoC** - Game logic, calculation, display, and file saving are all mixed together
3. **YAGNI** - Diamonds, rubies, and emeralds variables that aren't used
4. **DRY** - While not shown, if this treasure calculation is used elsewhere, we'd be repeating it

Here's a better version:

```
public class Position
{
    public int X { get; set; }
    public int Y { get; set; }

    public bool IsAdjacentTo(Position other)
    {
        return Math.Abs(X - other.X) <= 1 && Math.Abs(Y - other.Y) <= 1;
    }
}

public class Treasure
{
    public int Gold { get; set; }
    public int Silver { get; set; }

    public int GetTotalValue()
    {
        return Gold + Silver;
    }

    public void ApplyKeyBonus()
    {
        int bonus = GetTotalValue() / 2;
        Gold += bonus;
    }
}
```

```csharp
public class Player
{
    public Position Position { get; set; }
    public int Gold { get; set; }
    public bool HasKey { get; set; }

    public void AddGold(int amount)
    {
        Gold += amount;
    }
}

public class TreasureCalculator
{
    public static Treasure CalculateTreasure(int playerLevel, bool hasKey)
    {
        var treasure = new Treasure
        {
            Gold = playerLevel * 10,
            Silver = playerLevel * 5
        };

        if (hasKey)
        {
            treasure.ApplyKeyBonus();
        }

        return treasure;
    }
}

public class Display
{
    public static void ShowTreasureFound(Treasure treasure, bool hadKeyBonus)
    {
        Console.WriteLine("You open the chest!");
        Console.WriteLine($"You found {treasure.Gold} gold and " +
            $"{treasure.Silver} silver!");

        if (hadKeyBonus)
        {
            Console.WriteLine("Your key gave you a bonus!");
        }

        Console.WriteLine($"Total value: {treasure.GetTotalValue()}");
    }

    public static void ShowPlayerStatus(Player player)
    {
        Console.WriteLine($"Your gold: {player.Gold}");
    }

    public static void ShowTooFarMessage()
    {
        Console.WriteLine("You're too far from the chest!");
    }
}

public class SaveSystem
{
```

```csharp
    public static void SavePlayerProgress(Player player)
    {
        System.IO.File.WriteAllText("save.txt", $"Gold:{player.Gold}");
    }
}

public class ChestSystem
{
    public void OpenChest(Position chestPosition, Player player, int playerLevel)
    {
        if (!player.Position.IsAdjacentTo(chestPosition))
        {
            Display.ShowTooFarMessage();
            return;
        }

        Treasure treasure = TreasureCalculator.CalculateTreasure(playerLevel,
            player.HasKey);
        player.AddGold(treasure.GetTotalValue());

        Display.ShowTreasureFound(treasure, player.HasKey);
        Display.ShowPlayerStatus(player);

        SaveSystem.SavePlayerProgress(player);
    }
}
```

Usage Example:

```csharp
var player = new Player
{
    Position = new Position { X = 5, Y = 5 },
    Gold = 100,
    HasKey = true
};

var chestPos = new Position { X = 5, Y = 6 };
var chestSystem = new ChestSystem();
chestSystem.OpenChest(chestPos, player, 5);
```

Expected Output:

```
You open the chest!
You found 87 gold and 25 silver!
Your key gave you a bonus!
Total value: 112
Your gold: 212
```

Much better! Now:

- Each class has ONE responsibility (SoC)
- No unused variables (YAGNI)
- Code is simpler and easier to understand (KISS)
- Treasure calculation is in one place and can be reused (DRY)
- Classes only interact with what they need to know about (Least Knowledge)

Wrap-up: What You've Learned

Coding principles aren't just arbitrary rules made up by grumpy programmers, they're lessons learned from decades of people writing code, maintaining code, and fixing broken code at 2 AM while regretting their life choices. I probably would have more hair left if I knew this when I started programming.

Key Takeaways

- **DRY** keeps you from copy-pasting the same code everywhere. Write it once, use it everywhere, change it in one place.
- **KISS** reminds you that simple is better than clever. Your future self will thank you for writing code that's easy to understand.
- **YAGNI** stops you from building features you don't need yet. Focus on what matters now, not what might maybe possibly matter someday.
- **SoC** keeps different parts of your code separate. Game logic, graphics, sound, input, etc. They should all mind its own business.
- **Premature Optimization** warns you not to waste time making code fast before you even know if it's slow. Make it work, then make it fast (if needed).
- **Least Knowledge** teaches your code to only talk to its direct friends, not dig through chains of objects.

These principles overlap and reinforce each other. Following one often helps you follow others naturally. And while they're not hard rules that you'll get arrested for breaking, they'll make your coding life SO much easier.

Remember, the best code isn't the cleverest code, it's the code that's easy to read, easy to change, and easy to maintain. That's what these principles are all about.

Now go forth and write code that doesn't make future-you want to travel back in time and slap past-you!

Debugging

"If debugging is the process of removing bugs, then programming must be the process of putting them in." — Edsger Dijkstra

When your code doesn't work the way you expect, you enter the world of debugging, one of the most critical skills in all of programming. Every software system ever created, from the apps on your phone to the operating systems running hospitals and airports, has been debugged extensively. Netflix engineers debug streaming issues that affect millions of viewers. NASA programmers debug spacecraft code where a single error could end a billion-dollar mission. Game developers debug collision systems, AI behavior, and rendering pipelines. No matter what kind of software you build, you'll spend a significant portion of your time investigating why things aren't working and fixing them.

Debugging isn't just about finding typos or syntax errors; it's about developing a systematic approach to understanding what your code is actually doing versus what you think it's doing. Professional developers use a combination of tools and techniques, pausing execution to inspect program state, tracking variables as they change, measuring performance to find bottlenecks, and maintaining detailed logs to investigate issues that happened in the past. Learning to debug effectively transforms you from someone who gets frustrated when code breaks to someone who can methodically track down any problem. This appendix serves as your reference guide for these essential techniques, whether you're debugging your first program or investigating a complex issue in a system you've built.

<h3 align="center">Core Concepts Covered</h3>

- ✓ Setting breakpoints to pause and inspect running code
- ✓ Stepping through code execution line by line to understand program flow
- ✓ Inspecting and monitoring variable values during execution
- ✓ Modifying code during debugging sessions to test fixes immediately
- ✓ Measuring code performance to identify slow sections
- ✓ Effective logs for tracking program behavior and diagnosing production issues
- ✓ Developing a systematic, scientific approach to isolating and resolving problems

Figuring Out Why It Doesn't Work

 **Trivia:**

During the Manhattan Project, physicists' calculations couldn't determine if their first atomic bomb test would work properly or accidentally ignite the atmosphere and destroy all life on Earth. They couldn't test it safely; the only test WAS the real test. Physicist Enrico Fermi jokingly took bets on the outcome. Modern programmers can test code in safe "sandbox" environments, but imagine debugging when testing might end the world.

Welcome to the debugging appendix! If you're reading this, you're either:

1. Working through the book systematically and want to learn about debugging before you need it (smart move!)
2. Something in your code isn't working and you need help figuring out why (we've all been there!)
3. You've finished the main chapters and are ready to learn the professional techniques for hunting down bugs

No matter which category you're in, you're in the right place. This appendix is designed to be your reference guide whenever you encounter problems with your code. You can read it front-to-back, or jump directly to the section that addresses your current issue, whatever works best for you.

If you haven't encountered any bugs yet in your learning journey, don't worry. You will. And when you do, come back here. These techniques will make much more sense when you have an actual problem to solve.

The Bug Hunt Begins

Let's talk about debugging. No, not the act of removing actual insects from your computer (although that did happen to early computers in the 1940's a moth got stuck in a relay and coined the term "computer bug"). Debugging is the process of finding and fixing errors in your code. And trust me, you're going to be doing a LOT of it.

Here's the truth, writing code is maybe 30% of programming. The other 70% is figuring out why your code doesn't work, even though you're ABSOLUTELY SURE it should. It's like when the Prince falls through a floor tile you were certain was solid, you know something's wrong, you just need to figure out what.

Think of debugging like being a detective in your own crime scene, except you're both the detective AND the criminal. You wrote the code that's misbehaving, and now you need to track down exactly where you messed up.

Blaming the Computer (Then Yourself)

Debugging is the systematic process of identifying, analyzing, and removing errors (bugs) from your code.

These bugs can be:

- **Syntax errors**: You wrote something the compiler doesn't understand (like writing "foreac" instead of "foreach")
- **Runtime errors**: Your code compiles fine but crashes when it runs (like trying to divide by zero)
- **Logic errors**: Your code runs without crashing, but it doesn't do what you want (the Prince jumps left when you press right)

The first two types are annoying but usually easy to find. The third type? That's the nightmare. That's when your code runs perfectly fine according to the computer, but produces completely wrong results. It's like programming the Prince to run away from the exit instead of toward it.

Breakpoints: Your Time-Stopping Power

Remember in a game where you could quick-save before attempting a hard battle so you can retry until you succeed? Breakpoints are kind of like that, except instead of saving your game, you're freezing time in your code.

A **breakpoint** is a marker you place in your code that tells the debugger: "Hey, when you get to this line, STOP EVERYTHING." The program will pause right before executing that line, and you can examine what's happening. You can check the values of all your variables, see what methods have been called, and basically investigate the crime scene while everything is frozen in time.

Here's how breakpoints help you:

1. **Pause execution**: Your program stops running at exactly the line you marked
2. **Inspect variables**: You can see the current value of every variable in scope
3. **Control flow**: You decide when to continue, step forward, or jump around

Think of it like this, when our Prince are about to jump across a spike pit, wouldn't it be awesome if you could freeze time, float over to check if you're going to make it, see exactly where your feet will land, and then decide whether to proceed? That's what breakpoints do for your code.

Setting Breakpoints (F9)

In both VS Code and Visual Studio, setting a breakpoint is super simple:

- Click in the left margin (the gutter) next to the line number where you want to pause
- A red dot appears which is your breakpoint
- Run your program in debug mode
- When execution reaches that line, everything freezes

You can set as many breakpoints as you want. This is useful when you're not sure exactly where the problem is, so you set up a few checkpoints along the way.

Stepping Through Code

Once your program is paused at a breakpoint, you have several options for how to proceed. This is called "stepping" through your code, and it's one of the most powerful debugging techniques you'll ever learn.

Step Over (F10)

This moves to the next line of code in your current method. If that line calls another method, it executes the entire method and stops at the next line.

Imagine the Prince is standing at a door. "Step Over" means he walks through the door and emerges on the other side. You don't see what happened inside, you just know he made it through.

```
int health = 100;
int damage = 30;
health = CalculateDamage(health, damage); // Step Over executes this whole method
Console.WriteLine(health); // And stops here
```

Step Into (F11)

This takes you inside the method that's about to be called. If you're at a line that calls a method, Step Into will jump into that method and pause at its first line.

Using our door analogy, "Step Into" means the Prince opens the door, and you follow him inside to see exactly what he does in there. Maybe he pulls a lever, maybe he picks up a potion, you get to see everything.

```
int health = 100;
int damage = 30;
health = CalculateDamage(health, damage); // Step Into goes inside this method
// You're now at the first line of CalculateDamage

int CalculateDamage(int currentHealth, int dmg)
{   // You're now here
    return currentHealth - dmg;
}
```

Step Out (Shift + F11)

This finishes executing the current method and returns to where it was called from. It's useful when you've stepped into a method but realize, "Nope, the bug isn't here."

You followed the Prince through the door, watched him grab a potion, and now you fast-forward back to the hallway where he exits the room.

```
int CalculateDamage(int currentHealth, int dmg)
{
    int result = currentHealth - dmg; // You're paused somewhere in here
    // Step Out finishes this method and returns you to...
    return result;
}

health = CalculateDamage(health, damage);
Console.WriteLine(health); // ...here
```

Continue (F5)

This resumes normal execution until the program ends or hits another breakpoint. It's like unpausing the game where everything runs at full speed until you hit your next checkpoint.

 **Pro Tip:**

You can also use "Run to Cursor" in most debuggers. Right-click on a line and select "Run to Cursor", your program will run normally until it reaches that line, like setting a temporary breakpoint. This is super handy when you want to skip ahead without setting a permanent breakpoint.

The Debug Mindset

Keep in mind, debugging isn't just about tools. It's a mindset. When your code doesn't work, you need to approach it scientifically:

1. **Reproduce the bug**: Can you make it happen consistently? If the Prince sometimes falls through floors randomly, that's harder to debug than if he ALWAYS falls through the same floor tile.
2. **Isolate the problem**: Where does it happen? Start broad and narrow it down. "The game crashes" becomes "The game crashes when I attack" becomes "The game crashes when I attack while jumping" becomes "The game crashes because I forgot to check if the enemy exists before attacking it."
3. **Form a hypothesis**: Based on what you see, guess what might be wrong. "I think the health variable is becoming negative when it shouldn't."
4. **Test your hypothesis**: Use breakpoints to check if you're right. If health is actually fine, then your hypothesis was wrong then move on to the next theory.
5. **Fix and verify**: Once you think you've found the bug, fix it and run through all the scenarios that were broken before to make sure they work now.

Debugging in VS Code

VS Code is lightweight and popular, so let's start here. If you are using Visual Studio, feel free to jump to the next section.

To debug in VS Code, you need to:

1. Install the C# Dev Kit extension if you haven't already
2. Open your project folder in VS Code
3. Set your breakpoints by clicking in the left margin
4. Start debugging by pressing F5 or clicking the Run and Debug button in the sidebar

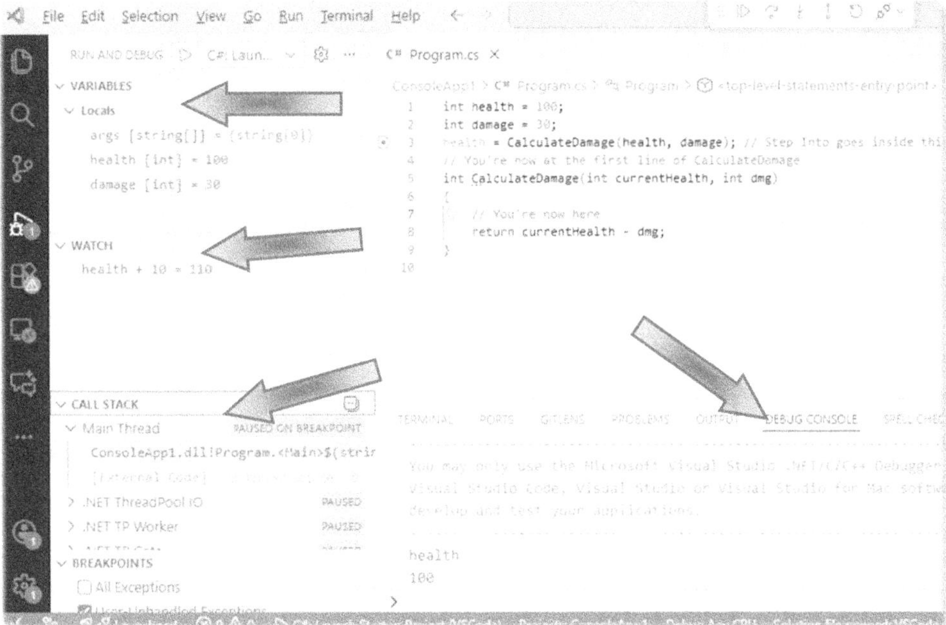

Once your program hits a breakpoint, you'll see several panels in the left sidebar:

Variables Panel: Shows all variables currently in scope and their values. This is GOLD when debugging. You can expand objects to see their properties, and even change values on the fly to test different scenarios.

Watch Panel: You can add specific expressions here to monitor continuously. For example, if you want to constantly watch what `health + 10` equals, add it to the watch panel and it updates automatically as you step through code.

Call Stack Panel: Shows the chain of method calls that got you to this point. Think of it like a breadcrumb trail. "Main called StartGame, which called PlayerTurn, which called Attack, and now we're here."

Debug Console: At the bottom, you can type expressions to evaluate them on the spot. Want to know what `playerName.ToUpper()` would return right now? Type it in the debug console and it'll show you immediately.

VS Code Debug Controls

When paused at a breakpoint, you'll see a small toolbar at the top:

From left to right:
- **Continue (F5)**: Resume execution
- **Step Over (F10)**: Execute this line and move to the next

- **Step Into (F11)**: Go inside the method being called
- **Step Out (Shift+F11)**: Finish this method and return to the caller
- **Restart**: Stop and restart debugging from the beginning
- **Stop**: End the debugging session

 **Pro Tip:**

Learn the keyboard shortcuts! When you're debugging a tricky problem, you'll be stepping through code a LOT. Using F10 and F11 instead of clicking buttons will save you lots of time and keep you in the flow.

Debugging in Visual Studio

Visual Studio (the full version, not VS Code) is a more heavyweight IDE with even more debugging power. The concepts are the same, but you get more bells and whistles.

Setting breakpoints works the same, click in the margin to place that red dot. But Visual Studio gives you extra options:

Conditional Breakpoints: Right-click on a breakpoint and add a condition. The debugger will only pause if that condition is true.

This is AMAZING when you're in a loop that runs 1,000 times, but you only care about iteration 743 where the bug happens.

```
for (int i = 0; i < 1000; i++)
{
    ProcessEnemy(i); // Set a breakpoint with condition: i == 743
}
```

Hit Count Breakpoints: Tell the debugger to pause only after this line has been hit a certain number of times. Useful for "the bug only happens the third time I enter this room" scenarios.

Data Breakpoints: In some cases, you can set a breakpoint that triggers when a specific variable's value changes. This is next-level debugging for when you have no idea where a variable is being modified.

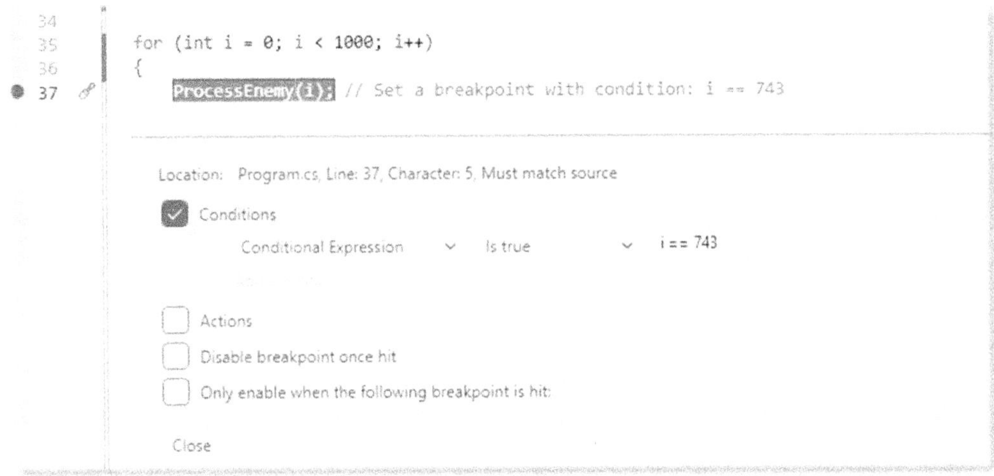

Visual Studio Debug Windows

Visual Studio has all the same panels as VS Code (Variables, Watch, Call Stack), but with extras:

Autos Window: Automatically shows variables that are relevant to the current line and previous line. It's like the debugger is reading your mind about what you want to inspect.

Locals Window: Shows all local variables in the current scope. This is similar to VS Code's Variables panel but with more detailed information.

Immediate Window: Similar to the Debug Console in VS Code. You can type expressions, call methods, even change variable values right here to test "what if" scenarios.

Watch Window: Visual Studio actually has multiple Watch windows (Watch 1, Watch 2, Watch 3, Watch 4), so you can organize different groups of watched expressions. This is useful for complex debugging sessions where you're tracking many different things.

Diagnostic Tools: Shows you memory usage and CPU performance while debugging. This is advanced stuff, but when you're wondering "why is my game suddenly running at 5 FPS?" this window has answers.

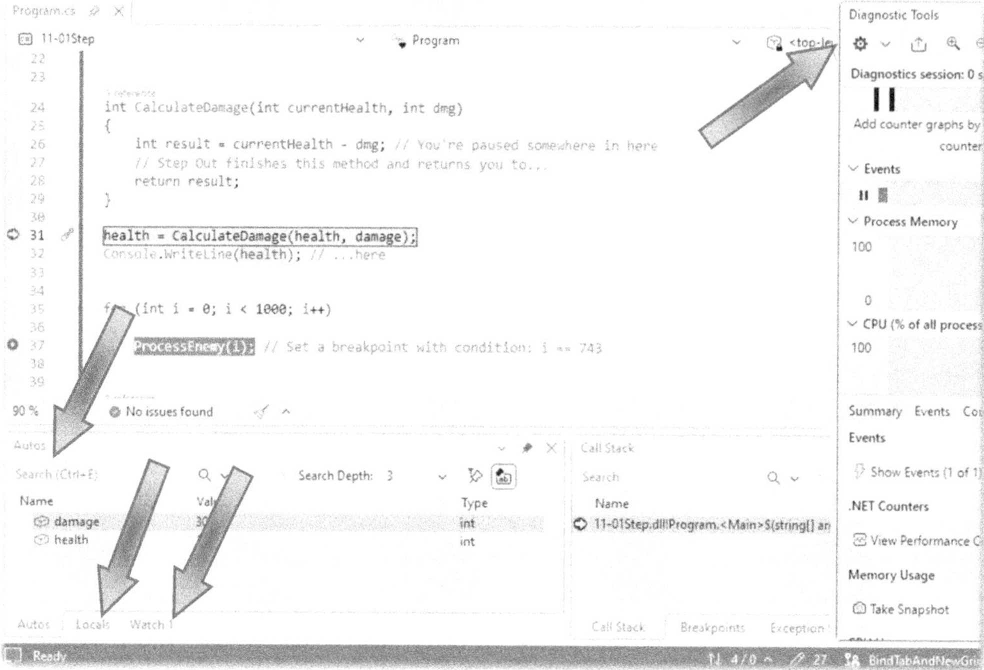

Inspecting Variables: X-Ray Vision for Your Code

Now that you understand the debugging windows available in both VS Code and Visual Studio, let's dive into the specific techniques you'll use most often to inspect what's actually happening in your code. These are your hands-on tools for investigating variables and expressions.

Hovering Over Variables

The simplest way to check a variable's value is to just hover your mouse over it while debugging. Seriously, it's that easy.

In both VS Code and Visual Studio, when you're paused at a breakpoint, hover your mouse cursor over any variable name in your code. A little tooltip pops up showing you its current value.

```
int playerHealth = 85;
int maxHealth = 100;
string playerName = "Prince";
```

Hover over playerHealth and you'll see: `playerHealth = 85`. Hover over `playerName` and you'll see: `playerName = "Prince"`:

Something really cool is if you hover over an object (not just a simple number or string), you can drill deeper into it. The tooltip will show a little arrow or plus sign that you can click to expand the object and see all its properties.

Here's an object with some values set:

```
Player prince = new Player
{
    Name = "Prince",
    Health = 85,
    MaxHealth = 100,
    CurrentWeapon = "Sword"
};
```

Hover the mouse pointer over `prince` and you'll see the whole object. Expand it to see:

This is incredibly useful because you can quickly check values without opening extra windows or typing commands. Just point and look. It's like having detective vision in the Batman Arkham games, just hover your mouse over something and instantly see all its details.

> ## Pro Tip:
>
> You can also hover over entire expressions, not just variables. Hover over `playerHealth + 10` and the debugger will evaluate it and show you the result. Hover over `playerName.ToUpper()` and it'll show you "PRINCE". This is super handy for testing small bits of logic on the fly.

The Watch Window: Your Surveillance System

Sometimes you want to keep an eye on specific variables continuously as you step through code. That's what the Watch window is for, it's like setting up security cameras on the variables you care about most.

Adding Watches in Visual Studio

In Visual Studio, while debugging:

1. Go to **Debug** → **Windows** → **Watch** → **Watch 1** (or press Ctrl+Alt+W, then 1)
2. In the empty row at the bottom of the Watch window, type the variable name you want to watch
3. Press Enter

Now as you step through your code, that variable's value will update automatically in the Watch window. You can add as many watches as you want.

Adding Watches in VS Code

VS Code also has a Watch section in its debug sidebar:

1. While debugging, look at the left sidebar
2. Find the **Watch** section (it's usually below Variables)
3. Click the + button
4. Type your variable name or expression
5. Press Enter

Just like in Visual Studio, you can watch variables or entire expressions. The Watch section updates automatically as you step through your code.

Quick Watch: The Instant Investigation Tool

Sometimes you don't want to add something to your Watch window permanently, you just want to quickly check a value or test an expression right now. That's what Quick Watch is for.

Quick Watch in Visual Studio

While paused at a breakpoint in Visual Studio:

1. Right-click on any variable in your code
2. Select **Quick Watch** (or press Shift+F9)
3. A dialog opens showing the variable's current value

But what's nice about the Quick Watch dialog is you can type NEW expressions at the top. Want to see what `playerHealth - 50` would be? Type it in. Want to see if `enemies.Count >
10`? Type it in. The debugger evaluates it instantly.

You can also add the expression to your main Watch window directly from Quick Watch by clicking "Add Watch."

Quick Watch in VS Code

VS Code doesn't have a traditional "Quick Watch" dialog like Visual Studio, but it has something similar through the Debug Console:

1. While paused at a breakpoint, look at the bottom panel
2. Click the **Debug Console** tab
3. Type any expression you want to evaluate
4. Press Enter

The Debug Console will immediately evaluate your expression and show the result. You can check variables, test calculations, even call methods.

 **Pro Tip:**

In Visual Studio's Quick Watch, you can expand objects just like hovering by clicking the arrows to drill into properties. You can even expand collections to see all their items. If you have a list of 50 enemies, you can browse through all of them in Quick Watch.

Edit and Continue: Time-Travel Debugging

Here's something that feels like magic when you first discover it. In Visual Studio (and in some cases VS Code), you can actually change your code while debugging, then rewind and try the new code without restarting your entire program.

This feature is called "Edit and Continue" and it's like having a time machine. You spot a bug, fix it on the spot, pull back the run line, and watch your fixed code execute without ending your debug session.

How It Works in Visual Studio

Let's say you're debugging this code:

```
int playerHealth = 100;
int damage = 30;

playerHealth = playerHealth - damage; // Paused here with a breakpoint
Console.WriteLine($"Health: {playerHealth}");
```

You're paused at the subtraction line. You step over it, and you see `playerHealth` becomes 70. But wait, you just realized you forgot to check if the player has a shield that should reduce damage by half!

Here's what you do:

1. **Edit the code** right now while still paused. Add the shield check:

```
int playerHealth = 100;
int damage = 30;
bool hasShield = true;

if (hasShield)
{
    damage = damage / 2;
}

playerHealth = playerHealth - damage; // You're still paused around here
Console.WriteLine($"Health: {playerHealth}");
```

2. **Drag the yellow arrow** (the execution pointer in the margin) back up to before the line you just edited. That yellow arrow shows where the debugger is currently paused. You can literally drag it to an earlier line.
3. **Step through again** and watch your new code execute with the shield logic included.

```
10        int playerHealth = 100;
11        int damage = 30;
12        bool hasShield = true;
13
14        if (hasShield)
15        {
16            damage = damage / 2;
17        }
18
19        playerHealth = playerHealth - damage; // You're still paused around here
20        Console.WriteLine(value: $"Health: {playerHealth}");
21
```

This is INSANELY useful. You don't have to stop debugging, restart the program, navigate back to the bug location, and try again. You just fix it and rewind right there.

 **Important limitations:**

- You can't add new methods or classes mid-debug
- You can't change method signatures (the parameters or return type)
- Some complex changes might not work and the debugger will tell you

But for most everyday bug fixes like changing a calculation, fixing a condition or adding a check it works beautifully.

Edit and Continue in VS Code

VS Code's support for Edit and Continue is more limited than Visual Studio's, but you can still make small edits and restart from your current breakpoint. The workflow is slightly different:

1. Make your code changes while paused
2. Use the **Restart** button in the debug toolbar

3. Your breakpoint will hit again with the new code

It's not quite as seamless as Visual Studio's "drag the arrow back" feature, but it still beats stopping, editing, recompiling, and running from scratch.

 **Pro Tip:**

Practice dragging that execution arrow in Visual Studio. You can move it forward too (though be careful, skipping code can lead to weird states). This is especially useful in loops. If you're debugging a loop that runs 100 times and you found the bug on iteration 47, you can drag the arrow back to the start of the loop body and watch iteration 47 again with your fix.

Performance Debugging with Stopwatch

Sometimes your code works correctly, but it's just too slow. Maybe your Prince is running at 10 frames per second instead of 60. It works, but it feels like you're playing through molasses. This is when you need to do performance debugging.

C# has a built-in tool called `Stopwatch` that measures exactly how long pieces of code take to run. It's like having a precision timer that can measure down to tiny fractions of a second.

Here's how to use it:

```csharp
using System;
using System.Diagnostics;

class PerformanceTest
{
    static void Main()
    {
        Stopwatch stopwatch = new Stopwatch();

        // Start timing
        stopwatch.Start();

        // Code you want to measure
        int total = 0;
        for (int i = 0; i < 1000000; i++)
        {
            total += i;
        }

        // Stop timing
        stopwatch.Stop();

        Console.WriteLine($"Total: {total}");
        Console.WriteLine($"Time taken: {stopwatch.ElapsedMilliseconds} ms");
        Console.WriteLine($"Time taken: {stopwatch.Elapsed.TotalSeconds} seconds");
    }
```

```
}
```

Expected Output:

```
Total: 1783293664
Time taken: 2 ms
Time taken: 0.0021086 seconds
```

The `Stopwatch` class is straightforward:

- `Start()`: Begin timing
- `Stop()`: Stop timing
- `ElapsedMilliseconds`: How many milliseconds passed
- `Elapsed`: A TimeSpan object with more detailed timing info
- `Restart()`: Reset to zero and start timing again

Real-World Performance Testing

Let's say you're implementing collision detection for your Prince, and you have two different approaches. Which one is faster?

Use Stopwatch to find out:

```csharp
using System;
using System.Diagnostics;

class CollisionPerformance
{
    static void Main()
    {
        int enemies = 1000;

        // Test Method 1: Simple collision check
        Stopwatch sw1 = new Stopwatch();
        sw1.Start();

        for (int i = 0; i < enemies; i++)
        {
            bool collision = SimpleCollisionCheck(i);
        }

        sw1.Stop();
        Console.WriteLine($"Simple collision: {sw1.ElapsedMilliseconds} ms");

        // Test Method 2: Optimized collision check
        Stopwatch sw2 = new Stopwatch();
        sw2.Start();

        for (int i = 0; i < enemies; i++)
        {
            bool collision = OptimizedCollisionCheck(i);
        }

        sw2.Stop();
        Console.WriteLine($"Optimized collision: {sw2.ElapsedMilliseconds} ms");
```

```csharp
        // Compare
        double improvement = ((double)(sw1.ElapsedMilliseconds -
            sw2.ElapsedMilliseconds) / sw1.ElapsedMilliseconds) * 100;
        Console.WriteLine($"Optimization improved by: {improvement:F2}%");
    }

    static bool SimpleCollisionCheck(int enemyId)
    {
        // Simulate some collision math
        Thread.Sleep(0); // make sure its slower
        double distance = Math.Sqrt(enemyId * enemyId + enemyId * 2);
        return distance < 100;
    }

    static bool OptimizedCollisionCheck(int enemyId)
    {
        // Simulate faster collision check (skip the expensive Sqrt)
        int distanceSquared = enemyId * enemyId + enemyId * 2;
        return distanceSquared < 10000; // 100 * 100
    }
}
```

Expected Output (numbers will vary):

```
Simple collision: 5 ms
Optimized collision: 0 ms
Optimization improved by: 100.00%
```

This is how developers figure out which code is faster. In actual game development, performance matters enormously. When you're trying to maintain 60 FPS (frames per second), you have only about 16 milliseconds to do EVERYTHING for that frame. Update all enemy positions, check all collisions, render all graphics, play all sounds. Every millisecond counts.

When to use Stopwatch:
- Comparing different algorithms or approaches
- Identifying slow sections of code (bottlenecks)
- Verifying those optimizations actually helped
- Testing if a library or method is fast enough for your needs

 **Pro Tip:**

Always test performance multiple times and average the results. Run your Stopwatch test in a loop 10 or 100 times, then divide the total time by the number of runs. Single measurements can be misleading because the computer might be busy with other things.

Remember, premature optimization is dangerous (it's cover in the principles chapter), but when you DO need to optimize, Stopwatch can work well for measuring whether your changes actually helped.

Logging: Your Black Box Recorder

Before fancy debuggers existed, programmers debugged by adding print statements everywhere. And you know what? It still works. Sometimes it's the fastest way to figure out what's happening.

```
Console.WriteLine("=== Starting Combat ===");
Console.WriteLine($"Player health: {playerHealth}");
Console.WriteLine($"Enemy health: {enemyHealth}");

int damage = CalculateDamage();
Console.WriteLine($"Damage calculated: {damage}");

playerHealth -= damage;
Console.WriteLine($"Player health after damage: {playerHealth}");

if (playerHealth <= 0)
{
    Console.WriteLine("Player died!");
}
```

Expected Output:

```
=== Starting Combat ===
Player health: 100
Enemy health: 80
Damage calculated: 25
Player health after damage: 75
```

This is called "logging" or "print debugging," and honestly, professional developers still do this ALL THE TIME. Why?

- **It's fast**: No need to set breakpoints and step through
- **It works everywhere**: Even in situations where you can't attach a debugger
- **You can see patterns**: When you log 100 iterations of a loop, you can see patterns emerge that you might miss stepping through one at a time

Why Logging Is Critical for Production Systems

But logging isn't just a crude debugging technique. It's actually THE ONLY way to debug certain kinds of problems, especially in **production systems** with live applications that real users are using right now.

Imagine you've released your Prince game to thousands of players. One player reports that their game crashed yesterday at 3:47 PM when they tried to open a specific door on level 5. But when you try to reproduce it today, everything works fine. What do you do?

You can't attach a debugger to code that ran yesterday. You can't set breakpoints in the past. You can't step through a game session that's already over. The only evidence you have is what your program or game in this case wrote to a log file. This is why professional applications write detailed logs to files:

```csharp
using System;
using System.IO;

class GameLogging
{
    static void Main()
    {
        string playerName = "Prince_47";
        int playerId = 12847;

        LogMessage("INFO", $"Combat started: Player {playerName} (ID: {playerId})");
        LogMessage("INFO", $"Player HP: 100, Enemy HP: 80");

        try
        {
            int damage = 25;
            LogMessage("INFO", $"Damage calculated: {damage}");
        }
        catch (Exception ex)
        {
            LogMessage("ERROR", $"Combat failed for player {playerName}:{ex.Message}");
        }
    }

    static void LogMessage(string level, string message)
    {
        string logEntry = $"[{DateTime.Now:yyyy-MM-dd HH:mm:ss}] [{level}] {message}";
        File.AppendAllText("game_log.txt", logEntry + Environment.NewLine);
        Console.WriteLine(logEntry);
    }
}
```

Expected Output (both console and in game_log.txt):

```
[2024-12-14 15:23:47] [INFO] Combat started: Player Prince_47 (ID: 12847)
[2024-12-14 15:23:47] [INFO] Player HP: 100, Enemy HP: 80
[2024-12-14 15:23:47] [INFO] Damage calculated: 25
```

Professional logging includes:

- **Timestamps**: Exactly when things happened
- **Log levels**: INFO (general info), WARNING (something unexpected), ERROR (something failed), DEBUG (detailed developer info)
- **Context**: User IDs, relevant data, what was happening

When to use logging vs debugging:
- Use the **debugger** when developing on your computer and can reproduce the bug
- Use **logging** when the bug happens in production, happened in the past, or is hard to reproduce

In reality, you use BOTH. Log everything important during development so when users encounter bugs in production, you can investigate what happened. The debugger helps you understand problems right now and logs help you understand problems that happened yesterday.

>  **Pro Tip:**
>
> In real applications, developers use logging frameworks like Serilog or NLog instead of `Console.WriteLine`. These frameworks handle writing to files, filtering by level, and managing log file sizes automatically. But for learning, `Console.WriteLine` is perfectly fine for quick debugging, and the concept of logging important events with context is what matters

The downside of simple logging? Your code gets cluttered with debug statements that you might need to remove later. But for quick investigations and for having a record of what happened in production, logging is essential and irreplaceable.

Debug Output: When Breakpoints Aren't Enough

There's a special type of logging that's perfect for development but automatically disappears when you release your game: `Debug.WriteLine()`.

The problem with `Console.WriteLine()` for debugging is that you have to remove all those statements before releasing your program. `Debug.WriteLine()` solves this. It works similarly to `Console.WriteLine()`, but only outputs when you're running in Debug mode during development.

When you build for release, the compiler automatically removes all `Debug.WriteLine()` statements:

```csharp
using System;
using System.Diagnostics;

class DebugLogging
{
    static void Main()
    {
        int playerHealth = 100;
        int damage = 25;

        Debug.WriteLine("=== Combat Debug Info ===");
        Debug.WriteLine($"Player health: {playerHealth}");
        Debug.WriteLine($"Applying damage: {damage}");

        playerHealth -= damage;

        Debug.WriteLine($"New health: {playerHealth}");

        Console.WriteLine("Combat complete!"); // This goes to the console/terminal
    }
}
```

Where Debug Output Goes

Here's the key difference: `Debug.WriteLine()` and `Console.WriteLine()` go to **different places**:

Visual Studio:
- `Console.WriteLine()` appears in the **console window** (the black terminal that pops up)
- `Debug.WriteLine()` appears in the **Output window** (View → Output, or Ctrl+Alt+O, make sure "Debug" is selected in the dropdown)

VS Code:
- `Console.WriteLine()` appears in the **Terminal** panel at the bottom
- `Debug.WriteLine()` appears in the **Debug Console** tab (next to Terminal when debugging)

So, when you run the code above in Debug mode:

- **Output/Debug Console** shows:

```
=== Combat Debug Info ===
Player health: 100
Applying damage: 25
New health: 75
```

- **Console/Terminal** shows:

```
Combat complete!
```

When you build in Release mode and run:

- **Output/Debug Console** shows: Nothing (all Debug.WriteLine removed)
- **Console/Terminal** shows:

```
Combat complete!
```

When to Use Each Type

- **Debug.WriteLine()**: Temporary debugging info during development that goes to the Output/Debug Console and automatically disappears in release builds
- **Console.WriteLine()**: Messages that go to the console/terminal, useful for quick debugging or information you want users to see
- **File logging**: Permanent records written to files for investigating production bugs

>  **Pro Tip:**
>
> You can use `Debug.Assert(condition, "message")` to check assumptions during development. For example: `Debug.Assert(playerHealth > 0, "Health should never be zero here!");` If the condition fails, the debugger breaks with your message. This only runs in Debug mode and helps catch logic errors early.

The beauty of `Debug.WriteLine()` is you can be as verbose as you want during development without cluttering the user-facing console. When you release, it all vanishes automatically like having collision boxes visible in your dev build that disappear in the final game.

When Debugging Gets Philosophical

The fact of the matter is sometimes the bug isn't in the code you're looking at. Sometimes you're debugging the wrong thing entirely.

Let's say your Prince game has a bug where enemies don't take damage. You spend hours debugging your `Attack` method, stepping through it line by line, and it looks PERFECT. The damage calculation is correct, the enemy's health is being reduced... but enemies still don't die.

Then you realize: You're modifying a copy of the enemy, not the actual enemy in the game. The bug isn't in the `Attack` method at all, it's in how you're passing the enemy object around.

This is why the "isolate the problem" step is so important. Make sure you're debugging the right thing. If you're convinced a specific method is broken, but you've stepped through it 50 times and it looks fine... maybe it's not broken. Maybe the problem is somewhere else.

The "Rubber Duck" Technique

Here's a weird but effective debugging technique used by some professional developers. Explain your code to a rubber duck or your teddy bear or your R2-D2, whatever you have around you.

Seriously.

When you explain your code line by line to someone (or something) else, you often spot the bug yourself. It forces you to slow down and think about what each line actually does versus what you think it does.

"Okay Mr. Booboo, here I'm checking if the player is on spikes OR if spikes are up, and then… wait, that's wrong! It should be AND not OR!"

Some programmers keep a toy on their desk for this purpose. Some explain it to their cat, their houseplant, or their patient (or annoyed) partner. The point is verbalizing the logic in simple terms often reveals the flaw.

Just talk through your code aloud. Yes, you'll look weird. Yes, it works anyway.

Fun Experiment: Debug the Spike Trap

Here's some buggy code for a spike trap for our Prince. The spikes should come up every 3 seconds and deal damage if the player is standing on them. But something's wrong, sometimes the player takes damage when the spikes are down!

The Challenge

Use breakpoints, stepping, and variable inspection (hovering, watches, or Quick Watch) to find the bug:

```csharp
using System;

class SpikeTrap
{
    static void Main()
    {
        int playerHealth = 100;
        bool playerOnSpikes = true;
        int spikeTimer = 0;
        bool spikesUp = false;

        Console.WriteLine("=== Prince vs Spike Trap ===");

        for (int seconds = 0; seconds < 10; seconds++)
        {
            spikeTimer++;

            if (spikeTimer >= 3)
            {
                spikesUp = !spikesUp;
                Console.WriteLine($"Second {seconds}: Spikes are now " +
                    $"{(spikesUp ? "UP" : "DOWN")}");
                spikeTimer = 0;
            }

            if (playerOnSpikes || spikesUp)
            {
                playerHealth -= 10;
                Console.WriteLine($"Second {seconds}: " +
                    $"Player took 10 damage! Health: {playerHealth}");
            }
        }

        Console.WriteLine($"\nFinal health: {playerHealth}");
    }
}
```

What you should do:

1. Set a breakpoint at the start of the loop
2. Add a watch for `playerOnSpikes && spikesUp` to see what the damage condition SHOULD be
3. Step through the code watching the values of `spikeTimer`, `spikesUp`, and `playerOnSpikes`
4. Hover over the condition on line 23 to see what it evaluates to
5. Pay attention to the condition that deals damage
6. Find the bug and fix it
7. Use Edit and Continue if you're in Visual Studio, fix the bug and drag the execution arrow back to test your fix

Try finding the bug yourself first!

Hint: Look carefully at line 23. That `||` operator might be suspicious...

Example Answer

The bug is on line 23. The condition should use && (AND) not || (OR). As written, the player takes damage if they're on the spikes OR if the spikes are up. But we want damage only when BOTH conditions are true, the player is on the spikes AND the spikes are up.

Expected Output (Fixed):

```
=== Prince vs Spike Trap ===
Second 2: Spikes are now UP
Second 2: Player took 10 damage! Health: 90
Second 5: Spikes are now DOWN
Second 8: Spikes are now UP
Second 8: Player took 10 damage! Health: 80

Final health: 80
```

This is a perfect example of a logic error. The code ran without crashing, but it did the wrong thing. By stepping through with a debugger and watching the variable values (either by hovering, using watches, or Quick Watch), you could see exactly when and why the damage was being applied incorrectly.

Wrap-up: What You've Learned

You now know the essential skills for hunting down bugs in your code!

Key Takeaways

- **Breakpoints** let you freeze your program at specific lines so you can inspect what's happening. They're your time-stopping power in the code world.
- **Stepping** (Step Over, Step Into, Step Out) gives you precise control over how your code executes, letting you follow the flow line by line or jump in and out of methods as needed.
- **Variable inspection** comes in multiple flavors: hover over variables to see values instantly, use the Watch window to monitor specific variables continuously, and use Quick Watch or the Debug Console to evaluate expressions on the fly. You can even drill into objects to see all their properties.
- **Edit and Continue** in Visual Studio lets you fix bugs mid-debugging and rewind to test your fixes without restarting, making you feel like a time-traveling debugging wizard.
- **Stopwatch** helps you measure performance and identify slow code, which is crucial when you need to optimize for speed like keeping a game running at 60 FPS or processing a large tables data.
- **Logging** is essential for both quick debugging during development and investigating issues in production systems where you can't attach a debugger. Good logs with timestamps, context, and log levels help you understand what happened when bugs occur in the wild.
- **The debugging mindset** is about being systematic: reproduce the bug, isolate where it happens, form theories about why, test those theories, and fix the root cause.
- Both **VS Code and Visual Studio** give you powerful debugging tools. Visual Studio is a full-featured IDE that works out of the box on Windows so just install it, create a project, and start debugging with no configuration needed. It also offers more advanced debugging features like Edit and Continue with execution arrow dragging, conditional breakpoints, and detailed performance diagnostics. VS Code is more lightweight, works on Windows, Mac, and Linux, and is highly customizable, but requires installing extensions (like C# Dev Kit) and some configuration before you can debug C# code.

Remember, debugging isn't a sign that you're a bad programmer. The best programmers aren't the ones who write perfect code on the first try (nobody does that). They're the ones who can efficiently track down bugs when they appear, whether that's through debugger breakpoints during development or through well-designed logs in production. And now, so can you.

Continuing Your Journey

"The only way to do great work is to love what you do." — Steve Jobs

So, you've made it through! You've learned the fundamentals, written your first programs, and probably wrestled with more than a few bugs along the way. However, mastering the basics is just the beginning. There's a whole world of software development out there waiting for you.

Think of this book as your foundation. You've learned the core concepts that every professional developer uses daily. It's like building a house, who dug deep and laid the foundation on the rock. And when a flood arose, the stream broke against that house and could not shake it, because it had been well built. Now you're ready to build on that foundation. The good news? Everything you learn from here on out builds on what you already know.

The Adventure Continues

 **Trivia:**

In 1991, 21-year-old student Linus Torvalds posted a message online: "I'm doing a (free) operating system (just a hobby, won't be big and professional)." That "hobby" became Linux, which now runs most of the world's servers, every Android phone, the International Space Station, and the world's fastest supercomputers. Torvalds made it open-source, allowing thousands of programmers worldwide to improve it for free. Today, 95% of the world's top 1 million web servers run Linux. A college student's "hobby project" powers most of the internet because he let others build on his work.

Here are some areas you'll want to explore as you continue developing your skills. Don't feel like you need to learn everything at once. Professional developers spend their entire careers learning new things. The key is **to learn what you need, when you need it**.

Generics

Remember how we used `List<string>` and `Dictionary<string, int>` throughout this book? Those angle brackets `< >` are generics in action. Generics let you write code that works with any type of data, one of the most powerful features in C#.

Right now, you've been using generics that other people created. The next step is learning to create your own. This lets you write reusable code that different parts of your application can use, which is exactly what professional developers do when building large software systems.

Garbage Collection and Memory Management

You might have noticed we never talked about cleaning up after ourselves. That's because C# has a garbage collector, an invisible janitor that cleans up memory you're no longer using. But understanding how it works can help you write faster, more efficient programs.

You'll learn about things like `IDisposable` and the `using` statement (not the one at the top of your files, confusingly, C# reuses that word). This is especially important when working with files, database connections, or anything that uses resources your computer needs to track.

The garbage collector is great, but it's not magic. Learning when and how it runs can help you avoid creating applications that pause unexpectedly, something users definitely notice, especially in responsive web applications or real-time systems.

Streams

No, not video streams (though those use this concept too). Streams are C#'s way of handling data that flows, whether it's reading a large file piece by piece, downloading data from the internet, or processing information that's too big to fit in memory all at once.

This is crucial for real-world applications. Imagine a banking system processing millions of transactions, or a web application handling file uploads. You can't load everything into memory at once, sometimes you need to process data in manageable chunks, and that's where streams come in.

Reflections

Reflection is used when software needs to inspect, understand, or interact with types at runtime, rather than at compile time. It is essential in frameworks and tools that work generically, such as serialization libraries, dependency injection containers, ORMs, testing frameworks, and plugin systems.

You can use reflection to discover what methods a class has, what properties it contains, and even create objects without knowing their type at compile time. It's powerful stuff, but use it wisely. Reflection is slower than normal code and should be used sparingly. You'll find it in frameworks, testing tools, and serialization libraries.

Dependency Injection

Remember how we talked about not creating dependencies directly in your classes? Dependency Injection (often called DI) is the formal pattern for handling this. Instead of a class creating everything it needs, you "inject" those dependencies from outside.

It sounds complicated, but it's really about making your code more flexible and easier to test. Most modern C# applications like web APIs to mobile apps uses dependency injection extensively. It's one of those concepts that seems confusing at first but becomes second nature once you understand it.

Unit Testing

Something that might sound boring but is actually critical for professional development is testing your code automatically. Unit tests are small programs that verify your code works correctly. They're like having an assistant who checks your work every time you make a change.

Professional developers write tests for their code because manually testing everything after each change is time-consuming and error-prone. Tests also give you confidence to refactor (improve) your code without worrying about breaking existing functionality. In many companies, writing tests is just as important as writing the actual code.

Design Patterns and Algorithms

Design patterns are proven solutions to common programming problems. They're the best practices that experienced developers have discovered over decades of building software. Once you learn them, you'll start recognizing them everywhere.

Similarly, algorithms are step-by-step procedures for solving specific problems, like finding the shortest path through a network of connections, sorting large amounts of data efficiently, or searching through information quickly.

These aren't things you memorize all at once. You learn them gradually as you encounter the problems they solve in real projects.

Networking and APIs

Want to build web applications? Create mobile apps that talk to a server? Integrate with other services like payment processors or email systems? You'll need to learn about networking and APIs (Application Programming Interfaces).

APIs are how different software systems communicate with each other. When you use a weather app, it's talking to a weather service's API. When you log into a website using your Google account, that website is using Google's authentication API. Understanding how to work with APIs is essential for modern software development.

Developer Tools: Git, NuGet, Docker, and more

Professional programmers use tools that sound intimidating but are actually incredibly helpful:

Git is version control. It's like having infinite save points for your code. Made a change that broke everything? Just load an earlier save. Want to try an experimental feature without risking your working code? Git handles that too.

NuGet is C#'s package manager. Instead of writing every piece of functionality from scratch, you can use NuGet to download and install packages (libraries) that other developers have created. Need to work with JSON? There's a NuGet package for that. Want to connect to a database? NuGet has you covered. It's like having access to thousands of pre-built tools that you can add to your projects with a single command.

Docker helps you package your program with everything it needs to run, so it works the same on any computer. No more "but it works on my machine!" situations.

These tools might seem overkill for small projects, but once you start using them, you'll wonder how you ever lived without them.

What Should You Learn First?

Here's my suggestion for your next steps:

1. **Get comfortable with Git** - Start using it now, even for small projects. Future you will thank present you.
2. **Learn about Generics** - They're everywhere in C#, and understanding them opens up a lot of doors.
3. **Pick up Unit Testing basics** - It'll change how you think about writing code.
4. **Explore Design Patterns** - But learn them as you need them, not all at once.

After that? Follow your interests. Want to make web apps? Learn about APIs and networking. Building desktop applications? Dive into design patterns and advanced C# features. The best way to learn is to build stuff you care about.

The Sequel

I have started work on a follow-up book that will take you from where you are now to intermediate and advanced topics. It'll dive deeper into many of the concepts mentioned in this appendix like generics, dependency injection, unit testing, design patterns, and more.

Until that book is available, don't wait around. Start exploring these topics on your own. The beauty of programming is that you can learn by doing. Pick a topic that interests you, find some tutorials or documentation online, and start experimenting. By the time the next book comes out, you'll already have some experience under your belt, which will make the advanced concepts even easier to grasp.

The Truth About Professional Development

Software development is vast and constantly evolving. Even experienced developers are always learning new technologies, frameworks, and techniques.

What separates beginners from professionals isn't knowing everything, it's knowing how to learn, how to solve problems, and how to write code that other people can understand and maintain. Those skills develop over time through practice and experience.

You're Not Done Yet

Remember your first variable declaration? Or when you finally understood how loops work? Those moments of understanding are just the beginning. Programming is a skill that grows with practice and experience.

The journey from here is yours to shape. Maybe you'll build web applications, develop mobile apps, create data analysis tools, or work on systems that millions of people use every day or start by writing your very own first game! The foundation you've built with this book, understanding variables, loops, methods, classes, and all the core concepts will serve you regardless of which path you choose.

So, take a moment to appreciate what you've learned. Then pick your next topic and keep going. The best way to become a better programmer is to keep programming, keep learning, and keep building things.

And hey, if you ever feel stuck or overwhelmed, remember that every professional developer was once exactly where you are now, wondering if they'd ever really "get it." They did, and so will you.

Your software development journey is just beginning. Make it count.

Now go build something useful, something interesting, or just something that is fun!

Quick Reference

Built-in value types

C# type/keyword	Range	Size	Description
bool	true or false	1 byte	Boolean value representing true or false
char	U+0000 to U+FFFF	2 bytes	Unicode UTF-16 character
DateTime	00:00:00.0000000 UTC, January 1, 0001 to 23:59:59.9999999 UTC, December 31, 9999	8 bytes	Represents dates and times
TimeSpan	-10,675,199 days to 10,675,199 days	8 bytes	Represents a time interval (duration)
Guid	00000000-0000-0000-0000-000000000000 to FFFFFFFF-FFFF-FFFF-FFFF-FFFFFFFFFFFF	16 bytes	Globally unique identifier
DateOnly	January 1, 0001 to December 31, 9999	4 bytes	Represents a date without time (.NET 6+)
TimeOnly	00:00:00.0000000 to 23:59:59.9999999	8 bytes	Represents a time without date (.NET 6+)

Integral numeric types

C# type/keyword	Range	Size	Description
sbyte	-128 to 127	1 byte	Signed 8-bit integer for small numeric values
byte	0 to 255	1 byte	Unsigned 8-bit integer, commonly used for binary data
short	-32,768 to 32,767	2 bytes	Signed 16-bit integer for small to medium numeric values
ushort	0 to 65,535	2 bytes	Unsigned 16-bit integer for positive small to medium values
int	-2,147,483,648 to 2,147,483,647	4 bytes	Signed 32-bit integer, the most commonly used integer type

uint	0 to 4,294,967,295	4 bytes	Unsigned 32-bit integer for positive values
long	-9,223,372,036,854,775,808 to 9,223,372,036,854,775,807	8 bytes	Signed 64-bit integer for very large numeric values
ulong	0 to 18,446,744,073,709,551,615	8 bytes	Unsigned 64-bit integer for very large positive values

Floating-point numeric types

C# type/keyword	Approximate range	Precision	Size	Description
Float	$\pm1.5 \times 10{-}45$ to $\pm3.4 \times 1038$	~6-9 digits	4 bytes	Single-precision floating-point, used when memory is limited
Double	$\pm5.0 \times 10{-}324$ to $\pm1.7 \times 10308$	~15-17 digits	8 bytes	Double-precision floating-point, the default for decimal numbers
Decimal	$\pm1.0 \times 10{-}28$ to $\pm7.9228 \times 1028$	28-29 digits	16 bytes	High-precision decimal type, ideal for financial and monetary calculations

Basic Collection types

C# Collection Type	Ordered	Duplicates	Description
Array (T[])	Yes	Yes	
List<T>	Yes	Yes	Dynamic array, most commonly used collection
Dictionary<TKey, TValue>	No	No (keys)	Key-value pairs with fast key lookups
HashSet<T>	No	No	Unordered collection of unique elements
Queue<T>	Yes (FIFO)	Yes	First-In-First-Out collection
Stack<T>	Yes (LIFO)	Yes	Last-In-First-Out collection
LinkedList<T>	Yes	Yes	Doubly-linked list, efficient insertions/deletions

SortedList<TKey, TValue>	Yes (by key)	No (keys)	Sorted key-value pairs, stored as array
SortedDictionary<TKey, TValue>	Yes (by key)	No (keys)	Sorted key-value pairs, stored as tree
SortedSet<T>	Yes (sorted)	No	Sorted collection of unique elements

Basic C# Operators

Category	Operator	Name	Description	Example
Arithmetic	+	Addition	Adds values or concatenates strings	5 + 3
	-	Subtraction	Subtracts values	5 – 3
	*	Multiplication	Multiplies values	5 * 3
	/	Division	Divides values	10 / 2
	%	Remainder/Modulus	Gets remainder	10 % 3
	++	Increment	Increases value by 1	i++ or ++i
	--	Decrement	Decreases value by 1	i-- or –i
Assignment	=	Assignment	Assigns value	x = 5
	+=	Addition assignment	x = x + y	x += 5
	-=	Subtraction assignment	x = x - y	x -= 5
	*=	Multiplication assignment	x = x * y	x *= 5
	/=	Division assignment	x = x / y	x /= 5
	%=	Remainder assignment	x = x % y	x %= 5
Comparison	==	Equality	Tests equality	5 == 5
	!=	Inequality	Tests inequality	5 != 3
	<	Less than	Compares values	5 < 10
	>	Greater than	Compares values	10 > 5

	<=	Less than or equal	Compares values	5 <= 5
	>=	Greater than or equal	Compares values	10 >= 5
Logical	&&	Logical AND	Short-circuit AND	x > 0 && y > 0
	`	`		Logical OR
	!	Logical NOT	Inverts boolean	!true
Conditional	?:	Ternary conditional	Returns value based on condition	x > 0 ? "+" : "-"
Member Access	.	Member access	Accesses a member of a type	person.Name
	[]	Indexer	Accesses array/collection element	array[5]
	()	Method invocation	Calls a method	Console.WriteLine()
Type	new	Object creation	Creates new instance	new Person()
	typeof	Type information	Gets Type object	typeof(int)
	(T)	Cast	Explicit type conversion	(int)3.14
String	+	Concatenation	Joins strings	"Hello" + " World"
	$""	String interpolation	Embeds expressions in strings	$"Value: {x}"

Basic Control Flow

Control Flow	Syntax	Description	Example

if	if (condition) { }	Executes block if condition is true	if (x > 0) {
			Console.WriteLine("Positive");
			}

if-else	if (condition) { } else { }	Executes first block if true, else second block	if (x > 0) { ... } else { ... }
else if	if (cond1) { } else if (cond2) { }	Chains multiple conditions	if (x > 0) { ... } else if (x < 0) { ... }
switch	switch (value) { case x: break; }	Multi-way branch based on value	switch (day) { case 1: ...; break; default: ...; }

switch expression	var result = value switch { pattern => result };	Pattern matching expression (C# 8+)	var type = num switch { > 0 => "Positive", < 0 => "Negative", _ => "Zero" };
for	for (init; condition; increment) { }	Loop with counter	for (int i = 0; i < 10; i++) { ... }
foreach	foreach (var item in collection) { }	Iterates through collection	foreach (var name in names) { ... }
while	while (condition) { }	Loop while condition is true	while (x < 100) { x++; }
do-while	do { } while (condition);	Executes at least once, then loops	do { x++; } while (x < 100);
Break	break;	Exits the current loop or switch	for (...) { if (found) break; }
Continue	continue;	Skips to next iteration of loop	for (...) { if (skip) continue; }
Return	return; or return value;	Exits method, optionally with value	return result;
Goto	goto label;	Jumps to labeled statement (rarely used)	goto ErrorHandler;
try-catch	try { } catch (Exception e) { }	Exception handling	try { ... } catch (IOException ex) { ... }
try-finally	try { } finally { }	Always executes finally block	try { ... } finally { file.Close(); }
try-catch-finally	try { } catch { } finally { }	Exception handling with cleanup	try { ... } catch (Exception ex) { ... } finally { ... }
Throw	throw; or throw exception;	Throws or re-throws exception	throw new ArgumentException("Invalid");
Pattern matching (is)	if (obj is Type variable) { }	C# 7.0+	Type test with variable declaration

Glossary

Term	Description
.csproj	C# Project file – contains settings and information about your project like which files to include and what libraries to use.
.sln	Solution file – contains information about one or more projects and how they relate to each other.
2D Array	A two-dimensional array that represents a grid with rows and columns.
3D Array	A three-dimensional array that represents a cube with width, height, and depth.
Absolute value	The distance of a number from zero (always positive)
Abstract Class	A class that cannot be instantiated directly and is meant only to be inherited from. Can contain both regular methods and abstract methods.
Abstract Method	A method declared in an abstract class that has no implementation. Child classes must override and implement it.
Access Modifier	Keywords (public, private, internal, protected) that control who can access class members
Action	A built-in delegate type for methods that return void (do something but don't return a value)
Aggregate Function	A function that processes a collection and returns a single value, like .Sum(), .Average(), .Max(), or .Min()
AggregateException	An exception that contains multiple inner exceptions from failed parallel or async operations
Alpha	The transparency level of a color, from 0 (invisible) to 255 (solid/opaque)
AND operator (&&)	Returns true only if both conditions are true
Anonymous Method	A method without a name, typically created using lambda syntax
Anonymous Type	A nameless type created using new { Property = value } syntax, often used with .Select()
AppData	A Windows folder where applications store user-specific data and settings

Argument	The actual value passed to a method when calling it
ArgumentException	An exception thrown when a method receives an invalid argument
ArgumentOutOfRangeException	An exception thrown when an argument value is outside the allowed range
Array	A fixed-size collection of items accessed by index, starting at 0.
Assembly	A compiled unit of code (usually a .dll or .exe file)
Async Exception	An exception that occurs in an asynchronous method and is delivered when the task is awaited
Async/Await	Keywords used to write asynchronous code that runs operations in the background without blocking
Asynchronous (Async)	A programming pattern where tasks can run "in the background" without blocking other code from executing. Opposite of synchronous (sync), where each task must finish before the next begins.
Auto-Property	A property where the compiler generates the backing field automatically
Await	A keyword that tells the program to pause at this line until an async operation completes, but allows other code to run in the meantime. Can only be used inside async methods.
Background Work	Operations that happen without blocking the main program flow, like loading files while a game continues running.
Base Case	The condition in a recursive method that stops it from calling itself, preventing infinite loops
Base Class	The parent class that other classes inherit from. Also called a parent class or superclass.
Binary	Another name for a compiled executable file or the bin folder where they're stored. Called this because computers read it as 1s and 0s (not human-readable).
Block Scope	The limited area inside curly braces (like loops or if statements) where a variable exists
Block/Blocking	When code stops and waits for an operation to complete before continuing. Causes freezing in UI applications.
Boolean (bool)	A value that is either true or false, used for yes/no decisions
Bottleneck	A part of the code that slows down the entire program, like a narrow section of road that causes traffic jams.

Boxing	Converting a value type to a more general type (e.g., int to double)
Braces	The curly bracket symbols { and } used to group code together and define scope.
Break	Keyword that exits a switch case or loop
Breakpoint	A marker in your code where the debugger will pause execution so you can inspect what's happening
Brush	A tool used to fill shapes with color, gradients, or patterns (like a paint bucket)
Bug	An error or flaw in code that causes it to behave incorrectly or crash
Call	To execute a method by writing its name with parentheses
Call Stack	The sequence of method calls that led to the current point in execution, like a trail of breadcrumbs
Camel Case	A naming style where the first word is lowercase and each following word starts with a capital letter (e.g., playerHealth)
Canvas	The drawing surface where graphics are rendered (in our case, the Form window)
Case	One possible value in a switch statement
Case-sensitive	When capitalization matters. In C#, Console and console are treated as completely different things.
Cast	Converting a value from one type to another
Character (char)	A single letter, number, or symbol (e.g., 'A', '5', '!')
Class	A blueprint or template that defines the structure and behavior of objects in your code.
Clean Code	Code that is easy to read and understand because it's well-organized and uses clear names.
ClientSize	The interior size of a window, excluding borders and title bar
Closure	When a lambda captures variables from the surrounding scope
Code Editor	A special text editor designed for writing programming code (like VS Code). Has features like syntax highlighting and code completion to make programming easier.
Collection	A group of items stored together, like an array or list.

Command Palette	In VS Code, a searchable menu (Ctrl+Shift+P or Cmd+Shift+P) that gives you quick access to all commands and features.
Command Prompt	Windows' terminal program where you can type text commands to control your computer and run programs.
Comment	Text in code that the computer ignores, used to explain code to humans.
Comparison operators	Symbols that compare two values (==, !=, >, <, >=, <=)
Compile/Compilation	The process of translating human-readable code into machine language that a computer can execute.
Composition	When a class contains instances of other classes as properties (has-a relationship) rather than inheriting from them.
Compound assignment	Operators like +=, -=, *=, /= that modify and assign in one step
Computational complexity	How the amount of work grows as input size increases (important for performance).
Concatenation	Joining strings together for example using the + operator
Condition	An expression that evaluates to either true or false
Conditional Breakpoint	A breakpoint that only pauses execution when a specific condition is true
Console	The text-based window where your program displays output and can receive input.
Console Application	A program that runs in a console/terminal window and uses text-based input and output.
Constructor	A special method that runs when creating a new object; same name as the class
Contains	A method that checks if a specific item exists in a collection.
ContainsKey	A method that checks if a specific key exists in a Dictionary.
Continue	A keyword that skips the rest of the current iteration and moves to the next one.
Convert Class	A helper class with methods like Convert.ToInt32() for flexible type conversions
Coordinates	The X and Y position of a point on the screen, where (0,0) is the top-left corner
Count	A property that returns the number of items in a collection like a List or Dictionary.

Coupling	How much one class depends on or knows about another class's internal details
CPU-bound	Work that requires heavy processing power from the computer's processor, like complex calculations or generating large amounts of data.
Cross-platform	Software that can run on multiple operating systems like Windows, Mac, and Linux
CSV	Comma-Separated Values; a simple format where values are separated by commas
Custom Exception	A programmer-created exception type designed for specific error situations
DateTime	A type that represents a specific point in time (date and time)
Deadlock	A situation where your program gets stuck waiting for something that will never happen, often caused by blocking async code incorrectly. The program essentially freezes permanently.
Debug Console	A window where you can type and evaluate code expressions while debugging
Debug Mode	A version of your compiled program that includes extra information to help find and fix errors. Slower but easier to troubleshoot.
Debugging	The process of finding and fixing errors (bugs) in your code.
Deconstruct	Breaking apart a tuple into separate variables
Decoupling	Reducing dependencies between different parts of code so they can work independently
Decrement	Decreasing a value, usually by 1 (like i--).
Default	The case in a switch that runs when no other cases match
Deferred Execution	When a LINQ query is defined but not executed until the results are actually needed (like in a foreach loop)
Delegate	A type that represents references to methods with a specific parameter list and return type
Dependency	External code or libraries that your project relies on to work properly.
Dequeue	Removing an item from the front of a queue.

Derived Class	A class that inherits from a base class. Also called a child class or subclass.
Deserialization	Converting stored data back into objects
Dictionary	A collection that stores key-value pairs for fast lookups by key.
Directory	A folder on disk that can contain files and other folders
Dispatcher	A tool in WPF applications used to explicitly run code on the main/UI thread. Similar to Invoke in Windows Forms but with WPF-specific syntax.
Dispose	A method that releases resources (like pens and brushes) when you're done using them
DLL	Dynamic Link Library – a file containing compiled code that can be shared and used by multiple programs.
Double	A number that can have decimal places with high precision (e.g., 3.14, 5.5, -2.789)
Double Buffering	A technique to prevent flickering by drawing to an off-screen buffer first before displaying
Doubly-linked List	A linked list where each node keeps track of both the previous and next items.
Edit and Continue	A feature that allows you to modify code while debugging and test the changes without restarting
Else	Part of an if statement that runs when the condition is false
Else if	Allows checking multiple different conditions in sequence
Encapsulation	Hiding implementation details and only exposing what's necessary, often using access modifiers like public, private, and protected.
Enqueue	Adding an item to the back of a queue.
Enum (Enumeration)	A type that lets you define a set of named values instead of using confusing numbers
Error	A problem in your code that prevents it from compiling or running. Must be fixed before the program will work.
Error List	A panel in Visual Studio that displays all errors, warnings, and messages in your code, with the ability to jump directly to each issue.

Escape Character	The backslash (\) used to include special characters in strings like quotes or newlines
Event	A mechanism that allows an object to notify other objects when something happens.
EventArgs	A class that contains data about an event; inheriting from this is the standard pattern for event data
EventHandler	A built-in delegate type specifically designed for events in .NET
Exception	An unexpected event or error that occurs during program execution that can be caught and handled
Executable File (.exe)	A compiled program file that can be run directly by your computer's operating system. On Windows these end in .exe, on Mac/Linux they often have no extension.
Execution Pointer	The yellow arrow in the debugger margin showing which line of code will execute next
Extension	Add-on software that gives a program new features. VS Code uses extensions to support different programming languages.
Field	A variable declared at the class level, accessible to all methods in the class
FIFO	First-In-First-Out, the first item added is the first item removed (like a line at a store).
File	A collection of data stored on disk with a name and extension like .txt or .json
File Extension	The letters after the dot in a filename (like .cs or .exe) that indicate what type of file it is.
FileStream	An object that provides access to a file for reading or writing data
Finally	A code block that always executes after try-catch, regardless of whether an exception occurred
Flatten()	A method on AggregateException that unwraps nested AggregateExceptions into a single flat list
Float	A number with decimal places but less precision than double; needs an 'f' suffix (e.g., 2.5f)
FormatException	An exception thrown when trying to convert data to the wrong format (like text to a number)
FPS	Frames Per Second - the number of full screen "images" displayed each second to create animation

Fragile	Code that breaks easily when you make changes, like a house of cards that collapses if you touch one card.
Frame Rate	How many times per second the screen is redrawn, measured in FPS (frames per second)
Freeze/Frozen	When a program becomes unresponsive and stops processing user input or updating the display. Bad user experience!
Func	A built-in delegate type for methods that return a value (calculate or get something)
Game Loop	The repeating cycle of updating game state and drawing to the screen
GDI+	Graphics Device Interface Plus - the Windows component that handles drawing graphics like shapes, images, and text
Generics	A way to create classes and collections that work with any type while remaining type-safe (e.g., List<T>).
GetType()	A method that returns the runtime type of an object
Global Variable	A variable declared at the class level that can be accessed by all methods in that class (also called a field)
Gracefully	Handling errors in a controlled way that doesn't crash the program
Graphics	An object that provides methods for drawing shapes, text, and images
GroupBy	A LINQ method that organizes items into groups based on a key value
Hash Code	A unique number calculated from a key, used to quickly locate data in a hash table.
Hash Table	The underlying data structure used by dictionaries to provide fast lookups.
HashSet	A collection that stores unique items with no duplicates and provides fast lookups.
HasValue	A property on nullable types that returns true if the variable contains a value (not null)
I/O (Input/Output)	Reading data into a program (input) or writing data out from a program (output)

IDE	Integrated Development Environment – a complete package with editor, compiler, debugger, and other tools all in one (like Visual Studio). More powerful and convenient than a simple code editor.
IEnumerable	The interface that represents a sequence of items that can be enumerated (looped through); LINQ operates on IEnumerable
If statement	A code structure that runs certain code only when a condition is true
Immediate Execution	When a LINQ query executes immediately and returns a result, like when using .ToList(), .Count(), or .First()
Immediate Window	Visual Studio's version of the Debug Console where you can evaluate expressions during debugging
Immutable	Data that cannot be changed after it's created; strings in C# are immutable
Increment	Increasing a value, usually by 1 (like i++).
Indentation	Spaces or tabs at the beginning of lines that show code hierarchy and make it more readable.
Index	The numerical position of an item in a collection (starting at 0).
IndexOutOfRangeException	An exception thrown when trying to access an array element that doesn't exist
Infinite loop	A loop that never ends because its condition never becomes false.
Inheritance	When one class (child/derived) gets all the properties and methods from another class (parent/base), allowing code reuse and creating relationships between classes.
Instance	Another word for object; a specific occurrence of a class
Instantiate	To create an actual object instance from a class blueprint.
Integer (int)	A whole number with no decimal point (e.g., 1, 42, -7)
Integer division	Division between whole numbers that discards the decimal part
IntelliSense	A code editor feature that suggests code as you type and shows information about functions and methods.
Interface	A contract that defines methods a class must implement, but contains no actual code. Classes can implement multiple interfaces.

Intermediate Language (IL)	A platform-independent language that C# code is compiled into. The .NET runtime then converts IL to actual machine code when the program runs.
Interpolation	Embedding variables inside strings using $"{}" syntax for cleaner code
Invalidate	A method that tells a form or control that it needs to be redrawn
Invoke	A method used in Windows Forms applications to explicitly run code on the main/UI thread. Used when working with background threads that need to update the user interface. OR Calling/executing a delegate or event to trigger all subscribed methods
IsCompletedSuccessfully	A task property that indicates whether the task completed without errors
IsFaulted	A task property that indicates whether the task completed due to an exception
Iteration	One complete pass through a loop's code.
JSON	JavaScript Object Notation; a popular text-based format for storing structured data
Key-Value Pair	A pair of related data where the key is used to look up the value (like a word and its definition).
Lambda	An anonymous (unnamed) method written inline using the => syntax
Length	A property that returns the number of items in an array.
Liability	Something that causes problems or creates extra work, like unused code that still needs to be maintained.
Library	A collection of pre-written code that provides useful functions you can use in your programs.
Lifetime	How long a variable exists in memory before being cleaned up
LIFO	Last-In-First-Out, the last item added is the first item removed (like a stack of plates).
LinkedList	A collection where each item points to the next item, useful for frequent insertions/removals.
LINQ	Language Integrated Query, a set of methods for querying and manipulating collections using a readable, SQL-like syntax

List	A dynamic collection that can grow or shrink automatically, more flexible than arrays.
Local Variable	A variable declared inside a method or block that only exists within that method or block
Log Level	A category indicating the severity of a log message (DEBUG, INFO, WARNING, ERROR)
Logging	Writing messages to console or files to track what code is doing, essential for debugging issues that occur in production
Logic Error	A bug where code runs without crashing but produces incorrect results due to flawed logic
Logical operators	Symbols that combine multiple conditions (&&, ||, !)
Loop	A programming structure that repeats code multiple times.
Loosely Coupled	Classes that have minimal dependencies on each other's internal implementations
Main Thread (UI Thread)	The primary thread of execution in a program, especially important in games and UI apps where all screen updates and user input must be handled on this thread.
Math class	Built-in C# collection of mathematical functions
Method	A named block of code that performs a specific task and can be called multiple times throughout your program
Method Chaining	Calling multiple methods in sequence, where each returns a value that the next method operates on
Modulus (%)	Math operator that returns the remainder after division
nameof()	A keyword that returns the name of a variable, method, or type as a string
Namespace	An organizational container for classes, like a folder for your code.
Nested loop	A loop inside another loop, often used for grids or tables.
new keyword	Creates a new instance of a class and calls its constructor
Node	An individual element in a linked list that contains data and references to neighboring nodes.
NOT operator (!)	Flips true to false or false to true
NuGet	A package manager for C# that lets you download and use external libraries in your projects.

Null	A special value meaning "nothing" or "no value"
Null-Coalescing Operator (??)	An operator that provides a default value when a variable is null
Null-Safe Operator	The ?. operator that checks if something is null before trying to use it
Nullable Type	A value type (like int or bool) that can also hold null by adding a ? after the type
Object	An instance of a class; the actual "thing" created from the blueprint
Object (base type)	The base type that all other types in C# inherit from
OR operator (||)	Returns true if at least one condition is true
out	A keyword requiring a method to assign a value to a parameter before completing
Override	Replacing a method inherited from a base class with a new implementation
Parallel processing	Running multiple operations at the same time using multiple processor cores.
Parameter	A variable in a method definition that receives data when the method is called
Parentheses ()	Used to group conditions together to control the order they're evaluated
Parse	Converting text (string) into another type like a number using methods like int.Parse()
PascalCase	Naming convention where each word starts with a capital letter (HealthPoints)
PATH	An environment variable that tells your computer where to find executable programs. Adding something to PATH lets you run it from any folder in the terminal.
Path	The location of a file on disk, like "C:\Users\Name\file.txt"
Pattern Matching	A feature that lets you check the type of an object and work with it in a type-safe way using keywords like is, as, and switch.
Pen	A tool used to draw outlines and lines with a specific color and thickness (like a pencil or marker)
Polymorphism	The ability to treat objects of different types the same way through a common parent class or interface, but have them behave differently.

Pop	Removing an item from the top of a stack.
Predicate	A function that returns true or false, commonly used in LINQ methods like .Where() to filter items
Production System	A live application that real users are actively using, where you cannot pause execution to debug
Profile	Testing code performance to measure how fast it runs and find slow parts that actually need optimization.
Project	A collection of code files and settings that work together to create a single program.
Projection	Transforming items in a collection into a different form, typically using .Select()
Property	A class member that looks like a field but has getter/setter logic
Publish	Another term for firing/raising an event (making the event happen)
Push	Adding an item to the top of a stack.
Query	A request to retrieve or transform data from a collection
Queue	A First-In-First-Out (FIFO) collection where items are processed in the order they were added.
Quick Watch	A feature that lets you instantly inspect a variable or evaluate an expression without adding it to the Watch window
Race condition	A bug that occurs when multiple operations try to access/modify the same data simultaneously in unpredictable order.
Random	A class that generates pseudo-random numbers within specified ranges
Readable Format	Data stored as text that humans can open and read (like JSON or XML)
Record	A special type designed for immutable data with value-based equality
Recursion	When a method calls itself, usually with modified parameters until reaching a stopping condition
ref	A keyword that allows a method to modify the original variable passed to it, not just a copy
Refactor	Restructuring existing code without changing what it does, usually to make it cleaner or easier to maintain.

Reference Type	A type where a reference to data is copied (classes)
Release Mode	A version of your compiled program optimized for speed and size, without debugging information. Used for final distribution.
Responsive	When a program continues to accept user input and update its display smoothly, even while doing background work. The opposite of frozen.
Return Value	The data that a method sends back to the code that called it
RGB	Red-Green-Blue color model where colors are created by mixing these three primary colors in values from 0-255
Runtime	The .NET runtime is the engine that runs your compiled C# programs, handling memory, security, and converting IL to machine code.
Scope	The region of code where something (like a variable or method) can be accessed.
SDK	Software Development Kit – a collection of tools needed to build applications for a specific platform. The .NET SDK lets you build C# programs.
Sealed	A keyword that prevents a class from being inherited or prevents a method from being overridden further.
SelectMany	A LINQ method that flattens nested collections into a single sequence
Sender	The object parameter in an event handler that represents who fired the event
Serialization	Converting objects into a format that can be stored or transmitted
Solution	A container that can hold one or more related projects. Used to organize complex applications.
Source Code	The human-readable code that programmers write, stored in files like Program.cs.
Stack	A Last-In-First-Out (LIFO) collection where the most recently added item is removed first.
Stack Overflow	An error that occurs when a program uses too much memory from excessive method calls, often from infinite recursion
Statement	A single instruction in your code, typically ending with a semicolon in C#.

Static	A member or class that exists only once and is shared across all instances
Step Into	Enter into a method that's being called so you can debug inside it
Step Out	Finish executing the current method and return to where it was called from
Step Over	Execute the current line and move to the next one, without going inside any methods that are called
Stopwatch	A class used to measure how long code takes to execute, useful for performance testing
String	Text made up of multiple characters, like words or sentences
StringBuilder	A class for efficiently building strings by avoiding the performance cost of string immutability.
Struct	A lightweight value type, similar to a class but stored differently
Subscribe	Registering a method to be called when an event fires (using the += operator)
Switch expression	Modern, compact syntax for switch statements that returns a value
Switch statement	A structure for handling multiple specific values of a single variable
Synchronization Context	A mechanism that ensures code resumes on the correct thread after an await operation, particularly important for UI applications. C# uses this automatically when you use await properly.
Synchronous (Sync)	Traditional programming where each operation must complete before the next one starts. Like waiting in a single-file line.
Syntax Error	An error caused by breaking the grammatical rules of the programming language, like forgetting a semicolon or misspelling a keyword.
Syntax Highlighting	When a code editor displays different parts of your code in different colors to make it easier to read.
Task	An object representing ongoing work that will complete in the future. Like a promise that says "I'm working on it, I'll let you know when I'm done."
Task	A type that represents an asynchronous operation that may or may not return a value

Task.Delay()	An async-friendly method that waits for a specified time without blocking the thread. Returns a Task that completes after the delay.
Task.WhenAll	A method that waits for multiple async operations to complete simultaneously
Task<T>	A Task that will return a value of type T when it completes (e.g., Task<int> returns an integer, Task<string> returns a string).
Terminal	A program that lets you type commands to interact with your computer. Also called Command Prompt on Windows, Terminal on Mac, and various names on Linux.
Thread	A separate path of execution in your program. Async uses threads behind the scenes to do work simultaneously.
Thread.Sleep()	A synchronous method that completely blocks the current thread for a specified time. Freezes everything on that thread.
Throw	The action of creating and sending an exception to signal that something went wrong
Tick	A single occurrence of a timer's interval event (like one frame in animation)
Tightly Coupled	When parts of code depend heavily on each other's internal details, making changes difficult and risky.
Timer	An object that triggers an event repeatedly at a specified interval
TimeSpan	A type that represents a duration or length of time
ToString()	A method inherited from Object that converts an object to its string representation
Try-Catch	A code block structure that attempts code and catches errors if they occur
TryGetValue	A Dictionary method that attempts to get a value by key and returns whether it succeeded.
TryParse	A method that attempts to convert data without throwing exceptions, returning true or false instead
Tuple	A lightweight data structure that groups multiple related values together
Type	The kind of data a variable holds (number, text, true/false, etc.)
Type Casting	Converting data from one type to another, often used between number types with (int) or (double)

Type-safe	Code that prevents you from accidentally using the wrong data type, catching errors at compile time.
typeof()	An operator that returns type information for a specified type
Unboxing	Converting a general type to a specific value type (e.g., double to int)
Unsubscribe	Removing a method from an event's list of listeners (using the -= operator)
Value Property	A property on nullable types that returns the actual value when it's not null
Value Type	A type where data is copied (structs, primitives)
Variable	A named container that stores data your program needs to remember, like a labeled box
Variables Panel	A debugger window that displays all variables currently in scope and their values
Verbatim String	A string prefixed with @ that treats backslashes as regular characters and preserves formatting
Virtual Method	A method in a base class that can be overridden by child classes to provide different behavior.
Visibility	Where in the code a variable can be accessed and used
void	A keyword indicating that a method doesn't return any value
Warning	A potential problem in your code that won't stop it from running but might cause issues. Should be addressed when possible.
Watch Panel	A debugger window where you can monitor specific variables or expressions while debugging
Windows Forms	A framework for building desktop applications with windows, buttons, and other visual controls in C#. Uses Invoke for thread management.
Workload	In Visual Studio, a pre-packaged set of tools and features for a specific type of development (like desktop apps or web apps).
WPF (Windows Presentation Foundation)	A modern framework for building desktop applications in C# with advanced graphics and styling. Uses Dispatcher for thread management.
XML	eXtensible Markup Language; a text-based format using tags to structure data

Zero-indexed	Counting that starts at 0 instead of 1, used for array and list indices.

Index